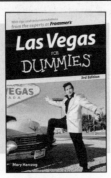

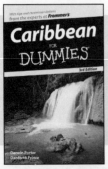
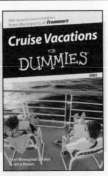

London
FOR
DUMMIES®
4TH EDITION

by Donald Olson

WILEY

Wiley Publishing, Inc.

London For Dummies,® 4th Edition

Published by
Wiley Publishing, Inc.
111 River St.
Hoboken, NJ 07030-5774
www.wiley.com

WILEY

About the Author

Donald Olson is a novelist, playwright, and travel writer. His newest novel, *Confessions of a Pregnant Princess,* was published in 2005 under the pen name Swan Adamson. An earlier Swan Adamson novel, *My Three Husbands,* has been translated into French and published in several European countries. Donald Olson's novel *The Confessions of Aubrey Beardsley,* was published in the United Kingdom by Bantam Press, and his play, *Beardsley,* was produced in London. His travel stories have appeared in *The New York Times, Travel & Leisure, Sunset, National Geographic* books, and many other publications. His guidebooks *London For Dummies, Best Day Trips from London, Irreverent London, Germany For Dummies,* and *Frommer's Vancouver & Victoria* are all published by Wiley Publishing, Inc. London is one of Donald's favorite cities, and England is one of his favorite countries. *England For Dummies* won a 2002 Lowell Thomas Travel Writing Award for best guidebook.

Dedication

This book is dedicated to all those Londoners who showed the world in July, 2005, that they were stronger than any terrorists.

Author's Acknowledgments

I would like to thank Gary Larson and Stephen Brewer for their help and comradeship while I was researching this new edition of *London For Dummies*.

Publisher's Acknowledgments

We're proud of this book; please send us your comments through our Dummies online registration form located at www.dummies.com/register/.

Some of the people who helped bring this book to market include the following:

Editorial

Editors: Melissa Bennett;
Project Editor, Elizabeth Kuball;
Development Editor, Marc Nadeau;
Assistant Editor

Copy Editor: Laura Miller

Cartographer: Andrew Murphy

Editorial Manager: Tamara Ahrens

Editorial Assistant:
Lindsay Thompson

Senior Photo Editor: Richard Fox

Cover Photo: Guardsmen standing
together, © Steve Vidler/
eStock Photo

Back Photo: Tower Bridge at Night,
© Bruno Perousee/
AGE Fotostock, Inc.

Cartoons: Rich Tennant
(www.the5thwave.com)

Composition Services

Project Coordinator: Jennifer Theriot

Layout and Graphics: Carl Byers,
Denny Hager, Joyce Haughey,
Lynsey Osborn

Proofreaders: Joe Niesen,
TECHBOOKS Production Services

Indexer: TECHBOOKS Production
Services

Publishing and Editorial for Consumer Dummies

Diane Graves Steele, Vice President and Publisher, Consumer Dummies

Joyce Pepple, Acquisitions Director, Consumer Dummies

Kristin A. Cocks, Product Development Director, Consumer Dummies

Michael Spring, Vice President and Publisher, Travel

Kelly Regan, Editorial Director, Travel

Publishing for Technology Dummies

Andy Cummings, Vice President and Publisher, Dummies
Technology/General User

Composition Services

Gerry Fahey, Vice President of Production Services

Debbie Stailey, Director of Composition Services

Contents at a Glance

Introduction 1

Part I: Introducing London 7
Chapter 1: Discovering the Best of London 9
Chapter 2: Digging Deeper into London 17
Chapter 3: Deciding When to Go 28

Part II: Planning Your Trip to London 37
Chapter 4: Managing Your Money 39
Chapter 5: Getting to London 51
Chapter 6: Catering to Special Needs or Interests 59
Chapter 7: Taking Care of the Remaining Details 69

Part III: Settling into London 81
Chapter 8: Arriving and Getting Oriented 83
Chapter 9: Checking In at London's Best Hotels and B&Bs 103
Chapter 10: Dining and Snacking in London 143

Part IV: Exploring London 183
Chapter 11: Discovering London's Top Attractions 185
Chapter 12: Shopping the Local Stores 237
Chapter 13: Following an Itinerary: Four Great Options 257
Chapter 14: Going Beyond London: Five Great Day Trips........263

Part V: Living It Up after Dark:
London Nightlife 287
Chapter 15: Applauding the Cultural Scene 289
Chapter 16: London's Best Pubs, Clubs, and Bars 299

Part VI: The Part of Tens 309
Chapter 17: Striking a Pose: Ten (Or So)
Famous London Statues 311
Chapter 18: Making Amens: Ten Noteworthy
London Churches...315
Chapter 19: Ale's Well that Ends Well:
Ten Historic London Pubs 319
Chapter 20: Ten Important Royals — Past and Present 323

Appendix: Quick Concierge 333
Index 341

Maps at a Glance

London's Neighborhoods 90
London Accommodations Overview 112
Hotels in Westminster and Victoria 115
Hotels in the West End...116
Hotels from Knightsbridge to Earl's Court 118
Hotels from Marylebone to Notting Hill 120
Restaurants in and around the City...148
Restaurants in Westminster and Victoria 149
Restaurants in the West End 150
Restaurants from Knightsbridge to Earl's Court 152
Restaurants from Marylebone to Notting Hill....................................154
London's Top Sights...186
The British Museum...190
St. Paul's Cathedral...201
The Tower of London...205
Westminster Abbey 207
More London Sights 210
Hampstead..227
Shopping in Knightsbridge and Chelsea 246
Shopping in the West End 248
Day Trips from London 264
Bath 267
Brighton..271
Canterbury 274
Stratford-upon-Avon..277
Salisbury 282
London Pubs, Clubs, and Bars 300

Table of Contents

Introduction *1*

About This Book...1
Conventions Used in This Book 2
Foolish Assumptions 3
How This Book Is Organized...3
 Part I: Introducing London 3
 Part II: Planning Your Trip to London 4
 Part III: Settling into London...4
 Part IV: Exploring London..4
 Part V: Living It Up after Dark: London Nightlife 4
 Part VI: The Part of Tens...5
 Quick Concierge...5
Icons Used in This Book..5
Where to Go from Here..6

Part 1: Introducing London *7*

Chapter 1: Discovering the Best of London 9

The Best Places to Soak Up London's History 9
The Best Museums..11
The Best of British Cuisine 12
The Best Places to Shop in London 13
The Best of London's Performing Arts 14
The Best Urban Charms 15

Chapter 2: Digging Deeper into London 17

The Main Events: A Brief History of London 17
 Pre-history and the arrival of the Romans 17
 Northern invaders 18
 William the Conqueror 18
 Magna Carta...18
 Hundred Years' War 18
 Tudor and Elizabethan England.....................................18
 Civil War 19
 Fire, plague, and rebuilding...19
 New lines of succession 19
 The Victorian Empire 19
 England in the World Wars 20
 The welfare state...20
 Queen Elizabeth II...20
 London at the millennium...20

Mayor Ken...21
New Labour 21
Terrorist bombings..22
Building Blocks: An Overview of English Architecture 22
Dining English Style, from Traditional to Modern 23
Visiting the Local Pub...24
Background Check: Finding London
    on Page and Screen...25

Chapter 3: Deciding When to Go 28

Revealing the Secrets of the Seasons 28
    Abloom in the spring...29
    Summer fun in the sun 30
    Chock-full of culture in the fall 30
    Wonderful in winter 31
Perusing a Calendar of Events....................................32
    January...32
    February...32
    March 32
    April..32
    May...33
    June..33
    July...34
    August 34
    September...34
    October 35
    November 35
    December..35

Part II: Planning Your Trip to London 37

Chapter 4: Managing Your Money 39

Planning Your Budget 39
    Transportation 40
    Lodging...41
    Dining 41
    Sightseeing...42
    Shopping and nightlife 42
Cutting Costs — But Not the Fun 43
Handling Money 44
    Making sense of pounds and pence 45
    Exchanging your currency....................................45
    Using ATMs and carrying cash.............................46
    Charging ahead with credit cards.........................47
    Toting traveler's checks......................................47
Dealing with a Lost or Stolen Wallet.............................48

Chapter 5: Getting to London 51

Flying to London 51
  Finding out which airlines fly there......................51
  Getting the best deal on your airfare 52
  Booking your flight online 53
Arriving by Other Means...................................54
  Taking the train 54
  Riding a ferry or hovercraft.............................55
Joining an Escorted Tour 55
Choosing a Package Tour 57
  Locating package tours 57
  Checking out airline and hotel packages.................58

Chapter 6: Catering to Special Needs or Interests....59

Traveling with the Brood: Advice for Families.............59
  Locating family-friendly accommodations
    and restaurants 60
  Planning your trip together 60
  Preparing for a long trip................................61
  Hiring a babysitter while on your trip 61
Making Age Work for You: Tips for Seniors 62
Accessing London: Advice for Travelers
  with Disabilities 62
  Joining escorted tours 64
  Dealing with access issues 64
  Taking health precautions 66
Following the Rainbow: Gay and Lesbian Travelers.........66

Chapter 7: Taking Care of the Remaining Details.......69

Getting a Passport..69
  Applying for a U.S. passport.............................69
  Applying for other passports 70
  Entering England with your passport 71
  Dealing with a (gulp) lost passport 71
Renting a Car in London — Not!..............................71
Playing It Safe with Travel and Medical Insurance 72
Staying Healthy When You Travel..........................73
Staying Connected by Cellphone or E-Mail................74
Keeping Up with Airline Security Measures 78

Part III: Settling into London..............................81

Chapter 8: Arriving and Getting Oriented....................83

Getting through Passport Control and Customs.............83
Making Your Way to Your Hotel...........................84
  Arriving at Heathrow....................................84
  Arriving at calmer Gatwick.............................86

Touching down at another airport 87
Arriving by train...88
Figuring Out the Neighborhoods 88
The City of London: The heart of it all....................92
The West End: Downtown London 92
Central London: Parks, museums, and more 95
Finding Information After You Arrive 97
Getting Around London...97
Taking the Underground (subway)...........................98
Riding a bus 100
Hailing a taxi 101
Walking on your own two feet.............................101

Chapter 9: Checking In at London's Best Hotels and B&Bs...103

Getting to Know Your Options 103
Understanding the pros and cons of B&Bs 103
Exploring hotel choices 104
Finding the Best Room at the Best Rate.......................106
Finding the best rate 106
Surfing the Web for hotel deals.............................107
Reserving the best room....................................108
Arriving without a Reservation 108
London's Top Hotels...109
Runner-Up Hotels 137
Index of Accommodations by Neighborhood..................139
Index of Accommodations by Price............................140

Chapter 10: Dining and Snacking in London 143

Getting the Dish on the Local Scene...............................143
Discovering the top dining areas...........................144
Eating with the locals 145
Trimming the Fat from your Budget 146
London's Best Restaurants 146
Dining and Snacking on the Go.................................172
Sandwich bars 172
Fish and chips 173
Department-store restaurants................................174
Treating Yourself to Tea 175
Casual tea rooms and pâtisseries.............................175
Elegant spots for high tea...................................176
Planning a Picnic 177
Index of Restaurants by Neighborhood 178
Index of Restaurants by Cuisine................................179
Index of Restaurants by Price 181

Part IV: Exploring London 183

Chapter 11: Discovering London's Top Attractions...185

The Top Attractions from A to Z 188
Finding More Cool Things to See and Do 208
    Sights for history buffs 209
    Attractions for art lovers 212
    Literary landmarks 214
    All manner of intriguing museums 216
    Activities for teens 218
    Places that please kids 219
    To see or not to see: Shakespeare sights 220
    Ships ahoy! Nautical London 221
    Architectural highlights and stately homes 222
    Parks and gardens 224
    A quaint village just a Tube ride away 226
    Royal castles and palaces 226
    Greenwich: The center of time and space 229
Seeing London by Guided Tour 230
    Bus tours 231
    Boat tours 231
    An amphibious tour 232
    Walking tours 233
Index of Top Attractions by Neighborhood 233
Index of Attractions by Type 234

Chapter 12: Shopping the Local Stores 237

Surveying the Shopping Scene 237
    Getting the VAT back 238
    Getting your goodies through Customs 240
Checking Out the Big Names 241
Shopping the Street Markets 244
    Chelsea and Antiquarius 244
    Covent Garden 244
    Portobello Road 244
Discovering the Best Shopping Neighborhoods 245
    Knightsbridge: Home of Harrods 245
    The West End: More famous shopping streets
        and stores 247
Index of Stores by Merchandise 254

Chapter 13: Following an Itinerary:
Four Great Options 257

London in Three Days 257
London in Five Days 259

London in Seven Days 259
London with Kids 260

Chapter 14: Going Beyond London: Five Great Day Trips..................................263

By Train or by Car: Weighing the Options 263
Taking the train 265
Taking a car: Driving on the left,
passing on the right..265
Bath: Hot Mineral Springs and Cool
Georgian Magnificence 266
Getting there..266
Finding information and taking a tour 266
Seeing the sights 268
Dining locally...269
Spending the night..269
Brighton: Fun beside the Seaside.............................270
Getting there..270
Finding information 270
Seeing the sights 270
Dining locally...272
Spending the night..272
Canterbury: Tales from the Great Cathedral 273
Getting there..273
Finding information and taking a tour 273
Seeing the sights 274
Dining locally...276
Spending the night..276
Stratford-upon-Avon: In the Footsteps of the Bard..........276
Getting there..276
Finding information and taking a tour 278
Seeing the sights 278
Seeing a play at the Royal Shakespeare
Theatre 280
Dining locally...280
Spending the night..281
Salisbury and Stonehenge: Gothic Splendor
and Prehistoric Mysteries 281
Getting there..281
Finding information 282
Seeing the sights 282
Dining locally...284
Spending the night..284

Part V: Living It Up after Dark: London Nightlife 287

Chapter 15: Applauding the Cultural Scene 289

Getting the Inside Scoop 289
Finding Out What's Playing and Getting Tickets.............290
Getting tickets 291
Using ticket agencies....................................291
Raising the Curtain on the Performing Arts 292
Theater...292
Opera..295
Symphony 296
Dance..297
Rock concerts..297

Chapter 16: London's Best Pubs, Clubs, and Bars.....299

Enjoying a Pint: London Pubs............................299
Focusing on the Music: The Best Jazz
and Blues Clubs 303
Laughing the Night Away: Comedy Clubs 304
Shaking Your Groove Thing: The Best Dance Clubs 304
Unwinding in Elegance: Posh Hotel Bars 305
Seeking Spots for Night Owls................................306
Stepping Out: Gay Clubs and Discos 306

Part VI: The Part of Tens 309

Chapter 17: Striking a Pose: Ten (Or So) Famous London Statues 311

Admiral Lord Nelson.......................................311
Charles I 311
Duke of York and Edward VII 312
Henry VIII 312
James II and George Washington...........................313
Oliver Cromwell...313
Peter Pan...313
Prince Albert...314
Queen Boudicca 314
Winston Churchill and Abraham Lincoln....................314

Chapter 18: Making Amens: Ten Noteworthy London Churches...315

Church of St. Bartholomew the Great 315
Church of St. Stephen Walbrook 316

St. Botolph's 316
St. Dunstan's-in-the-West 316
St. George the Martyr Church......................................317
St. Margaret's Westminster 317
St. Martin-in-the-Fields 317
St. Mary-le-Bow...317
Southwark Cathedral 318
Temple of Mithras 318

Chapter 19: Ale's Well that Ends Well: Ten Historic London Pubs 319

Anchor Inn 319
Coal Hole 319
George Inn 320
King's Head and Eight Bells 320
Lamb and Flag 320
Red Lion Public House 320
Salisbury 321
Williamson's Tavern..321
Ye Olde Cheshire Cheese 321
Ye Olde Watling...321

Chapter 20: Ten Important Royals — Past and Present 323

Queen Boudicca (a.d. 30?–60):
Braveheart of the Britons..323
Alfred the Great (849–899): A Warrior and a Scholar 324
William the Conqueror (1028–1087):
Winner Takes All..325
Henry II (1133–1189): Family Plots.............................326
Henry VIII (1491–1547): Take My Wife — Please! 326
Elizabeth I (1533–1603): Heart and Stomach of a King...327
George III (1738–1820): "My Lords and Peacocks . . . "...328
George IV (1762–1830): A Dandy King
for the Regency...329
Queen Victoria (1819–1901): Mother of Monarchs 330
Queen Elizabeth II (1926–): Monarchy Amidst Media 331

Appendix: Quick Concierge *333*

Fast Facts 333
Toll-Free Numbers and Web Sites 338
Where to Get More Information 339

Index *341*

Introduction

● ●

*F*or all its historic panache, time-honored traditions, quaint corners, and associations with royal pomp and ceremony, London is very much a modern European city. London is a rich blend of the very old and the very new — from the 900-year-old Tower of London to the 6-year-old Tate Modern gallery. And the city is big, in both size and population; more than 9 million people reside in the 622-square-mile megalopolis known as Greater London.

For first-time visitors, London can be a bit of a challenge. If you have a bit of advance planning and some useful information under your belt, making the trip will be easier than you thought. London may be far from where you live, but for many people, a trip to England is like going home.

About This Book

London For Dummies, 4th Edition, is meant to be used as a reference. You can start at the first page and read all the way through. If you do, you'll end up with an unusually complete knowledge of London essentials. On the other hand, you may not need parts of this book because you've already been to London or know the basics of international travel. You're after quick, easy-to-find specifics. In that case, you can easily flip to the part that you need or home in on a specific chapter. The philosophy behind this book is quite simple: I wanted to create the kind of guide that I wished I'd had on my first trips to London — informative, practical, down-to-earth, and fun.

When you travel, unexpected surprises create the most memorable moments and provide the stories that you take back with you. But the other side of travel is details and planning. Questions about where to eat and sleep aren't small issues when you're away from home. They can make or break a trip — I know that. So what I offer here is based on my own experience in traveling, living, and working in London.

You should know, however, that travel information is subject to change at any time — especially prices. Therefore, I suggest that you write or call ahead for confirmation when making your travel plans. The authors, editors, and publisher cannot be held responsible for the experiences of readers while traveling. Your safety is important to us, however, so we encourage you to stay alert and be aware of your surroundings. Keep a close eye on cameras, purses, and wallets — all favorite targets of thieves and pickpockets.

Conventions Used in This Book

I recently tried to extract some information from a guidebook and found so many symbols that I needed training in hieroglyphics to interpret them all. I'm happy to report that the user-friendly *London For Dummies,* 4th Edition, travel guide isn't like that. I keep the use of symbols and abbreviations to a minimum, as follows:

✔ The credit card abbreviations are AE (American Express), DC (Diners Club), MC (MasterCard), and V (Visa).

✔ I include the London postal area (SW7, for example) in all street addresses, in case you want to look up the street in a *London A to Z* or other London street reference map.

✔ I give the nearest Tube/Underground (subway) stop for all destinations (for example, Tube: Piccadilly Circus).

✔ I list all prices first in British pounds sterling (£), and then in U.S. dollars ($) rounded to the nearest dollar (when prices are under $10, I round them to the nearest nickel). Although the exchange rate fluctuates daily, in this book, I use the rate £1 = $1.85.

✔ The London city code, 020, precedes all London telephone numbers in this book (a different code applies in a few cases). The local London number follows the city code. If you're calling London from outside the United Kingdom, you must dial the U.K. country code (44), followed by 20 and the local number. If you're calling London from elsewhere within the United Kingdom, dial 020 before the number. If you're calling London from within London, just dial the local number.

I also apply a few conventions to the listings of hotels, restaurants, and attractions, as follows:

✔ I list the hotels, restaurants, and top attractions in alphabetical order, so you can easily move among the maps, worksheets, and descriptions.

✔ For those hotels, restaurants, and attractions that you can find on a map in this book, I include a page reference in the listing information. If a hotel, restaurant, or attraction is outside the city limits or in an out-of-the-way area, it may not be mapped.

✔ I give exact prices for every hotel, restaurant, and attraction. Please note, however, that prices are subject to change, and an additional 17.5 percent *VAT* (value-added tax) is added to restaurant meals and may be added to hotel bills. (I note in the individual hotel listings if the price does not include the VAT.)

✔ I use a system of dollar signs ($) to show a range of costs for hotels or restaurants. The dollar signs for hotels correspond to *rack rates* (nondiscounted standard rates) and reflect a hotel's low to high rates for a double room. For restaurants, the dollar signs denote the *average* cost of dinner for one person, including appetizer, main course, dessert, a nonalcoholic drink, tax, and a tip. Check out the following table to decipher the dollar signs:

Cost	Hotel	Restaurant
$	$175 or under	$25 or under
$$	$176–$275	$26–$40
$$$	$276–$375	$41–$60
$$$$	$376–$475	$61 and up
$$$$$	$476 and up	

✔ I divide the hotels into two categories — my personal favorites and those that don't quite make my preferred list but still get my hearty seal of approval. Don't be shy about considering these "runner-up" hotels if you can't get a room at one of my favorites or if your preferences differ from mine — the amenities that the runners-up offer and the services that each provides make all these accommodations good choices to consider as you determine where to rest your head at night.

Foolish Assumptions

As I wrote this book, I made some assumptions about you and what your needs may be as a traveler. You may be an inexperienced traveler looking for guidance when determining whether to take a trip to London and how to plan for it. You may be an experienced traveler, but you don't have a lot of time to devote to trip planning, or you don't have a lot of time to spend in London after you get there — you want expert advice on how to maximize your time and enjoy a hassle-free trip. Or you may be looking for a carefully selective guidebook, one that focuses only on the places that will give you the best or most unique experiences in London. If you fit any of these criteria, then *London For Dummies,* 4th Edition, gives you the information that you're looking for!

How This Book Is Organized

This book has six parts, plus an appendix. You can read all the parts independently — so if you want to zero in on restaurants or hotels, you can turn right to that part. Or you can read the book sequentially to find out all that you need to know about planning and visiting the City by the Thames. The parts include the following.

Part 1: Introducing London

This part introduces London and gives you some excellent reasons for going there. I give you a rundown of the best London has to offer, from hotels to historic sights, and then take you deeper into the city's culture, providing information to help you appreciate London's history, architecture, and cuisine. You can use this part to help you decide on the best time of year for your visit, and I recommend some books and movies that may whet your appetite and increase your enjoyment.

Part II: Planning Your Trip to London

This part helps take some of the wrinkles out of trip planning. First, you can get some tips on managing your money and planning a realistic budget. You can also find information on getting to London by air or by crossing over (or under) the English Channel from Europe. Included here are all the options for airlines, tips on how to get the best fare, plus the lowdown on package tours and whether they can save you money. I provide special tips for families, travelers with disabilities, seniors, and gays and lesbians. This part also covers the details that you need to take care of or consider before your trip begins — from passports to health insurance.

Part III: Settling into London

This part tells you what you need to know after you arrive. A bit of orientation is in order, including detailed information on the ways, means, and costs of getting from the airport into the city. The thumbnail sketches of London neighborhoods can help you decide where you want to stay and what areas you may want to explore. You can find everything that you need to know about getting around town — whether you travel on foot, on the public transit, or in a taxi. I explain what kind of accommodations you can expect for your money and describe London's best hotels and B&Bs. After that, I talk about the city's dining scene, provide you with an appetizing survey of London's best restaurants, and provide a list of places for quick, casual meals; simple or glamorous teas; down-to-earth fish-and-chips joints; and picnic possibilities.

Part IV: Exploring London

This part is dedicated to seeing the sights — from the absolute must-sees to lesser-known haunts — and fascinating places that are only a quick train or Tube ride away. You can find all kinds of guided tours and shopping coverage that steers you to a whole range of big stores (yes, including Harrods) and small specialty shops. I also provide four sample itineraries that maximize your sightseeing but won't leave you gasping for breath. And if you want to explore beyond London, check out my five great day trips — to Bath, Stonehenge, and more.

Part V: Living It Up after Dark: London Nightlife

This part introduces you to the performing arts, with an emphasis on London's fabulous theater scene, and all manner of after-dark entertainment possibilities. I clue you in to the best sources for finding out what's going on around town and tell you how to get tickets. I also fill you in on some of the city's best pubs, clubs, bars, and discos.

Part VI: The Part of Tens

This part allows me to squeeze in some extra people, places, and things that you may want to know about but that don't really fit in elsewhere in the book. My lists include ten famous London statues, ten special London churches, ten historic pubs, and ten important royals — past and present.

Quick Concierge

This appendix includes an A-to-Z directory of fast facts that you need to know, such as how the telephone system works, what numbers to call in an emergency, and what taxes you must pay. I also provide a list of toll-free telephone numbers and Web sites for airlines and hotel chains serving London, and tell you where to go for more information on London.

Icons Used in This Book

These five icons appear in the margins throughout this book:

 Bargain Alert is my favorite icon — and I suspect it may be yours, too. I'm not cheap, but I love to save money and find out about special deals. Every time I tell you about something that can save you money, I include the Bargain Alert icon.

 The Best of the Best icon highlights the best London has to offer in all categories — hotels, restaurants, attractions, shopping, and nightlife.

 I'm not an alarmist, so you won't find too many Heads Up icons in this book. If you see one, it means that I want you to be aware of something, such as ticket agencies claiming to sell "reduced-price tickets" or the double-tipping scam that you may encounter in a restaurant. London, you'll be pleased to know, isn't the kind of city that requires too many warning labels.

 Traveling with children? Keep your eyes peeled for the Kid Friendly icon. If the icon is in front of a hotel name, the hotel welcomes families with children and may even provide extras for kids. If it's in front of a restaurant name, the kids will enjoy the food or the atmosphere, and the staff will be welcoming to youngsters. And if the icon is in front of an attraction name, kids will (probably) enjoy something about the place.

 When was the last time you read a travel book that filled you in on local gossip, as well as all the mundane facts? For the London Tattler icon (named after the famous London newspaper, *The Tatler,* published from 1709 to 1711), I include only the most newsworthy scandals — I mean stories — to report on. I throw in these tidbits about well-known Londoners and curious bits of London lore just for the fun of it.

The Tip icon highlights useful bits of information that can save you time or enhance your London experience. A Tip alerts you to something (like a special guided tour or a way to avoid standing in long lines) that you may not otherwise consider or even know about.

Where to Go from Here

To London, of course! This book, which gives you the tools you need to make the most of your trip, is a very good place to start your journey. Because the book covers all the basics, it's an excellent guide to help you plan, anticipate, and understand exactly what you want to see and do in London. Whatever your plan, I hope that you think of me as your guide or companion on the journey. I love London. My goal is to help you have a great time while you're there.

Part I
Introducing London

"I think Philip was inspired by our trip last year touring the Great Gothic Decks of London."

In this part . . .

Are you a stranger to London? Well, now's the time to be introduced. This part helps you put a face to the place. In Chapter 1, I give a general overview of the best this great city has to offer, sketching in some details so you know what you can find there — including the newest attractions. Chapter 2 helps you understand London from a historical, architectural, and gastronomical perspective and gives you a few suggestions for books and movies that may add to your London knowledge. If you haven't decided when to go, Chapter 3 fills you in on what London offers during each season and why you find some times better than others for a visit.

Chapter 1

Discovering the Best of London

. . . .

In This Chapter

▶ Discovering London's greatest historic landmarks

▶ Exploring London's world-famous museums

▶ Tasting the best of British cuisine

▶ Enjoying London's performing arts and nightlife

▶ Experiencing the urban charms of London

. . . .

So, you're going to London. Gives you a thrill just thinking about it, right? The capital of the U.K. is one of the world's top destinations, visited year-round by millions from all corners of the globe. In fact, international travel surveys consistently rank London as one of the most popular holiday destinations in the world. After you arrive, you can make your way through one of the most historic, cultured, and exciting cities on earth. You have every reason to feel a tingle of anticipation.

This chapter gives you an at-a-glance reference to the absolute best — the best of the best — that London has to offer. In the categories that I outline, you'll find some of the things that make visiting London so much fun and so endlessly fascinating. I discuss each of these places in detail later in this book; you can find them in their indicated chapters, marked with a "Best of the Best" icon.

The Best Places to Soak Up London's History

The great historic landmarks in London never fail to stir the imagination: They've been witness to so much — from glorious triumphs to bloody tragedies — that it's almost impossible to remain unmoved when visiting them. In Chapter 11, you'll find more details on the sites listed in this section:

> ✔ An almost perceptible aura of legend pervades the **Tower of London,** which was built over 900 years ago. When visiting the Tower, you walk on a piece of ground where the great dramas and

terrors of a turbulent kingdom were played out, where Elizabeth I was held captive while still a princess, and where Sir Thomas More and Anne Boleyn (second wife of Henry VIII and mother of the future Elizabeth I) were beheaded.

✔ No less venerable is **Westminster Abbey,** a magnificent Gothic church that ranks as the most historically significant religious structure in England. Stepping into Westminster Abbey, you enter the place where England's kings and queens have been crowned since William the Conqueror claimed the throne in 1066 and where some of England's greatest figures are buried or memorialized.

✔ Most of London's most historic sites are or were Royal domains, and Royal watching is a sport almost as popular as horse racing. Okay, so you're probably not going to get invited to the Queen's Garden Party, but you can see where those famous parties take place — and stroll through the Royal staterooms — by visiting **Buckingham Palace,** the queen's London residence and a seat of today's Royal power and intrigue.

✔ If you missed the Changing of the Guard at Buckingham Palace or want another dose of that Royal pomp and pageantry, **Windsor Castle** is less than an hour away. Reputedly the queen's favorite castle, Windsor has a 900-year history that stretches back to the time of William the Conqueror. Many of the rooms that you visit today were remodeled in the time of Queen Victoria.

✔ **Hampton Court Palace** is one of the most magnificent of former Royal palaces, and you can easily get there in 30 minutes by train from Central London (or, more romantically, by taking a boat on the Thames). In addition to visiting dozens of staterooms in this 16th-century Tudor palace where Henry VIII once resided, you can enjoy the splendid gardens with their famous maze.

✔ Although you can't see the rooms where the late Princess Diana actually lived, you can get into her former home, **Kensington Palace,** situated at the western side of Kensington Gardens. In addition to the vast, visitable staterooms, this mostly 18th-century palace, where Victoria was born in 1819, houses a remarkable costume exhibit that includes Royal raiment through the ages.

✔ Occupying a spot right on the River Thames, the **Houses of Parliament** and their landmark clock tower containing Big Ben, have been a familiar sight to Londoners for nearly 150 years. In the summer, fascinating tours of this seat of power let you see the House of Commons and the House of Lords. Or you can just admire the buildings from the outside and wait for the hourly boom of Big Ben.

✔ **St. Paul's Cathedral** with its landmark dome is dear to the hearts of Londoners and is used for events of national significance. A masterpiece by the architect Sir Christopher Wren, the cathedral was built following the Great Fire that swept through London in 1666.

Pomp, ceremony, and scandal: The Royals

In London, the Royals are spied on the way movie stars are in America. The paparazzi furor lessened a bit after Princess Diana's death, but it still exists.

I never really gave much thought to royalty, except as a footnote to history, until one day several years ago. I was passing St. James's Palace just as Princess Diana and Princess Anne were being hustled into a waiting limo. There they were, two princesses, going about the mysterious routines of royalty. I saw them for maybe three seconds and stood there like a slack-jawed yokel as the limo pulled away.

From the Queen on down, the monarchy is a huge business (they actually call themselves **"The Firm"**), and you can't avoid it. Buy a London paper any day that you're there, and you can find some juicy tidbit about Prince Charles, his new wife Camilla Parker-Bowles (the Duchess of Cornwall), Prince William, Prince Andrew, Prince Harry, Princess Anne, or some other member of The Firm. (I provide a few juicy items of my own in this book with my "London Tattler" asides.)

The Best Museums

If you're a dedicated museum maven, London's selection will keep you going for days, weeks, months, even years. This city is loaded with every conceivable kind of treasure from all over the world. And, amazingly enough, entrance to all the great national museums is free. You can read more about all of London's top museums in Chapter 11:

✔ The venerable **British Museum,** with its unparalleled collection of antiquities, comes out on top — the magnificent Parthenon sculptures (formerly called the Elgin Marbles) understandably hold pride of place there, but you'll be amazed by the superlative Egyptian and Roman collections, as well as the ancient treasures found in England.

✔ The **National Gallery** houses the nation's greatest collection of British and European paintings from the 13th to the 20th centuries. Here, you find works by Italian masters, such as Leonardo da Vinci and Raphael; canvases by every great French Impressionist; a stunning Rembrandt collection; and paintings by great British artists, such as Turner and Constable.

✔ If you tire of the great Western European masterworks hanging in the National Gallery, you can walk next door to see images of pop icons like Elton John and Princess Di in the **National Portrait Gallery.** Here, you'll find a visual who's who of every famous Brit in history, captured in paint, stone, bronze, and photographs.

✔ Keen on decorative and applied arts? Then head over to the **Victoria & Albert Museum,** a linchpin in the cluster of great South

Kensington museums. The V&A, as it's called, houses wonderfully decorated period rooms, a comprehensive fashion collection, Italian Renaissance sculpture, and acres more.

✔ The other two outstanding museums in South Kensington are the **Natural History Museum** and the **Science Museum.** Animatronic dinosaurs, including a hungry T. Rex, are the cold-blooded stars in the Natural History Museum's famed dinosaur exhibit, but while you're there, check out the mind-boggling collection of gems. In the Science Museum, you come face to face with legends from the world of science and technology.

✔ London's South Bank is really buzzing with the addition of the stunning **Tate Modern.** Housed in a former power station on the river, the museum exhibits an international roster of contemporary greats.

✔ **Tate Britain** holds the world's greatest collection of British art. Wander through rooms filled with works by William Blake, Turner, Hogarth, Sir Joshua Reynolds, Constable, and all the Pre-Raphaelites.

✔ London lovers will love the **Museum of London,** probably the world's most comprehensive city museum, which features an amazing collection of Roman antiquities (the museum incorporates part of a 2,000-year-old Roman wall) and tells the fascinating story of London through the ages.

✔ You can also enjoy masterpieces in museums that were built as private palaces, such as **Spencer House,** former home of Princess Diana's family; **Apsley House,** home of the first Duke of Wellington; and **Hertford House,** home of the Wallace Collection, a national museum.

The Best of British Cuisine

Once upon a time, you could always count on getting lousy meals in London. The nation's dull, insular, uninspired cooking was the joke of Europe. That reputation began to change in the 1980s, with the influx of new cooking trends that favored foods from France and Italy. Since then, London has become a food capital (allegedly with more Michelin-starred restaurants than Paris). You can find my list of top London restaurants in Chapter 10. For a handy reference guide to English cuisine, see the Cheat Sheet at the front of this book:

✔ London is the best place to find restaurants serving inventive Modern British cuisine. Reserve a table at **Rules, The Ivy, Langan's Bistro, Veronica's, The Oratory,** or **Boxwood Café** — to name just a few — and let your taste buds do the talking.

✔ Traditionalists need not despair: All those wonderful "Old English" faves are still around — eggs, kippers, beans, and fried tomatoes for breakfast; bubble and squeak; roast beef and Yorkshire pudding;

meat pies; fish and chips; toad in the hole; cottage pie; sticky toffee pudding; and trifle. You'll find the old English comfort foods at pubs and restaurants such as **The Stockpot, Founders Arms, Simpson's-in-the-Strand, Porter's English Restaurant,** and many others.

✔ Some would say that Indian cooking is the new national cuisine of England. Well, it's certainly one of multiethnic London's faves, and Indian restaurants are often far more affordable. Like other cuisines, Indian cooking in England has been undergoing many changes. **Veeraswamy** is the oldest Indian restaurant in London, but the interior is cool and contemporary. You can also find great Indian cooking at **Mela** and **Noor Jahan.**

✔ If French cooking is your idea of heaven, you don't lack for dining options in London. Both traditional and nouvelle French restaurants remain alive and well. You may want to try the classiest of them all, **Aubergine;** other choices include **Oxo Tower Brasserie,** with its stunning river views, **Criterion Grill,** or **Brasserie St. Quentin.**

✔ And don't forget that London boasts more ethnic restaurants than anywhere else in the U.K., so almost any kind of cuisine can be on the tip of your tongue. For delectable tapas and Spanish/Moroccan food, go to **Moro.** For slurpy and superlative Japanese noodles, head for **Wagamama.** At **Ken Lo's Memories of China,** you can feast on food inspired by a Chinese master chef. For fresh New Zealand mussels and the most delicious New Zealand dessert, known as Pavlova, **Suze in Mayfair** is your best bet.

The Best Places to Shop in London

It's not just my credit cards speaking: I'm here to tell you that London is one of the world's great shopping cities — possibly the greatest. Why? The sheer variety of what's available.

Trend-setting London is to the United Kingdom what New York City is to the United States: the place where it happens first (or ultimately ends up). London is where you can put the eyeball on what's hot, British style. You see the latest hardcore **street fashions** side by side with the quintessentially traditional.

Not into new? In London, you can hunt for an old engraving, try on a cocktail dress from the '50s, paw through bric-a-brac at an outdoor market stall, or wander through the London silver vaults in your quest for a Georgian soup ladle.

For my complete rundown of London shopping, see Chapter 12:

✔ Is **Harrods** the most famous department store in the world? Quite possibly so. See for yourself if it deserves all the hype. And be sure to visit the Food Halls.

✔ **Fortnum & Mason** is the queen's London grocer, and it's probably the only store in the world where you'll see cans of soup displayed on wooden shelves along carpeted aisles. Other departments include china, crystal, leather, antiques, and stationery — plus, you can dine at the store's famous restaurants.

✔ Shopaholics hold **Oxford Street** in very high regard. Lined with major department stores like **Selfridges** and **Marks & Spencer**, and chockablock with dozens upon dozens of moderate to upscale shops, it's a rendezvous point for shoppers of all ages from all over the world. Motto: Big Names, Reasonable Prices.

✔ **Knightsbridge** is a flash-and-cash point of the highest order, home of the aforementioned Harrods, the smaller **Harvey Nichols,** and a lot of luxurious designer boutiques where real and wannabe aristocrats shop for "the season."

✔ Time and money just fly when you visit the super-chic boutiques of **Covent Garden, Bond Street,** and **King's Road** in Chelsea. In these certified shopping zones, you can find everything a super-chic fashionista could ever want.

✔ Hidden away from the hoi polloi, the 200-year-old shops on **Jermyn Street** cater to traditionalists who want the finest goods available. Many of the shops on Jermyn Street have *Royal Warrants* — that is, they're allowed to advertise that they sell to the Royal family. Look for custom-made shirts and suits, hand-tooled leather shoes, and fabulous toiletry shops, such as **Floris** and **Taylors of Old Bond Street.**

✔ What reader wouldn't be tempted by the wonderland of bookstores on **Charing Cross Road?** It's a reader's feast and a browser's paradise, with major U.K. independent bookstores like **W & G Foyle,** major U.K. chains like **Waterstone's,** and smaller specialized bookstores like **Murder One** all represented.

The Best of London's Performing Arts

London is a world capital, and that includes being a world capital of the performing arts. When the sun goes down, the curtain comes up. For a description of London's major performing arts venues, see Chapter 15:

✔ For many visitors, going to the **theater** is reason enough to go to London. When actors of the highest caliber are on the boards — as they always are in London — you don't need to think twice about going to the theater. You just go. The London theater scene is phenomenal, prices are lower than in New York, and seeing a **West End** play adds to any trip's enjoyment. Take your pick: long-running international-hit musicals, light comedies, hard-hitting dramas, new works in "fringe" venues, everything from William Shakespeare to Oscar Wilde to Neil LaBute and beyond.

✔ Opera buffs (and *buffos*) appreciate the fact that London has two major opera companies. International stars appear at the historic **Royal Opera** in Covent Garden, where operas are performed in their original languages. A few blocks away is the **English National Opera,** where every opera is sung in English by mostly British singers and the productions tend to be more adventuresome.

✔ Every night, lovers of classical music have an embarrassment of riches to choose from. London is home to two world-class symphony orchestras. The **London Symphony Orchestra** plays at the Barbican Center, where good seats cost as little as £5 ($9.25). The **Royal Philharmonic Orchestra** performs at Cadogan Hall and the Royal Albert Hall. Other renowned London or U.K. orchestras perform regularly in the city, as do renowned chamber music ensembles. A summer highlight are the Proms concerts at Royal Albert Hall, featuring an international roster of the best orchestras and soloists in the world.

✔ Dance aficionados can enjoy an evening at the **Royal Ballet** and/or the **English National Ballet,** both of which have regular London seasons. Smaller dance companies, from traditional to cutting edge, are at home in venues throughout the city.

The Best Urban Charms

London is one great city that has actually gotten better over the years. In deference to the millennium year 2000, the city dusted itself off and tarted itself up in ways that benefit residents and visitors alike. Old museums have been revamped with stunning results, such as the Great Court in the British Museum, and new museums, such as Tate Modern, have opened (see "The Best Museums," earlier in this chapter). Sleek new bridges now span the Thames, and riverside areas have seen a flurry of development. Trafalgar Square has been joined to the National Gallery, making pedestrian access a breeze rather than a chore. All in all, London has shaken off its old mantle of hidebound traditionalism, has embraced multiculturalism, and is now as high-tech as a hyperlink.

But the old fabric of London still remains and invites exploration. Despite all the improvements in public transit, London remains a city where walking is a joy that reveals no end of simple urban pleasures:

✔ London is blessed with marvelous **parks.** You may have heard of them: **Hyde Park, Kensington Gardens, St. James's Park, Green Park,** and **Regent's Park** (all described in Chapter 11). These carefully groomed havens, where you can stroll beneath stately trees, lounge on the grass, watch ducks in a pond, or admire the color of the springtime daffodils, were former Royals-only hunting grounds. Now they're part of every Londoner's life and life's blood, the green lungs of an otherwise congested city.

✔ What could be more fun than just wandering around **London's streets?** Try it. Pick a neighborhood — the City, Soho, Chelsea — then just stroll at will, taking note of the wealth of architectural styles, the curious reminders of days gone by, and the array of local sights, such as the blue, "famous-person-lived-here" plaques on house fronts. On some streets, you can almost hear the horses' hooves clopping on the cobblestones as they did up until about 1915.

✔ The **South Bank** and **Southwark** areas on the "other" side of the river have been opened up for pedestrians and show off an ancient area of London that's been completely revitalized. You can enjoy a waterside walk with city views from Westminster Bridge to Tower Bridge.

✔ The variety of **architectural styles** adds to the beauty of the city. Because the Great Fire of 1666 burned down most of medieval London, the building and house styles that you see tend to range from the sober neoclassical of the early 18th century, to the more elegantly light-hearted Regency style of the early 19th century, to the heavier and less graceful Victorian period of the mid- to late 19th century. The human scale of London streets, with their long terraces of attached brick, stone, and stucco homes built around leafy squares, gives the city a charm and character that intrigues and delights the eye. London grew from a series of villages, and you can still find that villagelike character in many London neighborhoods (for a list of those neighborhoods, see Chapter 8, and for more on London architecture, see Chapter 2).

Chapter 2

Digging Deeper into London

In This Chapter

▶ Perusing the main events in London's history

▶ Admiring London's architecture

▶ Discovering English food and beer

▶ Finding books and movies about London

*T*his chapter helps you find out more about London and deepens your experience of England. I distill the essence of London's complicated and tumultuous past so you can get a clear, quick sense of the major epochs. Then I highlight the main architectural trends, whet your appetite with a primer on English food and drink, and recommend some excellent books and movies about the capital of the U.K.

The Main Events: A Brief History of London

London's history is inextricably intertwined with the larger history of England. Endless tomes have been written on individual monarchs, colorful personalities, architectural styles, and historical epochs in English history. But I'm going to be as brief as a bikini and give you a history that covers only the bare essentials in the following sections.

Pre-history and the arrival of the Romans

Over 2,500 years ago, a Celtic tribe was living beside the River Thames in the region that would later become London.

When the Romans conquered England in A.D. 43, they suppressed or subdued the local Celts. The legendary Queen Boudicca (or Boadicea) was a Celtic warrior queen who fought back the invading Romans. You can see a statue of her on Westminster Bridge in London. The Romans brought their building and engineering skills to England and erected a 1-square-mile fort they called Londinium. This square mile eventually became the City of London, the earliest area to be developed. In the City, you can still see the remains of Roman walls and a temple where Roman soldiers worshipped a Persian god called Mithras (see Chapter 18).

Northern invaders

With the Roman Empire's breakup in A.D. 410, Jutes, Angles, and Saxons from northern Europe invaded England and formed small kingdoms. For the next 600 years or so, the Anglo-Saxon kingdoms fought off Viking raiders. The capital of England at this time was in Winchester, in the Anglo-Saxon kingdom of Wessex. Because of its strategic position on the Thames, London grew as an important center of trade.

William the Conqueror

The next major transitional period in England — and London — started in 1066, when William of Normandy (1028–1087) fought and killed Harold, the Anglo-Saxon king of England, at the Battle of Hastings. William and his French nobles took over the land, moved their power base to London, and built fortified castles — including Windsor Castle and the Tower of London (both described in Chapter 11) — that still stand today. Every monarch up to the present day claims descent from William the Conqueror and, like him, has been crowned at Westminster Cathedral (Chapter 11) in London.

Magna Carta

King John, a Plantagenet, signed the Magna Carta in 1215, granting more rights to the nobles. What about the common man and woman? As serfs and vassals in a closed, hierarchical, class-ridden society, their lot wasn't an easy one. Geoffrey Chaucer (1342–1400), who lived and worked in London, was the first writer to give us some recognizable portraits of folks who lived during the medieval period, in *The Canterbury Tales*.

Hundred Years' War

At home and abroad, war and bloodshed tore England apart for more than 300 years. The Hundred Years' War between France and England began in 1337. There was also the War of the Roses, fought between the Houses of York and Lancaster.

Tudor and Elizabethan England

Henry VIII, the Tudor king famous for taking six wives, brought about the next great shift in what had been Catholic England. In 1534, he dissolved all the monasteries and became head of the Church of England. He nabbed Hampton Court Palace (Chapter 11) from Cardinal Wolsey and made it one of his royal residences. Henry's second wife, Anne Boleyn, was beheaded at the Tower of London in 1536. Henry and Anne Boleyn's daughter, Elizabeth I, ruled during a period of relative peace, power, and prosperity. The Elizabethan period was England's Golden Age, the time when Shakespeare's plays were being performed at the Globe Theatre (Chapter 15) in London.

Civil War

In 1603, James VI of Scotland became King James I (1566–1625) of England, uniting the crowns of England and Scotland. But conflicts between monarchs and nobles were endless. Charles I (1600–1649), seeking absolute power, dissolved Parliament in 1629. He was beheaded in London after Oliver Cromwell (1599–1658) led a bitter civil war between Royalists and Parliamentarians. Cromwell's armies destroyed churches and royalist strongholds throughout the country. Cromwell was elevated to Lord Protectorate of the Realm, but by 1660 a new king, Charles II (1630–1685), was on the throne. This time, however, his powers were limited.

Fire, plague, and rebuilding

London, which had been growing steadily, was devastated by two back-to-back catastrophes, the Great Plague of 1665 and the Great Fire of 1666.

Under the brilliant architect Sir Christopher Wren (1632–1723), a new London emerged from the ashes of the Great Fire. Brick and stone replaced timber as the primary building material. Wren's masterpiece, St. Paul's Cathedral (Chapter 11), was built on the site of the old cathedral and dozens of Wren churches were erected in the City of London. England's steadily growing naval might was centered at Greenwich (Chapter 11), where Wren designed the Royal Naval College, today a UNESCO World Heritage Site.

New lines of succession

When James II (1633–1701) tried to reinstate Catholicism in England, he was deposed in 1688 and succeeded by his daughter Mary (1662–1694) and William of Orange (1650–1702), thus assuring a Protestant line of succession. William and Mary renovated and lived in Kensington Palace (Chapter 11). The children of Queen Anne (1665–1714), the next monarch, predeceased her, leaving the kingdom without an heir when Anne died. George of Hanover (1660–1727) was chosen to be the next king of England, thus ushering in the reign of the Hannoverians who preceded Victoria.

The Victorian Empire

England reached its zenith of power and prestige during the reign of Victoria (1837–1901), who ruled over an empire so vast that "the sun never set" on it. Victoria was born at Kensington Palace and moved to the grander Buckingham Palace when she was crowned in 1837. Following the death of her husband, Prince Albert of Saxe-Coburg, the queen had the Albert Memorial (Chapter 11) erected in Kensington Gardens, where it still stands.

The Industrial Revolution spawned major societal changes during this period, moving England away from its agrarian past and into a mechanized future. Charles Dickens (1812–1870) and other social reformers exposed the wretched working and living conditions in Victorian London and throughout England. After a fire, the Houses of Parliament were rebuilt and reopened in 1857. The late Victorian age was the time of Sherlock Holmes, a fictional London detective created by Arthur Conan Doyle, and Jack the Ripper, a real-life serial killer who terrorized London's East End.

England in the World Wars

England suffered terrible losses during World War I (1914–1918) but emerged victorious. During World War II, from the fall of France in 1940 until the United States entered the war in 1941, England stood alone against Hitler. Winston Churchill (1874–1965), the country's prime minister during the war years, frequently held cabinet meetings in a secret warren of underground rooms called the Cabinet War Rooms (Chapter 11), which are preserved just as they were during his tenure. With strictly rationed food, mandatory blackouts, and terrible bombing raids that destroyed whole sections of London and killed tens of thousands of civilians, life in wartime London had a profound effect on its citizens. Shortages continued for many years afterward.

The welfare state

A major societal shift occurred in 1945 when the Labour Party began to dismantle the empire and introduced the welfare state. Under the National Health System, every citizen in the United Kingdom can receive free health care (the quality of the care is another story). It wasn't until Margaret Thatcher and the Tory Party came into power during the 1980s that England began privatizing formerly state-run agencies, such as the railroad (with what some say are disastrous results).

Queen Elizabeth II

Queen Elizabeth II ascended the throne in 1952. The fairy-tale wedding of her son Prince Charles to Lady Diana Spencer at St. Paul's Cathedral in 1981 was the last high point for the House of Windsor (which changed its name from the German Saxe-Coburg during World War II). Charles and Diana's subsequent divorce seemed to unleash a floodgate of Royal scandals, with the result that the popularity of the British monarchy is at an all-time low. Following her divorce, Diana (1961–1997) lived at Kensington Palace (Chapter 11), where grieving Londoners left a sea of floral tributes following her death in a car crash.

In 2002, Queen Elizabeth II celebrated her 50th anniversary on the throne.

London at the millennium

In anticipation of the year 2000, London went on an all-out public-relations blitz to show the world that "Rule, Britannia" had become "Cool Britannia." The giant Millennium Dome was a giant fiasco, but the British Airways London Eye (Chapter 11), an enormous observation wheel, remains one of London's most popular attractions.

Mayor Ken

In 2000, Ken Livingstone, former Labour Member of Parliament, was elected to the newly created post of Mayor of London (not to be confused with the Lord Mayor of London, an ancient ceremonial position in the City of London). During his controversial tenure — he was re-elected for a second term in 2004 — Mayor Ken has instituted major changes in the public-transportation system, including the introduction of London's *congestion charge,* a fee that any driver entering Central London during specific hours of the day must pay.

New Labour

In 2001, Tony Blair was elected to a second term as prime minister, and New Labour, with its centrist approach, was firmly in control of the government. But in the 2005 elections, the party lost one-third of its seats as voters expressed their discontent with Blair's continuing support of the war in Iraq.

Recent Royal events

In 2005, Prince Charles, the heir to the British throne, finally married his long-time mistress, Camilla Parker-Bowles, in a ceremony that his mother, Queen Elizabeth, did not attend. The wedding was something of a highlight — if you can call it that — in a Royal year full of royal embarrassments. For one thing, it became apparent that the British public did not want Camilla to be their eventual queen. She will, though, unless the governments of England and 15 Commonwealth nations change the law. In the meantime, the pre-queen is addressed as Her Royal Highness the Duchess of Cornwall.

Earlier in the year, the British public was shocked to see a picture of Prince Harry, youngest son of Charles and his first wife, Princess Diana, wearing a World War II German desert uniform with a Nazi swastika on his armband. It seems that the party-boy prince didn't realize that wearing such an outfit to a costume party would offend. Harry was forced to apologize — just about the time a former art teacher charged that she painted the paintings Harry submitted for his art exams at Eton. Not a minute too soon, Harry was packed off to Sandhurst Military Academy for the usual pseudo-military training of a Royal.

Then news erupted that Prince Andrew and Prince Edward, younger sons of Queen Elizabeth, were in essence receiving royal housing benefits that made them look like welfare cheats. Andrew (Fergie's ex), whose wealth is estimated at £13 million ($24 million), has paid no annual rent for a 30-room lodge in Windsor Great Park. Edward, with a fortune estimated at £9 million ($17 million), pays £10,000 ($18,500) a year for a 57-room house set on 87 acres in Bagshot Park. No wonder the Queen was so eager to claim that the monarchy — which costs every citizen of the U.K. about $1.12 a year — provided the British taxpayers with real value for their money. It must have warmed the heart of every hardworking commoner.

Terrorist bombings

In July 2005, one day after exultant Londoners learned that their city had been chosen to host the 2012 Olympics, terrorists detonated bombs in the London Underground and on a double-decker bus, killing 56 people and wounding hundreds more. Londoners stood together and carried on, showing the world that they would not be cowed by acts of violence. A second bombing attempt a week later failed but had tragic consequences when police shot and killed a man suspected of terrorism.

Building Blocks: An Overview of English Architecture

The period in which a building was constructed (or reconstructed), is found in its architectural and decorative details. In a country like England, where the age of buildings can span a thousand-year period (a few Anglo-Saxon churches are even older than that), many different styles evolved. The architectural periods are often named for the monarch or royal family reigning at the time. You can enhance your enjoyment of London's abundance of historic buildings if you know a few key features of the different styles. Keep in mind that little remains from before the Great Fire of 1666, which destroyed most of London — Westminster Abbey and the Tower of London are the two most notable exceptions. The following list gives you a brief primer in English architectural history from Norman to Victorian times:

- ✔ **Norman (1066–1189):** Round arches, barrel vaults, and highly decorated archways characterize this period's Romanesque style.

- ✔ **Early English Gothic (1189–1272):** The squat, bulky buildings of the Norman period gave way to the taller, lighter buildings constructed in this style.

- ✔ **Decorated Gothic (1272–1377):** Buildings in this style have large windows, *tracery* (ornamental work with branching lines), and heavily decorated gables and arches.

- ✔ **Perpendicular Gothic (1377–1483):** Large *buttresses* (exterior side supports) allowed churches to have larger windows than ever before. Tracery was more elaborate than in previous Gothic buildings, the four-centered arch appeared, and *fan vaulting* (a decorative form of vaulting in which the structural ribs spread upward and outward along the ceiling like the rays of a fan) was perfected.

- ✔ **Tudor (1485–1553):** During this period, buildings evolved from Gothic to Renaissance styles. Large houses and palaces were built with a new material: brick. England has many half-timbered Tudor and Elizabethan domestic and commercial buildings. This method of construction used brick and plaster between visible wooden timbers.

✔ **Elizabethan (1553–1603):** The Renaissance brought a revival of classical features, such as columns, *cornices* (prominent rooflines with brackets and other details), and *pediments* (decorative triangular features over doorways and windows). The many large houses and palaces of this period were built in an E or H shape and contained long galleries, grand staircases, and carved chimneys.

✔ **Jacobean (1603–1625):** In England, Inigo Jones used the symmetrical, classically inspired Palladian style that arrived from Italy. Buildings in this style incorporate elements from ancient Greece and Rome.

✔ **Stuart (1625–1688):** Elegant classical features, such as columns, cornices, and pediments, are typical of this period, in which Sir Christopher Wren was the preeminent architect.

✔ **Queen Anne (1689–1714):** Buildings from the English baroque period mix heavy ornamentation with classical simplicity.

✔ **Georgian and Regency (1714–1830):** During these periods, elegant terraced houses were built; many examples survive in Brighton and Bath. Form and proportion were important elements; interior decoration inspired by Chinese motifs became fashionable.

✔ **Victorian (1830–1901):** A whole range of antique styles emerged — everything from Gothic and Greek Revival to pseudo-Egyptian and Elizabethan. Hundreds of English churches were renovated during the Victorian era.

Dining English Style, from Traditional to Modern

Not so very long ago, English cooking was the joke of Europe. That began to change in the 1980s, with the influx of new cooking trends that favored foods from France and Italy. Since then, London has become a major food capital, and the rest of the country has raised its food consciousness considerably. London is the best place to find restaurants serving inventive Modern British and ethnic cuisines of every sort. Spicy Indian cooking is England's second "national" cuisine. You can find scores of Indian and other ethnic restaurants throughout the city.

But traditionalists in search of all those wonderful Old English faves won't be at a loss. It's true that many Londoners now opt for a latte and a muffin at Starbucks for their breakfast, but you can still find places that serve a good greasy "fry-up" with eggs, kippers, beans, and fried tomatoes. And old comfort foods like bubble and squeak (mashed potatoes mixed with cabbage) and bangers and mash (sausages with mashed potatoes) are still around, too. The great traditional "roasts" are served at places like Simpson's-in-the-Strand, where a server at your table will slice your roast beef or roast lamb and dish up your Yorkshire pudding. When traditional, nonfancy English dishes are done well, they're super-satisfying and delicious.

Other traditional dishes loved by Londoners include meat and fish pies, *shepherd's pie* (ground beef topped with mashed potatoes and baked), and fish and chips. And for dessert? At restaurants like Porter's English Restaurant, you can still find *sticky toffee pudding* (sponge cake smothered in warm butterscotch sauce), *spotted dick* (steamed, raisin-filled sponge cake covered with custard), and *trifle* (sherry-soaked sponge cake layered with raspberry preserves, covered with custard sauce, and topped with whipped cream).

While you're in London, you can also look forward to the world of afternoon tea. Teas can be as simple or fancy as you want — nothing more than a cup of tea and a pastry in a patisserie, or an elaborate affair with scones, clotted or whipped cream, preserves, cakes, and sandwiches served in a luxurious hotel lobby.

See Chapter 10 for a list of my recommended London restaurants and spots for tea, and check out the Cheat Sheet at the front of this book for a glossary of English food terms.

Visiting the Local Pub

The pub (short for public house) is an English institution. London is awash with historic pubs where you can sit all evening with a pint of ale, bitter, stout, or cider, and soak up the local color. You can even do a *pub crawl,* walking (upright) from pub to pub and sampling the diverse brews on tap. Although you can get a hard drink at both bars and pubs, when you're in a pub, you're better off confining yourself to beer.

A beer primer: Are you bitter or stout?

Most of the pubs in London and throughout the United Kingdom are *tied* to a particular brewery and sell only that brewery's beers (you see the name of the brewery on the sign outside). Independent pubs can sell more brands than a tied pub. Either way, you still have to choose from what may seem like a bewildering variety. The colorful names of individual brews don't provide much help — you can only wonder what Pigswill, Dogs Bollocks, Hobgoblin, Old Thumper, Pommies Revenge, or Boondoggle taste like. Depending on all sorts of factors — the water, the hops, the fermentation technique, and so on — the brewery crafts the taste of any beer, whether on draught or in a bottle. You can get a few U.S. and international brands, but imports are more expensive than the homegrown products.

When ordering beer in a pub, specify the type, the brand, and the amount (pint or half-pint) you want. Asking the bartender to recommend something based on your taste preferences is perfectly okay. Just remember that most English beer is served at room temperature. The following brief descriptions of beer will come in handy in a pub:

✔ **Bitter** is what most locals drink. It's a clear, yellowish, traditional beer with a strong flavor of hops. *Real ale* is a bitter that's still fermenting ("alive") when it arrives from the brewery; it's pumped and served immediately.

✔ **Ale** isn't as strong as bitter and has a slightly sweeter taste. You can order *light* or *pale ale* in a bottle; *export ale* is a stronger variety.

✔ **Lager,** when chilled, is probably the closest you can come to an American-style beer. Lager is available in bottles or on draught.

✔ **Shandy** is equal parts bitter and lemonade (sometimes limeade or ginger beer); it's for those who like a sweet beverage that's only partially beer-like in taste.

✔ **Stout** is a dark, rich, creamy version of ale. Guinness is the most popular brand. A *black and tan* is half lager and half stout.

 Parliament has instituted the strict hours that most pubs adhere to: Monday through Saturday from 11 a.m. to 11 p.m. and Sunday from noon to 10:30 p.m. Americans, take note: You don't have to (and aren't expected to) pay a service charge in a pub, and you *never* tip the bartender; the best you can do is offer to buy him or her a drink — an acceptable practice in England. Ten minutes before closing, a bell rings, signaling that the time has come to order your last round.

Background Check: Finding London on Page and Screen

Has any country produced as many great and enduring writers as England has? It's impossible in a brief survey to even scratch the surface. The wonderful thing about London — at least, if you love literature — is that it figures in so many great works. All over the city, you encounter blue plaques on the front of buildings identifying what famous person lived there and when. Many of those famous residents were writers. Here are a few of my recommendations:

✔ *History of Britain,* **by Simon Schama:** This highly readable three-volume history of Britain by the noted historian accompanied a program of the same name on the BBC History Channel.

✔ *London,* **by Edward Rutherfurd:** London is the main character in this fascinating historical novel that follows the fates of families and fortunes over 2,000 years.

- ✔ *London: A Biography,* **by Peter Ackroyd:** When you get Peter Ackroyd going, you can't shut him up — so it's a good thing he has such fascinating material to so endlessly talk about.

- ✔ *Oliver Twist,* **by Charles Dickens:** Dickens set many of his novels in London; one of the most enduring is this story of a boy in Victorian London who survives an almost comically nightmarish world of orphanages and crime.

- ✔ *The Cazalet Chronicles,* **by Elizabeth Jane Howard:** The four novels *(The Light Years, Marking Time, Confusion, Casting Off)* in this compulsively readable series chronicle the life of a middle-class family in London and on the south coast of England between the two world wars.

- ✔ *The Line of Beauty,* **by Alan Hollinghurst:** A Booker Prize–winner, Hollinghurst's brilliantly realized novel sketches a portrait of London during the Thatcher years.

- ✔ *Mrs. Dalloway,* **by Virginia Woolf:** One of Woolf's most accessible and popular books, this novel, written in 1925, takes place during one day in the life of Clarissa Dalloway, an exemplary London hostess, as she prepares for a big party.

- ✔ *Saturday,* **by Ian McEwan:** McEwan's latest novel evokes the life of an upper-middle-class family in London today.

- ✔ *Watching the English,* **by Kate Fox:** An entertaining pop-psych book that deals humorously with the "hidden rules" of English behavior as it relates to class and "Englishness."

- ✔ *White Teeth,* **by Zadie Smith:** The profoundly hilarious story of two immigrant families in North London.

Other useful travel guides

Frommer's Born to Shop London (Wiley) is a must for travelers eager to cruise London with a credit card. This book covers everything from top department stores to tiny boutiques and helps you find the best, brightest, most unique, and most quintessentially English goods.

Frommer's London from $95 a Day (Wiley) is a time-honored bible for budget-minded travelers who want to visit London but don't want to spend a fortune doing so. I can heartily recommend this book because I wrote it.

Frommer's Memorable Walks in London (Wiley) is an excellent resource for those travelers who want to explore the city in depth and on foot. Each walking tour provides clear, easy-to-follow directions and describes important sights along the way.

The Brits are great filmmakers and beat Hollywood cold when it comes to honesty in acting, re-creation of period detail, and human-scale cinematic storytelling. If you've ever watched British television, you know how completely it differs from American TV. The characters actually look like human beings and inhabit recognizable worlds.

Over the past 30 years or so, television imports from the BBC and other U.K. television producers have been shown in the U.S. on *Masterpiece Theatre, Mystery!,* and cable channels, winning legions of fans. Many of these popular series are set in London. They're available on video and DVD:

- ✔ *Absolutely Fabulous:* Hilarious, over-the-top sitcom about two over-the-top women in '90s London.

- ✔ *Cazalet Chronicles:* The fortunes of a middle-class London family between the world wars.

- ✔ *The Forsythe Saga:* An Edwardian tale of family intrigue.

- ✔ *Upstairs, Downstairs:* Rich London family above, servants below, and stories from both sides at the turn of the 20th century.

For a cinematic look at London, you may want to check out the following films:

- ✔ *About a Boy:* You can see a lot of London shots in this well-told story of a narcissistic Londoner (Hugh Grant) who becomes surrogate father to an awkward boy.

- ✔ *Closer:* A chic anomie pervades the lives of four rather unlikable characters whose lives intersect in London today.

- ✔ *Darling:* A John Schlesinger film from way back in the 1960s, starring a young Vanessa Redgrave as a fashionable victim of fashion.

- ✔ *Georgy Girl:* London in the swingin' '60s with a young, overweight Lynn Redgrave playing a good-hearted oaf living with a cold-hearted bitch (Charlotte Rampling).

- ✔ *Love, Actually:* Londoners dealing with contemporary life and romance.

- ✔ *Midnight Lace:* Doris Day is menaced in London circa 1960 by a mysterious caller; you can see many shots of the city.

- ✔ *Notting Hill:* A romantic comedy starring Hugh Grant as the owner of a London bookstore and Julia Roberts as an American movie star (quite a stretch).

- ✔ *Sunday, Blood Sunday:* An adult drama from the early '70s starring Glenda Jackson and Peter Finch as Londoners in love with the same guy.

Chapter 3

Deciding When to Go

In This Chapter

▶ Going in season or out

▶ Knowing how rainy it really is

▶ Checking a calendar of special events

*L*ondon is one of those cities that's popular year-round. So popular, in fact, that according to VisitBritain (formerly the British Tourist Authority), more than 13.4 *million* tourists from around the globe visited London in 2004 (the last year for which figures are available), with nearly 2.8 million of them from the States (17 percent of the total).

Arriving in London at any time of year without advance hotel reservations is not a wise idea. If you plan to visit between April and mid-October, making hotel reservations is essential. Although you can find agencies in London that can help you find a hotel or a B&B in peak season (see Chapter 9), you never know quite what you're getting or where it will be. In Chapter 9, you can find descriptions of my recommended London hotels.

Revealing the Secrets of the Seasons

London weather is what you might call "changeable." Predicting what the weather will be like in any given season is difficult. England is an island, after all, and the seas surrounding it, as well as its northerly location, determine its weather patterns. In general, however, the climate is fairly mild year-round, rarely dipping below freezing or rising above 80°F/27°C (at least for extended periods). Table 3-1 gives you an idea of London's temperature and rainfall variations.

Table 3-1	London's Average Temperatures and Rainfall	
Month	*Temp (°F/°C)*	*Rainfall (in.)*
January	40/4	2.1
February	40/4	1.6

Month	Temp (°F/°C)	Rainfall (in.)
March	44/7	1.5
April	49/9	1.5
May	55/13	1.8
June	61/16	1.8
July	64/18	2.2
August	64/18	2.3
September	59/15	1.9
October	52/11	2.2
November	46/8	2.5
December	42/6	1.9

London can be drizzly, muggy, dry and hot, or clammy. It can also be "glorious, with clear skies and gentle breezes, or bone-chilling cold. Some days you get a bit of everything: rain, spots of sun, drizzle, clearing, and more rain. But whatever the weather, whatever the season, London is well worth seeing. The following sections let you know what's happening in London, season by season, so that you can pick the best time to go for you.

Abloom in the spring

London is at its green, blooming best in April and May. Highlights of the season include the following:

✔ The great London parks and gardens and the surrounding countryside are at their peak of lushness. The Chelsea Flower Show is the quintessential spring event.

✔ Airfares are lower than in summer.

✔ The sky stays light well into the evening.

But keep in mind these springtime pitfalls:

✔ During the half-term school holidays in late February and for three weeks around Easter, visitors pour into London. As a result, the major attractions have longer lines (*queues* in Britspeak), and you may have a harder time finding a hotel room.

✔ The weather is always unpredictable.

- ✔ Public transportation is reduced during holiday periods.

- ✔ Many museums, stores, and restaurants close on Good Friday, Easter, and Easter Monday.

Summer fun in the sun

Notoriously chilly London becomes irresistible under the sun. Many tourists flock to London throughout the summer to enjoy the fine weather, but that fine weather can turn into rain or a fine, gray drizzle in July and August. The crowds descend in summer for several reasons:

- ✔ Everyone moves outdoors at the slightest hint of fine weather, and London buzzes with alfresco theaters, concerts, and festivals (see Chapter 15).

- ✔ The evenings are deliciously long and often cool, even if the day has been hot.

- ✔ The evening stays light until 10 p.m. or even later.

But keep in mind:

- ✔ If you believe the weather statistics, July and August are the months of highest rainfall in London, so skies can stay gray and cloudy.

- ✔ Occasional summer heat waves can drive the mercury into the 80s and even 90s, making July and August hot and muggy. Many businesses and budget-class hotels don't have air-conditioning.

- ✔ Aggravated by London's soot, plus gas and diesel fumes, a hot spell can lead to excessive air pollution.

- ✔ Most overseas visitors (30 percent of travelers) converge on the city from July to September. Lines for major attractions can be interminably long.

- ✔ Centrally located hotels are more difficult to come by, and their high-season rates apply.

- ✔ Booking your hotel in advance is essential during this time of year (see Chapter 9).

Chock-full of culture in the fall

The golden glow of autumn casts a lovely spell over London. The air is crisp, and the setting sun gives old stone buildings and church spires a mellow patina. Fall is my favorite time of year to be in London, and I can think of only one disadvantage to counteract the many advantages, which include the following:

- ✔ After mid-September, fewer tourists are around, so the city feels less crowded and you encounter more Londoners than visitors.

✔ With the drop in tourism, hotel rates and airfares may go down as well.

✔ London's cultural calendar springs to life.

✔ Although you may experience rain at this time of year, you're just as likely to encounter what Americans call "Indian summer."

One thing to look out for: Like every season in England, autumn can bring rain.

Wonderful in winter

Londoners love to be cozy, and there's no better time for coziness than winter. Although most overseas visitors to London arrive during the warmer months, the number of visitors from *within* the United Kingdom is highest between January and March. What do they know that you should know? Consider the points that make winter wonderful:

✔ London in winter is a bargain. London's off-season is November 1 to December 12 and December 25 to March 14. Winter off-season rates for airfares and hotels can sometimes be astonishingly low — airline package deals don't get any cheaper (see Chapter 5). At these times, hotel prices can drop by as much as 20 percent. If you arrive after the Christmas holidays, you can also take advantage of London's famous post-Christmas sales (more on these sales in Chapter 12).

✔ Although the winter winds may blow, nothing in London stops — in fact, everything gets busier. The arts — theater, opera, concerts, and gallery shows — are in full swing.

✔ London develops a lovely buzz during the Christmas season: The stores are decorated, lights are lit, carols are sung, special holiday pantomimes are performed, and the giant Norwegian spruce goes up in Trafalgar Square.

Naturally, visiting London in the winter has its downside. Consider these points:

✔ Although the Yuletide holidays are always jolly, they also add up to another peak tourist season from mid-December to Christmas. You know what that means: bigger crowds and higher prices. The city is virtually shut down on December 25 and 26 and January 1. Stores, museums, and other attractions close, and public transportation is severely curtailed. On December 26 (Boxing Day), you may have problems finding any kind of open restaurant.

✔ Wintertime London may be gray and wet for weeks on end; by mid-winter, the skies get dark by about 3:30 p.m. The English usually keep their thermostats set about 10° lower than Americans do. Rather than turn up the heat, the English don their *woollies* (long underwear). You should do the same — or be prepared for a chronic case of goose pimples.

Perusing a Calendar of Events

London hums with festivals and special events of all kinds, some harking back to centuries past. Before you leave for London, write or call **VisitBritain** (see the Quick Concierge, at the end of this book, for addresses and phone numbers) and request a copy of its monthly *London Planner,* which lists major events, including theater and the performing arts.

January

In January, the **London Parade,** also called the New Year's Day Parade, features marching bands, floats, and the Lord Mayor of Westminster in a procession from Parliament Square to Berkeley Square. Call ☎ 020/8566-8586 for more details. January 1 (noon to 3 p.m.).

February

Late January or early February brings the **Chinese New Year,** marked by colorful street celebrations on and around Gerrard and Lisle streets in Soho's Chinatown. Call ☎ 020/7851-6686 for more information. Date varies.

March

St. Patrick's Day is a big to-do in London, which has the third-largest Irish population, after Dublin and New York. There are no parades, but you see lots of general merriment. March 17.

The **BADA Antiques & Art Fair** (formerly known as the Chelsea Antiques Fair) draws antiques lovers to Duke of York Square in London's Chelsea for six days. For more information, call ☎ 020/7589-6108. Mid-March.

April

At the **Oxford and Cambridge Boat Race** between Putney Bridge and Mortlake Bridge, rowing eights from the two famous universities compete for the Beefeater Cup. The Hammersmith Mall makes a good viewing spot. Last Thursday in March or first Saturday in April. (Check the local press for the exact date or go to www.theboatrace.org.)

The **London Marathon** was first held in 1981 and has become one of the most popular sporting events in the city. Over 46,000 runners — men and women, champion athletes and first-timers — take part. The 26.2-mile race begins in Greenwich, winds its way past the Tower of London and along the Thames, and finishes in the Mall in front of Buckingham Palace, one of the best viewing spots. For more information, call ☎ 020/7902-0199 or check out www.london-marathon.co.uk. Mid-April.

May

The **Football Association FA Cup Final** is held at Wembley Stadium. Remember that *football* in the United Kingdom is what people in the United States call *soccer,* and tickets are difficult to obtain given the sport's popularity. Contact the Box Office, Wembley Stadium Ltd., Wembley HA9 0DW (☎ **020/8795-9000;** www.thefa.com). Mid-May.

One of London's most famous spring events, the **Chelsea Flower Show,** held on the grounds of the Chelsea Royal Hospital, draws tens of thousands of visitors from around the world. You probably want to order tickets at least two months in advance; in the States, you can order them from Keith Prowse at ☎ **800-669-7469** or 212-398-4175. For more information, contact the Royal Horticultural Society, Vincent Square, London SW1P 2PE (☎ **020/7834-4333;** www.rhs.org.uk). Third week in May.

June

The juried **Royal Academy Summer Exhibition** presents more than 1,000 works of art by living artists from all over the United Kingdom. For more information, call the Royal Academy at ☎ **020/7300-8000** (www.royal academy.org.uk). Early June through July.

April 21 is Queen Elizabeth's birthday, but her birthday parade, **Trooping the Colour,** takes place in mid-June. The Horse Guards celebrate "Ma'am's" birthday in Whitehall with an equestrian display full of pomp and ceremony. For free tickets, send a self-addressed envelope and International Reply Coupon (or U.K. stamps) from January 1 to February 28 to Brigade Major Horseguards, Whitehall, London SW1A 5BJ (☎ **020/7414-2279**). Mid-June.

The most prestigious horseracing event in England is **Royal Ascot,** held at the Ascot Racecourse (near Windsor in Berkshire, about 30 miles from London) in the presence of the Royal family. For information, call ☎ **01344/876-876** or visit the Web site at www.ascot.co.uk. You can order tickets online for this event. *Note:* In 2005, Royal Ascot was held in York while the Ascot racecourse was being refurbished; it will do so again in 2006. Mid- to late June.

Kenwood, a lovely estate at the top of Hampstead Heath, is the pastoral setting for the **Kenwood Lakeside Concerts,** a summer season of Saturday night, open-air concerts. For more information, call ☎ **020/7413-1443** (www.picnicconcerts.com). Mid-June to early September.

The world's top tennis players whack their rackets at the **Wimbledon Lawn Tennis Championships,** held at Wimbledon Stadium. Getting a ticket to this prestigious event is complicated. From August 1 to December 31, you can apply to enter the public lottery for next year's tickets by sending a self-addressed stamped envelope to All England Lawn Tennis Club, P.O. Box 98, Church Rd., Wimbledon, London SW19

5AE. For more information, call ☎ **020/8944-1066** or 020/8946-2244 (recorded information), or visit www.wimbledon.com. Late June to early July.

The **City of London Festival** presents a series of classical concerts, poetry readings, and theater in historic churches and buildings, including St. Paul's Cathedral and the Tower of London. For more information, call ☎ **020/7377-0540** or visit www.colf.org. Late June to mid-July.

July

Pride in the Park, the U.K.'s largest gay and lesbian event, begins with a march and parade from Hyde Park to Parliament Square, followed by live music, dancing, and fun. For more information, visit www.pridelondon.org. First Saturday in July.

The **Henley Royal Regatta,** one of England's premiere sporting and social events, is a championship rowing event with a long tradition. The regatta takes place on the Thames just downstream from Henley, an Oxfordshire town 35 miles west of London. For more information, call ☎ **01491/572-153** or go to www.hrr.co.uk. First week in July.

The **Hampton Court Flower Show,** held on the palace grounds in East Molesey, Surrey (part of Greater London), shows off one of the loveliest gardens in England. For more information, call Hampton Court Palace ☎ **0870/752-7777** or go to www.hrp.org.uk. Second week in July.

In July, you can see the much-loved **BBC Henry Wood Promenade Concerts.** Known as the Proms, this series of classical and popular concerts is held at the Royal Albert Hall. To book by credit card, call the box office at ☎ **020/7589-8212** or visit www.royalalberthall.com or www.bbc.co.uk/proms. Mid-July to mid-September.

August

Buckingham Palace opens to the public August through September (see Chapter 11).

During the **Notting Hill Carnival,** steel bands, dancing, and Caribbean fun take over in the streets of Notting Hill (Portobello Road, Ladbroke Grove, and All Saints Road). This enormous street fair is one of Europe's largest. For more information, check magazine listings or call ☎ **020/8964-0544.** Bank Holiday weekend in August (last Mon in Aug).

September

The **Thames Festival** celebrates the mighty river, with giant illuminated floats. For more information, call ☎ **020/7401-2255** or visit www.thamesfestival.org. Mid-September.

During the **London Open House Weekend,** over 400 buildings usually closed to visitors open their doors for free. For more information, call ☎ 09001/600-061 or visit www.londonopenhouse.org. Third weekend in September.

October

The **Chelsea Crafts Fair** is the largest such fair in Europe. Contact the Crafts Council for details at ☎ 020/7806-2512 (www.craftscouncil.org.uk). Last two weeks of October.

November

Although based at the National Film Theatre on the South Bank, the **London Film Festival** presents screenings all over town. Call ☎ 020/7815-1433 in November for recorded daily updates on what's showing where; or check the Web site www.lff.org.uk. Late October to early November.

On **Guy Fawkes Night,** bonfires and fireworks commemorate Guy Fawkes's failure to blow up King James I and Parliament in 1605. Check the weekly entertainment magazine *Time Out* (www.timeout.com/london) for locations. November 5.

For the **State Opening of Parliament,** the queen in all her finery sets out from Buckingham Palace in her royal coach and heads to Westminster, where she reads out the government's program for the coming year. (This event is televised.) For more information, call ☎ 020/7291-4272 or visit www.parliament.uk. First week in November.

The new Lord Mayor of London goes on the grand **Lord Mayor's Procession** through the City from Guildhall to the Royal Courts of Justice in his gilded coach; festivities include a carnival in Paternoster Square and fireworks on the Thames. For more information, call ☎ 020/7606-3030 or visit www.lordmayorsshow.org. Early November.

December

Christmas lights go on in Oxford Street, Regent Street, Covent Garden, and Bond Street. Mid-November to early December.

The **lighting ceremony** of the huge Norway spruce Christmas tree in Trafalgar Square officially announces the holiday season. First Thursday in December.

Trafalgar Square is the focus of **New Year's Eve** celebrations. December 31.

Part II
Planning Your Trip to London

The 5th Wave   By Rich Tennant

"Welcome to our nonstop flight to London. Will you be sitting among the heather with us sir, or back in the moors?"

In this part . . .

This part is all about the nitty-gritty of trip planning. Chapter 4 helps you manage the money side of your trip — that means planning a workable budget based on real prices in London and converting your money into English pounds and pence when you get there; in this chapter, you can find everything you need to know about using ATMs and credit cards in London, as well as how to save money by following some useful cost-cutting tips. Chapter 5 covers all your transportation options for getting to London by plane, train, or boat, and it gives you some tips on escorted tours and money-saving package tours. Chapter 6 is full of special trip-planning advice for London-bound families, seniors, travelers with disabilities, and gays and lesbians. Chapter 7 goes through some last-minute details, such as getting a passport, dealing with travel and medical insurance, staying healthy while you travel, and more.

Chapter 4

Managing Your Money

● ●

In This Chapter

▶ Planning a realistic budget for your trip

▶ Pricing things in London

▶ Uncovering hidden expenses

▶ Using credit cards, traveler's checks, and ATMs

▶ Considering money-saving tips

● ●

*O*kay, you want to go to London. You're excited and eager to pack, but can you really afford it? At this point, a financial reality check is in order. London is an expensive city, no two ways about it. But adding everything up, your trip to London can cost Americans about the same as a trip to New York, San Francisco, or Los Angeles.

Planning Your Budget

You can easily budget for your London trip, but holding down costs while you're there may be another matter. (The city's shopping and dining is so enticing — and expensive.) Table 4-1 gives you an idea of some basic costs.

Table 4-1	What Things Cost in London
Item	*Cost in U.S. $*
Transportation from Heathrow to Central London by Underground	$7
Transportation from Gatwick to Central London by train	$22
One-way Underground fare within Central London	$3.70
Double room at the Cadogan Hotel	$453–$630
Double room at Hazlitt's 1718	$374–$471

(continued)

Table 4-1 *(continued)*

Item	Cost in U.S. $
Double room with breakfast at St. Margaret's Hotel	$170–$180
Double room at Luna Simone Hotel	$111–$148
Double room at Astons Apartments (self-catering)	$166
Pub meal for one at The Museum Tavern	$12
Lunch for one at Oxo Tower Brasserie, excluding wine	$40
Set-price dinner for one at Rules, excluding wine	$45
Dinner for one at The Oratory, excluding wine	$25
Pizza at Gourmet Pizza Company	$12
Afternoon tea for one at the Lanesborough	$47
Coffee and cake at Pâtisserie Valerie	$9
Pint of beer at a pub	$4.50
Admission to the Tower of London (adult/child)	$27/$18
Admission to Madame Tussaud's (adult/child)	$32/$31
Theater ticket	$10–$100

Note: As a general rule, except for tips in restaurants (12.5 to 15 percent) and to cab drivers (15 percent), you don't have to tip excessively in London. But if you stay in an expensive hotel, give the porters who carry your bags £1 ($1.85) per bag and doormen who hail you cabs £1 ($1.85) per cab.

Transportation

You may think a trip to London is prohibitively expensive because of the transatlantic flight, but you can often find bargain airfares to this popular spot that are cheaper than what you'd pay when flying within the U.S. For more-specific information on airlines and airfares, see Chapter 5.

I have some other good news that can save you a bundle: You don't need to rent a car in London. (If you want to rent a car to explore the areas surrounding London, see Chapter 14.) The London Underground (called the **Tube**) is fast, convenient, and easy to use. Special reduced-price transportation passes, called Visitor Travelcards, make getting around the city relatively inexpensive. You also can get reduced-price day and multiday passes at any Tube station after you arrive; see Chapter 8 for more information.

Lodging

The cost of accommodations takes the biggest bite from your budget. Fortunately, because you have to book your rooms well in advance, you'll know this expense before you leave on vacation.

Chapter 8 gives you an idea of London neighborhoods and their suitability as your home base. Chapter 9 tells you what you can expect for your money, shows you how to get the best rate, and gives you my recommended list of top-notch B&Bs and hotels in all price ranges and locations.

Rates vary considerably from B&B to B&B and from hotel to hotel, so I can't really give you a reliable average. For the recommendations in this book, however, the rates are *generally* £95 and under ($175 and under) for an inexpensive property, £96 to £149 ($176–$275) for a moderately priced one, £150 to £203 ($276–$375) for an expensive one, and £204 to £257 ($376–$475) for a very expensive one. After that, you hit the stratosphere of £258-plus ($475-plus) for a luxury B&B or hotel. Keep in mind that many midrange London hotels and all B&Bs include at least a continental breakfast as part of the room rate, so you can save a few pounds there.

The rack rates that I list are not the lowest, special-deal rates that you'll probably be able to find on the hotel's Web site. You may be surprised at how much you can save from the "official" price of a room.

Britain's version of a sales tax is called the **value-added tax (VAT).** Brace yourself: The tax amounts to 17.5 percent. The VAT is part of the reason that prices in London are so high. The tax is added to the total price of consumer goods (the price on the tag already includes it) and to hotel and restaurant bills. The VAT is not a hidden expense, but not all quoted room rates, especially in the luxury tier, include the tax. Be sure to ask whether your quoted room rate includes the VAT. (In the hotel listings in Chapter 9, I tell you if the rate doesn't include the VAT.)

Dining

In recent years, London has emerged as one of the great food capitals of the world, known for the variety of its restaurants and the overall quality of the cooking. I can't fudge the fact that eating at the top restaurants costs you a pretty penny, but there are also countless pubs, local restaurants, cafes, and sandwich shops where you can dine cheaply and well. In addition, many of the best London restaurants offer two- and three-course fixed-price meals that can be real bargains.

If you eat lunch and dinner at the moderately priced restaurants that I recommend in Chapter 10, expect to pay £25 to £50 ($46–$93) per person per day for meals, not including alcoholic drinks (assuming that breakfast is included in your hotel rate). If you have breakfast at a cafe rather than your hotel and are content with coffee and a roll, expect to pay about £3.50 to £6 ($6.50–$11). Depending on the restaurant, an old-fashioned English breakfast with eggs, bacon or sausage, toast, and tea or coffee can run anywhere from £6 to £12 ($11–$22). Likewise, a simple afternoon tea at a cafe sets you back about £5 to £7 ($9.25–$13), but a lavish high tea at one of the great London hotels may run £25 ($46) or more. For specifics on restaurants, inexpensive cafes and sandwich shops, and places for afternoon tea, see Chapter 10.

On top of the VAT, a few restaurants add a service charge of 12.5 to 15 percent to your bill. If they do, the menu has to state this policy. This charge amounts to mandatory tipping, so if your credit-card charge receipt comes back with a space for you to add a tip, put a line through it.

Sightseeing

Your budget for admission fees depends, of course, on what you want to see. Some of London's top attractions are pricey indeed: an adult ticket to the **Tower of London** costs £15 ($28). But many other outstanding attractions in London — the **British Museum, National Gallery, National Portrait Gallery, Tate Britain,** and **Tate Modern** — are completely free. So are the **Natural History Museum,** the **Science Museum,** and the **Victoria & Albert Museum.** Strolling through London's great parks or viewing **Buckingham Palace** (okay, from the outside) and the **Changing of the Guard** won't cost you a penny. From my suggestions in Chapter 11, you can weed out the must-see sights from the maybes.

Keep in mind that if you're a senior or a student, you can often get a reduced-price admission, and most attractions offer reduced family rates that are good for two adults and two children.

Shopping and nightlife

Shopping and entertainment are the most flexible parts of your budget. You don't have to buy anything at all, and you can hit the sack right after dinner instead of seeing a play or dancing at a club. You know what you want. Flip through the shopping options in Chapter 12 and the entertainment and nightlife venues in Chapters 15 and 16. If anything strikes you as something you can't do without, budget accordingly. (Keep in mind that a pint in a pub sets you back about £2.50/$4.65, whereas a theater, opera, or concert ticket can cost anywhere from £5/$9.25 to over £100/$185.)

If you're not a resident of the European Union, you can get a VAT refund on purchases made in the United Kingdom. (This refund doesn't include hotels and restaurants.) See Chapter 12 for details.

Cutting Costs — But Not the Fun

 Throughout this book, Bargain Alert icons highlight money-saving tips and/or great deals. Check out some additional cost-cutting strategies:

✔ **Go in the off-season.** If you can travel at nonpeak times (Oct to mid-Dec or Jan–Mar), you'll find hotel prices can be as much as 20 percent less than during peak months.

✔ **Travel on off days of the week.** Airfares vary, depending on the day of the week. If you can travel on a Tuesday, Wednesday, or Thursday, you may find cheaper flights to London. See if you can obtain a cheaper rate by flying on a different day.

✔ **Try a package tour.** For popular destinations like London, you can make just one call to a travel agent or packager to book airfare, hotel, ground transportation, and even some sightseeing. You pay much less than if you tried to put the trip together yourself (see Chapter 5).

✔ **Reserve a hotel room with a kitchen.** In London, these rooms are called *self-catering units.* With your own kitchen, you can do at least some of your own cooking. You may not feel as if you're on vacation if you do your own cooking and wash your own dishes, but you'll save money by not eating in restaurants two or three times a day. Parents traveling with small children may find this strategy particularly useful.

✔ **Always ask for discount rates.** Membership in AAA, frequent-flier programs, trade unions, AARP, or other groups may qualify you for discounts on plane tickets, hotel rooms, or even meals.

✔ **Always ask if any special room rates are in effect.** Hotels are eager to fill their rooms and now offer many different rates, including "promotional" rates and lower weekend rates. In most cases, you'll find these special rates on the hotel's Web site.

✔ **Ask if your kids can stay in your room with you.** A room with two double beds usually doesn't cost any more than one with a queen-size bed. And many hotels won't charge you the additional person rate if that person is pint-sized and related to you. Even if you have to pay a few pounds extra for a rollaway bed, you save hundreds by not taking two rooms.

✔ **Use pay phones rather than the phone in your hotel room.** You may find the telephone in your hotel room convenient, but avoid using it if you're on a budget. A local call that costs 20p (35¢) at a phone booth may cost you £1 ($1.85) or more from your hotel room. If you plan to make a number of calls during your trip, get a phone card (see the details about using phones in the Quick Concierge, at the end of this book) and use pay phones.

✔ **Try expensive restaurants at lunch rather than dinner.** At most top restaurants, prices at lunch are considerably lower than those at dinner, and the menu often includes many of the dinnertime specialties. Also, look for the fixed-price menus.

✔ **Walk a lot.** London is large but completely walkable. A good pair of walking shoes can save you money on taxis and other local transportation. As a bonus, you get to know the city and its inhabitants more intimately, and you can explore at a slower pace.

✔ **Skip the souvenirs.** Your photographs and your memories should be the best mementos of your trip. If you're worried about your budget, do without the T-shirts, key chains, and other trinkets.

Handling Money

Money makes the world go around, but dealing with an unfamiliar currency can make your head spin. In London, you pay for things in pounds and pence, meaning you have to convert your own currency into British pounds sterling. When it comes to carrying money in London, should you bring traveler's checks or use ATMs? What about paying with credit cards? In the following sections, I tell you what you need to know about each option.

Ways to save in London and beyond

Visitor Travelcards are not sold in England. In the United States and Canada, you can buy a voucher for a Visitor Travelcard before you leave home. After you arrive in England, you exchange the voucher for the appropriate card at any London Underground ticket window. Two kinds of cards are available: the *All Zone* and the *Central Zone,* which is good for everything in Central London, the area that contains the city's main attractions (see Chapter 11). Both cards allow unlimited travel on the Tube and bus and are available in three-, four-, or seven-day increments. Prices for the Central Zone card are $24 for adults and $10 for children for three days; $29 for adults and $11 for children for four days; and $36 for adults and $14 for children for seven days. You can buy Visitor Travelcards by contacting a travel agent, by calling RailEurope at ☎ 877-272-7245 in the U.S. or 800-361-7245 in Canada, or by going to www.raileurope.com.

If you plan to travel around England by train, consider getting a BritRail pass. You must buy these passes before you arrive (they aren't sold in England), but they offer considerable savings over individual fares. You have many options: a choice of either first or standard class, senior passes for those over 60, travel-time periods from four consecutive days to one month, and Flexipasses allowing you to travel a certain number of days within a set time period. You can also get a London Plus card that's great for day trips around London. You can find information on the various rail passes in Chapter 14.

Making sense of pounds and pence

Britain's unit of currency is the **pound sterling (£)**. Every pound is divided into **100 pence (p)**. Coins come in denominations of 1p, 2p, 5p, 10p, 20p, 50p, £1, and £2. Notes are available in £5, £10, £20, and £50 denominations. As with any unfamiliar currency, British pounds and pence take a bit of getting used to. The coins have different sizes, shapes, and weights according to value. Each bank note denomination has its own color and bears a likeness of the queen. All currency is drawn on the Bank of England.

Exchanging your currency

The **exchange rate,** which fluctuates every day, is the rate that you get when you use your own currency to buy pounds sterling (see Table 4-2). In general, **$1 = 54p (or £1 = $1.85)**. These are *approximate* figures, but they're what I use for all prices in this guide (rounded to the nearest dollar if the amount is over $10). When you're about to leave on your trip, check with your bank or look in the newspaper to find out the current rate.

Table 4-2		Simple Currency Conversions	
U.S. Dollars to U.K. Pounds		*U.K. Pounds to U.S. Dollars*	
U.S.	*U.K.*	*U.K.*	*U.S.*
$1	54p	£1	$1.85
$5	£2.70	£2	$3.70
$10	£5.40	£5	$9.25
$20	£10.80	£10	$18.50
$50	£27	£20	$37
$100	£54	£50	$92.50

Changing money (either cash or traveler's checks) into a foreign currency makes many people nervous, especially if they're changing money for the first time. You needn't fear. Changing money is a simple operation. Just remember that every time you exchange money, you need to show your passport.

If you want some pounds in hand when you arrive at the airport in London, you can exchange currency before you leave home at many banks and at foreign exchange services at international airports. Otherwise, you can easily change cash or traveler's checks in London by using a currency-exchange service called a **bureau de change.** These services are available at major London airports, any branch of a major bank, all major rail and Underground stations in Central London, post offices, and American Express or Thomas Cook offices. Unless located in a bank or travel agency, most *bureaux de change* are open daily from 8 a.m. to 9 p.m.

Every major bank in Central London has a foreign currency window where you can exchange traveler's checks or cash. Weekday hours for banks are generally 9:30 a.m. to 4:30 p.m., but a few open earlier. Some banks (usually based in busy shopping areas) are open all day Saturday. All banks are closed on public holidays, but many branches have 24-hour banking lobbies with ATMs or ATMs on the street outside. Banks in London and throughout the U.K. include **Barclays Bank** (☎ 020/7441-3200), **HSBC** (☎ 0845/743-4445), **Midland Bank** (☎ 020/7599-3232), and **NatWest** (☎ 020/7395-5500). These banking companies all have branches throughout the city.

Reputable London banks and *bureaux de change* exchange money at a competitive rate but charge a commission (typically 1 to 3 percent of the total transaction) and a small additional fee (usually £3/$5.55). Some currency-exchange services now guarantee you the same exchange rate when you return pounds for dollars.

All U.K. *bureaux de change* and other money-changing establishments are required to display exchange rates and full details of any fees and rates of commission with clarity and equal prominence. Rates must be displayed at or near the entrance to the premises. Rates fluctuate from place to place, and so do fees, so shopping around sometimes pays.

Steer clear of *bureaux de change* that offer good exchange rates but charge a heavy commission (up to 8 percent). You find them in major tourist sections of London (some are open 24 hours). Some hotels also cash traveler's checks, but their commission is often considerably higher than at a bank or *bureau de change*. Before exchanging your money, always check to see the exchange rate, how much commission you'll have to pay, and whether additional fees apply.

You can avoid paying a second commission fee by using American Express traveler's checks and cashing them at an **American Express** office. The main office is in London at 6 Haymarket, SW1 (☎ 020/7930-4411; Tube: Piccadilly). Its foreign exchange bureau is open Monday through Friday from 9 a.m. to 5:30 p.m., on Saturday from 9 a.m. to 6 p.m., and on Sunday from 10 a.m. to 5 p.m. For the addresses of other American Express offices in London, see the Quick Concierge, at the end of this book.

Using ATMs and carrying cash

The easiest and best way to get cash away from home is from an ATM (automated teller machine). You'll find ATMs, or *cashpoints* as they're sometimes called in England, all over London. The **Cirrus** (☎ 800/424-7787; www.mastercard.com) and **PLUS** (☎ 800/843-7587; www.visa.com) networks span the globe; look at the back of your bank card to see which network you're on, then call or check online for ATM locations in

London. Be sure that you know your personal identification number (PIN) before you leave home and find out your daily withdrawal limit before you depart. Some banks will allow you to withdraw cash only from your checking account, not from your savings. Also keep in mind that many banks impose a fee every time that you use your card at a different bank's ATM, and that fee may cost more for international transactions (up to $5 or more) than for domestic ones (where it rarely goes over $1.50). On top of this fee from your bank, the bank from which you withdraw cash may charge its own fee. For international withdrawal fees, ask your bank.

 Citibank customers who use ATMs at **Citibank International** (☎ 020/ 7234-5678) — with branches at 332 Oxford St., W1 (Tube: Marble Arch), and 336 Strand, WC2 (Tube: Charing Cross) — pay no transaction fee.

Charging ahead with credit cards

Credit cards are a safe way to carry money: They also provide a convenient record of all your expenses, and they generally offer relatively good exchange rates. You can also withdraw cash advances from your credit cards at banks or ATMs, provided you know your PIN. If you've forgotten yours, or didn't even know you had one, call the number on the back of your credit card and ask the bank to send it to you. It usually takes five to seven business days to arrive by mail, though some banks will provide the number over the phone if you tell them your mother's maiden name or some other personal information.

Keep in mind that when you use your credit card abroad, most banks assess a 2 percent fee above the 1 percent fee that Visa, MasterCard, and American Express charge for currency conversion on credit charges. But credit cards still may be the smart way to go when you factor in things like exorbitant ATM fees and higher traveler's check exchange rates (and service fees).

 Some credit card companies recommend that you notify them of any impending trip abroad so that they don't become suspicious when you use the card numerous times in a foreign destination and block your charges. Even if you don't call your credit card company in advance, you can always call the card's toll-free emergency number if a charge is refused — a good reason to carry the phone number with you. But perhaps the most important lesson here is to carry more than one card with you on your trip; a card may not work for any number of reasons, so having a backup is the smart way to go.

Toting traveler's checks

These days, traveler's checks are less necessary because most cities have 24-hour ATMs that allow you to withdraw cash as needed. However, keep in mind that you'll likely be charged an ATM withdrawal fee if the bank isn't your own, so if you're withdrawing money every day, you may want to go with traveler's checks — provided that you don't mind showing identification every time you want to cash one.

You can get traveler's checks at almost any bank. **American Express** offers denominations of $20, $50, $100, $500, and (for cardholders only) $1,000. You pay a service charge ranging from 1 to 4 percent. You can also get American Express traveler's checks over the phone by calling ☎ 800/221-7282; Amex gold and platinum cardholders who use this number are exempt from the 1 percent fee.

Visa offers traveler's checks at Citibank locations nationwide, as well as at several other banks. The service charge ranges between 1.5 percent and 2 percent; checks come in denominations of $20, $50, $100, $500, and $1,000. Call ☎ 800/732-1322 for information. AAA members can obtain Visa checks without a fee at most AAA offices or by calling ☎ 866/339-3378. **MasterCard** also offers traveler's checks. Call ☎ 800/223-9920 for a location near you.

 If you choose to carry traveler's checks, be sure to keep a record of their serial numbers separate from your checks in the event that they are stolen or lost. You'll get a refund faster if you know the numbers.

 Never pay for hotels, meals, or purchases with traveler's checks denominated in any currency other than British pounds. You get a bad exchange rate if you try to use them as cash.

Dealing with a Lost or Stolen Wallet

Be sure to contact all of your credit-card companies the minute you discover your wallet has been lost or stolen and file a report with the police. In London, call ☎ 192 for directory assistance, free from public pay phones, to find out the precinct nearest you. Your credit card company or insurer may require a police report number or record of the loss. Most credit card companies have an emergency toll-free number to call if your card is lost or stolen; they may be able to wire you a cash advance immediately or deliver an emergency credit card in a day or two. Call the following emergency numbers in the U.K.:

- ✔ **American Express:** ☎ 01273/696-933

- ✔ **MasterCard:** ☎ 01702/362-988

- ✔ **Visa:** ☎ 01604/230-230

If you need emergency cash over the weekend when all banks and American Express offices are closed, you can have money wired to you via **Western Union** (☎ 0800/833-833 in the U.K.; www.westernunion.co.uk).

Identity theft or fraud are potential complications of losing your wallet, especially if you've lost your driver's license along with your cash and credit cards. Notify the major credit-reporting bureaus immediately; placing a fraud alert on your records may protect you against liability for criminal activity. The three major U.S. credit-reporting agencies are

Equifax (☎ 800/766-0008; www.equifax.com), **Experian** (☎ 888/
397-3742; www.experian.com), and **TransUnion** (☎ 800/680-7289;
www.transunion.com). Finally, if you lose all forms of photo ID, call
your airline and explain the situation; they may let you board the plane
if you have a copy of your passport or birth certificate and a copy of the
police report that you've filed.

If you follow four basic rules, you can minimize the risk of a crime happening to you:

- ✔ Don't keep your wallet in your back pocket or in your backpack, but do keep it out of sight.

- ✔ Don't leave your purse, briefcase, backpack, or coat unattended in any public place.

- ✔ Ladies: Don't hang your purse over the back of your chair in crowded or outdoor cafes or restaurants.

- ✔ Don't flash your money or credit cards around.

Earning their keep: Royal expenses

In 2005, in an attempt to prove how cheap royalty is, Buckingham Palace said the
queen costs U.K. taxpayers the equivalent of 61p ($1.15) per person per year. That
amount adds up to the yearly total of £36.8 million ($68 million) which the queen
receives in public money to carry out her duties and maintain her palaces. But that
figure doesn't include the unknown but rising cost of security or the ceremonial duties
of the armed services.

Does the House of Windsor earn its keep? According to published reports, members
of the royal family carried out 2,900 official engagements in 2004. The royals spent
some £514,000 ($950,900) on garden parties, £432,000 ($799,200) on food and kitchens,
and £6,000 ($11,100) on wines and beverages. Travel costs included £2.2 million ($4 million) on helicopters, £812,000 ($1.5 million) on civilian air travel, £534,000 ($987,900) with
the RAF, and £782,000 ($1.4 million) on the Royal Train.

Chapter 5

Getting to London

● ●

In This Chapter

▶ Evaluating the benefits of using a travel agent
▶ Planning the trip on your own
▶ Traveling by plane, train, or ferry
▶ Deciding whether to travel on your own or take an escorted tour
▶ Discovering the advantages of package tours

● ●

*N*ow that you've decided to visit London, you'll need to find a way to get there. In this chapter, I discuss your options for direct, non-stop flights and give you some ideas on how you can save money on your flight (and your hotel). What are the pros and cons of taking an escorted tour? You can find answers to your basic travel questions in this chapter.

Flying to London

London's airports are among the busiest in the world, with direct or connecting flights from all over the globe. Finding a flight won't be difficult, choosing one from the many that are offered may require some research and comparison shopping for the lowest fare.

Finding out which airlines fly there

Most regularly scheduled international flights from the United States, Canada, Australia, and New Zealand arrive at London's Heathrow and Gatwick airports. Flights from the Continent land at Heathrow, Gatwick, Stansted, or London City. Luton, the smallest of London's five airports, is a destination for charter flights from the Continent.

Here's a brief description of each of the London airports, who flies to them, and how to travel from them to Central London (see the Quick Concierge, at the end of this book, for the contact information of the airlines in this list):

   ✔ **Heathrow,** the main international airport, is 15 miles west of Central London. It's served by **Air Canada** (Canadian flights from Calgary, Montreal, Ottawa, St. John's, Toronto, and Vancouver);

Air New Zealand (Australian flights from Sydney; New Zealand flights from Auckland); **American** (U.S. flights from Boston, Chicago, Los Angeles, Miami, and New York); **British Airways** (U.S. flights from Boston, Chicago, Detroit, Los Angeles, Miami, Newark, New York JFK, Philadelphia, San Francisco, Seattle, and Washington Dulles; Australian flights from Brisbane, Melbourne, Perth, and Sydney; New Zealand flights from Auckland); **Continental** (U.S. flights from Los Angeles, Newark, New York JFK, San Francisco, and Washington Dulles); **Icelandair** (U.S. flights from Baltimore, Boston, Minneapolis/ St. Paul, and New York JFK); **Qantas** (Australian flights from Melbourne, Perth, and Sydney; New Zealand flights from Auckland); **United** (U.S. flights from Boston, Chicago, Los Angeles, Newark, New York JFK, San Francisco, and Washington Dulles); and **Virgin Atlantic** (U.S. flights from Chicago, Newark, New York JFK, San Francisco, and Washington Dulles). For information on getting into London from Heathrow, see Chapter 8.

✔ **Gatwick** is a smaller airport about 25 miles south of London. It's served by **American** (U.S. flights from Boston, Dallas/Ft. Worth, and Raleigh/Durham); **British Airways** (U.S. flights from Atlanta, Baltimore, Charlotte, Dallas/Ft. Worth, Denver, Houston, Miami, New York JFK, Orlando, Phoenix, and Tampa); **Continental** (U.S. flights from Boston, Cleveland, Houston, Miami, Newark, and Orlando); **Delta** (U.S. flights from Atlanta and Cincinnati); **Northwest** (U.S. flights from Detroit and Minneapolis/St. Paul); **Qantas** (Australian flights from Sydney); and **Virgin Atlantic** (U.S. flights from Boston, Las Vegas, Miami, Newark, Orlando, and San Francisco). For information on getting into London from Gatwick, see Chapter 8.

✔ **Stansted,** 50 miles northeast of London, handles national and European flights. The Stansted Sky Train to Liverpool Street Station takes 45 minutes and costs £13 ($24).

✔ **London City,** only 6 miles east of Central London, services European destinations. A bus charges £5 ($9.25) per person to take passengers on the 25-minute trip from the airport to Liverpool Street Station.

✔ **Luton,** 28 miles northwest of London, services mostly charter flights. You can travel by train from the airport to King's Cross Station for £9.50 ($18); the trip takes about an hour.

Getting the best deal on your airfare

Competition among the major U.S. airlines is unlike that of any other industry. Every airline offers virtually the same product (basically, a coach seat is a coach seat is a . . .), yet prices can vary by hundreds of dollars.

Business travelers who need the flexibility to buy their tickets at the last minute and change their itineraries at a moment's notice — and who want to get home before the weekend — pay the premium rate, known as the *full fare*. But if you can book your ticket far in advance, stay over Saturday night, and travel midweek (Tues, Wed, or Thurs), you can qualify for the least expensive price — usually a fraction of the full fare. On most flights, even the shortest hops within the United States, the full fare costs close to $1,000 or more, but a 7- or 14-day advance-purchase ticket may cost less than half of that amount. Obviously, planning ahead pays.

The airlines also periodically hold sales, in which they lower the prices on their most popular routes. These fares have advance-purchase requirements and date-of-travel restrictions, but you can't beat the prices. As you plan your vacation, keep your eyes open for these sales, which tend to take place in seasons of low travel volume — in England, that's basically October through March. You almost never see a sale around the peak summer vacation months of July and August, or around Thanksgiving or Christmas, when many people fly, regardless of the fare they have to pay.

Consolidators, also known as bucket shops, are great sources for international tickets, although they usually can't beat the Internet on fares within North America. Start by looking in Sunday newspaper travel sections; U.S. travelers should focus on the *New York Times, Los Angeles Times,* and *Miami Herald.*

Bucket-shop tickets are usually nonrefundable or rigged with stiff cancellation penalties, often as high as 50 to 75 percent of the ticket price, and some put you on charter airlines with questionable safety records.

Several reliable consolidators are worldwide and available on the Net, and most of them offer flights to London. **STA Travel** (☎ 800/781-4040; www.statravel.com), the world's leader in student travel, offers good fares for travelers of all ages. **ELTExpress** (☎ 800/872-8800; www.flights.com) started in Europe and has excellent fares worldwide, but particularly to that continent. Flights.com also has "local" Web sites in 12 countries. **FlyCheap** (☎ 800/FLY-CHEAP; www.1800flycheap.com) is owned by package-holiday megalith MyTravel and has especially good access to fares for international destinations. **Air Tickets Direct** (☎ 800/778-3447; www.airticketsdirect.com) is based in Montreal and leverages the currently weak Canadian dollar for low fares.

Booking your flight online

The "big three" online travel agencies, **Expedia** (www.expedia.com), **Travelocity** (www.travelocity.com), and **Orbitz** (www.orbitz.com), sell most of the air tickets bought on the Internet. (Canadian travelers should try www.expedia.ca and www.travelocity.ca; U.K. residents can go for expedia.co.uk and opodo.co.uk.) Each agency has different business deals with the airlines and may offer different fares on the same flights, so shopping around is wise. Expedia and Travelocity will also send you an **e-mail notification** when a cheap fare becomes available to your favorite destination. Of the smaller travel-agency Web sites, **SideStep** (www.sidestep.com) receives good reviews from users. It's a browser add-on that purports to search over 100 sites at once.

Great **last-minute deals** are available through free weekly e-mail services provided directly by the airlines. Most of these deals are announced on Tuesday or Wednesday and must be purchased online. Most are only valid for travel that weekend, but some (such as Southwest's) can be booked weeks or months in advance. Sign up for weekly e-mail alerts at airline Web sites or check mega-sites that compile comprehensive lists of last-minute specials, such as **Smarter Living** (smarterliving.com). For last-minute trips, www.site59.com in the U.S. and www.lastminute. com in Europe often have better deals than the major-label sites.

If you're willing to give up some control over your flight details, use an opaque fare service like **Priceline** (www.priceline.com) or **Hotwire** (www.hotwire.com). Both services offer rock-bottom prices in exchange for travel on a "mystery airline" at a mysterious time of day, often with a mysterious change of planes en route. The mystery airlines are all major, well-known carriers — and the possibility of being sent from Philadelphia to Chicago via Tampa is remote. But your chances of getting a 6 a.m. or 11 p.m. flight are pretty high. Hotwire tells you flight prices before you buy; Priceline usually has better deals than Hotwire, but you have to play their "name our price" game. *Note:* In 2004, Priceline added non-opaque service to its roster. You now have the option to pick exact flights, times, and airlines from a list of offers — or opt to bid on opaque fares as before.

Great last-minute deals are also available directly from the airlines themselves through a free e-mail service called *E-savers.* Each week, the airline sends you a list of discounted flights, usually leaving the upcoming Friday or Saturday and returning the following Monday or Tuesday. You can sign up for all the major airlines at one time by logging on to **Smarter Living** (www.smarterliving.com), or you can go to each individual airline's Web site. Airline sites also offer schedules, flight booking, and information on late-breaking bargains.

Arriving by Other Means

If you're traveling to London from another destination in Europe, you don't have to fly to get there. Train and car ferries and high-speed hovercrafts cross the English Channel throughout the year from ports in France, Holland, and Belgium. And the Eurostar high-speed train zips beneath the channel through the *Chunnel,* a tunnel beneath the English Channel.

Taking the train

London has several train stations, and the one you arrive at depends on your point of departure from the Continent. The three-hour Eurostar service connecting Paris and Brussels to London via the Chunnel arrives at Waterloo International Station. Trains from Amsterdam arrive at Liverpool Street Station. Other London train stations include Euston, King's Cross, Paddington, and Victoria stations.

The trains in England and the rest of the United Kingdom are separate from those in continental Europe, so a Eurail pass isn't valid in the U.K. If you're going to travel within England or the rest of the United Kingdom, check out the various BritRail passes available (see Chapter 7 for more information).

Several types of Eurostar fares are available. Senior fares for those over 60 and youth fares for those under 26 can cut the price of a first-class fare by 20 percent or more. The same reductions apply for passengers traveling with validated Eurail and BritRail passes. To check out current and special promotional fares for Eurostar, visit RailEurope's Web site at www.raileurope.com.

Riding a ferry or hovercraft

Crossing times for the car, train, and passenger ferries that regularly crisscross the English Channel can be anywhere from 90 minutes to 5 hours, depending on the point of departure. Various *hovercrafts* (high-speed ferries with propellers that lift them off the surface of the water) skim over the water in as little as half an hour. Frequent train service to London is available from all the channel ports. The following is a list of the major ferry and hovercraft companies:

✔ **Hoverspeed UK Limited** (☎ **0870/5240-241** in the U.K.; www.hover speed.co.uk) operates hovercrafts that zip across the channel between Calais and Dover in 35 minutes; the SuperseaCats (jet-propelled catamarans) run between Newhaven and Dieppe in 55 minutes.

✔ **P&O European Ferries** (☎ **561/563-2856** in the U.S. or **0870/ 242-4999** in the U.K.; www.poportsmouth.com) offers daily ferry/ car crossings between Cherbourg and Portsmouth (crossing time is five hours) and Le Havre and Portsmouth (five and a half hours).

✔ **P&O Stena Line** (☎ **0870/5980333** in the U.K.; www.poferries.com) operates ferries between Calais and Dover (crossing time is 75 minutes).

✔ **Sea France Limited** (☎ **01304/212-696** in the U.K.; www.seafrance. co.uk) runs ferries between Dover and Calais (crossing time is 90 minutes).

Joining an Escorted Tour

You may be one of the many people who love escorted tours. The tour company takes care of all the details and tells you what to expect at each leg of your journey. You know your costs up front and don't get many surprises. Escorted tours can take you to the maximum number of sights in the minimum amount of time with the least amount of hassle.

If you decide to go with an escorted tour, I strongly recommend purchasing travel insurance, especially if the tour operator asks you to pay up front. But don't buy insurance from the tour operator! If the tour operator doesn't fulfill its obligation to provide you with the vacation you paid for, there's no reason to think that it'll fulfill its insurance obligations either. Get travel insurance through an independent agency. (You can find out more about the ins and outs of travel insurance in Chapter 7.)

When choosing an escorted tour, along with finding out whether you have to put down a deposit and when final payment is due, ask a few simple questions before you buy:

✔ **What is the cancellation policy?** Can they cancel the trip if they don't get enough people? How late can you cancel if you're unable to go? Do you get a refund if you cancel? If they cancel?

✔ **How jam-packed is the schedule?** Does the tour schedule try to fit 25 hours into a 24-hour day, or does it give you ample time to relax or shop? If getting up at 7 a.m. every day and not returning to your hotel until 6 or 7 p.m. sounds like a grind, certain escorted tours may not be for you.

✔ **How large is the group?** The smaller the group, the less time you spend waiting for people to get on and off the bus. Tour operators may be evasive about this, because they may not know the exact size of the group until everybody has made reservations, but they should be able to give you a rough estimate.

✔ **Is there a minimum group size?** Some tours have a minimum group size, and they may cancel the tour if they don't book enough people. If a quota exists, find out what it is and how close they are to reaching it. Again, tour operators may be evasive in their answers, but the information may help you select a tour that's sure to happen.

✔ **What exactly is included?** Don't assume anything. You may have to pay to get yourself to and from the airport. A box lunch may be included in an excursion, but drinks may be extra. Beer may be included, but not wine. How much flexibility do you have? Can you opt out of certain activities, or does the bus leave once a day, with no exceptions? Are all your meals planned in advance? Can you choose your entree at dinner, or does everybody get the same chicken cutlet?

Here are a few companies that offer escorted tours to London and the rest of England (with prices per person, based on double occupancy):

✔ **Globus and Cosmos** (www.globusandcosmos.com) are well-known budget tour companies working in partnership. Current offerings include a five-day/three-night tour of London starting at $1,372, airfare included.

✔ **Maupintour** (www.maupintour.com) has an eight-day garden tour
   that includes two nights in London; admission to the Chelsea
   Flower Show; trips to the great gardens at Sissinghurst, Stourhead,
   and Blenheim Palace; plus excursions to Bath and Oxford. Prices
   start at $3,479, airfare not included. They also have an eight-day
   Christmas in London tour that includes side trips to the Cotswolds
   and Leeds Castle; prices start at $2,959, airfare not included.

✔ **Trafalgar Tours** (www.trafalgartours.com) provides tours to
   London and the rest of the U.K. Prices for the Week in London tour
   start at an amazingly low $675, airfare not included.

Choosing a Package Tour

For a lot of destinations, package tours can be a smart way to go. In
many cases, a package tour that includes airfare, hotel, and transportation to and from the airport costs less than the hotel alone on a tour that
you book yourself. That's because packages are sold in bulk to tour
operators, who resell them to the public.

Package tours vary greatly in what they provide. Some offer a better
class of hotels than others; others provide the same hotels for lower
prices. Some book flights on scheduled airlines; others sell charters. In
some packages, your choice of accommodations and travel days may be
limited. Some let you choose between escorted vacations and independent vacations; others allow you to add on a few excursions or escorted
day trips (also at discounted prices).

To find package tours, check out the travel section of your local Sunday
newspaper or the ads in the back of national travel magazines, such as
Travel + Leisure, National Geographic Traveler, and *Condé Nast Traveler.*
Liberty Travel (call ☎ 888/271-1584 to find the store nearest you;
www.libertytravel.com) is one of the biggest packagers in the
Northeast and usually boasts a full-page ad in Sunday papers.

Another good source of package deals is the airlines themselves. Most
major airlines offer air/land packages. Several big **online travel agencies** —
Expedia, Travelocity, Orbitz, Site59, and Lastminute.com — also do a
brisk business in packages.

Locating package tours

Information about package tours is available from a variety of sources.
Here are a few companies that offer packages to England:

✔ **British Travel International** (☎ 800/327-6097; www.british
   travel.com) is a good source for discount packages.

✔ **Liberty Travel** (☎ 888/271-1584; www.libertytravel.com), one
   of the biggest packagers in the northeastern United States, offers
   reasonably priced packages.

✔ **Trailfinders** (www.trailfinders.com), another good source for discount packages, has several offices in Australia: Brisbane (☎ 07/3229-0887), Cairns (☎ 07/4041-1199), Melbourne (☎ 03/9600-3022), Perth (☎ 08/9226-1222), and Sydney (☎ 02/9247-7666).

Checking out airline and hotel packages

Airlines are good sources for package tours, especially to London, because they package their flights together with accommodations. The following airlines offer packages to London:

✔ **American Airlines Vacations** (☎ 800/321-2121; www.aavacations.com)

✔ **British Airways Holidays** (☎ 800/247-9297; www.britishairways.com/holiday)

✔ **Continental Airlines Vacations** (☎ 800/525-0280; www.continental.com)

✔ **Northwest Airlines World Vacations** (☎ 800/800-1504; www.nwaworldvacations.com)

✔ **United Airlines Vacations** (☎ 800/328-6877; www.unitedvacations.com)

✔ **Virgin Atlantic Vacations** (☎ 888/937-8474; www.virgin.com/vacations)

Chapter 6

Catering to Special Needs or Interests

In This Chapter

▶ Visiting London with children
▶ Getting discounts and special tours for seniors
▶ Locating wheelchair-accessible attractions
▶ Finding lesbian- and gay-friendly communities and special events

*M*any of today's travelers have special interests or needs. Parents may want to take their children along on trips. Seniors may like to take advantage of discounts or tours designed especially for them. People with disabilities may need to ensure that sites on their itineraries offer wheelchair access. And gays and lesbians may want to know about welcoming places and events. In response to these needs, this chapter offers advice and resources.

Traveling with the Brood: Advice for Families

Traveling with children, from toddlers to teens, is a challenge — no doubt about it. Bringing the brood can put a strain on the budget and influence your choices of activities and hotels. But in the end, isn't sharing your experiences as a family great?

 Look for the Kid Friendly icon as you flip through this book. I use it to highlight hotels, restaurants, and attractions that are particularly family friendly. Zeroing in on these places can help you plan your trip more quickly and easily.

In addition, the following resources can help you plan your trip:

✔ **About Family Travel** (3555 S. Pacific Hwy., Medford, OR 97501; ☎ 541/535-5411; www.about-family-travel.com) can tailor a tour specifically for families traveling to London. Its services include arranging airfares, hotel rooms, transportation, and theater tickets, as well as providing tips on sights and destinations.

✓ **Familyhostel** (☎ 800/733-9753; www.learn.unh.edu/family hostel) takes the whole family, including kids ages 8 to 15, on moderately priced learning vacations, including England.

✓ **Family Travel Forum** (www.familytravelforum.com) is a comprehensive site that offers customized trip planning.

Admission prices for most London attractions are generally reduced for children 5 to 16 years old. Children under 5 almost always get in for free. If you're traveling with one or two children, always check to see whether the attraction offers a money-saving family ticket, which considerably reduces the admission price for a group of two adults and two children.

Locating family-friendly accommodations and restaurants

Most hotels can happily accommodate your family if you reserve your rooms in advance and make the staff aware that you're traveling with kids. The establishment may bring in an extra cot or let you share a larger room; these types of arrangements are common. Smaller bed-and-breakfasts (B&Bs) may present problems, such as cramped rooms and shared toilet facilities, and some places don't accept children at all. Ask questions before you reserve.

London has plenty of American-style fast-food places, including **Burger King, KFC, McDonald's,** and **Pizza Hut.** Teens probably want to check out the **Hard Rock Café** in Mayfair or the scene at the **Pepsi Trocadero** in **Piccadilly Circus,** which offers theme restaurants such as **Planet Hollywood** and the **Rainforest Café** (see Chapter 10).

Expensive restaurants are less welcoming toward young children. The menus aren't geared to the tastes of American youngsters, the prices can be high, and the staff can be less than accommodating.

To keep costs down, you can rent a hotel room with a kitchen (in England these rooms are called *self-catering units*) and prepare your own meals, as long as you don't mind cooking while on vacation. Another option, when the weather cooperates, is to take the family on a picnic. **Kensington Gardens** or **Hyde Park** may be just the ticket for an enjoyable afternoon (see Chapter 10 for more suggestions). You can also take advantage of pre-theater, fixed-price menus (usually served from 5:30–7 p.m.), which usually give you a good deal.

Planning your trip together

Letting your younger children read *Peter Pan* or *Peter Pan in Kensington Gardens,* and telling them about his statue there, can generate excitement about the trip. Slightly older children may want to read the *Harry Potter* series, which takes place in real and fictional settings in London and around the country. (If your kids have already read the *Harry Potter* series, they know that Harry lives in London — in fact, he leaves from Paddington Station to go off to sorcerer's school.) With the information in this book and some online investigating, you can also incite your kids' curiosity about historic sites such as the **Tower of London** and **H.M.S. Cutty Sark.** And most young people enjoy the prospect of a meal at the **Hard Rock Café** or a trip to **Madame Tussaud's** wax museum.

Some kid and adult activities can easily overlap. You may want to spend one afternoon in **Kensington Gardens.** After the entire family visits Kensington Palace, the kids can blow off steam in the new **Princess Diana Memorial Playground.** Many kid-oriented activities in London are just as interesting for parents. From the fantastic dinosaur exhibit in the **Natural History Museum** to the animatronic robots re-creating historic scenes at Madame Tussaud's, you *and* your kids have plenty that you can experience and enjoy together.

Preparing for a long trip

The shortest trip from the U.S. to London (which is from New York) is about 6 hours; airtime from Australia may be 25 hours, which is a lot of time for kids to sit still and be quiet. Although children can spend some of the journey time watching a movie (or two) on the plane, come prepared with extra diversions: games, puzzles, books — whatever you know will keep your kids entertained. Request from the airline a special kids' menu at least a day in advance. If your child needs baby food, bring your own and ask a flight attendant to warm it. Dealing with jet lag can be hard on adults but even harder on small children. Don't schedule too much for your first day in London. Get everyone comfortably settled and then take it from there.

Hiring a babysitter while on your trip

What you really need is a relaxing evening at the opera and a romantic late dinner. But you can't take Junior along on this special evening. What are your options? Ask your hotel staff if they can recommend a local babysitting service. Most of the hotels marked with a Kid Friendly icon in Chapter 9 can arrange for babysitting. London also has several respected and trustworthy babysitting agencies that provide registered nurses and carefully screened mothers, as well as trained nannies, to watch children. One old and trustworthy babysitting service is **Universal Aunts** (☎ **020/7386-5900;** www.universalaunts.co.uk), which charges ₤6.50 ($12) per daytime hour, ₤5 ($9.25) after 6 p.m. (four-hour minimum), plus a ₤3.50 ($6.50) agency fee.

A fully licensed childcare facility, **Pippa Pop-ins** (430 Fulham Rd., SW6 1DU; ☎ **020/7385-2458;** www.pippapopins.com), in Chelsea, provides a lovely toy-filled nursery staffed by experienced caregivers where you can safely park the little ones. Babysitting is available from 8 a.m. until 7 p.m. Monday through Friday; call for rates. A branch is located in Fulham at 165 New Kings Rd., SW6 (same phone number).

Making Age Work for You: Tips for Seniors

London won't present any problems for you if you're a senior who gets around easily. If you do have mobility issues, be aware when you plan your trip that not all hotels — particularly less expensive B&Bs — have elevators. The steep staircases in some places are a test for *anyone* with luggage. When you reserve a hotel, ask whether you'll have access to a *lift* (an elevator in Britspeak).

In most cities, including London, being a senior often entitles you to some terrific travel bargains, such as reduced admissions at theaters, museums, and other attractions. Carrying ID with proof of age can pay off in all these situations. *Note:* In London and the United Kingdom, you may find that some discounts are available only to members of a British association; public transportation reductions, for example, are available only to U.K. residents with British Pension books. But always ask, even if the reduction isn't posted.

The following sources can provide information on discounts and other benefits for seniors:

- ✔ **AARP** (formerly the American Association of Retired Persons; 601 E St. NW, Washington, DC 20049; ☎ 800/424-3410; www.aarp.org) offers member discounts on car rentals and hotels. AARP offers $12.50 yearly memberships that include discounts of 10 to 25 percent on Virgin Atlantic flights to London from nine U.S. cities.

- ✔ **Elderhostel** (11 Ave. de Lafayette, Boston, MA 02110-1746; ☎ 877/426-8056; www.elderhostel.org) offers people 55 and older a variety of university-based educational programs in London and throughout England. These courses are value-packed, hassle-free ways to learn while traveling. The price includes airfare, accommodations, meals, tuition, tips, and insurance. And you'll be glad to know that you don't receive any grades. Popular London offerings have included "Inside the Parliament," "Legal London," "Classical Music and Opera in London," and "Treasures of London Galleries."

- ✔ **Grand Circle Travel** (347 Congress St., Boston, MA 02210; ☎ 800/959-0405; www.gct.com) is an agency that escorts tours for mature travelers to London. In 2003, they offered their popular 16-day London tour from $1,695, including hotels and airfare.

Accessing London: Advice for Travelers with Disabilities

A disability doesn't have to stop anybody from traveling — more options and resources are available today than ever before. Many hotels and restaurants are happy to accommodate people with disabilities.

Persons with disabilities are often entitled to special discounts at sight-seeing and entertainment venues in Britain. These discounts are called *concessions* (often shortened to *concs*).

Before departing on your trip, contact VisitBritain (see the Quick Concierge, at the end of this book, for addresses and phone numbers) to request a copy of its *Disabled Traveler Fact Sheet*, which contains some helpful general information. *Access London* ($19.95) is the best and most comprehensive London guide for people with disabilities and anyone with a mobility problem. The book provides full access information for all the major sites, hotels, and modes of transportation. You can order it at major online booksellers.

The United Kingdom has several information resources for disabled travelers. The best of these resources include the following:

- ✔ **Artsline** (☎ **020/7388-2227;** www.artsline.org.uk) provides advice on the accessibility of London arts and entertainment events.

- ✔ **The Society of London Theatres** (32 Rose St., London WC2E 9ET; www.officiallondontheatre.co.uk) offers a free guide called *Access Guide to London's West End Theatres.*

- ✔ **Holiday Care Service** (7th Floor, Sunley House, 4 Bedford Park, Croyden, Surrey CR0 2AP; ☎ **0845/1249971** in the U.K. or **020/8760-0072** outside the U.K.; www.holidaycare.org.uk) offers information and advice on suitable accommodations, transportation, and other facilities in England.

- ✔ **The National Trust** (☎ **020/7447-6742;** www.nationaltrust.org.uk) is a British organization that owns and operates hundreds of historic properties (castles, gardens, and more) throughout England. The free booklet *Information for Visitors with Disabilities* provides details on accessibility at each site. Contact The National Trust Disability Office, 36 Queen Anne's Gate, London SW1H 9AS, to obtain a copy. Although not all National Trust sites are accessible, the organization provides powered four-wheeled vehicles free of charge at more than 50 properties; you can drive yourself or have a companion or volunteer drive for you.

- ✔ **Royal Association for Disability and Rehabilitation** (RADAR; 12 City Forum, 250 City Rd., London EC14 8AF; ☎ **020/7250-3222;** www.radar.org.uk) publishes information for disabled travelers in Britain.

- ✔ **Tripscope, The Courtyard** (Evelyn Road, London W4 5JI; ☎ **08457/585641** within the U.K. or 0117/939-7782 from outside the U.K.; www.tripscope.org.uk) provides travel and transport information and advice, including airport facilities.

Some other helpful resources in the United States include the following:

- ✔ **American Foundation for the Blind** (11 Penn Plaza, Suite 300, New York, NY 10001; ☎ **800/232-5463**; www.afb.org) offers information on traveling with Seeing Eye dogs; the foundation also issues ID cards to the legally blind.

- ✔ **The Society for Accessible Travel & Hospitality** (347 Fifth Ave., Suite 610, New York, NY 10016; ☎ **212/447-7284**; www.sath.org) is a membership organization with names and addresses of tour operators specializing in travel for the disabled. You can call to subscribe to its magazine, *Open World.*

- ✔ **Travel Information Service** (www.mossresourcenet.org) provides general information and resources for the disabled traveler.

Joining escorted tours

You can find tours designed to meet the needs of travelers with disabilities. One of the best operators is **Flying Wheels Travel** (143 West Bridge, P.O. Box 382, Owatonna, MN 55060; ☎ **507/451-5005**; www.flyingwheels travel.com), which offers various escorted tours and cruises, as well as private tours in minivans with lifts.

Here are some other tour operators for London-bound travelers with disabilities:

- ✔ **Accessible Journeys** (☎ **800/846-4537**; www.disabilitytravel. com) offers tours of Britain and London in minibuses or motor coaches.

- ✔ **The Guided Tour** (☎ **800/783-5841**; e-mail: gtour400@aol.com) has one- and two-week guided tours for individuals, with one staff member for every three travelers.

- ✔ **Undiscovered Britain** (11978 Audubon Place, Philadelphia, PA 19116; ☎ **215/969-0542**; www.undiscoveredbritain.com) provides specialty travel and tours for individuals, small groups, or families traveling with a wheelchair user.

Dealing with access issues

The United Kingdom doesn't yet have a program like the Americans with Disabilities Act. More and more businesses are becoming accessible, however, and access in general is easier than ever before.

Not all hotels and restaurants in Britain provide wheelchair ramps. Most of the less expensive B&Bs and older hotels don't have elevators, or the elevators are too small for a wheelchair. Ask about this when you reserve your room or table.

All the top sights and many of the attractions in Chapter 11 are wheelchair accessible, but in some cases you must use a different entrance. Call the attraction to find out about special entrances, ramps, elevator locations, and general directions. Theaters and performing arts venues are often wheelchair accessible, as well (again, call first).

Trains throughout the United Kingdom now have wide doors, grab rails, and provisions for wheelchairs. To get more information or to obtain a copy of the leaflet *Rail Travel for Disabled Passengers,* contact Project Manager (Disability), British Rail, Euston House, Eversholt Street, London NW1 1DZ; ☎ **020/7922-6984.** You can also check out the **National Rail** Web site at www.nationalrail.co.uk, which has a section on disabled travel and contact information for the various train operating companies.

Disabled travelers will want to keep the following in mind when traveling around London:

✔ Although London's streets and sidewalks are generally kept in good repair, the city is old and not all streets have modern curb cuts.

✔ Not all the city's Underground (subway) stations have elevators and ramps.

✔ Low-floor wheelchair-accessible buses serve most stations in London.

✔ The city's black cabs are roomy enough for wheelchairs.

✔ Victoria Coach Station in Central London has Braille maps.

The following organizations provide access information and services for disabled travelers in London:

✔ **Transport for London** (☎ **020/7222-1234;** www.tfl.gov.uk/tfl/) publishes a free brochure called *Tube Access,* which helps travelers with disabilities plan a Tube journey, avoiding stairs and escalators. You can obtain this brochure at Underground stations in London.

✔ **Wheelchair Travel** (1 Johnston Green, Guildford, Surrey GU2 6XS; ☎ **1483/233-640** within the U.K. or 1483-237-668 from outside the U.K.; www.wheelchair-travel.co.uk) is an independent transport service for the disabled traveler arriving in London. The organization offers self-drive cars and minibuses (although I strongly discourage anyone, disabled or not, from driving in London) and can provide wheelchairs. Drivers who also act as guides are also available on request. Bring your own disabled stickers and permits from home if you're going to rent a self-drive vehicle.

Taking health precautions

Before you leave on your trip, talk to your physician about your general physical condition and your prescriptions for the time you're traveling, the medical equipment that you need to take, and how to get medical assistance when you're away. Carry all prescription medicines in their original bottles with the contents clearly marked, along with a letter from your doctor.

 Make a list of the generic names of your prescription drugs, in case you need to replace or refill them during your visit. Pack medications in your hand luggage. If you use a wheelchair, have a maintenance check before your trip. If you don't use a wheelchair but have trouble walking or become easily tired, consider renting a wheelchair to take with you as checked baggage.

Following the Rainbow: Gay and Lesbian Travelers

London has always been a popular destination for gays and lesbians, even in the days (prior to 1967) when homosexuality was a criminal offense in Britain. Today, with a more tolerant government at the helm and gay marriage an imminent possibility, gay pride is prominent. The city government has actually spent money to promote gay tourism. You can find gay theaters, gay shops, more than 100 gay pubs, famous gay discos, and gay community groups of all sorts. Click the "Gay and Lesbian" link on the VisitBritain Web site at www.visitbritain.com for information on gay venues and events throughout England.

Old Compton Street in Soho is the heart of London's Gay Village, filled with dozens of gay pubs, restaurants, and upscale bars/cafes. The **Earl's Court** area, long a gay bastion, is home to many gay pubs and restaurants.

Lesbigay events in London include the **London Lesbian and Gay Film Festival** in March, the **Pride Parade** and celebrations in June, and the big outdoor bash known as **Summer Rites** in August. You can obtain information and exact dates from the London Lesbian and Gay Switchboard at ☎ **020/7837-7324** or online at www.llgs.org.uk.

 Brighton (which I describe in Chapter 14) is one of the gayest seaside resort towns in Europe. From London, you can get to Brighton on the train in under an hour.

You may want to check out the following Web sites as you plan your trip. All are specifically geared to gay and lesbian travelers to London and the United Kingdom:

✔ www.gaybritain.co.uk

✔ www.gayguide.co.uk

✔ www.pinkpassport.com

In addition, several gay magazines, useful for their listings and news coverage, are available in gay pubs, clubs, bars, and cafes. The most popular are *Pink Paper* (www.pinkpaper.com) and *QX (Queer Xtra;* www.qxmagazine.co.uk). *Gay Times* (www.gaytimes.co.uk), a high-quality, monthly, news-oriented mag, is available at most news agents. Indispensable for its citywide listings (including gay listings), *Time Out,* with gay and lesbian listings, appears at newsstands on Wednesdays.

Gay's the Word (66 Marchmont St., WC1; ☎ **020/7278-7654;** www.gays theword.co.uk; Tube: Russell Square) is the city's only all-round gay and lesbian bookstore; the store stocks a fine selection of new and used books and current periodicals.

Chapter 7

Taking Care of the Remaining Details

In This Chapter

▶ Crossing borders: Passports

▶ Insuring yourself and your trip

▶ Taking care of your health: Medications and emergencies

▶ Using cellphones and e-mail in London

▶ Getting through airport security

*B*efore you depart for London to take that boat ride on the river Thames or visit the Tower of London, you need to take care of some final details. Do you have an up-to-date passport? Have you taken steps to meet your health needs while you're on your trip? Are you wondering how to use a cellphone or access e-mail while in London? Do you think you need to rent a car? This chapter gives you the information that you need.

Getting a Passport

A valid passport is the only legal form of identification accepted around the world. You can't cross an international border without one. Getting a passport is easy, but the process takes some time.

The U.S. Department of State's Bureau of Consular Affairs maintains www.travel.state.gov, a Web site that provides everything you ever wanted to know about passports (including a downloadable application), Customs, and other government-regulated aspects of travel.

Applying for a U.S. passport

If you're applying for a first-time passport, follow these steps:

1. Complete a **passport application** in person at a U.S. passport office; a federal, state, or probate court; or a major post office. To find your regional passport office, either check the **U.S. State Department**

Web site (http://travel.state.gov) or call the **National Passport Information Center** (☎ 877-487-2778) for automated information.

2. Present a **certified birth certificate** as proof of citizenship. (Bringing along your driver's license, state or military ID, or Social Security card is also a good idea.)

3. Submit **two identical passport-sized photos,** measuring 2 x 2 inches in size. You often find businesses that take these photos near a passport office. *Note:* You can't use a strip from a photo-vending machine because the pictures aren't identical.

4. Pay a **fee.** For people 16 and over, a passport is valid for ten years and costs $85. For children 15 and under, a passport is valid for five years and costs $70.

Allow plenty of time before your trip to apply for a passport; processing normally takes three weeks but can take longer during busy periods (especially spring).

If you have a passport in your current name that was issued within the past 15 years (and you were over age 15 when it was issued), you can renew the passport by mail for $55. Whether you're applying in person or by mail, you can download passport applications from the U.S. State Department Web site at http://travel.state.gov. For general information, call the **National Passport Agency** (☎ 202-647-0518). To find your regional passport office, either check the U.S. State Department Web site or call the **National Passport Information Center** (☎ 877-487-2778) for automated information.

Applying for other passports

The following list offers information for citizens of Australia, Canada, and New Zealand:

- ✔ **Australians** can visit a local post office or passport office, call the **Australia Passport Information Service** (☎ 131-232 toll-free from Australia), or log on to www.passports.gov.au for details on how and where to apply.

- ✔ **Canadians** can pick up applications at passport offices throughout Canada; at post offices; or from the central **Passport Office,** Department of Foreign Affairs and International Trade, Ottawa, ON K1A 0G3 (☎ 800-567-6868; www.ppt.gc.ca). Applications must be accompanied by two identical passport-sized photographs and proof of Canadian citizenship. Processing takes five to ten days if you apply in person or about three weeks if you apply by mail.

- ✔ **New Zealanders** can pick up a passport application at any New Zealand Passports Office or download it from their Web site. Contact the **Passports Office** at ☎ 0800/225-050 in New Zealand or 04/474-8100, or log on to www.passports.govt.nz.

Entering England with your passport

 If you're a citizen of the United States, Canada, Australia, or New Zealand, you must have a passport with at least two months remaining until its expiration to enter the United Kingdom. You need to show your passport at the Customs and immigration area when you arrive at a U.K. airport. After your passport is stamped, you can remain in the United Kingdom as a tourist for up to three months. No visa is required if you're going to stay in England or the rest of the United Kingdom for less than three months.

Keep your passport with you at all times. You need to show it only when you're converting traveler's checks or foreign currency at a bank or currency exchange. However, you may be asked to present your passport to the hotel clerk when you check in; after examining it, the clerk will return the passport to you. If you're not going to need your passport for currency exchanges, ask whether the hotel has a safe where you can keep it locked up.

Dealing with a (gulp) lost passport

Don't worry; if you lose your passport in England, you won't be sent to the Tower of London, but you need to take steps to replace it *immediately*. First, notify the police. Then go to your consulate or high commission office (they're all located in London — you'll find addresses and phone numbers in the Quick Concierge, at the end of this book). Bring all available forms of identification, and the staff can get started on generating your new passport. Always call first to verify the hours.

Renting a Car in London — Not!

Having a car in London is more trouble than it's worth for the following reasons:

✔ Maneuvering through London's congested and complicated maze of streets can be an endurance test even for Londoners.

✔ Finding your way through the city in heavy traffic while driving on the *left-hand* side of the road can turn even the best American driver into a gibbering nut case.

✔ Parking is difficult to find and expensive (street meters cost £1/$1.85 for 20 minutes).

✔ Gas (*petrol* in Britspeak) costs over $6 a gallon.

✔ Public transportation — especially the Tube — will get you everywhere you want to go at a fraction of the cost.

Do yourself a favor: Forget about renting a car. If you want to be with Londoners on their own turf (or in their own tunnels), the Tube (Underground) is a great way to do it. Even if you're planning excursions outside London, the trains are a better option. (However, see Chapter 14 for details on renting a car for day-tripping.)

Playing It Safe with Travel and Medical Insurance

Three kinds of travel insurance are available: trip-cancellation insurance, medical insurance, and lost-luggage insurance. The cost of travel insurance varies widely, depending on the cost and length of your trip, your age and health, and the type of trip that you're taking, but expect to pay between 5 percent and 8 percent of the vacation itself. Here's my advice on all three:

- ✔ **Trip-cancellation insurance** helps you get your money back if you have to back out of a trip, if you have to go home early, or if your travel supplier goes bankrupt. Allowed reasons for cancellation can range from sickness to natural disasters to the State Department declaring your destination unsafe for travel. (Insurers usually won't cover vague fears, though, as many travelers discovered who tried to cancel their trips in October 2001 because they were wary of flying.)

  A good resource is **"Travel Guard Alerts,"** a list of companies considered high-risk by Travel Guard International (www.travel insured.com). Protect yourself further by paying for the insurance with a credit card — by law, you can get your money back on goods and services not received if you report the loss within 60 days after the charge is listed on your credit card statement.

- ✔ For travel overseas, most health plans (including Medicare and Medicaid) do not provide coverage. Even if your plan does cover overseas treatment, most out-of-country hospitals, including those in England, make you pay your bills up front and send you a refund only after you've returned home and filed the necessary paperwork with your insurance company. As a safety net, you may want to buy **travel medical insurance.** If you require additional medical insurance, try **MEDEX Assistance** (☎ 410-453-6300; www.medexassist.com) or **Travel Assistance International** (☎ 800-821-2828; www.travel assistance.com; for general information on services, call the company's Worldwide Assistance Services, Inc., at ☎ 800-777-8710).

- ✔ **Lost-luggage insurance** is not necessary for most travelers. On international flights (including U.S. portions of international trips), baggage coverage is limited to approximately $9.07 per pound, up to approximately $635 per checked bag. If you plan to check items more valuable than the standard liability, see if your valuables are covered by your homeowner's policy, get baggage insurance as part of your comprehensive travel-insurance package, or buy Travel Guard's "BagTrak" product. Don't buy insurance at the airport — it's usually overpriced. Be sure to take any valuables or irreplaceable items with you in your carry-on luggage, because many valuables (including books, money, and electronics) aren't covered by airline policies.

If your luggage is lost, immediately file a lost-luggage claim at the airport, detailing the luggage contents. For most airlines, you must report delayed, damaged, or lost baggage within four hours of arrival. The airlines are required to deliver luggage, once found, directly to your house or destination free of charge.

For more information, contact one of the following recommended insurers: **Access America** (☎ 866-807-3982; www.accessamerica. com); **Travel Guard International** (☎ 800-826-4919; www.travel guard.com); **Travel Insured International** (☎ 800-243-3174; www. travelinsured.com); and **Travelex Insurance Services** (☎ 888-457-4602; www.travelex-insurance.com).

Staying Healthy When You Travel

Getting sick will ruin your vacation, so I *strongly* advise against it (of course, last time I checked, the bugs weren't listening to me any more than they probably listen to you).

For travel abroad, you may have to pay all medical costs up front and be reimbursed later. For information on purchasing additional medical insurance for your trip, see the preceding section.

Avoiding "economy-class syndrome"

Deep vein thrombosis, or as it's know in the world of flying, "economy-class syndrome," is a blood clot that develops in a deep vein. It's a potentially deadly condition that can be caused by sitting in cramped conditions — such as an airplane cabin — for too long. Symptoms of deep vein thrombosis include leg pain or swelling, or even shortness of breath.

During a flight (especially a long-haul flight), get up, walk around, and stretch your legs every 60 to 90 minutes to keep your blood flowing. Other preventative measures include frequent flexing of the legs while sitting, drinking lots of water, and avoiding alcohol and sleeping pills.

If you have a history of deep vein thrombosis, heart disease, or another condition that puts you at high risk, some experts recommend wearing compression stockings or taking anticoagulants when you fly; always ask your physician about the best course for you.

Talk to your doctor before leaving on a trip if you have a serious and/ or chronic illness. For conditions such as epilepsy, diabetes, or heart problems, wear a **MedicAlert identification tag** (☎ **888-633-4298;** www. medicalert.org), which immediately alerts doctors to your condition and gives them access to your records through MedicAlert's 24-hour hotline. Contact the **International Association for Medical Assistance to Travelers** (IAMAT; ☎ **716-754-4883** in the U.S. or 416-652-0137 in Canada; www.iamat.org) for tips on travel and health concerns in the countries that you're visiting.

Staying Connected by Cellphone or E-Mail

The three letters that define much of the world's **wireless capabilities** are GSM (Global System for Mobiles), a big, seamless network that makes for easy cross-border cellphone use throughout Europe and dozens of other countries worldwide. In the United States, T-Mobile, AT&T Wireless, and Cingular use this quasi-universal system; in Canada, Microcell and some Rogers customers are GSM; and all Europeans and most Australians use GSM.

If your cellphone is on a GSM system, and you have a world-capable multiband phone such as many Sony Ericsson, Motorola, or Samsung models, you can make and receive calls across developed areas throughout much of the world, from Andorra to Uganda. Just call your wireless operator and ask for "international roaming" to be activated on your account. Unfortunately, per-minute charges can be high — usually $1 to $1.50 in England and Western Europe.

That's why it's important to buy an "unlocked" world phone from the get-go. Many cellphone operators sell "locked" phones that restrict you from using any removable computer memory phone chip (called a **SIM card**) other than the ones they supply. Having an unlocked phone allows you to install a cheap, prepaid SIM card (found at a local retailer) in your destination country. (Show your phone to the salesperson; not all phones work on all networks.) You'll get a local phone number — and much, much lower calling rates. Getting an already locked phone unlocked can be a complicated process, but it can be done; just call your cellular operator and say you'll be going abroad for several months and want to use the phone with a local provider.

For many, **renting** a phone is a good idea. While you can rent a phone from any number of overseas sites, including kiosks at airports and at car-rental agencies, I suggest renting the phone before you leave home. That way, you can give loved ones and business associates your new number, make sure the phone works, and take the phone wherever you go — especially helpful for overseas trips through several countries, where local phone-rental agencies often bill in local currency and may not let you take the phone to another country.

Phone rental isn't cheap. You'll usually pay $40 to $50 per week, plus airtime fees of at least $1 a minute. If you're traveling to England, though, local rental companies often offer free incoming calls within their home country, which can save you big bucks. The bottom line: Shop around.

Rent-a-phone (☎ 800-400-7221 in the U.S. or 0800/317-540 in the U.K.) is an international cellphone rental company with offices in the U.S. and U.K.; per-minute charges from England are generally about $1.99 per minute to the U.S. and Europe, and the phones can be delivered to your door in the U.S. before you leave. In Terminal 1 and Terminal 2 at Heathrow Airport, you can buy a range of mobile phones and services, including SIM cards, at **Primus** (☎ 020-8607-5960).

Two good wireless rental companies are **InTouch USA** (☎ 800-872-7626; www.intouchglobal.com) and **RoadPost** (☎ 888-290-1606 or 905-272-5665; www.roadpost.com). Give them your itinerary, and they'll tell you what wireless products you need. InTouch will also, for free, advise you on whether your existing phone will work overseas; simply call ☎ 703-222-7161 between 9 a.m. and 4 p.m. eastern standard time or go to www.intouchglobal.com/travel.htm.

You have any number of ways to check your e-mail and access the Internet on the road. Of course, using your own laptop — or even a personal digital assistant (PDA) or electronic organizer with a modem — gives you the most flexibility. But even if you don't have a computer, you can still access your e-mail and even your office computer from cybercafes.

It's hard nowadays to find a city in England that *doesn't* have a few cybercafes, though you won't find any in smaller towns and villages. Although there's no definitive directory for cybercafes — these are independent businesses, after all — two places to start looking are at www.cybercaptive.com and www.cybercafe.com.

Aside from formal cybercafes, most **youth hostels** nowadays have at least one computer on which you can access the Internet. And most **public libraries** across the world offer Internet access free or for a small charge. If you want to save money, avoid **hotel business centers** unless you can use the service for free.

Most major airports now have **Internet kiosks** scattered throughout their gates. These kiosks, which you also see in shopping malls, hotel lobbies, and tourist-information offices around the world, give you basic Web access for a per-minute fee that's usually higher than cybercafe prices. The kiosks' clunkiness and high price mean that you probably want to avoid them whenever possible.

Surfing at Internet cafes in London

The handy www.netcafeguide.com has a pretty good London listing, including the **easyInternetCafe** chain. There are 18 of these giant Internet cafes in the capital — but *cafe* is really a misnomer, because the hundreds of screens in the largest locations make them look like telemarketing sweatshops, and you don't hear any conversation, just the clicking of keyboards.

The charging system is radical because surfers buy credit, not minutes. The minimum you'll spend is £2 ($3.70), and the amount of time you get for that is in inverse proportion to how busy the branch is. The rate is adjusted every five minutes and posted on video screens, a bit like a stock exchange. Your ticket has a user ID, which notes the current rate when you first log on. That becomes your rate. You'll never pay more, but if things quiet down, your credit will buy more time — a pound could be worth up to six hours, or so they claim. easyEverything never closes, so avoid afternoons and early evenings, and surf with the creatures of the night and early morning.

Check www.easyeverything.com for new branches to add to this list: 358 Oxford St., W1 (Tube: Bond Street); 9–16 Tottenham Court Rd., W1 (Tube: Tottenham Court Road); 160–166 Kensington High St., W8 (Tube: Kensington High Street); 456–459 Strand, WC2 (Tube: Charing Cross); and 9–13 Wilton Rd., SW1 (Tube: Victoria). As befitting a large chain, the telephone number for all locations is ☎ 020/7241-9000.

To retrieve your e-mail, ask your **Internet service provider (ISP)** if it has a Web-based interface tied to your existing e-mail account. If your ISP doesn't have such an interface, you can use the free **mail2web** service (www.mail2web.com) to view and reply to your home e-mail. For more flexibility, you may want to open a free, Web-based e-mail account with **Yahoo! Mail** (http://mail.yahoo.com). (Microsoft's Hotmail is another popular option, but Hotmail has severe spam problems.) You may be able to get your home ISP to forward your e-mail to the Web-based account automatically.

If you need to access files on your office computer, look into a service called **GoToMyPC** (www.gotomypc.com). The service provides a Web-based interface for you to access and manipulate a distant PC from anywhere — even a cybercafe — provided that your "target" PC is on and has an always-on connection to the Internet (such as with Road Runner cable). The service offers top-quality security, but if you're worried about hackers, use your own laptop rather than a cybercafe computer to access the GoToMyPC system.

If you're bringing your own computer, the buzzword in computer access to familiarize yourself with is **Wi-Fi** (wireless fidelity), and more and more hotels, cafes, and retailers are signing on as wireless *hotspots* from which you can get a high-speed connection without cable wires, networking hardware, or a phone line. You can get a Wi-Fi connection one of several ways. Many laptops sold in the last year have built-in Wi-Fi capability (an 802.11b wireless Ethernet connection). Mac owners have their own networking technology, Apple AirPort. If you have an older computer, you can plug an 802.11b/**Wi-Fi card** (around $50) into your laptop.

You sign up for wireless access service much as you do cellphone service, through a plan offered by one of several commercial companies that have made wireless service available in airports, hotel lobbies, and coffee shops, primarily in the U.S. (followed by the U.K. and Japan). **T-Mobile Hotspot** (www.t-mobile.com/hotspot) serves up wireless connections at Starbucks coffee shops throughout England. **Boingo** (www.boingo.com) and **Wayport** (www.wayport.com) have set up networks in airports and high-class hotel lobbies. iPass providers also give you access to a few hundred wireless hotel-lobby setups. Best of all, you don't need to be staying at the Four Seasons to use the hotel's network; just set yourself up on a nice couch in the lobby. The companies' pricing policies can be byzantine, with a variety of monthly, per-connection, and per-minute plans, but in general, you pay around $30 a month for limited access — and as more and more companies jump on the wireless bandwagon, prices are likely to get even more competitive.

There are also places that provide **free wireless networks** in cities around the world. To locate these free hotspots, go to www.personal telco.net/index.cgi/WirelessCommunities.

If Wi-Fi is not available at your destination, most business-class hotels throughout England and the rest of the U.K. offer dataports for laptop modems, and many offer free high-speed Internet access using an Ethernet network cable. You can bring your own cables, but most hotels rent them for around $10. **Call your hotel in advance** to see what your options are.

In addition, major ISPs have **local access numbers** around the world, allowing you to go online by simply placing a local call. Check your ISP's Web site or call its toll-free number and ask how you can use your current account away from home, and how much it will cost. If you're traveling outside the reach of your ISP, the **iPass** network has dial-up numbers in most of the world's countries. You'll have to sign up with an iPass provider, who will then tell you how to set up your computer for your destination(s). For a list of iPass providers, go to www.ipass.com and click "Individuals Buy Now." One solid provider is **i2roam** (☎ 866-811-6209 or 920-235-0475; www.i2roam.com).

Wherever you go, bring a **connection kit** of the right power and phone adapters, a spare phone cord, and a spare Ethernet network cable — or find out whether your hotel supplies them to guests.

North American current runs 110V, 60 cycles; the standard voltage throughout Britain is 240V AC, 50 cycles. You need a current converter or transformer to bring the voltage down and the cycles up. Two-pronged

North American plugs won't fit into the three-pronged square British wall sockets, so you also need a three-pronged square adapter and converter if you use North American laptops or appliances while in England. Plug adapters and converters are available at most travel, luggage, electronics, and hardware stores. Some plug adapters are also current converters. Most contemporary laptop computers automatically sense the current and adapt accordingly.

Keeping Up with Airline Security Measures

With the federalization of airport security, security procedures at U.S. airports are more stable and consistent than ever. Generally, you'll be fine if you arrive at the airport **one hour** before a domestic flight and **two hours** before an international flight; if you show up late, tell an airline employee and she'll probably whisk you to the front of the line.

Bring a **current, government-issued photo ID** such as a driver's license or passport. Keep your ID at the ready to show at check-in, the security checkpoint, and sometimes even the gate. (Children under 18 do not need government-issued photo IDs for domestic flights, but they do for international flights to most countries.)

In 2003, the TSA phased out **gate check-in** at all U.S. airports. And **e-tickets** have made paper tickets nearly obsolete. If you have an e-ticket, you can beat the ticket-counter lines by using airport **electronic kiosks** or even **online check-in** from your home computer. Online check-in involves logging on to your airline's Web site, accessing your reservation, and printing out your boarding pass — and the airline may even offer you bonus miles to do so! If you're using a kiosk at the airport, bring the credit card that you used to book the ticket or your frequent-flier card. Print out your boarding pass from the kiosk and simply proceed to the security checkpoint with your pass and a photo ID. If you're checking bags or looking to snag an exit-row seat, you'll be able to do so using most airline kiosks. Even the smaller airlines are employing the kiosk system, but always call your airline to make sure these alternatives are available. **Curbside check-in** is also a good way to avoid lines, although a few airlines still ban curbside check-in; call before you go.

Security checkpoint lines are getting shorter than they were immediately after September 11, 2001, but some doozies remain. If you have trouble standing for long periods of time, tell an airline employee; the airline will provide a wheelchair. Speed up security by **not wearing metal objects** such as big belt buckles. If you've got metallic body parts, a note from your doctor can prevent a long chat with the security screeners. Keep in mind that only **ticketed passengers** are allowed past security, except for folks escorting disabled passengers or children.

Federalization has stabilized **what you can carry on** and **what you can't.** The general rule is that sharp things are out, nail clippers are okay, and food and beverages must be passed through the x-ray machine — but that security screeners can't make you drink from your coffee cup. Bring food in your carryon rather than checking it, because explosive-detection machines used on checked luggage have been known to mistake food (especially chocolate, for some reason) for bombs. Travelers in the U.S. are allowed one carry-on bag, plus a "personal item" such as a purse, briefcase, or laptop bag. Carry-on hoarders can stuff all sorts of things into a laptop bag; as long as it has a laptop in it, it's still considered a personal item. The Transportation Security Administration (TSA) has issued a list of restricted items; check its Web site (www.tsa.gov/public/index.jsp) for details.

Airport screeners may decide that your checked luggage needs to be searched by hand. You can now purchase luggage locks that allow screeners to open and relock a checked bag if hand-searching is necessary. Look for Travel Sentry certified locks at luggage or travel shops and Brookstone stores (you can buy them online at www.brookstone.com). These locks, approved by the TSA, can be opened by luggage inspectors with a special code or key. For more information on the locks, visit www.travelsentry.org. If you use something other than TSA-approved locks, your lock will be cut off your suitcase if a TSA agent needs to hand-search your luggage.

Part III
Settling into London

©RICHTENNANT

WHILE ON VACATION IN LONDON, BILL AND DENISE WATCH A LOCAL FAMILY WORKING ON THE TRADITIONAL THATCHED ROOF COTTAGE, THATCHED ROOF SATELLITE DISH, AND THATCHED ROOF JEEP CHEROKEE.

In this part . . .

In this part, I help you settle into London. In Chapter 8, you can find out how to get from the airport into the city, and I introduce you to London's neighborhoods; I also tell you everything you need to know about public transportation, including ways to save a bundle on bus and Tube tickets. Chapter 9 tells you what you can expect in terms of accommodations and their price ranges, focuses on finding a good hotel for the best possible rate, and gives you my list of London's best hotels, all described and cross-indexed by price and location. In Chapter 10, I introduce you to London's dining scene, telling you about the variety of cuisines you'll discover and recommending dozens of my favorite London restaurants, from pubs and fish-and-chips joints to the hottest of haute hang-outs, all cross-referenced so you can easily find what you're looking for. I also give you a list of places for a quick snack or a formal high tea.

Chapter 8

Arriving and Getting Oriented

In This Chapter

▶ Making it through Customs

▶ Traveling from the airport (or train station) to your hotel

▶ Getting familiar with the London neighborhoods

▶ Finding help and information after you arrive

▶ Traveling around the city

Although London is among the world's largest cities, both in size and population, its neighborhoods were once small, separate villages. With urban roots (and routes) that hark back to Roman times, London isn't always the easiest city to navigate. Streets aren't organized in a grid, and although most have been paved and modernized, a few old lanes here and there still have cobblestones. This quaint, villagelike quality is one reason for London's enduring charm, but charm is little comfort when you're lost in a strange place. This chapter helps you get your bearings. Neighborhood boundaries come later in this chapter, too. First, you need to get from the airport or train station into Central London.

Getting through Passport Control and Customs

Have your passport ready because your first stop after deplaning is passport control (for details on getting a passport, see Chapter 7). The procedure is fairly routine. On the plane you fill out a *landing card* that asks for your name, home address, passport number, and the address where you'll be staying in London. Present the completed card with your passport to the official at Passport Control. The official may ask for the following information:

✔ How long you'll be staying (you must stay less than three months if you don't have a visa)

✔ Where you plan to stay

✔ Whether the trip is for business or pleasure (don't be afraid to say pleasure)

✔ What your next destination will be

✔ How much money you have with you

Although you may think that the question about your finances is snoopy impertinence, officials have good reason to ask. They want to verify that people entering England won't apply for some kind of welfare or national health-insurance benefits and become a burden on the country.

Officials may stamp your passport without asking a thing. After your passport is stamped, proceed to pick up your luggage. From there, you wind your way out through the Customs Hall.

At the Customs area, you get two choices: "Nothing to Declare" and "Goods to Declare." Chances are you won't be declaring anything, in which case you'll walk right through. Limits on imports for visitors 17 and older entering England include the following:

✔ 200 cigarettes, 50 cigars, or 250 grams (8.8 oz.) of loose tobacco

✔ 2 liters (2.1 qt.) of still table wine

✔ 1 liter of liquor over 22 percent alcohol content or 2 liters of liquor under 22 percent

✔ 2 fluid ounces of perfume

If you fall within these limits, go through the "Nothing to Declare" area at Customs. You may, however, be stopped for a random luggage search. Don't take it personally if this happens. Unless you're smuggling in contraband, you have nothing to worry about.

For details on duty-free shopping and limits on what you can bring back home, see Chapter 12.

Making Your Way to Your Hotel

You're in London — well, almost. First, you have to get from the airport or train station to your hotel. I fill you in on all your options in the following sections.

Arriving at Heathrow

About 15 miles west of Central London, Heathrow (☎ **020/8759-4321**; www.baa.co.uk) is the largest of London's airports, as well as one of the world's busiest, with four passenger terminals (and a fifth under construction) serving flights from around the globe. Moving walkways and signposts that mark just about everything make the trek through the long corridors easy. You'll probably arrive at Terminal 3 or 4:

🖊 Terminal 3 is for non-British, long-haul flights.

🖊 Terminal 4 is for British Airways intercontinental flights.

After clearing Customs (see the section "Getting through Passport Control and Customs," earlier in this chapter), you enter the main concourse of your terminal. You can pick up a free map and general info from the **Tourist Information Centre** in the Underground concourse of Terminals 1, 2, and 3 (open Oct–May daily 8 a.m.–6 p.m. and June–Sept Mon–Sat 8 a.m.–7 p.m.). You can also find ATMs, hotel booking agencies (see Chapter 9), theater booking services, and several banks and *bureaux de change* where you can swap your dollars or traveler's checks for pounds and pence.

You have several options for getting into the city. The **London Underground** (☎ 020/7222-1234), called the *Underground* or the *Tube,* is the London subway system and the cheapest mode of public transportation for most Central London destinations (see the inside back cover of this book for a map of the Underground system). All terminals at Heathrow link up with the Tube system. Follow the Underground signs to the ticket booth. The Piccadilly Line gets you into Central London in about 45 minutes for a fare of £3.80 ($7.05). Underground trains run from all four Heathrow terminals every five to nine minutes Monday through Saturday 5:30 a.m. to 11:30 p.m. and Sunday 6 a.m. to 11 p.m.

The one potential hassle with the Underground is that the Tube trains don't have luggage racks. Stash your bags as best you can — behind your legs, on your lap, or near the center doors where there's more space. Keep in mind that during rush hour the trains become increasingly packed as you get closer to London. To reach your hotel on the Underground, you may have to change trains or take a cab from the Underground station closest to your destination.

If the Underground is closed, you can ride the **N97 night bus** from Heathrow to Central London. Buses (located in front of the terminals) run every 30 minutes Monday through Saturday midnight to 5 a.m. and Sunday 11 p.m. to 5:30 a.m. The trip takes about an hour; a one-way fare costs £1.50 ($2.80).

The buses operated by **National Express** (☎ 08705/747777; www.nationalexpress.com) may be a better alternative to the Underground if you have lots of heavy luggage. Two routes are available: The **National Express** bus goes from Heathrow to **Victoria Station** via Cromwell Road, Knightsbridge, and Hyde Park Corner; the **Route A2 Airbus** goes to **Kings Cross Station** via Bayswater, Marble Arch, Euston, and Russell Square. Travel time for both takes about 75 minutes, and the fare (which you can pay on the bus) costs £8 ($15). Up to three buses per hour depart daily from 4 a.m. to 11:23 p.m. from the coach station in front of Heathrow's Terminals 3 and 4.

The **Heathrow Express** (☎ 0845/600-1515; www.heathrowexpress.co.uk) is a dedicated train line running from all four Heathrow terminals to London's Paddington Station in only 15 minutes. The trains have air-conditioning, ergonomically designed seating, and plenty of luggage space. The standard-class fare costs £14 ($26). You can buy tickets at the airport or onboard the train. Service runs Monday through Saturday 5:07 a.m. to 11:32 p.m. and Sunday 5:07 a.m. to midnight. All the major airlines have check-in counters right at Paddington, so when you're returning from London to the airport, you can conveniently check your luggage *before* boarding the train; then when you arrive at Heathrow, you can go directly to your departure gate without further check-in.

If you're travel-weary, you may want the luxury of taking a **taxi** directly to your hotel. Taxis are especially cost effective if four or five people are traveling together. You can order one at the Taxi Information booths in Terminal 3 (☎ 020/8745-4655) or Terminal 4 (☎ 020/8745-7302). Expect to pay about £45 ($83), plus tip (15 percent of the total fare), for a trip of about 45 minutes. Cabs are available 24 hours a day. Wheelchair facilities are available at all times for the disabled.

Arriving at calmer Gatwick

Gatwick (☎ 08700/002468; www.baa.co.uk) is considerably smaller than Heathrow but basically provides the same services, except that there's no tourist information office here. Gatwick is about 28 miles south of Central London and handles national and international flights from some U.S. airlines; international flights come in at the South Terminal. Gatwick also has a North Terminal.

 If you land at Gatwick rather than Heathrow, you have fewer transportation options into Central London. The highway system from Gatwick into London is far less efficient than from Heathrow, so buses, minivans, or cabs can end up taking two to three hours in heavy traffic.

Your quickest way of getting into Central London from Gatwick is the convenient **Gatwick Express train** (☎ 0845/101-515; www.gatwickexpress.co.uk). You can board the train right in the South Terminal, and in about 30 minutes, you'll be at Victoria Station. The trip costs £12 ($22) Express class. Trains run daily every 15 minutes from 6:50 a.m. to 1:30 a.m.

Slightly less expensive, the **Thameslink train** (☎ 08457/48-4950; www.thameslink.co.uk) runs between Gatwick and King's Cross Station for £9.50 ($18). Service is every 15 minutes daily from 3:45 a.m. to 12:15 a.m.; trip time is about 45 minutes.

Hotelink (☎ 01293/552251; www.hotelink.co.uk) runs a minibus service from Gatwick directly to your hotel for £20 ($37).

For 24-hour taxi service between Gatwick and Central London, call

- 🖉 Gatwick Airport Cars (☎ **01293/562-291**)
- 🖉 Gatwick Goldlines Cars (☎ **01293/568-368**)

You can order a taxi at the Taxi Information booth when you arrive at Gatwick Airport. Fares for both companies are the same: £65 ($120), plus tip, for the journey that takes about 90 minutes.

Touching down at another airport

If you fly into London from elsewhere in Europe, you may arrive at an airport other than Heathrow and Gatwick. The following sections help you navigate from these less-used facilities.

Stansted: For national and European flights

Stansted (☎ **08700/000303**) is a single-terminal airport used for national and European flights. The airport is about 33 miles northeast of Central London. The **Stansted Express** (☎ **0845/600-7245**) to Liverpool Street Station takes 45 minutes and costs £15 ($28). Trains run every half-hour daily 4:30 a.m. to 11 p.m. The **Route A6 Airbus** (☎ **08705/747777**) makes the journey to Victoria Coach Station in about 1 hour and 40 minutes and costs £8 ($15). Taxi fare into the city averages about £60 ($111), plus tip.

London City Airport: European destinations only

London City Airport (☎ **020/7646-000**) is a mere 10 miles east of the city center, and it services only European destinations. A **blue shuttle bus** (☎ **020/7646-0000**) takes passengers from the airport to Liverpool Street Station in 25 minutes for £5 ($9.25). The buses run every 10 minutes daily 6 a.m. to 9:30 p.m. A taxi to the vicinity of Marble Arch costs about £25 ($46), plus tip.

Luton: Serving European charters

Luton (☎ **01582/405-100**) services European charter flights. This small, independent airport is about 33 miles northwest of the city. The **Greenline 757 Bus** (☎ **08706/087261**) runs from the airport to Victoria Coach Station on Buckingham Palace Road daily every hour 5:30 a.m. to midnight; the trip takes about 75 minutes and costs £8 ($15).

You can also take the 24-hour **Railair Coach Link** to Luton Station (3 miles away), which connects with the Thameslink City Flyer train to King's Cross Station in Central London. The fare costs £9.50 ($18); trip time takes one hour.

Taxis into the city cost about £50 ($93), plus tip.

Arriving by train

If you're coming from the Continent, you cross the English Channel and disembark at one of the United Kingdom's Channel ports. The ports closest to London are Dover, Folkestone, and Ramsgate to the east and Newhaven, Portsmouth, and Southampton to the south. The *QEII* cruise ship also docks at Southampton.

Trains connecting with ferries on the U.K. side of the Channel generally go to Liverpool Street Station, Victoria Station, or Waterloo International. Waterloo International (part of Waterloo Station) is also where the Eurostar Chunnel trains arrive from Paris and Brussels. On the Eurostar, you don't have to make any train-to-boat-to-train transfers along the way. For more on the Eurostar, see Chapter 5.

All London stations link to the Underground system. Just look for the Underground symbol (a circle with a line through it). The stations connect to the Underground as follows:

- ✔ **Liverpool Street** is on the Circle, East London, Metropolitan, and Central Lines.

- ✔ **Victoria** is on the District, Circle, and Victoria lines.

- ✔ **Waterloo** is linked to the Northern and Bakerloo lines.

Taxis wait outside all train stations. See the section "Getting Around London," later in this chapter, for more information on the London Underground and taxis.

London's train stations are swarming with activity. You find bookstores, *bureaux de change* (currency exchange facilities), restaurants, newsstands, and many of the services that airports traditionally offer. While passing through, you can stock up on maps and brochures, and if you arrive in London without a hotel reservation, you can book a room at hotel reservation agencies.

 Keep in mind that the United Kingdom, like the rest of Europe, uses the 24-hour clock for rail and other timetables, which means that 0530 is 5:30 a.m., 1200 is noon, and 1830 is 6:30 p.m. Don't be confused: Just continue counting up from noon: 1300 = 1 p.m., 1400 = 2 p.m., 1500 = 3 p.m., and so on up to 2400 (midnight). In this book, I stick to the American a.m. and p.m. system. Like most of the rest of the world, London goes on daylight saving time from April through October.

Figuring Out the Neighborhoods

Londoners orient themselves by neighborhood (see the "London's Neighborhoods" map on p. 90). Sounds simple enough, but with

London's confusing and sometimes oddly named streets and its seemingly endless plethora of neighborhoods, you may have a hard time telling where one neighborhood begins and another leaves off. For orientation purposes, I give you major streets as boundary markers. But be aware that the neighborhoods frequently bleed beyond these principal arteries.

To help you find your way around, I strongly suggest that you buy a copy of *London A to Z* (ask for *London A to Zed,* because *z* is pronounced *zed*). You can pick up this indexed London street map at just about any bookstore or newsstand (you may want to get it while you're at the airport).

Although **Greater London** encompasses a whopping 622 square miles, the main tourist portion covers only a fraction (25 sq. miles at the most) of that distance. Most sites within this 25-mile range are convenient to the Underground system (the Tube). You may have a short (ten-minute or less) walk from the Tube stop to your destination, but London is flat, and for walkers it's a dream.

London is divided into **postal districts,** like zip codes in the United States. All London street addresses include a designation such as SW1 or EC3. (In London, the postal districts are related to where they lie geographically from the original post office, which was at St. Martin-le-Grand in the City.) Addresses in the City of London, the easternmost portion of Central London, have designations such as EC2, EC3, or EC4. As you move west, the codes change to W, WC, SW, NW, and so on.

You don't need to bother yourself with postal districts except when you're looking up streets in *London A to Z* (many streets in different parts of London have the same name) or mailing something to London. When you actually hit the streets, the postal district designations aren't as important as the nearest Tube stop.

London grew up along the north and south banks of the **Thames River,** which snakes through the city in a long, loose S-curve. This great tidal river played a fundamental role in London's growth, development, and prosperity. London's major tourist sights, hotels, and restaurants are on the river's north bank, and many of the city's famous performing-arts venues are on the South Bank.

Central London, on the north bank of the Thames, is considered the city center — the area covered by the Circle Line Underground route. Paddington Station anchors the northwestern corner, Earl's Court marks the southwestern corner, Tower Hill sits at the southeast corner, and Liverpool Street Station anchors the northeastern corner. Central London is divided into three areas: the **City,** the **West End,** and **West London.** In the descriptions that follow, I start at the City and move west from there.

London's Neighborhoods

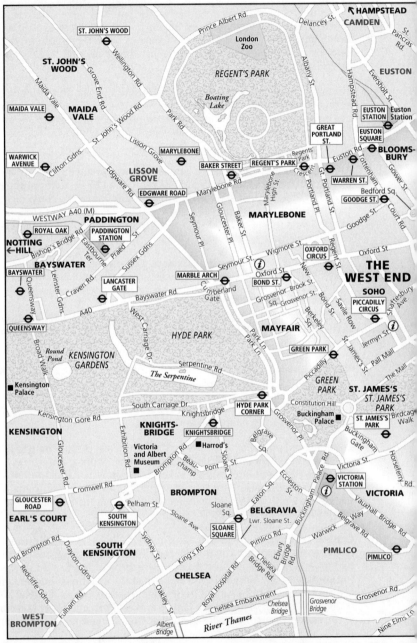

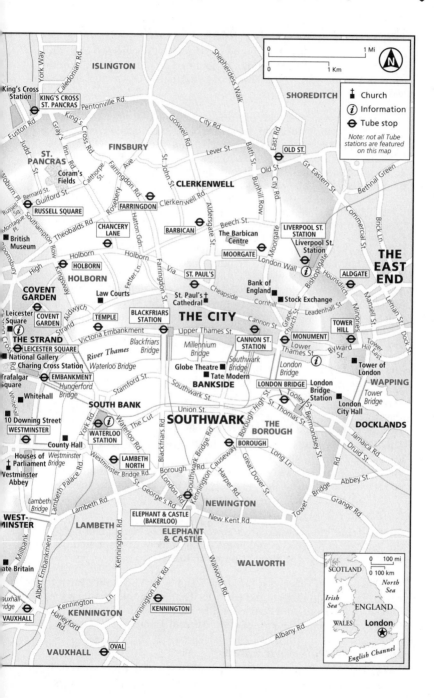

The City of London: The heart of it all

A self-governing entity that extends south from Chiswell Street to the river Thames, the City of London is bounded on the west by Chancery Lane and to the east by the **Tower of London,** the City's most important historic monument.

Fleet Street, associated with printing and publishing since the 1500s but now a little forlorn since the departure of most of its newspaper offices, cuts through the center of the district to Ludgate Circus, where it becomes Ludgate. Follow that road and you get to **St. Paul's Cathedral,** its massive dome beautifully illuminated at night. St. Paul's is just one of the buildings built atop the ancient area known as the City.

Covering the original 1 square mile that the Romans called Londinium, the City encompasses the territory between Moorfields to the north and the Thames to the south and from Aldgate to the east and Temple Bar to the west. Today, this area is the Wall Street of England, home to the **Bank of England,** the **Royal Exchange,** and the **Stock Exchange,** as well as the new **Lloyds of London** building and the **NatWest Tower,** London's second tallest building. You also find the **Museum of London,** the remains of the **Roman Temple of Mithras,** the church of **St. Stephen Walbrook** (designed by Christopher Wren), the Wren-designed **Monument** that commemorates the Great Fire of London in 1666, and the **Barbican Centre,** a mega-arts complex of theaters and concert halls.

Liverpool Street Station is the main rail terminus in this area. The major Tube stops are Bank, Barbican, Blackfriars, Liverpool Street Station, Moorgate, St. Paul's, and Tower Hill.

The West End: Downtown London

The West End (that is, west of the City) is "downtown" London. The West End is known for the theater, entertainment, and shopping areas around Piccadilly Circus and Leicester Square. But a host of neighborhoods make up the West End. I describe them briefly in the sections that follow.

Holborn

Abutting the City of London to the west is the old borough of Holborn, the legal heart of London and home to the **Inns of Court, Lincoln's Inn Fields, Old Bailey,** and **Royal Courts of Justice.**

This "in-between" district is bounded roughly by Theobald's Road to the north, Farringdon Road to the east, the Thames to the south, and Kingsway, Aldwych, and Lancaster Place to the west. The major Tube stops are Aldwych, Blackfriars, Holborn, and Temple.

The Strand and Covent Garden

The northern section of the Strand, the area west of Holborn, is Covent Garden, with Shaftesbury Avenue as its northern boundary. Covent

Garden has many theaters, eateries, and shops and is home to the **Royal Opera House** and **Covent Garden Market,** one of the busiest shopping areas in London. Covent Garden is an area for strolling, shopping, and stopping for tea or a meal.

Formerly one of the premier streets in England, the Strand (the same name as the neighborhood) runs from Trafalgar Square to Fleet Street; the Strand is the principal thoroughfare along the southern edge, with Charing Cross Road to the west and Kingsway, Aldwych, and Lancaster Place to the east. **Cleopatra's Needle,** an Egyptian obelisk dating from about 1475 B.C. and moved to England in 1878, is located in the Victoria Embankment on the north side of the Hungerford Bridge. The major Tube stops are Charing Cross, Covent Garden, and Leicester Square.

Bloomsbury

Just north of Covent Garden, New Oxford Street and Bloomsbury Way mark the beginnings of the Bloomsbury district, home of the **British Museum** and several colleges and universities, as well as the only surviving London home of novelist Charles Dickens.

This intellectual pocket of Central London was home to the famed Bloomsbury Group, whose members included novelist Virginia Woolf and historian Lytton Strachey. Bloomsbury is bounded to the east by Woburn Place and Southampton Row, to the north by Euston Road, and to the west by Tottenham Court Road. The major Tube stops are Euston Square, Goodge Street, Russell Square, and Tottenham Court Road.

Soho

This lively area is full of restaurants, cafes, bars, pubs, and nightclubs and is popular with the gay community. London's **Gay Village** centers around Old Compton Street. Gerrard Street is one of the main streets of **Chinatown.** Much of Soho used to be a down-to-earth Italian neighborhood, but the area later became known for its strip joints and porn palaces. You still see remnants of the sex 'n' sleaze era, but most of it is now gone, and things are going upscale.

The Soho neighborhood occupies the maze of densely packed streets north of Shaftesbury Avenue, west of Charing Cross Road, east of Regent Street, and south of Oxford Street. The major Tube stops are Covent Garden, Leicester Square, and Tottenham Court Road.

Piccadilly Circus, Leicester Square, and Charing Cross

This area, just west of the Strand, is "downtown" London or Theatreland. Piccadilly Circus, with its landmark statue of Eros, is the area's major traffic hub and best-known tourist destination, feeding into Regent Street and Piccadilly. The **Royal Academy of Arts** is just west of Piccadilly Circus. A few minutes' walk to the east puts you at Leicester Square and Shaftesbury Avenue, where you find most of the West End theaters. From Leicester Square, Charing Cross Road runs south to **Trafalgar Square,** with its delightful fountains and four immense bronze lions guarding its corners. Around the square, you see the **National Gallery** and the **National Portrait Gallery. Charing Cross Road** is well known for its bookshops. The Tube stops are Charing Cross, Leicester Square, and Piccadilly Circus.

Mayfair

Elegant and exclusive, Mayfair is luxury-hotel and luxury-shopping land. The area is nestled among Regent Street on the east, Oxford Street on the north, Piccadilly on the south, and Hyde Park on the west. The major Tube stops are Bond Street, Hyde Park Corner, Marble Arch, and Piccadilly Circus.

Marylebone

In a sense, Marylebone (pronounced *Mar*-lee-bone) is "Medical London" because the area has several hospitals and the famous **Harley Street Clinic.** But perhaps the most famous street is Baker Street, home of the fictional Sherlock Holmes. **Madame Tussaud's** wax museum is on Marylebone Road.

Marylebone is the neighborhood north of Mayfair and Bloomsbury and is capped to the north by giant **Regent's Park** (Marylebone Road runs south of the park). Great Portland Street is the area's eastern boundary and Edgware Road the western. The major Tube stops are Baker Street, Marylebone, and Regent's Park.

St. James's

St. James's is "Royal London," a posh green haven beginning at Piccadilly and moving southwest to include **Green Park** and **St. James's Park,** with **Buckingham Palace** between them and **St. James's Palace** across from St. James's Park.

Pall Mall (pronounced *Pell Mell*), lined with exclusive "gentlemen's clubs," runs roughly east-west into the area and meets the north-south St. James's Street. Regent Street is the eastern boundary. The Tube stops are Green Park and St. James's Park.

Westminster

East and south of St. James's, Westminster draws visitors to **Westminster Abbey** and the **Houses of Parliament,** the seat of British government.

Westminster extends from Northumberland Avenue just south of Charing Cross to Vauxhall Bridge Road, with the Thames to the east and **St. James's Park** to the west. Victoria Station, on the northwestern perimeter, is a kind of axis for Belgravia, Pimlico, and Westminster. The Tube stops are St. James's Park, Victoria, and Westminster.

Pimlico

The pie-shaped wedge of London extending west from Vauxhall Bridge Road to Buckingham Palace Road is Pimlico. Crowning the area to the north is Victoria Station. Near the Vauxhall Bridge is the **Tate Britain** gallery. The Tube stops are Pimlico and Victoria.

Belgravia

A posh quarter long favored by aristocrats, Belgravia is where many foreign embassies are located. Beginning west of Victoria Station and Green Park, Belgravia extends south to the river and west to Sloane Street; **Hyde Park** is its northern boundary. The Tube stops are Hyde Park, Sloane Square, and Victoria.

Central London: Parks, museums, and more

West of the West End, you find Central London's residential, cultural, and shopping attractions, including beautiful gardens and popular museums.

Knightsbridge

West of Belgravia is the fashionable residential and shopping district of Knightsbridge, bounded to the north by **Hyde Park** and to the west by Brompton Road. Here you find **Harrods,** the famed department store that has been a London shopping staple for a century and a half. Running through the neighborhood is pretty Beauchamp (pronounced *Beech*-um) Place with its expensive boutiques. The Tube stops are Knightsbridge and Sloane Square.

Chelsea

South of Knightsbridge and west of Belgravia, artsy, trendy Chelsea begins at Sloane Square and runs south to Cheyne Walk and Chelsea Embankment along the Thames. The famous King's Road acts as its northern boundary and Chelsea Bridge Road its eastern border. To the west, the area extends as far as Earl's Court Road, Redcliffe Gardens, and Edith Grove. In Chelsea, you find **Carlyle's House** and the lovely and historic **Chelsea Physic Garden.** The annual Chelsea Flower Show is held on the grounds of Chelsea Royal Hospital. The Tube stop is Sloane Square.

South Kensington

Forming the green northern boundary of South Kensington are **Kensington Gardens** and **Hyde Park.** South Ken is London's museum capital and is packed with hotels and restaurants. Tourists enjoy the attractions of the **Natural History Museum, Science Museum,** and **Victoria & Albert Museum.**

South Kensington is bounded to the south by Brompton Road, to the west by Gloucester (pronounced *Glos*-ter) Road, and to the east by Fulham Road. The Tube stops are Gloucester Road and South Kensington.

Kensington

The residential neighborhood of Kensington fills in the gap between **Kensington Gardens** and **Holland Park,** with Notting Hill Gate and Bayswater Road marking the northern boundary. Kensington Church Street runs north-south between Notting Hill Gate and Kensington High Street. The Tube stop is High Street Kensington.

Earl's Court

This down-to-earth neighborhood has long been a haven for budget travelers (particularly Australians — hence its nickname, Kangaroo Court) and for gays and lesbians. Earl's Court is gradually being renovated, but some streets still look a bit down at the heels. This area offers no major tourist attractions, but it does have some good hotels and B&Bs.

The area begins south of West Cromwell Road and extends south to Lillie Road and Brompton Road. Its western boundary is North End Road, and its eastern boundary is Earl's Court Road. The Tube stop is Earl's Court.

Notting Hill

Beginning north of Holland Park, Kensington Gardens, and Hyde Park (Holland Park Avenue and Bayswater Road run along the northern perimeter of the parks), you find the antiques shops of Notting Hill and the rising subneighborhood of Notting Hill Gate.

The area is bounded by Clarendon Road to the west, Queensway to the east, and Wesbourne Grove to the north. The most famous street, Portobello Road, runs north-south through the center. The neighborhood served as a backdrop for the 1999 movie *Notting Hill,* starring Julia Roberts and Hugh Grant. The Tube stops are Bayswater, Notting Hill Gate, and Queensway.

Bayswater and Paddington

Picking up where Notting Hill ends, Bayswater runs east to meet Marylebone at Edgware Road. The roaring A40 (Westway) highway acts as its northern boundary. Paddington Station is in the northwestern corner of Bayswater.

This commercial area isn't much to look at. The neighborhood offers no major tourist attractions, but it does have many budget B&Bs. The Tube stops are Edgware Road, Lancaster Gate, Marble Arch, and Paddington.

The South Bank

You most likely won't be staying on the South Bank, but you may go there for a play, an exhibition, or a concert at one of its internationally known arts and performance venues or museums. The Tube stops are London Bridge, Southwark, and Waterloo.

The **Hayward Gallery,** the **National Film Theatre,** the **Royal National Theatre,** and the **South Bank Centre** (which contains **Royal Festival Hall** and two smaller concert halls) are all clustered beside the river within easy walking distance of Waterloo Station. Closer to Westminster Bridge is the city's newest high-rise attraction: the **British Airways London Eye** observation wheel.

For a scenic route to the South Bank, take the Tube to Embankment, on the north bank, and walk across the Thames on the new Hungerford pedestrian bridge. The **Jubilee Walkway,** a breezy riverside path, extends south from the arts complexes to the **London Aquarium** and north to the new **Tate Modern,** the **Globe Theatre** (a re-creation of the Elizabethan outdoor theater used by William Shakespeare), **Southwark Cathedral,** and **Tower Bridge.** The new pedestrian-only **Millennium Bridge** spans the Thames from the **Tate Modern** to **St. Paul's.**

Finding Information After You Arrive

You can find hotel- and theater-booking agencies, a currency exchange, and a lot of free brochures on river trips, walking tours, and day trips from London at the **Britain & London Visitor Centre,** 1 Regent St., Piccadilly Circus, SW1 (Tube: Piccadilly Circus), which provides tourist information to walk-in visitors (no phone assistance is available). The center is open Monday 9:30 a.m. to 6:30 p.m., Tuesday through Friday 9 a.m. to 6:30 p.m., and Saturday and Sunday 10 a.m. to 4 p.m.

Tourist Information Centres are found in the following locations (call ☎ 020/7234-5800 for information for all Tourist Information Centres):

- ✔ **City of London,** St. Paul's Churchyard (St. Paul's Cathedral), open Easter through September daily 9:30 a.m. to 5 p.m.; October through Easter Monday through Friday 9:30 a.m. to 5 p.m. and Saturday 9:30 a.m. to 12:30 p.m.

- ✔ **Waterloo International Terminal Arrivals Hall,** open daily 8:30 a.m. to 10:30 p.m.

Getting Around London

You can choose many ways to get around London. If you travel for any distance, the fastest mode of transportation in this enormous city is the

Tube (the subway system). Many of the slower but more scenic buses are double-deckers. Most convenient (unless you're stuck in a traffic jam) is to go by taxi. But walking is the most fun of all. When you're on foot, you see more and can explore some of the leafy squares and cobbled lanes that contribute to London's enduring charm.

For general London travel information, call **Transport for London** at ☎ **020/7222-1234** or visit their Web site, www.tfl.gov.uk. You can get free bus and Underground maps and buy Travelcards and bus passes at any major Underground station or at the London Travel Information Centres in the stations at King's Cross; Liverpool Street; Oxford Circus; Piccadilly Circus; St. James's Park; Victoria; and Heathrow Terminals 1, 2, and 3.

Taking the Underground (subway)

London has the oldest and most comprehensive subway system in the world. The Tube is fast and convenient, and just about everyone but the Royals use it. Everywhere you'll want to go is near a Tube stop, each of which is clearly marked by a red circle with a horizontal line through it. For an Underground map, see the inside back cover of this book.

Using the Underground

Thirteen Underground lines crisscross the city and intersect at various stations where you can change from one train to another. On Underground maps, every line is color-coded (Bakerloo is brown, Piccadilly is dark blue, and so on), which makes planning your route easy. All you need to know is the name of your stop and the direction you're heading. After you figure out which line you need to take, look on the map for the name of the last stop in the direction you need to go. The name of the last stop on the line appears on the front of the train and sometimes on electronic signboards that display the name of the arriving train. (The one exception to this rule is the Circle Line, which runs in a loop around Central London.) Inside all but the oldest trains are electronic signs, recorded voices, or both, which announce the name of each approaching stop.

Most of the Underground system operates with automated entry and exit gates. You feed your ticket into the slot, the ticket disappears and pops up again like a piece of toast, the gate bangs open, and you remove your ticket and pass through. At the other end, you do the same to get out, but the machine keeps the ticket (unless your ticket is a multiuse Travelcard, which the machine returns to you). Ticket collectors are located at some stations outside of Central London.

Traveling to your destination by Underground may require transferring from one Underground line to another. All Underground maps clearly show where various lines converge. Signs in the stations direct you from one line to another. To get from one line to another, you go through tunnels (which the Brits call *subways*), and you may have to go up or down a level or two.

Underground service stops around midnight (a little earlier on less-used lines). Keep this in mind when you're out painting the town red. If you miss the last train, you have to take a taxi or one of the night buses.

Buying tickets

You can purchase Underground tickets at the ticket window or from one of the automated machines that you can find in most stations. Machines can change £5, £10, and £20 notes. Fares to every station are posted.

For fare purposes, the city is divided into zones. **Zone 1** covers all Central London. **Zone 6** extends as far as Heathrow to the west and Upminster to the east. Make sure that your ticket covers all the zones that you're traveling through (no problem if you're staying in Central London), or you may have to pay a £10 ($19) penalty fare.

A **single-fare one-way ticket** within one zone costs £2 ($3.70) for an adult and 60p ($1.10) for a child from 5 to 15 years of age. You don't have to pay more than this to reach any sight in Central London (provided you're also traveling from within Central London). Tickets are valid for use on the day of issue only.

 If you're going to travel by Underground, you can save time and money by buying a book of ten tickets, called a *carnet*. **Carnet tickets** are valid in Zone 1 only. Each ticket is good for a single ride on any day. The price is £17 ($31) for an adult and £5 ($9.25) for a child. With a Travelcard (see the following section), you can save even more.

Saving with Travelcards

 To make the most of London's public transportation system, consider buying a **Travelcard,** which allows unlimited travel by Underground *and* bus. You can purchase these cards at any Tube station window or machine in the following increments:

- ✔ A **Day Travelcard** for Zones 1 and 2 (everything in Central London) costs £4.70 ($8.70) for an adult and £2 ($3.70) for a child; the card is valid after 9:30 a.m. weekdays and all day Saturday and Sunday.

- ✔ The **3-Day Travelcard** for Zones 1 and 2 costs £15 ($28) for an adult and £7.50 ($14) for a child.

- ✔ A **7-day Travelcard** for Zone 1 (all Central London) costs £19 ($35) for an adult and £7.50 ($14) for a child.

- ✔ The **Family Travelcard** is good for families or groups of one or two adults traveling with one to four children; to use it, you must travel together as a group. The Family Travelcard is valid after 9:30 a.m. Monday to Friday and all day Saturday and Sunday. Rates for one day of travel in Zones 1 and 2 are £3.10 ($5.75) for an adult and 80p ($1.50) for a child.

Another great way to save money on London transportation is the **Visitor Travelcard,** which you can buy in the United States and Canada before leaving home. For details, see Chapter 4.

Riding a bus

Distinctive red double-decker buses are very much a part of London's snarled traffic scene, but not all London buses are double-deckers, and some aren't red. The one drawback to bus travel, especially for first-timers, is that you need to know the streets of London so you can get off at the correct stop. Get a free bus map at one of the Travel Information Centres (see "Finding Information After You Arrive," earlier in this chapter), or you may overshoot your destination. On the plus side, riding the bus is cheaper than taking the Tube; you don't have to contend with escalators, elevators, or tunnels; and you get to see the sights as you travel.

A concrete post with a red or white sign on top reading LONDON TRANSPORT BUS SERVICE clearly marks each bus stop. Another sign shows the routes of the buses that stop there. If the sign on top is red, the stop is a request stop, meaning you must hail the approaching bus as you would a taxi (don't whistle — just put up your hand). If the sign is white, the bus stops automatically. Be sure to check the destination sign on the front of the bus to make certain that the bus travels the entire route. Have some coins with you, because the driver won't change banknotes.

The bus network is divided into two fare zones to simplify cash transactions. **Zone 1** covers all Central London, including all the main tourist sites. The bus fare for adults is £1.20 ($2.20), 40p (75¢) for children. Children 16 and under ride free if they have a **Child Photocard;** you must supply your own passport-size photo to obtain this free ID card, which is available at Tube stations or one of the Travel Information Centres.

A **1-day bus pass** can be used all day but isn't valid on N-prefixed night buses (see the next paragraph). You can purchase this and bus passes good for longer periods at most Underground stations, selected news agents, and the Travel Information Centres. A one-day bus pass for all Central London costs £3 ($5.55) for an adult and £1 ($1.85) for a child age 5 to 15. A **7-day bus pass** for Central London costs £11 ($20) for an adult and £4 ($7.40) for a child 5 to 15. *Note:* Children must have a **Child Photocard** ID in order to buy and use any of these passes (see the preceding paragraph).

At the witching hour of midnight, buses become **night buses** (N), and their routes change. Nearly all night buses pass through Trafalgar Square, Central London's late-night magnet for insomniacs.

Hailing a taxi

Taking a taxi is a safe and comfortable way to get around the city. Riding in the old-fashioned, roomy black taxis is a pleasure. Today, there are also many smaller and newer-model taxis. London cabs of any size or color aren't cheap. The fare starts at £1.40 ($2.60) for one person, with 40p (75¢) for each additional passenger. Then you have to deal with the surcharges: 10p (20¢) per item of luggage; 60p ($1.10) weeknights 8 p.m. to midnight; 90p ($1.70) from midnight until 7 a.m.; 60p ($1.10) Saturday and Sunday until 8 p.m. and 90p ($1.65) after that. The meter leaps 20p (35¢) every 111 yards or 90 seconds. Tip your cabbie 10 to 15 percent of the total fare.

You can hail a cab on the street. If a cab is available, the yellow or white FOR HIRE sign on the roof is lit. You can order a **radio cab** by calling ☎ **02072/720-272** or 02072/535-000. Be aware that if you call for a cab, the meter starts ticking when the taxi receives notification from the dispatcher.

London is one city where you don't have to worry about whether the cab driver knows where he's going. When it comes to finding a street address, London cabbies are among the most knowledgeable in the world. Their rigorous training, which includes an exhaustive street test called "The Knowledge," gives them an encyclopedic grasp of the terrain.

Walking on your own two feet

Sure, you can hop from one place to the next using the Tube, a bus, or a cab. But if you really want to get acquainted with the charming hodge-podge and monumental grandeur of London, bring along a good pair of walking shoes and explore on foot. Everywhere you turn, you see entic-ing side streets, countrylike lanes, little *mews dwellings* (former stables converted into homes), and picturesque garden squares. London's great parks are as safe to walk in as its streets. (In fact, crime is less prevalent in London than in many other major cities, and all the neighborhoods included in this book are safe.)

If you want to follow a detailed stroll or two around the city, perhaps of Dickens's London or of Westminster and Whitehall, check out the 11 tours in *Frommer's Memorable Walks in London,* by Richard Jones (Wiley).

A 7-mile walk commemorating the life of Princess Diana passes through four of London's royal parks — St. James's Park, Green Park, Hyde Park, and Kensington Gardens. Along the way are 90 plaques that point out sites associated with Diana, including Kensington Palace (her home for 15 years), Buckingham Palace, St. James's Palace (where she shared an office with Prince Charles), and Spencer House (her family's mansion, now a museum).

When you walk in London (or anywhere in England), remember:

✔ **Traffic moves on the opposite side of the street from what you're accustomed to.** This sounds simple enough on paper, but in practice, you need to keep reminding yourself to look in the "wrong" direction when crossing a street. Throughout London, you see LOOK RIGHT or LOOK LEFT painted on street crossings.

✔ **Pedestrian crossings are marked by striped lines (called *zebra crossings*) on the road.** Flashing lights near the curb indicate that drivers must stop and yield the right of way when a pedestrian steps out into the zebra to cross the street.

Chapter 9

Checking In at London's Best Hotels and B&Bs

In This Chapter
▶ Getting the lowdown on London's accommodations types
▶ Knowing what to expect from a hotel in your price range
▶ Finding the best room for the best rate
▶ Reviewing a list of London favorites

*L*ondon hotel rooms run the gamut from a basic tiny bedroom with a shared bathroom down the hall to elegant, sumptuous splendor. Many travelers don't care where they stay, as long as they can stay there cheaply. The reasoning is, "I'm only going to be in a hotel room to sleep." That assumption may be true, but I also know that a cheap-at-all-costs hotel room can color your mood and turn a potentially memorable vacation into something unnecessarily dreary.

This chapter is devoted to London hotels and B&Bs. You can find details about what to expect for your money, get the lowdown on ways to get the best rooms at the best rates, and check out a list of specific hotels and B&Bs that I heartily recommend.

Getting to Know Your Options

Accommodations in London are available in varying price ranges and degrees of luxury. Places to stay generally fit into one of two categories: hotels and bed-and-breakfast inns (B&Bs). The following sections provide a rundown on the quirks and perks of each type of accommodations.

Understanding the pros and cons of B&Bs

B&Bs are small, family-run hotels with differing degrees of comfort and service. Because B&Bs are often private homes (or what were once private homes), amenities vary widely, especially in the bathroom facilities. Nearly all B&B rooms contain wash basins, but you may have to share a bathroom down the hall. The facilities are usually kept scrupulously clean. Keep in mind that *en-suite* (in the room) baths are generally so small that you feel as if you haven't left the airplane, and the super-small showers can be a trial.

The décor in many of the lowest-priced B&Bs is unimaginative and unimpressive. Coming back to a small room with mismatched furniture, pink walls, and a tiny bathroom down the hall with no hot water may be an inconvenience that you're willing to suffer for the sake of saving money, but I don't recommend any such places in this book. The more popular and well-appointed B&Bs are more expensive, but their comforts and conveniences are worth the price.

What about the breakfast part of the B&B? Well, gone are the days when the staff of every B&B cooked you up a *full English breakfast* of eggs, sausages, bacon, fried tomatoes, and beans. Some B&Bs still do serve an English breakfast, but others put out a *continental buffet,* which is a breakfast of cereals, fruits, and breads. The B&B descriptions in this book say either "English breakfast included" or "continental breakfast included," so you know what to expect.

Licensed B&Bs, like hotels, are inspected regularly, and the quality of B&Bs has improved tremendously over the years. I recommend them for people who don't require many extras, although the most successful B&Bs continually upgrade their services or offer some enticing amenities. For example, many B&Bs now provide cable TVs and direct-dial phones in the rooms.

If you want to do some additional B&B research, the following three agencies have useful Web sites:

- ✔ **London Bed and Breakfast:** www.londonbandb.com (☎ 800/872-2632 in the U.S. or 020/7351-3445 in London)

- ✔ **London Bed and Breakfast Agency Ltd.:** www.londonbb.com (☎ 020/7586-2768 in London)

- ✔ **Uptown Reservations:** www.uptownres.co.uk (☎ 020/7351-3445 in London)

If you're physically disabled in any way, B&Bs may not be the choice for you. B&Bs usually don't have elevators, so you may have to carry your luggage up steep, narrow stairs. Be sure to check how accessible the B&B is before you make your reservations.

Exploring hotel choices

You find a wide choice of hotels in London. Most of the moderately priced hotels provide breakfast with a room rental. At a four- or five-star hotel, you pay a hefty price to eat breakfast on the premises. The rooms in a self-catering hotel are equipped with small kitchens, so you can make your own breakfast in your room or go out to a nearby cafe or restaurant.

Boutique and deluxe hotels

London offers a few *boutique hotels*. These hotels are midrange in size but not price; sumptuously furnished, they offer state-of-the-art amenities and full service. The **Montague** in Bloomsbury and **41** in Victoria/Westminster are two of the best.

A more traditional choice is one of London's older deluxe hotels. The **Cadogan Hotel** in Chelsea, **The Gore** in South Kensington, and **Hazlitt's 1718** in Soho have all been around for a century or more. These hotels offer a distinctly English kind of style, full of charm and character.

The older deluxe hotels are offset by the hippest-of-the-hip: the **St. Martin's Hotel,** an Ian Schrager concoction in a converted office block.

Chain properties

But maybe you *always* stay at one of the chain hotels — a **Crowne Plaza,** a **Hyatt,** or a **Marriott** — places that are basically the same no matter where they are: They rely on their brand name and a no-surprise approach to win customers. London is chock-full of chain hotels, if that's what you fancy. Most of them cater to large groups, and you may feel rather anonymous in them. On the other hand, these hotels are usually well equipped for people with disabilities and families with children.

Landmark hotels

At the top of the hotel spectrum, in both price and prestige, are the landmark hotels: **Claridge's,** the **Dorchester,** the **Park Lane Sheraton,** and **The Savoy.** These famous hotels are among the best in the world. In each of them, you can expect glamorous public salons, a generously proportioned and well-decorated room with a large private bath, an on-site health club or access to one nearby, and top-of-the-line service.

Self-catering options

You can also consider staying at a *self-catering hotel,* where *you* do the cooking in the kitchen in your own hotel room. For short stays and for one or two people, self-catering hotels don't always beat the competition's price. But for families and travelers who can't afford or don't want to eat every meal out, self-catering hotels can be a budget-saver. For comfort and convenience, **Astons Apartments** in South Kensington is among the best.

One of the most economical ways to stay in London is to rent a self-catering flat. The owners register their flats with rental agencies; minimum rental time is usually one week. You can find a small studio flat in Central London that sleeps two and is fully equipped for under £500 ($925) per week. One of the best agencies to help you find a flat is the **Independent Traveller** (☎ **01392/860807;** www.gowithit.co.uk).

Finding the Best Room at the Best Rate

The maximum rate that a hotel charges for a type of room is the *rack rate*. If you walk in off the street and ask for a room for the night, the hotel may charge you this top rate. Hotel rates, like airline fares, change all the time, and it's impossible to list the most current "specials" a hotel is offering on its Web site. So the rack rate is what I use as a hotel price guide in this book.

Be aware that you don't have to pay the rack rate. Hardly anybody does. Just ask for a cheaper or discounted rate. The result is often favorable when savvy travelers make this request. Hotels in London are eager to fill their beds, and most of them are willing to negotiate a room rate. Read on for more strategies on getting a good rate.

Finding the best rate

The rate you pay for a room depends on many factors, and the way you make your reservation is the most important. The following strategies can help you get the best rate available:

- ✔ **Call around.** I recommend that you call both the U.S. toll-free number and the local London number for the prospective hotel. I know that calling both sources takes time and costs money, but the quoted rates can vary so widely that you may save a bundle. (Smaller and less expensive B&Bs and hotels generally don't have toll-free numbers in the States, so you have to call, fax, or e-mail those establishments directly.)

- ✔ **Ask about discounts.** If you make your reservation with a large chain hotel, be sure to mention membership in AARP, frequent-flier programs, and any other corporate rewards program. Budget hotels and small B&Bs rarely offer these organization discounts, but with larger hotels, you never know when the mention may be worth a few pounds off your room rate.

- ✔ **Travel off-season and on weekends.** Room rates change with the season and as occupancy rates rise and fall. You're less likely to receive discount rates if a hotel is close to full, but if it's nearly empty, you may be able to negotiate a significant discount. Expensive hotels catering to business travelers are most crowded on weekdays and usually offer big discounts for weekend stays.

You may be able to save 20 percent or more by traveling off-season, which is mid-October to mid-December and January to March.

- ✔ **Choose a package tour.** The best rates of all will probably be with an air/hotel package (see Chapter 5). With these packages, which are sometimes astonishingly cheap, you have to choose a hotel that's part of the package. Airline package hotels tend to be larger chains. So what? The money you save may amount to hundreds of dollars.

✔ **Use a travel agent.** A travel agent may be able to negotiate a better room rate than you could get by yourself. The hotel gives the agent a discount in exchange for steering his or her business toward that hotel.

Surfing the Web for hotel deals

Another great source for finding hotel deals is the Internet. Nowadays, almost all hotels, even those in the budget range, have Web sites. (I list each hotel's Web site with the other hotel information, later in this chapter.) Special promotional offers are often available only on the hotel's Web site, so it pays to do some checking.

You can also use search engines to help you locate a London hotel. Although the major travel-booking Web sites (Arthur Frommer's Budget Travel Online, Travelocity, Microsoft Expedia, Yahoo!, and Smarter Living) offer hotel booking, you may be better off using a Web site devoted to lodging because more-general sites don't list all types of properties. Some lodging sites specialize in a particular type of accommodations, such as bed-and-breakfast inns, which aren't on the more mainstream booking services. Other services, such as TravelWeb (see the following list), offer weekend deals on major chain properties that cater to business travelers and have more empty rooms on the weekends.

Some good all-purpose Web sites that you can use to track down and make online reservations at hotels in London include the following:

✔ **All Hotels on the Web** (www.all-hotels.com) doesn't actually include *all* the hotels on the Web, but it does have tens of thousands of listings throughout the world, including London. Bear in mind that each hotel in the list has paid a fee ($25 and up) for placement, so the list is not objective, but more like online brochures.

✔ **British Hotel Reservation Centre** (www.bhrc.co.uk) lists current and seasonal specials at selected London hotels.

✔ **HotelDiscount.com** (www.hoteldiscount.com) lists bargain rates at hotels in U.S. and international cities, including London. If you click "London" and input your travel dates, the site provides a list of the best prices for a selection of hotels in various neighborhoods.

✔ **Independent Traveller** (www.gowithit.co.uk) lists hundreds of self-catering accommodations in London. These are private flats, not hotels, and are available for a one-week minimum period; they can be a fantastic bargain.

✔ **London Bed & Breakfast** (www.londonbandb.com) can provide inexpensive accommodations in select private homes.

✔ **London Bed and Breakfast Agency Ltd.** (www.londonbb.com) is another reliable B&B-finder in London.

✔ The **Londontown** (www.londontown.com) Web site has a long list of hotels to choose from, including some with special offers.

- **SeniorSearch U.K.** (www.wiredseniors.com/ageofreason) is a site for seniors looking for special hotels and other forms of accommodations, including home and apartment exchanges.

- **TravelWeb** (www.travelweb.com) lists more than 16,000 hotels worldwide, focusing on chains, such as Hyatt and Hilton. You can book almost 90 percent of the properties online. Its Click-It Weekends, updated each Monday, offers weekend deals at many leading chains.

- **Uptown Reservations** (www.uptownres.co.uk) provides listings for dozens of B&Bs in private homes in London.

Reserving the best room

After you know where you're staying, asking a few more questions can help you land the best possible room. For example:

- **Ask about staying in a corner room.** They're usually larger, quieter, and brighter, but they may cost a bit more.

- **Ask about staying in a room in the back of the building.** In London, especially, traffic noise can be loud and annoying. In the back, you may get a room that overlooks a quiet garden.

- **If your London hotel is a high-rise, request a room on a high floor.** Being farther away from the street means your room may be quieter. Plus, a higher room may give you the added bonus of a better view.

- **Ask whether the hotel is renovating.** If the answer is yes, request a room away from the renovation work, and make sure you ask again when you check in.

- **If you have any physical impairments, be sure to ask whether the hotel has a *lift* (elevator).** Many small and older hotels in London do not have elevators. If the hotel lacks a lift, ask whether a ground-floor (first floor) room is available.

- **Inquire about the location of restaurants, bars, and meeting facilities, which can be noisy.**

- **If you aren't happy with your room when you arrive, return to the front desk right away.** If another room is available, the staff should be able to accommodate you, within reason.

Arriving without a Reservation

Whatever your hotel choice in London, I want to remind you again: *Booking ahead is a good idea.* Why waste precious vacation time searching for a hotel? If you do arrive without a reservation, your first option is to start calling the hotels directly. Keep in mind that smaller B&Bs don't accept reservations late in the evening. You can also book rooms through the trustworthy agencies in the following list, but the first one doesn't have phone service so you must show up in person.

- ✔ **The Britain & London Visitor Centre** (1 Regent St.; Tube: Piccadilly Circus) is open weekdays 9 a.m. to 6:30 p.m. (from 9:30 a.m. on Mon) and on Saturday and Sunday 10 a.m. to 4 p.m. (Sat June–Sept 9 a.m.–5 p.m.). The Visitor Centre doesn't have phone service, so you have to show up in person to get help reserving a room somewhere.

- ✔ **British Hotel Reservation Centre** (☎ 020/7340-1616; www.bhrc.co.uk) offers a 24-hour phone line. The center provides free reservations and discounted rates at all the leading hotel groups and the major independents. This agency operates a reservations desk (open daily 6 a.m. to midnight) at the Underground station of Heathrow Airport.

- ✔ **First Option Hotel Reservations** (☎ 020/7808-3861) is another hotel booking service. This hotel booking agency operates kiosks at the following Central London rail stations: Charing Cross (☎ 020/7976-1171); Euston (☎ 020/7388-7435); Kings Cross, by Platform 8 (☎ 020/7837-5681); Paddington (☎ 020/7723-0184); and Victoria, by Platform 9 (☎ 020/7828-4646).

London's Top Hotels

Every recommended hotel in this chapter has a $ symbol to help you home in on your price limit. These symbols reflect a hotel's high- and low-end rack rates for a double room. Table 9-1 shows what you can expect in terms of accommodations type, room size, and standard amenities in the five price categories.

Table 9-1	Key to Hotel Dollar Signs	
Dollar Sign(s)	**Price Range**	**What to Expect**
$	Less than £95/$176	These accommodations are relatively simple and more likely to be found in B&Bs than hotels. Rooms will likely be small, and in-room amenities such as a telephone and televisions are not necessarily provided. You may have to share a bathroom. In a B&B, you will get breakfast.

(continued)

Table 9-1 *(continued)*

Dollar Sign(s)	Price Range	What to Expect
$$	£96–£149/$176–$275	A bit classier, these midrange accommodations offer more room, more extras (such as irons, hair dryers, or a microwave), and a more convenient location than the preceding category. You probably get breakfast.
$$$	£150–£203/$276–$375	Higher-class still, these accommodations begin to look more upscale and service begins to factor in. Many chain hotels are in this category. You'll have a roomier private bathroom, cable TV, and other in-room amenities, and there will probably be a cafe or restaurant on the premises. You may or may not get breakfast.
$$$$	£204–£257/$376–$475	Hotels in this category will generally meet high international standards and be found in upscale neighborhoods. Porter and room service will be available. Think fine furnishings, larger bathrooms with designer toiletries, high-quality bedding, chocolates on your pillow, a classy restaurant, and a knowledgeable concierge. There will be a fine breakfast available, but you'll probably have to pay for it.
$$$$$	£257/$475 and up	These top-rated accommodations generally come with luxury amenities, such as valet parking, 24-hour room service, a gourmet restaurant, on-site spa and health club, large bathrooms, high-end furnishings and high-quality sheets, DVD/CD players, turn-down service — it's all great, and you pay through the nose for it. Breakfast will be available but not included in the price. The great London "name" hotels fall into this category.

Sorry, you can't escape that annoying **17.5 percent value-added tax (VAT).** In general, the quoted room rate includes the VAT (except for rooms at the upper end of the price scale). Be sure to ask, though, so you won't get an unpleasant surprise when you're checking out. Unless I note otherwise, the VAT is included in the rates for my recommended hotels.

The Abbey Court
$$–$$$$ **Notting Hill**

This small, graceful hotel, with a flower-filled front patio and a rear conservatory where breakfast is served, is located in a renovated mid-Victorian townhouse near Kensington Gardens. The 22 charming guest rooms feature 18th- and 19th-century country antiques and marble bathrooms equipped with Jacuzzi tubs, showers, and heated towel racks. You can enjoy 24-hour room service and take advantage of the services of the concierge, who can help arrange for babysitting.

See map p. 120. 20 Pembridge Gardens, W2 4DU. ☎ *020/7221-7518. Fax: 020/7792-0858.* www.abbeycourthotel.co.uk. *Tube: Notting Hill Gate (then a five-minute walk north on Pembridge Gardens Road). Rack rates: £110–£250 ($204–$463) double. AE, MC, V.*

Abbey House
$ **Kensington**

For tranquility and affordability in a great location (next to Kensington Gardens and Palace), this small, family-run B&B can't be beat. Although modernized, the 1860s-era building retains many original features. The 16 spacious guest rooms (some triples and quads suitable for families) have central heating and wash basins; every two units share a bathroom. The décor is cheerful and practical.

See map p. 118. 11 Vicarage Gate (off Kensington Church Street), W8 4AG. ☎ *020/ 7727-2594.* www.abbeyhousekensington.com. *Tube: High Street Kensington (then a five-minute walk east on Kensington High Street and north on Kensington Church Street). Rack rates: £74 ($137) double without bathroom. English breakfast included. No credit cards accepted.*

Aster House
$$–$$$ **South Kensington**

Found at the end of an early Victorian terrace, this beautifully renovated (in 2000) nonsmoking charmer was named "Bed and Breakfast of the Year" by the London Tourism Awards in 2001 and 2002. Each of the 12 guest rooms is individually decorated in English country-house style, some with four-poster, half-canopied beds and silk wallpaper. The new bathrooms come with power showers. The breakfasts, served in the glassed-in garden conservatory, are more health-conscious than those served in most English B&Bs.

See map p. 118. 3 Sumner Place (near Onslow Square), SW7 3EE. ☎ *020/7581-5888. Fax: 020/7584-4925.* www.asterhouse.com. *Tube: South Kensington (then a five-minute walk west on Old Brompton Road and south on Sumner Place). Rack rates: £145–£195 ($268–$361) double. Continental breakfast included. MC, V.*

London Accommodations Overview

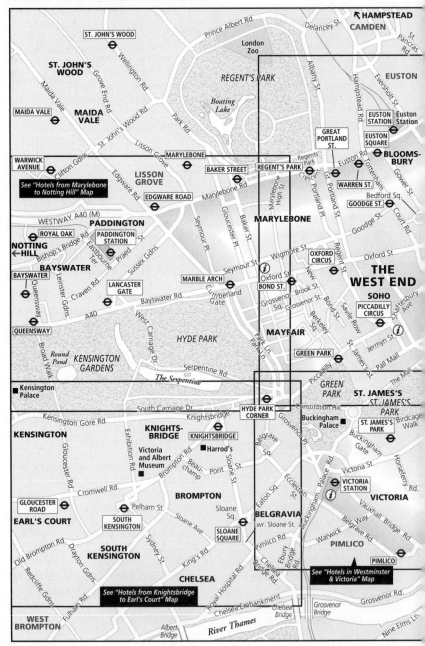

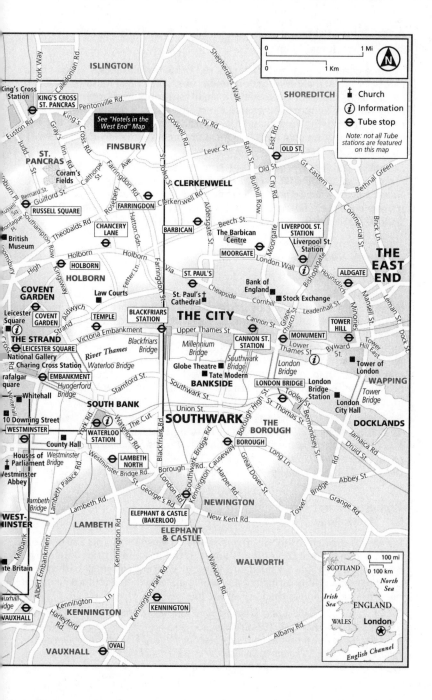

Astons Apartments
$-$$ South Kensington

In three carefully restored Victorian red-brick townhouses, Astons offers value-packed self-catering accommodations, some ideal for families. Each studio has a compact kitchenette, a small bathroom, and bright functional furnishings. The more expensive executive studios feature larger bathrooms, more living space, and extra pizzazz in the décor. If you like the idea of having your own cozy London apartment (with daily maid service), you can't do better.

See map p. 118. 31 Rosary Gardens (off Hereford Square), SW7 4NQ. ☎ **800/525-2810** *in the U.S. or 020/7590-6000. Fax: 020/7590-6060.* www.astons-apartments.com. *Tube: Gloucester Road (then a five-minute walk south on Gloucester Road and west on Hereford Square; Rosary Gardens is 1 block farther west). Rack rates: £90–£125 ($167–$231) double. Rates don't include 17.5 percent VAT. AE, MC, V.*

Avonmore Hotel
$-$$ Kensington

This small hotel is in a quiet neighborhood easily accessible to West End theaters and shops. You'd be hard-pressed to find more for your money: Each of the nine guest rooms offers a tasteful décor and an array of amenities not usually found in this price range. A few years ago, this establishment was voted London's best private hotel by the Automobile Association (AA), and the high standards that earned that honor are still maintained. An English breakfast is served in a cheerful breakfast room; a bar and limited room service are also available, and the hotel can arrange for babysitting.

See map p. 118. 66 Avonmore Rd. (northwest of Earl's Court), W14 8RS. ☎ **020/7603-4296.** *Fax: 020/7603-4035.* www.avonmorehotel.co.uk. *Tube: West Kensington (then a five-minute walk north on North End Road and Mattheson Road to Avonmore Road). Rack rates: £60–£90 ($111–$167) double without bathroom, £80–£110 ($148–$204) double with bathroom. English breakfast included. AE, MC, V.*

Bryanston Court Hotel
$$ Marylebone

Located in a neighborhood with many attractive squares, this 200-year-old hotel is one of Central London's finest in the moderate price range. The refurbished hotel has 54 small guest rooms (with equally small bathrooms) that are comfortably furnished and well maintained. You find a welcoming bar with a fireplace in the back of the lounge.

See map p. 120. 56–60 Great Cumberland Place (near Marble Arch), W1H 7FD. ☎ **020/7262-3141.** *Fax: 020/7262-7248.* www.bryanstonhotel.com. *Tube: Marble Arch (then a five-minute walk north on Great Cumberland Place to Bryanston Place). Rack rates: £120 ($222) double. Continental breakfast included. AE, DC, MC, V.*

Hotels in Westminster and Victoria

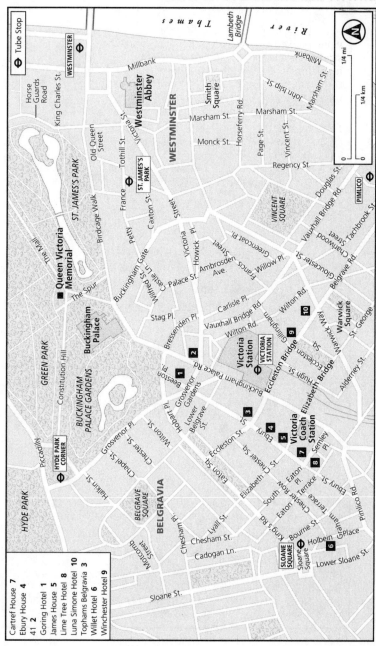

Cartref House **7**
Ebury House **4**
41 **2**
Goring Hotel **1**
James House **5**
Lime Tree Hotel **8**
Luna Simone Hotel **10**
Tophams Belgravia **3**
Willet Hotel **6**
Winchester Hotel **9**

Hotels in the West End

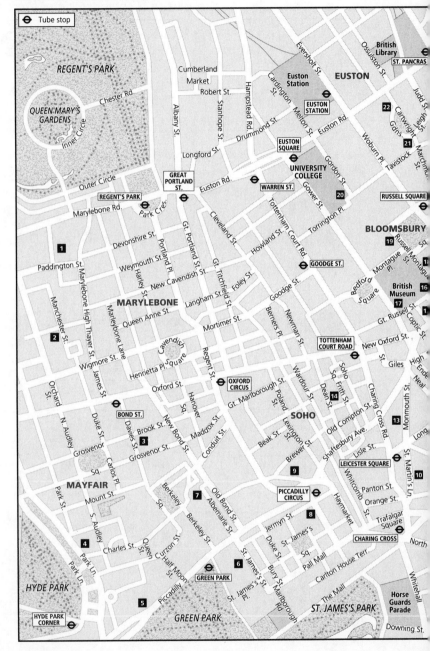

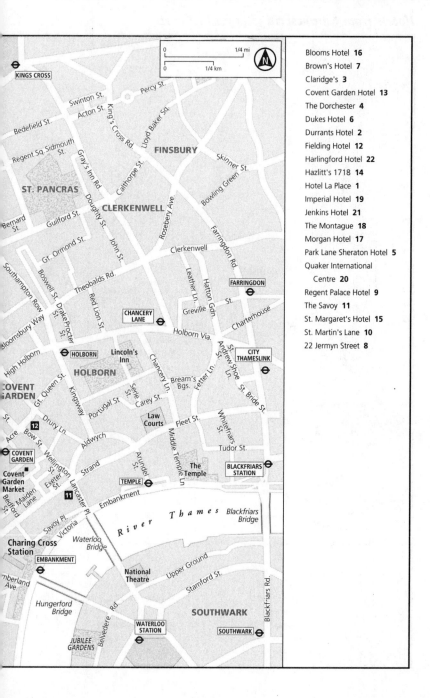

Blooms Hotel **16**
Brown's Hotel **7**
Claridge's **3**
Covent Garden Hotel **13**
The Dorchester **4**
Dukes Hotel **6**
Durrants Hotel **2**
Fielding Hotel **12**
Harlingford Hotel **22**
Hazlitt's 1718 **14**
Hotel La Place **1**
Imperial Hotel **19**
Jenkins Hotel **21**
The Montague **18**
Morgan Hotel **17**
Park Lane Sheraton Hotel **5**
Quaker International
   Centre **20**
Regent Palace Hotel **9**
The Savoy **11**
St. Margaret's Hotel **15**
St. Martin's Lane **10**
22 Jermyn Street **8**

Hotels from Knightsbridge to Earl's Court

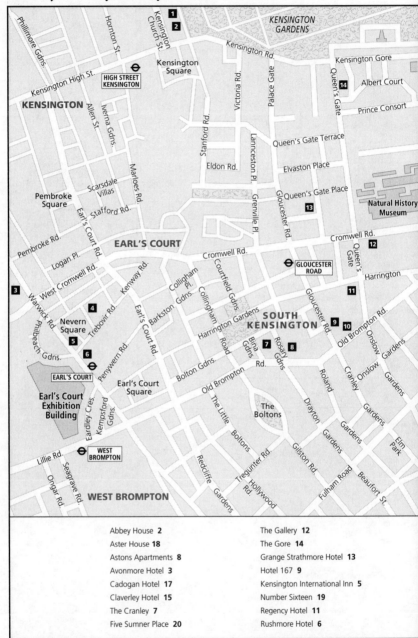

Abbey House **2**	The Gallery **12**
Aster House **18**	The Gore **14**
Astons Apartments **8**	Grange Strathmore Hotel **13**
Avonmore Hotel **3**	Hotel 167 **9**
Cadogan Hotel **17**	Kensington International Inn **5**
Claverley Hotel **15**	Number Sixteen **19**
The Cranley **7**	Regency Hotel **11**
Five Sumner Place **20**	Rushmore Hotel **6**

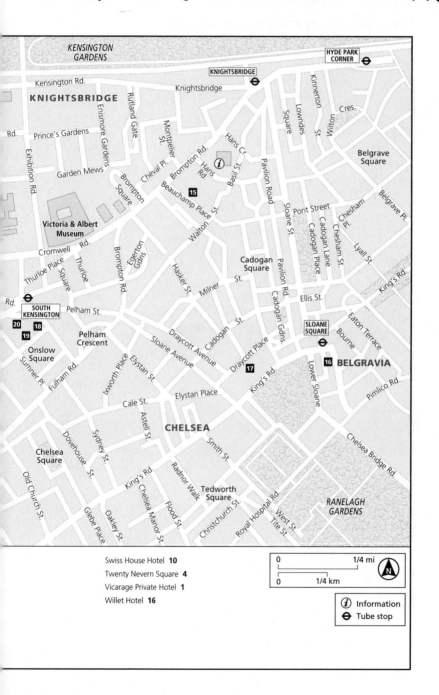

KENSINGTON GARDENS

HYDE PARK CORNER

KNIGHTSBRIDGE

Kensington Rd.

Knightsbridge

KNIGHTSBRIDGE

Kinnerton St.

Lowndes Square

Cres.

Wilton

Belgrave Square

Rd.

Prince's Gardens

Ensmore Gardens

Rutland Gate

Exhibition Rd.

Garden Mews

Montpelier St.

Cheval Pl.

Brompton Rd.

Hans Cr.

Hans Rd.

Basil St.

i

15

Pavilion Road

Belgrave Pl.

Beauchamp Place

Brompton Square

Pont Street

Chesham Pl.

Chesham St.

Lyall St.

Walton

Sloane St.

Cadogan Lane

Cadogan Place

Cromwell Rd.

Victoria & Albert Museum

Thurloe Place

Egerton Gdns

Cadogan Square

Pavilion Rd.

Ellis St.

King's Rd.

Thurloe Square

Thurloe

Brompton Rd.

Hasker St.

Milner St.

Cadogan Gdns

Eaton Terrace

Rd.

SOUTH KENSINGTON

Pelham St.

Cadogan St.

SLOANE SQUARE

Bourne

20 **18**

19

Pelham Crescent

Draycott Avenue

Sloane Avenue

Draycott Place

16 **BELGRAVIA**

Onslow Square

Summer Pl.

Fulham Rd.

Ixworth Place

Elystan St.

17

King's Rd.

Lower Sloane

Pimlico Rd.

Cale St.

Elystan Place

Dovehouse St.

Sydney St.

Astell St.

CHELSEA

Smith St.

Chelsea Bridge Rd.

Chelsea Square

King's Rd.

Radnor Walk

Tedworth Square

RANELAGH GARDENS

Old Church St.

Glebe Place

Oakley St.

Flood St.

Christchurch St.

Royal Hospital Rd.

West St.

Tite St.

Swiss House Hotel **10**
Twenty Nevern Square **4**
Vicarage Private Hotel **1**
Willet Hotel **16**

0   1/4 mi
0   1/4 km

N

i Information
⊖ Tube stop

Hotels from Marylebone to Notting Hill

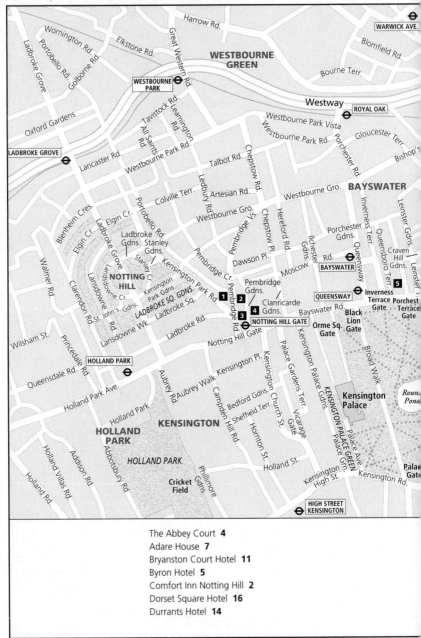

The Abbey Court **4**
Adare House **7**
Bryanston Court Hotel **11**
Byron Hotel **5**
Comfort Inn Notting Hill **2**
Dorset Square Hotel **16**
Durrants Hotel **14**

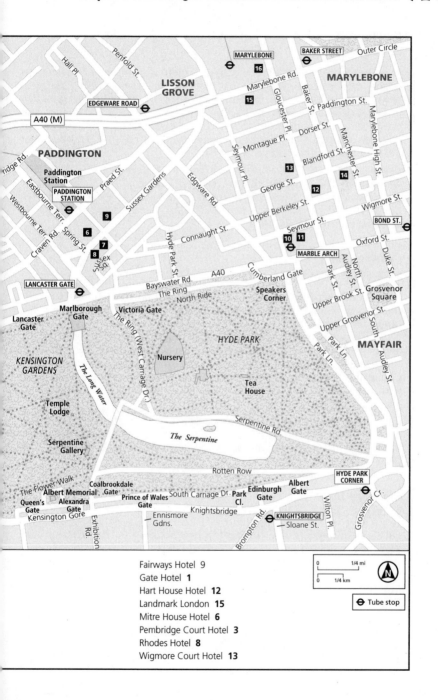

Fairways Hotel 9
Gate Hotel 1
Hart House Hotel **12**
Landmark London **15**
Mitre House Hotel **6**
Pembridge Court Hotel **3**
Rhodes Hotel **8**
Wigmore Court Hotel **13**

Byron Hotel
$$ Bayswater

The family-run 45-room Byron occupies a Victorian house that's been thoroughly modernized but hasn't lost its traditional atmosphere. The guest rooms have ample closets, tile baths, and good lighting. Breakfast is served in a cheery dining room. The staff members are pleasant and helpful, and the hotel can provide child cots and help with special requirements for children's meals. Considering the amenities offered, this establishment offers an especially good value.

See map p. 120. 36–38 Queensborough Terrace (off Bayswater Road), W2 3SH. ☎ *020/7243-0987. Fax: 020/7792-1957.* www.capricornhotels.co.uk. *Tube: Queensway (then a five-minute walk east on Bayswater Road and north on Queensborough Terrace). Rack rates: £120 ($222) double. English or continental breakfast included. AE, DC, MC, V.*

Cadogan Hotel
$$$$–$$$$$ Chelsea

You feel transported back to the Victorian era at this beautiful 69-room hotel, with a small wood-paneled lobby and sumptuous drawing room (good for afternoon tea), close to all the exclusive Knightsbridge shops. The Cadogan (pronounced Ca-*dug*-en) is the hotel where poet, playwright, and novelist Oscar Wilde was staying when he was arrested (room 118 is the Oscar Wilde Room). The large guest rooms, many overlooking the Cadogan Place gardens, are quietly tasteful and splendidly comfortable, with large bathrooms. The sedate Edwardian restaurant is known for its excellent cuisine.

See map p. 118. 75 Sloane St. (near Sloane Square), SW1X 9SG. ☎ **800/260-8338** *in the U.S. or 020/7235-7141. Fax: 020/7245-0994.* www.cadogan.com. *Tube: Sloane Square (then a five-minute walk north on Sloane Street). Rack rates: £245–£350 ($453–$648) double. Rates don't include 17.5 percent VAT. AE, MC, V.*

Claverley Hotel
$$–$$$$$ Knightsbridge

On a quiet Knightsbridge cul-de-sac a few blocks from Harrods, this cozy place is considered one of London's best B&Bs. The public rooms feature Georgian-era accessories, 19th-century oil portraits, elegant antiques, and leather-covered sofas. The 29 guest rooms are smart and cozy, with marble bathrooms with tubs and power showers. The price includes an excellent English breakfast.

See map p. 118. 13–14 Beaufort Gardens (off Brompton Road), SW3 1PS. ☎ **800/ 747-0398** *in the U.S. or 020/7589-8541. Fax: 020/7584-3410.* www.claverley hotel.co.uk. *Tube: Knightsbridge (then a two-minute walk south past Harrods on Brompton Road to Beaufort Gardens). Rack rates: £149–£259 ($276–$479) double. English breakfast included. AE, DC, MC, V.*

Comfort Inn Notting Hill
$$ Notting Hill

You'll get a lower room rate at this chain-hotel franchise if you book directly with them instead of through central reservations. Located on a quiet, pretty street off Notting Hill Gate, the Comfort Inn stretches across five terrace houses and has 64 fair-size rooms on the three upper floors. (There's an elevator.) Rooms have been redecorated with a nice traditional look and equipped with firm new beds; a few newly redone rooms are on a charming interior courtyard. Standard amenities include dataports, coffeemakers, and hair dryers. The bathrooms are also newly renovated.

See map p. 120. 6–14 Pembridge Gardens, W2 4DU. ☎ **020/7229-6666.** *Fax: 020/ 7229-3333.* www.1th-hotels.com. *Tube: Notting Hill Gate (then a two-minute walk north on Pembridge Gardens). Rack rates: £100 ($185) double. Continental breakfast included. AE, DC, MC, V.*

Covent Garden Hotel
$$$$–$$$$$ Covent Garden

Created from an 1850s French hospital and dispensary, this boutique hotel surrounds guests in luxury. No two of the 50 guest rooms are alike. Many rooms have large windows with rooftop views. The décor is a lush mix of antiques and fine contemporary furniture, and the granite-tiled bathrooms with glass-walled showers and heated towel racks are among the best in London. The wood-paneled public rooms are just as impressive. On-site **Brasserie Max** serves up eclectic bistro food and is a chic place to lunch. If you don't get enough exercise touring London, you can keep in shape at the small gym on the premises.

See map p. 116. 10 Monmouth St. (near Covent Garden Market), WC2H 9BH. ☎ **800/ 553-6674** *in the U.S. or 020/7806-1000. Fax: 020/7806-1100.* www.firmdale.com. *Tube: Leicester Square (then a five-minute walk north on St. Martin's Lane, which becomes Monmouth Street). Rack rates: £210–£305 ($389–$564) double. Rates don't include 17.5 percent VAT. AE, DC, MC, V.*

The Cranley
$$$–$$$$ South Kensington

On a quiet street near South Kensington's museums, the Cranley occupies a quartet of restored 1875 townhouses. Luxuriously appointed public rooms and 39 high-ceilinged, air-conditioned guest rooms — with original plasterwork, a blend of Victorian and contemporary furnishings, and up-to-the-minute, in-room technology — make this property a standout. The bathrooms are large and nicely finished, with tubs and showers. Rates include tea with scones in the afternoon and champagne and canapés in the evening.

See map p. 118. 10–12 Bina Gardens (off Brompton Road), SW5 0LA. ☎ **800/448-8355** *in the U.S. or 020/7373-0123. Fax: 020/7373-9497.* www.thecranley.com. *Tube: Gloucester Road (then a five-minute walk south on Gloucester Road, west on*

Brompton Road, and north on Bina Gardens). Rack rates: £190–£220 ($352–$407) double. AE, DC, MC, V.

Dorset Square Hotel
$$$$–$$$$$ **Marylebone**

This sophisticated, 38-room, luxury boutique hotel occupies a beautifully restored Regency townhouse overlooking Dorset Square, a private garden surrounded by graceful buildings. Inside and out, this hotel is the epitome of traditional English style. Each guest room is unique, filled with a superlative mix of antiques, original oils, fine furniture, fresh flowers, and richly textured fabrics. The bathrooms are marble and mahogany (just remember that some of those enticing little toiletries aren't free).

See map p. 120. 39–40 Dorset Square (just west of Regent's Park), NW1 6QN. ☎ **800/553-6674** *in the U.S. or 020/7723-7874. Fax: 020/7724-3328.* www.dorset square.co.uk. *Tube: Marylebone (then a two-minute walk east on Melcombe to Dorset Square). Rack rates: £210–£300 ($389–$555) double. Rates don't include 17.5 percent VAT. AE, MC, V.*

Durrants Hotel
$$$ **Marylebone**

Opened in 1789 off Manchester Square, this 92-room hotel provides an atmospheric London retreat. The pine-and-mahogany-paneled public areas, including an 18th-century letter-writing room and a wonderful Georgian room that serves as a restaurant, are quintessentially English. The guest rooms are generously proportioned (for the most part) and nicely furnished, with decent-size bathrooms.

See map p. 120. George Street (across from the Wallace Collection), W1H 6BJ. ☎ *020/7935-8131. Fax: 020/7487-3510.* www.durrantshotel.co.uk. *Tube: Bond Street (then a five-minute walk west on Oxford Street and north on Duke Street and Manchester Street). Rack rates: £165 ($305) double. AE, MC, V.*

Fairways Hotel
$ **Paddington**

This large, late-Georgian house from the 1820s is a real bargain. Stephen Adams, who took over the management from his parents (they ran the hotel for 25 years), made several improvements in 2002, laying new carpeting and redoing all the communal toilets and showers. All 17 rooms are different, the ones in back much quieter. Some of the private bathrooms are much smaller than others. Coffeemakers and hair dryers are in the rooms, but the phone is in the hallway and, to keep prices low, breakfast is not included in the low room rate.

See map p. 120. 186 Sussex Gardens, W2 1TU. ☎ *020/7723-4871. Fax: 020/7723-4871.* www.fairways-hotel.co.uk. *Tube: Paddington (then a five-minute walk). Rack rates: £60 ($111) double without bathroom, £70 ($130) double with bathroom. AE, DC, MC, V.*

Fielding Hotel
$$ Covent Garden

Named for author Henry Fielding (famous for *The History of Tom Jones*), the Fielding is on a beautiful old street (now pedestrian-only) lit by 19th-century gaslights and across from the Royal Opera House. The stairways are steep and narrow (the hotel has no elevator), and the 24 rather cramped guest rooms are undistinguished in decor, but they do have showers and toilets. Those quibbles aside, this quirky hotel is an excellent value. A small bar is on the premises, and the area is loaded with cafes, restaurants, and fabulous shopping.

See map p. 116. 4 Broad Court, Bow Street, WC2B 5QZ. ☎ **020/7836-8305.** *Fax: 020/7497-0064.* www.the-fielding-hotel.co.uk. *Tube: Covent Garden (then a five-minute walk north on Long Acre and south on Bow Street). Rack rates: £100–£130 ($185–$241) double. AE, DC, MC, V.*

Five Sumner Place
$$ South Kensington

This 14-room charmer — one of the best B&Bs in Kensington — occupies a landmark Victorian terrace house that has been completely restored in an elegant English style. The guest rooms are comfortably and traditionally furnished; all have bathrooms (a few have refrigerators, as well). You can enjoy a full range of services, including breakfast in a Victorian-style conservatory.

See map p. 118. 5 Sumner Place (just east of Onslow Square), SW7 3EE. ☎ **020/ 7584-7586.** *Fax: 020/7823-9962.* www.sumnerplace.com. *Tube: South Kensington (then a three-minute walk west on Brompton Road and south on Sumner Place). Rack rates: £130 ($241) double. English breakfast included. AE, MC, V.*

41
$$$$$ Westminster and Victoria

Overlooking Buckingham Palace Mews, this unique, 18-room boutique hotel is the epitome of luxury and offers superior personal service. The hotel lobby and breakfast room is an elegant conservatory that was once the waiting room for debutantes who were going to Buckingham Palace to be presented. Every detail in the beautifully furnished rooms, from the Frette sheets to the Penhaligon toiletries, is pure *luxe*. The staff here is wonderfully friendly.

See map p. 115. 41 Buckingham Palace Rd. (just north of Victoria Station), SW1W 0PS. ☎ **877/955-1515** *in the U.S. or 020/7300-0041. Fax: 020/7300-0141.* www. 41hotel.com. *Tube: Victoria (then a five-minute walk northeast along Buckingham Palace Road). Rack rates: £295–£315 ($546–$583) double. Rates don't include 17.5 percent tax. Continental breakfast included. AE, MC, V.*

The Gallery
$$–$$$ South Kensington

This relatively unknown 36-room hotel, located near the cultural and retail attractions in South Kensington and Knightsbridge, occupies two completely restored and converted Georgian residences. The elegant guest rooms are individually designed and include half-canopied beds and marble-tiled bathrooms. The lounge, with its rich mahogany paneling and moldings and deep colors, has the ambience of a private club. The overall decor is wonderfully Victorian, but every modern convenience is available, including wireless Internet. Two of the suites have their own roof terraces.

See map p. 118. 8–10 Queensberry Place (opposite the Natural History Museum), SW7 2EA. ☎ *020/7915-0000. Fax: 020/7915-4400.* www.eeh.co.uk. *Tube: South Kensington (then a five-minute walk west on Thurloe Street and Harrington Road and north on Queensberry Place). Rack rates: £145–£180 ($268–$333) double. Rates don't include 17.5 percent VAT. English breakfast included. AE, DC, MC, V.*

Gate Hotel
$–$$ Notting Hill

This tiny, three-story building dates from the 1820s (when people were evidently much smaller), so the six color-coordinated guest rooms are cramped but atmospheric, and the stairs are steep. The Gate is one of only two hotels along the length of Portobello Road, famous for its antiques shops and Saturday bric-a-brac stalls. Kensington Gardens is a five-minute walk away. Be sure to introduce yourself to Bilko, the talkative resident parrot.

See map p. 120. 6 Portobello Rd., W11 3DG. ☎ **020/7221-0707.** *Fax: 020/7221-9128.* www.gatehotel.com. *Tube: Notting Hill Gate (then a five-minute walk north on Pembridge Road and northwest on Portobello Road). Rack rates: £80–£99 ($148–$183) double. Continental breakfast included. MC, V.*

The Gore
$$$–$$$$ South Kensington

If you dream of the days of Queen Victoria, you'll definitely appreciate the Victorian-era charm of the Gore, which has been in more or less continuous operation since 1892. On a busy road near Kensington Gardens and the Royal Albert Hall, the Gore is loaded with historic charm: walnut-and-mahogany paneling, oriental rugs, and 19th-century prints. Each of the 54 guest rooms is unique, filled with high-quality antiques and elegant furnishings, including old commodes that conceal the toilets.

See map p. 118. 189 Queen's Gate (south of Kensington Gardens), SW7 5EX. ☎ **800/637-7200** *in the U.S. or 020/7584-6601. Fax: 020/7589-8127.* www.gore hotel.com. *Tube: Gloucester Road (then a ten-minute walk east on Cromwell Road and north on Queen's Gate). Rack rates: £190–£210 ($352–$389) double. Rates don't include 17.5 percent VAT. AE, DC, MC, V.*

Grange Strathmore Hotel
$–$$$ South Kensington

Formerly the residence of the 14th earl of Strathmore, the late Queen Mum's father, this hotel overlooks a private garden square just minutes from the South Ken museums. Some of the guest rooms feature a high-ceilinged spaciousness rare in London hotels, and bathrooms with tubs and showers. Plenty of hand-carved rosewood furniture and well-chosen fabrics decorate the rooms. One drawback is that on weekends, no general manager is on duty; also, service can sometimes be rather impersonal.

See map p. 118. 41 Queen's Gate Gardens (at the southeast corner of the gardens), SW7 5NB. ☎ **020/7584-0512.** *Fax: 020/7584-0246.* www.grangehotels.com. *Tube: Gloucester Road (then a two-minute walk north on Gloucester Road and east on Queen's Gate Gardens). Rack rates: £90–£150 ($167–$278) double. AE, MC, V.*

Harlingford Hotel
$ Bloomsbury

In the heart of Bloomsbury, this wonderfully personable and immaculately maintained hotel occupies three 1820s townhouses joined by an array of staircases (no elevators) and hallways. The 44 guest rooms (all unique) are pleasantly comfy, some graced with floral prints and double-glazed windows to cut down on noise; the best rooms are on the second and third levels. The bathrooms are very small, however. The hotel has family rooms and can provide cots for children. Guests have use of the tennis courts in Cartwright Gardens.

See map p. 116. 61–63 Cartwright Gardens (north of Russell Square), WC1H 9EL. ☎ **020/7387-1551.** *Fax: 020/7387-4616.* www.harlingfordhotel.com. *Tube: Russell Square (then a ten-minute walk northwest on Woburn Place, east on Tavistock Square, and north on Marchmont Street). Rack rates: £95 ($176) double. English breakfast included. AE, DC, MC, V.*

Hart House Hotel
$$ Marylebone

A Georgian townhouse built in 1782 and used by members of the French nobility during the French Revolution, Hart House is one of the most welcoming and professionally run B&Bs in London. It has retained its dignified entrance hall and polished paneling. The 16 rooms (all nonsmoking) are attractive and comfortable with small but immaculate bathrooms. Double-glazing on the windows screens out the traffic roar on Gloucester Place. Some very large rooms, perfect for families, have big bathtubs and showers, and the staff can help you arrange babysitting.

See map p. 120. 51 Gloucester Place, Portman Square (just north of Marble Arch), W1U 8JF. ☎ **020/7935-2288.** *Fax: 020/7935-8516.* www.harthouse.co.uk. *Tube: Marble Arch (then a five-minute walk north on Gloucester Place). Rack rates: £105 ($194) double. English breakfast included. AE, MC, V.*

Hazlitt's 1718
$$$$ Soho

Built in 1718 (you may have guessed it from the name), this intimate, 23-room gem offers old-fashioned atmosphere and a hip Soho location. Recent restoration exposed original wood paneling and other features hidden for years, but the hotel still lacks an elevator. The charming Georgian-era guest rooms feature mahogany and pine furnishings and antiques, as well as lovely bathrooms, many with claw-foot tubs. The back rooms are quieter; the front rooms are lighter, but without the quieting effect of double-glazed windows, you do hear the street noise.

See map p. 116. 6 Frith St., Soho Square (just west of Charing Cross Road), W1D 3JA. ☎ *020/7434-1771. Fax: 020/7439-1524.* www.hazlitts.co.uk. *Tube: Tottenham Court Road (then a ten-minute walk west on Oxford Street and south on Soho Street to Frith Street at the south end of Soho Square). Rack rates: £205–£255 ($379–$472) double. Rates don't include 17.5 percent VAT. AE, DC, MC, V.*

Hotel La Place
$$ Marylebone

This desirable hotel, north of Oxford Street, caters to women traveling alone. The interior has been upgraded to boutique-hotel standards (although the exterior isn't especially impressive); the 21 moderate-size guest rooms are done in classic English style, with mahogany furnishings, brocades, TV armoires, and writing desks. The bathrooms are as nice as the rooms. The hotel's **Jardin** is a chic, intimate wine bar/restaurant; you also find an Internet cafe on the premises.

See map p. 116. 17 Nottingham Place (near the southwest corner of Regent's Park), W1M 3FF. ☎ *020/7486-2323. Fax: 020/7486-4335.* www.hotellaplace.com. *Tube: Baker Street (then a five-minute walk east on Marylebone Road and south on Nottingham Place). Rack rates: £120–£139 ($222–$257) double. English breakfast included. AE, DC, MC, V.*

Hotel 167
$$ South Kensington

Hotel 167 attracts hip young visitors drawn by the price, and business people who like its central location (and the price). This hotel is bright and attractive, offering 16 comfortable guest rooms, each with a decent-size bathroom (some with showers, others with tubs). The rooms are furnished with a mix of fabrics and styles. Nearby Tube stations make the hotel convenient to the rest of London, and the busy neighborhood itself is fun to explore.

See map p. 118. 167 Old Brompton Rd., SW5 0AN. ☎ *020/7373-0672. Fax: 020/7373-3360.* www.hotel167.com. *Tube: South Kensington (then a ten-minute walk west on Old Brompton Road). Rack rates: £99–£110 ($178–$204) double. Continental breakfast included. AE, DC, MC, V.*

Imperial Hotel
$$ Bloomsbury

The décor is dated and the exterior epitomizes the worst of 1960s architecture, but so what? The 448-room Imperial is a full-service hotel and a terrific value. Nine floors are guest rooms; the third floor is entirely non-smoking. The hotel does plenty of tour-group business, but the rooms have stood up well to the traffic. They're all a decent size, with unusual triangular-shaped bay windows, good storage space, and workable bathrooms. Amenities include a restaurant, a late-hour Internet cafe, concierge, and room service.

See map p. 116. Russell Square, WC1B 5BB. ☎ **020/7278-7871.** *Fax: 020/7837-4653.* www.imperialhotels.co.uk. *Tube: Russell Square (the hotel is on the east side of the square). Rack rates: £98 ($181) double. English breakfast included. AE, DC, MC, V.*

James House and Cartref House
$ Westminster and Victoria

Sitting across the street from each other, with a total of 19 rooms between them, James House and Cartref House are among the top budget B&Bs in London. Each guest room is individually designed and comfortably furnished; some of the larger ones contain bunk beds, which makes them suitable for families. Fewer than half have private bathrooms. The English breakfast is hearty (but ends at 8:30 a.m.), and the place is remarkably well kept. Neither house has an elevator, but guests don't seem to mind. Both are completely smoke-free. It doesn't matter to which house you're assigned; both are winners.

See map p. 115. 108 and 129 Ebury St. (near Victoria Station), SW1W 9QD. James House ☎ **020/7730-7338;** *Cartref House* ☎ **020/7730-6176.** *Fax: 020/7730-7338.* www.jamesandcartref.co.uk. *Tube: Victoria Station (then a ten-minute walk south on Buckingham Palace Road, west on Eccleston Street, and south on Ebury Street). Rack rates: £70 ($130) double without bathroom, £85 ($157) double with bathroom. English breakfast included. AE, MC, V.*

Jenkins Hotel
$ Bloomsbury

This nonsmoking hotel offers a bit of Georgian charm, a great location near the British Museum and West End theaters, a nice comfortable atmosphere, a full breakfast, and a low price. The 15 guest rooms are small, but all have private bathrooms. You don't find reception or sitting rooms, or even an elevator, but you can still settle in and feel at home. Although the hotel has no special facilities for kids, it welcomes children.

See map p. 116. 45 Cartwright Gardens (just south of Euston Station), WC1H 9EH. ☎ **020/7387-2067.** *Fax: 020/7383-3139.* www.jenkinshotel.demon.co.uk. *Tube: Euston Station (then a five-minute walk east on Euston Road and south on Mabledon Place to the south end of Cartwright Gardens). Rack rates: £85 ($157) double. English breakfast included. MC, V.*

Kensington International Inn
$$ Earl's Court

This newly refurbished hotel on an elegant Victorian street near the Earl's Court Tube station has small rooms but a surprisingly chic contemporary décor that makes it stand out. All 60 rooms are done in pale wheaty colors and have sleek wooden headboards and furnishings. Bathrooms are small, too, with glass-walled showers. The hotel has a hip little bar, a conservatory lounge, and in-room amenities such as a trouser press, a coffeemaker, and a hair dryer. You may find a lower price on their Web site than the rack rates listed here.

See map p. 118. 4 Templeton Place, SW5 9LZ. ☎ *020/7370-4333. Fax: 020/7244-7873.* www.kensingtoninternationalinn.com. *Tube: Earl's Court (then a three-minute walk along Trebovir Road and north on Templeton Place). Rack rates: £130 ($241) double. Continental breakfast included. MC, V.*

Landmark London
$$$$$ Marylebone

The finest Victorian railway hotel in England when it opened in 1899, the Landmark was recently restored to its former glory. The hotel sits in a great location, particularly if you're with kids, because Madame Tussaud's wax museum and Regents Park are only around the corner. Built around an eight-story atrium, the 299 rooms are among London's largest and feature marble bathrooms. The hotel offers every amenity, including babysitting, a large health club, and an indoor pool.

See map p. 120. 222 Marylebone Rd. (half a block from Madame Tussaud's), NW1 6JQ. ☎ *800/323-7500 in the U.S. or 020/7631-8000. Fax: 020/7631-8080.* www.landmarklondon.co.uk. *Tube: Marylebone (the hotel is just a few steps away). Rack rates: £395–£455 ($731–$842) double. Rates don't include 17.5 percent VAT. AE, DC, MC, V.*

Lime Tree Hotel
$$ Westminster and Victoria

This attractive, brick-fronted townhouse is located near Buckingham Palace, Westminster Abbey, and the Houses of Parliament. It's nicely furnished, with deep cornices in the hall and statues and flowers in the alcoves up the stairs. The more expensive of the 26 rooms are quite luxurious, with swagged curtains, canopied beds, and pretty furniture; others are more simply furnished, but all are generally larger and have more amenities than you usually find in this price range. The bathrooms are small. The front rooms have small balconies overlooking Ebury Street; the rear rooms are quieter and look out over a small garden.

See map p. 115. 135–137 Ebury St. (near Victoria Station), SW1W 9RA. ☎ *020/7730-8191. Fax: 020/7730-7865.* www.limetreehotel.co.uk. *Tube: Victoria Station (then a five-minute walk north on Grosvenor Gardens and south on Ebury Street). Rack rates: £105–£125 ($194–$231) double. English breakfast included. AE, DC, MC, V.*

Luna Simone Hotel
$ Westminster and Victoria

The outside of this big, stuccoed, family-run hotel gleams bright white and all the guest rooms have been freshly renovated with private bathrooms installed. The 36 rooms vary widely in size, but with their pleasant décor and newly tiled bathrooms (all with showers), they beat all the dowdy, badly designed hotels and B&Bs for miles around. The reception area and smart-looking breakfast room (now totally nonsmoking) are also new. The look throughout is refreshingly light, simple, and modern.

See map p. 115. 47–49 Belgrave Rd., SW1V 2BB. ☎ *020/7834-5897. Fax: 020/7828-2474.* www.lunasimonehotel.com. *Tube: Victoria (then a 15-minute walk east along Belgrave Road; the hotel is just beyond Warwick Square). Rack rates: £60–£80 ($111–$148) double. English breakfast included. MC, V.*

Mitre House Hotel
$ Paddington

This fine, midsize hotel near Paddington Station stretches across four Georgian townhouses and is kept in tiptop shape. The assortment of accommodations makes it great for families: two-bedroom family suites come with a private bathroom, and superior family suites that face quiet, leafy Talbot Square have a toilet and tub/shower off a private corridor. All 69 rooms are above-average size for London; those at the back are quieter, though the view north across back alleys to Paddington isn't very inspiring. A pleasant lounge and bar, and even an elevator, are on-site.

See map p. 120. 178–184 Sussex Gardens, W2 1TU. ☎ *020/7723-8040. Fax: 020/ 7402-0990.* www.mitrehousehotel.com. *Tube: Lancaster Gate (a five-minute walk north on Lancaster Terrace and east on Sussex Gardens). Rack rates: £80 ($148) double. English breakfast included. AE, DC, MC, V.*

The Montague
$$$–$$$$ Bloomsbury

For service and sheer sumptuousness, you won't find a better hotel anywhere in the vicinity of the British Museum — which happens to be right across the street from the Montague. Every room in this immaculately kept property has been individually decorated and features every amenity you can think of, from twice-daily maid service with evening turndown to luxuriously equipped bathrooms. The airy gardenside conservatory is a delightful spot for afternoon tea or a cocktail, and the Chef's Table restaurant is an enjoyable spot for lunch or dinner.

See map p. 116. 15 Montague St. (east side of the British Museum), WC1B 5BJ. ☎ *877/955-1515 in U.S. or 020/7637-1001. Fax: 020/7637-2516.* www.montague hotel.com. *Tube: Russell Square (then a five-minute walk south across Russell Square to Montague Street). Rack rates: £150–£240 ($278–$444) double. Rates don't include 17.5 percent VAT. AE, MC, V.*

Number Sixteen
$$$–$$$$ South Kensington

Gardeners will appreciate the award-winning gardens at this luxuriously appointed B&B in four early-Victorian townhouses. The 40 guest rooms feature an eclectic mix of English antiques and modern paintings, and the bathrooms are large by London standards. The rooms look out over the private gardens of Sumner Place. On chilly days, you find a fire crackling in the drawing-room fireplace. Breakfast is served in the rooms, but if the weather's fine, you can have it in the garden and enjoy the fish pond and the bubbling fountain.

See map p. 118. 16 Sumner Place (north of Onslow Square), SW7 3EG. ☎ 800/ 592-5387 in the U.S. or 020/7589-5232. Fax: 020/7584-8615. www.numbersixteen hotel.co.uk. *Tube: South Kensington (then a five-minute walk west on Brompton Road and south on Sumner Place). Rack rates: £170–£250 ($315–$463) double. Continental breakfast included. Rates don't include 17.5 percent VAT. AE, DC, MC, V.*

Park Lane Sheraton Hotel
$$$–$$$$ Mayfair

Sometimes called the "Iron Lady of Piccadilly" because it's so well built, this landmark hotel opened in 1927. Executive rooms and suites are decorated with a warm mix of classic English furnishings and have beautiful marble bathrooms. The price goes up according to location (particularly if it's a suite overlooking Green Park), size, and décor. Every conceivable amenity is available. The Palm Court Lounge (see Chapter 10) is a swank place for afternoon tea, and two restaurants are on the premises.

See map p. 116. Piccadilly (across from Green Park), W1Y 8BX. ☎ 800/325-3535 in the U.S. or 020/7499-6321. Fax: 020/7499-1965. www.sheraton.com/parklane. *Tube: Green Park (then a three-minute walk southwest along Piccadilly). Rack rates: £154–£250 ($285–$463) double. AE, DC, MC, V.*

Quaker International Centre
$ Bloomsbury

If you want cheap, simple accommodations in a safe, friendly environment, this guesthouse run by the Quakers is a wonderful choice. Located in the heart of Bloomsbury, the hotel provides rooms that are spartan but completely adequate. None, however, has a private bathroom. The shared facilities are kept spotless. A comfy lounge and a rather plain breakfast room are on-site. This place isn't frilly or fancy, but that's why guests like it.

See map p. 116. 1–3 Byng Place (near Gordon Square), WC1E 7JH. ☎ 020/7387-5648. Fax: 020/7383-3722. E-mail: qic1@qic.org.uk. *Tube: Goodge Street (then a five-minute walk north on Tottenham Court Road and east on Torrington Place to Byng Place). Rack rates: £65 ($120) double. MC, V.*

Regency Hotel
$$–$$$ **South Kensington**

This hotel occupies six refitted Victorian terrace houses. A Chippendale fireplace graces the lobby, and five Empire chandeliers suspended vertically, one on top of the other, hang in one of the stairwells. The 210 modern guest rooms are subdued and attractive, with good-size bathrooms. The one downside is that the air-conditioning system on the west side of the building can be pretty loud on hot summer nights. Guests can use the health club with steam rooms and saunas.

See map p. 118. 100 Queen's Gate (near Royal Albert Hall), SW7 5AG. ☎ **800/223-5652** *in the U.S. or 020/7373-7878. Fax: 020/7370-9700.* www.regency-london.co.uk. *Tube: South Kensington (then a three-minute walk west on Old Brompton Road to Queen's Gate). Rack rates: £100–£160 ($185–$296) double. Rates don't include 17.5 percent VAT. English breakfast included. AE, DC, MC, V.*

Regent Palace Hotel
$–$$ **Piccadilly Circus**

One of Europe's largest hotels, the 920-room Regent Palace sits at the edge of Piccadilly Circus. The hotel has finally upgraded its utilitarian 1915 design. About a quarter of the guest rooms now contain toilets and showers; the others have sinks in the rooms and shared facilities in the halls (an attendant provides you with soap and towel). With a lobby that looks like an airport ticket counter (expect lines on weekends) and an endless flow of tourists, feeling anonymous here is easy. But step out the door and you're in the exciting heart of the West End. Rates are lower Sunday through Thursday.

See map p. 116. Glasshouse Street, Piccadilly Circus, W1B 5DN. ☎ **020/7734-0716.** *Fax: 020/7287-0238.* www.regentpalacehotel.co.uk. *Tube: Piccadilly Circus (then a two-minute walk north; the hotel sits at the fork of Glasshouse Street and Sherwood Street). Rack rates: £79–£89 ($146–$165) double without bathroom; £129–£139 ($239–$257) double with bathroom. AE, DC, MC, V.*

Rhodes Hotel
$ **Paddington**

The personable owner of the Rhodes recently spruced up the entire hotel, adding hand-painted, Greek-inspired murals to the public areas. Other improvements include air-conditioning in the main part of the hotel (though not in the annex, which is why rooms are cheaper there) and dataports for Internet access in all 18 guest rooms. The room décor is quite simple and comfortable; bathrooms are small but well kept. Room 220 has its own little private roof terrace, complete with table and chairs.

See map p. 120. 195 Sussex Gardens, W2 2RJ. ☎ **020/7262-0537.** *Fax: 020/7723-4054.* www.rhodeshotel.com. *Tube: Paddington (then a five-minute walk south on Spring Street or London Street to Sussex Gardens). Rack rates: £70–£85 ($130–$157) double. Continental breakfast included. MC, V.*

The Savoy
$$$$–$$$$$ **The Strand**

An opulent eight-story landmark from 1889, the Savoy offers 15 types of guest rooms (233 rooms in all), including some famous Art Deco ones with their original features. They're all spacious and splendidly decorated. The bathrooms, as large as some hotel rooms, are clad in red-and-white marble and have enormous glass-walled showers and heated towel racks. The most expensive rooms offer river views; others look out over the hotel courtyard. The **Savoy Grill** is one of London's most famous restaurants, and in the Thames Foyer you can get a superlative English tea (see Chapter 10). Check the Web site for special offers.

See map p. 116. The Strand (just north of Waterloo Bridge), WC2R 0EU. ☎ 800/63-SAVOY in the U.S. or 020/7836-4343. Fax: 020/7240-6040. www.savoy-group.co.uk. *Tube: Charing Cross (then a five-minute walk east along The Strand). Rack rates: £229–£409 ($424–$757) double. Rates don't include 17.5 percent VAT. AE, DC, MC, V.*

St. Margaret's Hotel
$–$$ **Bloomsbury**

The welcome that you get here inspires devoted loyalty. Mrs. Marazzi is the second generation of her family to run this nonsmoking B&B, which rambles over four houses. The 64 rooms are simple and immaculate, and no two are alike. Only about ten rooms have private bathrooms, but the Marazzis recently created some extra public bathrooms, so it's easy to survive the sharing experience. Some rooms look out onto the quiet communal garden that all the guests can use. Babysitting can be arranged.

See map p. 116. 26 Bedford Place, WC1B 5JL. ☎ 020/7636-4277. Fax: 020/7323-3066. www.stmargaretshotel.co.uk. *Tube: Russell Square (then a five-minute walk to Bedford Place on the south side of Russell Square). Rack rates: £64 ($118) double without bathroom, £92–£98 ($170–$181) double with bathroom. English breakfast included. MC, V.*

Swiss House Hotel
$–$$ **South Kensington**

Swiss House is a comfortable bargain B&B. It lacks an elevator and isn't stylish, but the 16 guest rooms are clean and nice, with pale walls, floral-print bedspreads, and small but serviceable bathrooms. The rear rooms are quieter and have views out into a garden. Located in the heart of South Ken (next door to Hotel 167), this hotel is well known to budget travelers, so book your reservations early. The hotel staff can arrange for babysitting.

See map p. 118. 171 Old Brompton Rd. (south of the Gloucester Road Tube station), SW5 0AN. ☎ 020/7373-2769. Fax: 020/7373-4983. www.swiss-hh.demon.co.uk. *Tube: Gloucester Road (then a five-minute walk south on Gloucester Road and west on Old Brompton Road). Rack rates: £95–£120 ($176–$222) double. Continental breakfast included. AE, DC, MC, V.*

Tophams Belgravia
$$–$$$ **Westminster and Victoria**

Completely renovated in 1997, Tophams includes five small, intercon-nected row houses. The flower-filled window boxes in the front add charm and color. The best of the 40 guest rooms are comfortably appointed, with private bathrooms and four-poster beds. The restaurant offers both tra-ditional and modern English cooking for lunch and dinner. The location is convenient for travelers planning to explore London by Tube or train. They offer a 10 percent discount to seniors over 60.

See map p. 115. 28 Ebury St. (around the corner from Victoria Station), SW1W 0LU. ☎ **020/7730-8147.** *Fax: 020/7823-5966.* www.tophams.co.uk. *Tube: Victoria Station (then a five-minute walk north on Grosvenor Gardens and south on Ebury Street). Rack rates: £140–£150 ($259–$278) double. English breakfast included. AE, DC, MC, V.*

Twenty Nevern Square
$$$ **Earl's Court**

This sumptuously refurbished boutique hotel in a Victorian townhouse overlooking Nevern Square shows off the gentrified side of Earl's Court. The look throughout is plush and glamorous, with great attention paid to detail. The 20 bedrooms are all individually designed with an emphasis on natural materials, such as linen, cotton, silk, and wood. The bathrooms are just as lovely. The hotel has its own bar and restaurant, Café Twenty.

See map p. 118. 20 Nevern Square, SW5 9PD. ☎ **020/7565-9555.** *Fax: 020/7565-9444.* www.twentynevernsquare.co.uk. *Tube: Earl's Court (then a two-minute walk along Trebovir Road to Nevern Square). Rack rates: £175–£195 ($324–$361) double. Continental breakfast included. AE, MC, V.*

The big splurge

In this chapter, you can get the lowdown on a few deluxe **$$$$$** hotels, among them the **Landmark London** and **The Savoy.** If you're looking for the plushest of the plush, here are a few more suggestions:

✔ **Brown's Hotel:** See map p. 116; 29–34 Albemarle St. (near Berkeley Square), W1A WIS40; ☎ **020/7493-6020;** Fax: 020/7493-9381; www.brownshotel.com.

✔ **Claridge's:** See map p. 116; Brook Street (near Grosvenor Square), W1A 2JQ; ☎ **800/223-6800** in the U.S. or 020/7629-8860; Fax: 020/7499-2210; www.savoy-group.co.uk.

✔ **The Dorchester:** See map p. 116; 53 Park Lane (at the east side of Hyde Park), W1A 2HJ; ☎ **800/727-9820** in the U.S. or 020/7629-8888; Fax: 020/7409-0114; www.dorchesterhotel.com.

22 Jermyn Street
$$$$ St. James's

This chic 18-room boutique hotel near Piccadilly Circus is an Edwardian townhouse on an exclusive street where almost every shop has a *royal warrant* (the sign of official royal patronage). In the richly appointed guest rooms, contemporary decor and fabrics mix with antique furnishings to create a stylish and comfortable ambience. The granite bathrooms are just as nice. Many amenities and 24-hour room service are available.

See map p. 116. 22 Jermyn St. (just south of Piccadilly Circus), SW1Y 6HL. ☎ *800-682-7808 in the U.S. or 020/7734-2353. Fax: 020/7734-0750.* www.22jermyn.com. *Tube: Piccadilly Circus (take Lower Regent Street exit; Jermyn Street is the first right outside the station). Rack rates: £210 ($389) double. AE, DC, MC, V.*

The Vicarage Hotel
$–$$ Kensington

The family-run Vicarage offers old-world English charm, hospitality, and a good value. The hotel is on a residential garden square close to High Street Kensington and Kensington Palace. The 18 guest rooms, individually furnished in Victorian style, can accommodate up to four; room 19 on the top floor is particularly charming. Some of the double and twin rooms have small bathrooms. The hotel welcomes children and will arrange for babysitting; however, the hotel isn't really equipped to deal with the needs of the under-3 set. Many guests return here year after year.

See map p. 118. 10 Vicarage Gate (west of Kensington Gardens), W8 4AG. ☎ *020/7229-4030. Fax: 020/7792-5989.* www.londonvicaragehotel.com. *Tube: Kensington High Street (then a ten-minute walk east on Kensington High Street and north on Kensington Church Street). Rack rates: £78 ($144) double without bathroom, £102 ($189) double with bathroom. English breakfast included. No credit cards.*

Wigmore Court Hotel
$–$$ Marylebone

This appealing Georgian-era B&B lacks an elevator but rewards anyone who is willing to climb up to a fifth-floor room with a four-poster bed. The 18 rooms are decorated with a pleasant mix of traditional styles and contain coffeemakers and hair dryers. The quieter rooms at the back look over a mews. Guests can use the kitchen and laundry facilities, a big bonus normally restricted to budget B&Bs.

See map p. 120. 23 Gloucester Place, W1H 3PB. ☎ *020/7935-0928. Fax: 020/7487-4254.* www.wigmore-hotel.co.uk. *Tube: Marble Arch (then a ten-minute walk east on Marble Arch and north on Gloucester Place). Rack rates: £78–£98 ($144–$181) double. English breakfast included. MC, V.*

Willett Hotel
$$–$$$ Chelsea

Part of a quiet, red-brick terrace, the Willett is noteworthy for its Victorian architectural details and very high standards. This is a dream location for shopaholics, just off Sloane Square and a five-minute walk to Chelsea's King's Road. Refurbished throughout in a traditional style that matches the building, the hotel has 19 rooms, each one different. Deluxe rooms have canopy beds, voluptuous swagged curtains and matching armchairs, and nice but not terribly large bathrooms. A porter to carry your bags and a secluded garden are on-site.

See map p. 118. Sloane Gardens, SW1 8DJ. ☎ *800/270-9206 in the U.S. or 020/7824-8415. Fax: 020/7730-4830.* www.eeh.co.uk. *Tube: Sloane Square. Rack rates: £130–£160 ($241–$296) double. Rates don't include 17.5 percent VAT. English breakfast included. AE, DC, MC, V.*

Winchester Hotel
$ Westminster and Victoria

One of the best choices along Belgrave Road, this 18-room hotel is owned and managed by Jimmy McGoldrick, who goes out of his way to make his customers happy. Guests have been returning for 20 years, and if you stay here you'll understand why. Jimmy's staff maintains an extremely high level of service and cleanliness. The recently refurbished guest rooms are comfortable and well decorated. Each room has a small private bathroom with a good shower. Guests are served a big English breakfast in a lovely and inviting room. A sleek modernity is displayed throughout that's rare in small London hotels.

See map p. 115. 17 Belgrave Rd., SW1 1RB. ☎ *020/7828-2972. Fax: 020/7828-5191.* www.winchester-hotel.net. *Tube: Victoria. Rack rates: £85 ($157) double. English breakfast included. No credit cards.*

Runner-Up Hotels

Adare House
$ Paddington

This well-maintained property near Hyde Park retains a modest homey ambience with small, immaculately clean, and comfortably furnished guest rooms. *See map p. 120. 153 Sussex Gardens, W2 2RY.* ☎ *020/7262-0633. Fax: 020/7706-1859.* www.adarehotel.co.uk.

Blooms Hotel
$$$$ Bloomsbury

With its cozy fireplace and period art, this 27-room hotel evokes a luxurious country-home atmosphere. *See map p. 116. 7 Montague St. (next to the British Museum), WC1B 5BP.* ☎ *020/7323-1717. Fax: 020/7636-6498.* www.grangehotels.com.

Dukes Hotel

$$$$–$$$$$ **St. James's**

Dukes provides charm, style, and tradition in a 1908 townhouse; babysitting is just one of its many amenities. *See map p. 116. 35 St. James's Place, SW1A 1NY.* ☎ *800-381-4702 in the U.S. or 020/7491-4840. Fax: 020/7493-1264.* www.dukeshotel.co.uk.

Ebury House

$ **Westminster and Victoria**

This B&B near Victoria Station is known for the warmth of its hospitality. *See map p. 115. 102 Ebury St., SW1W 9QD.* ☎ *020/7730-1350. Fax: 020/7259-0400.*

Goring Hotel

$$$$ **Westminster and Victoria**

The Goring has a great location, just behind Buckingham Palace, and top-notch service. This family-run property offers a particularly warm welcome to families. *See map p. 115. 15 Beeston Place, Grosvenor Gardens, SW1W 0JW.* ☎ *020/7396-9000. Fax: 020/7834-4393.* www.goringhotel.co.uk.

Morgans Hotel

$$ **Bloomsbury**

Every room is different in this attractive, air-conditioned, 18th-century townhouse hotel near the British Museum. *See map p. 116. 24 Bloomsbury St., WC1B 3QJ.* ☎ *020/7636-3735. Fax: 020/7636-3045.* www.morganshotel.co.uk.

Pembridge Court Hotel

$$$ **Notting Hill**

Antiques furnish this lovely hotel, located in Notting Hill Gate. Nearby parks and fun gifts for children make this hotel a good choice for families. *See map p. 120. 34 Pembridge Gardens, W2 4DX.* ☎ *020/7229-9977. Fax: 020/7727-4982.* www.pemct.co.uk.

Rushmore Hotel

$ **Earl's Court**

This gracious townhouse hotel is comfortable and well designed, with many special decorative touches. *See map p. 118. 11 Trebovir Rd., SW5 9LS.* ☎ *020/7370-3839. Fax: 020/7370-0274.* www.rushmore-hotel.co.uk.

St. Martin's Lane

$$$$–$$$$$ **Piccadilly Circus**

Developed by hotelier Ian Schrager, St. Martin's Lane appeals to those into trendy high design. *See map p. 116. 45 St. Martin's Lane, WC2N 4HX.* ☎ *020/7300-5500. Fax: 020/7300-5501.* www.schragerhotels.com.

Index of Accommodations by Neighborhood

Bayswater
Byron Hotel ($$)

Bloomsbury
Blooms Hotel ($$$$)
Harlingford Hotel ($)
Imperial Hotel ($$)
Jenkins Hotel ($)
The Montague ($$$–$$$$)
Morgans Hotel ($$)
Quaker International Centre ($)
St. Margaret's Hotel ($–$$)

Chelsea
Cadogan Hotel ($$$$–$$$$$)
Willett Hotel ($$–$$$)

Covent Garden
Covent Garden Hotel ($$$$–$$$$$)
Fielding Hotel ($$)

Earl's Court
Kensington International Inn ($$)
Rushmore Hotel ($)
Twenty Nevern Square ($$$)

Kensington
Abbey House ($)
Avonmore Hotel ($–$$)
The Vicarage Hotel ($–$$)

Knightsbridge
Claverley Hotel ($$–$$$$$)

Marylebone
Bryanston Court Hotel ($$)
Dorset Square Hotel ($$$$–$$$$$)
Durrants Hotel ($$$)
Hart House Hotel ($$)
Hotel La Place ($$)
Landmark London ($$$$$)
Wigmore Court Hotel ($–$$)

Mayfair
Park Lane Sheraton Hotel ($$$–$$$$)

Notting Hill
The Abbey Court ($$–$$$$)
Comfort Inn Notting Hill ($$)
Gate Hotel ($–$$)
Pembridge Court Hotel ($$$)

Paddington
Adare House ($)
Fairways Hotel ($)
Mitre House Hotel ($)
Rhodes Hotel ($)

Piccadilly Circus
Regent Palace Hotel ($–$$)
St. Martin's Lane ($$$$–$$$$$)

Soho
Hazlitt's 1718 ($$$$)

South Kensington
Aster House ($$–$$$)
Astons Apartments ($–$$)
The Cranley ($$$–$$$$)
Five Sumner Place ($$)
The Gallery ($$–$$$)
The Gore ($$$–$$$$)
Grange Strathmore Hotel ($–$$$)
Hotel 167 ($$)
Number Sixteen ($$$–$$$$)
Regency Hotel ($$–$$$)
Swiss House Hotel ($–$$)

St. James's
Dukes Hotel ($$$$–$$$$$)
22 Jermyn Street ($$$$)

The Strand
The Savoy ($$$$–$$$$$)

Westminster and Victoria
Ebury House ($)
41 ($$$$$)
Goring Hotel ($$$$)
James House and Cartref House ($)

Lime Tree Hotel ($$)
Luna Simone Hotel ($)
Tophams Belgravia ($$–$$$)
Winchester Hotel ($)

Index of Accommodations by Price

$

Abbey House (Kensington)
Adare House (Paddington)
Astons Apartments (South Kensington)
Avonmore Hotel (Kensington)
Ebury House (Westminster and Victoria)
Fairways Hotel (Paddington)
Gate Hotel (Notting Hill)
Grange Strathmore Hotel (South Kensington)
Harlingford Hotel (Bloomsbury)
James House and Cartref House (Westminster and Victoria)
Jenkins Hotel (Bloomsbury)
Luna Simone Hotel (Westminster and Victoria)
Mitre House Hotel (Paddington)
Quaker International Centre (Bloomsbury)
Regent Palace Hotel (Piccadilly Circus)
Rhodes Hotel (Paddington)
Rushmore Hotel (Earl's Court)
St. Margaret's Hotel (Bloomsbury)
Swiss House Hotel (South Kensington)
The Vicarage Hotel (Kensington)
Wigmore Court Hotel (Marylebone)
Winchester Hotel (Westminster and Victoria)

$$

The Abbey Court (Notting Hill)
Aster House (South Kensington)
Astons Apartments (South Kensington)
Avonmore Hotel (Kensington)
Bryanston Court Hotel (Marylebone)
Byron Hotel (Bayswater)

Claverley Hotel (Knightsbridge)
Comfort Inn Notting Hill (Notting Hill)
Fielding Hotel (Covent Garden)
Five Sumner Place (South Kensington)
The Gallery (South Kensington)
Gate Hotel (Notting Hill)
Grange Strathmore Hotel (South Kensington)
Hart House Hotel (Marylebone)
Hotel La Place (Marylebone)
Hotel 167 (South Kensington)
Imperial Hotel (Bloomsbury)
Kensington International Inn (Earl's Court)
Lime Tree Hotel (Westminster and Victoria)
Morgans Hotel (Bloomsbury)
Regency Hotel (South Kensington)
Regent Palace Hotel (Piccadilly Circus)
St. Margaret's Hotel (Bloomsbury)
Swiss House Hotel (South Kensington)
Tophams Belgravia (Westminster and Victoria)
The Vicarage Hotel (Kensington)
Wigmore Court Hotel (Marylebone)
Willett Hotel (Chelsea)

$$$

The Abbey Court (Notting Hill)
Aster House (South Kensington)
Claverley Hotel (Knightsbridge)
The Cranley (South Kensington)
Durrants Hotel (Marylebone)
The Gallery (South Kensington)
The Gore (South Kensington)
Grange Strathmore Hotel (South Kensington)
The Montague (Bloomsbury)
Number Sixteen (South Kensington)

Park Lane Sheraton Hotel (Mayfair)
Pembridge Court Hotel (Notting Hill)
Regency Hotel (South Kensington)
Tophams Belgravia (Westminster and Victoria)
Twenty Nevern Square (Earl's Court)
Willett Hotel (Chelsea)

$$$$

The Abbey Court (Notting Hill)
Blooms Hotel (Bloomsbury)
Cadogan Hotel (Chelsea)
Claverley Hotel (Knightsbridge)
Covent Garden Hotel (Covent Garden)
The Cranley (South Kensington)
Dorset Square Hotel (Marylebone)
Dukes Hotel (St. James's)
The Gore (South Kensington)
Goring Hotel (Westminster and Victoria)

Hazlitt's 1718 (Soho)
The Montague (Bloomsbury)
Number Sixteen (South Kensington)
Park Lane Sheraton Hotel (Mayfair)
The Savoy (The Strand)
St. Martin's Lane (Piccadilly Circus)
22 Jermyn Street (St. James's)

$$$$$

Cadogan Hotel (Chelsea)
Claverley Hotel (Knightsbridge)
Covent Garden Hotel (Covent Garden)
Dorset Square Hotel (Marylebone)
Dukes Hotel (St. James's)
41 (Westminster and Victoria)
Landmark London (Marylebone)
The Savoy (The Strand)
St. Martin's Lane (Piccadilly Circus)

Chapter 10

Dining and Snacking in London

· ·

In This Chapter

▶ Discovering what's new and what's hot

▶ Locating the best dining neighborhoods

▶ Reviewing my favorite restaurants in London

▶ Listing restaurants by neighborhood, cuisine, and price

· ·

*Y*ou can still find traditional English dishes in London: Yorkshire pudding, fish and chips, or *bangers and mash* (sausages and mashed potatoes). So if you want to sample the old cuisine, you won't be disappointed. But London now offers a vast array of culinary choices; more than 5,700 restaurants prepare the cuisines of more than 60 countries. This chapter explains what you need to know about new trends; traditional, modern, and ethnic cuisines; spots favored by locals; and finding a bargain. I list my favorite London dining spots, too.

For a glossary of English food terms, see the Cheat Sheet at the beginning of this book.

Getting the Dish on the Local Scene

London is now considered one of the food capitals of the world, and its restaurant scene is a volatile one. To be trendy and talked about, a London restaurant must have a celebrity owner, a celebrity chef, a solid reputation, a great view, a chic location, and/or an unmistakable ambience — and, of course, memorable food helps, too. But two trends are worth noting: The days of Sir Terence Conran's mega-eateries — places that held hundreds of diners — are pretty much over; and, in a city where even an ordinary meal can easily cost £25 ($46), Londoners are looking more and more toward ethnic foods and restaurants that don't charge exorbitant prices.

Multicultural London is always in the midst of culinary evolution. The local food horizon expanded as the postwar generation began to travel outside England, experiencing new cuisines, and as "exotic" foods became more readily available in the markets.

Traditional "plain English cooking" — undeniably hearty but sometimes considered dull — is certainly still prevalent in London, and the style is even enjoying renewed interest and respect. The best traditional dishes — game, lamb, meat and fish pies, and roast beef with Yorkshire pudding — are readily available. Modern British cuisine takes old standards and deliciously reinvents them with foreign influences and ingredients, mostly from France (sauces), the Mediterranean (olive oil, oregano, and garlic), and northern Italy (pasta, polenta, and risotto). Besides Modern British, London foodies continue to favor classic French and Italian cuisines.

Indian cooking has been a favorite ethnic food for some time. In fact, curry is now considered a "national" dish. London is filled with Indian restaurants (about 1,500 of them) serving curries and dishes cooked in clay tandoori pots. *Balti,* a thick curry from Pakistan, is one of the more recent ethnic must-try dishes in London. Other new influences making their way into Modern British cooking come from Thailand and Morocco.

For more on English cooking, see Chapter 2.

If you want to dine in a restaurant, reserving a table is always a good idea. At all but the "smartest" London restaurants, you can usually get a table on fairly short notice during the week, especially if you're willing to dine before 7 p.m. or after 9 p.m.

Nonsmoking sections are becoming more common in London's restaurants (not in pubs), but the sections aren't always effectively smoke-free. You may be in the same room as the smokers, just in a different area. If smoking bothers you, ask about the restaurant's nonsmoking section when you call to reserve your table.

Discovering the top dining areas

London offers a mouth-watering mix of restaurants; you can enjoy a wide variety of foods throughout the city. Soho and neighboring Covent Garden offer the most choices in the West End, with British, African, Caribbean, Mongolian, American (North and South), French, Italian, Spanish, Thai, Korean, Japanese, Middle Eastern, Eastern European, Modern European, Turkish, and vegetarian all represented. South Kensington makes up another eclectic grab bag of culinary choices.

Unlike some other large cities, ethnic restaurants aren't grouped together within specific areas of Central London. However, several Chinese restaurants are clustered along Lisle, Wardour, and Gerrard streets in Soho's Chinatown. And Notting Hill has long been a standby for low-price Indian and Caribbean restaurants.

Eating with the locals

Londoners, like the residents in any large city, have their favorite neighborhood eateries. Pubs, cafes, and wine bars are places where locals go for casual meals that aren't as expensive as restaurants.

Ordering up pub grub

If you're not into ethnic dining, then pubs are your best bet for getting a good meal for a low price. The food is generally traditional and down to earth: meat pies and *mash* (mashed potatoes), fish and chips, *mixed grills* (sausages and a chop or cutlet), salads, sandwiches, and the famous *ploughman's lunch* (bread and cheese, or pâté). Pub food may be prepackaged and frozen and then microwaved. However, more and more pubs resemble casual restaurants. There is a new genre of pub restaurants called *gastropubs,* where the cooking is fresher, more adventurous, and better prepared than at traditional pubs.

Pubs are drop-in places, and finding a table at lunchtime isn't always easy. Pubs don't accept reservations. Usually, you order your food from the serving counter and your drinks from the bar, and then seat yourself. Sometimes there is table service. Pub grub is generally washed down with beer, the British national drink. Draft beer in Britain is served at room temperature, as are most soft drinks. Bottled imported beer, served cold, is generally available but more expensive.

Unless a pub has a special *children's certificate,* kids under 14 are allowed only into the gardens and separate family rooms. The legal drinking age in the United Kingdom is 18, although restaurants can serve beer or cider to kids over 16 who order a meal. Pubs tend to be smoky.

Wining and dining at wine bars

Londoners may love to knock back a pint of beer at their local pub, but when it comes to dining, wine is the favored accompaniment. You can get wine in a pub, but the choices will be limited. Wine bars, on the other hand, are dedicated to good food and good grape, most of it imported from France, Australia, and South America. Wine bars are more upscale than pubs and usually less smoky. Like pubs, wine bars don't permit children under 14, except in gardens or family rooms. Be aware that a meal in a wine bar costs more than a similar meal in a pub.

Kicking back at cafes

London's cafes generally serve light, inexpensive food and offer limited menus. Most people enjoy a cup of coffee or pot of tea and a sandwich. The cakes and other sweets may tempt you, too.

Gays and lesbians on the lookout for low-priced meals in groovy gay-friendly environments flock to Soho's gay cafes and bars. These trendy hangouts serve good, low-priced meals and pay serious attention to decor.

Trimming the Fat from your Budget

If the thought of paying $50 dinner tabs gives you heartburn, you can visit pubs, cafes, sandwich bars, and pizza places to get good, economical food. And, of course, you can find fast-food chains throughout the city. Another alternative: Many of London's top restaurants offer *fixed-price meals* (also called *set-price* or *prix-fixe* meals), which allow you to order two to three courses from a limited menu for a set price that is cheaper than ordering the courses individually. Sometimes these bargains are called *pre-* or *post-theater menus,* and they're served only from about 5:30 to 7 p.m. and after 9:30 p.m. Wine is expensive, so forgo that if price is an issue. And try your splurge-dining at lunch, when prices are often one-third less than those at dinner and the food is the same.

 Restaurants automatically add that annoying 17.5 percent VAT (value-added tax) to your tab. They may tack on a moderate cover charge for bread (even if you don't eat it), as well.

 Plenty of unwary tourists double-tip without realizing it. Some restaurants add a service charge to your bill and also have a tip area on the credit-card receipt that you sign. Be aware that the words *service charge included* on a menu mean that a gratuity will automatically be added to your bill. When the bill arrives, you're not expected to leave any additional tip. If the menu says *service not included,* however, leave a tip of at least 15 percent for acceptable service.

 At the end of a meal, Americans ask for a "check," whereas Brits ask for the "bill."

London's Best Restaurants

London is home to more than 5,700 restaurants. As you can imagine, choosing which establishments to include in this chapter of my favorites was a monumental task. I try to cover as much of Central London as possible. If you want to get the flavor of merry old England, I include some of the oldest and most respected London restaurants serving traditional English food. For the more chic and trendy among you, I include restaurants that serve the best of Modern British cuisine, as well as hybrids of British/French and British/Continental. For people on a budget — or who just want to eat in a down-to-earth, amiable environment — I also review some of the best London pubs. All the establishments are easy to get to, and you can reach all of them by taking the Underground (Tube) system and perhaps walking a bit. For indexes of the restaurants by neighborhood, cuisine, and price, see the end of this chapter. For locations, see the maps in this chapter.

Each restaurant I review is given one to four dollar signs ($). The dollar signs indicate the average price of a meal, including an appetizer, entree, and nonalcoholic beverage. Table 10-1 lists the dollar amounts used for each dollar sign. Please bear in mind that if you order the most expensive entree and a bottle of wine, a $$ restaurant will become a $$$$ restaurant. On the other hand, if you order from a set-price menu, a $$$$ restaurant tab may dip down to $$.

Table 10-1	Key to Restaurant Dollar Signs
Dollar Sign(s)	*Price Range*
$	$25 or less
$$	$26–$40
$$$	$41–$60
$$$$	$61 and up

 The Kid Friendly icon in front of a restaurant name indicates that the place is suitable for families with children. These restaurants welcome families and may offer a children's menu.

 Note that restaurant prices in this chapter do not include the 17.5 percent VAT (value-added tax). Unfortunately, you can't avoid paying this extra expense.

 Aubergine

$$$$ **Chelsea   FRENCH**

You compete with celebrities, royalty, and commoners for the privilege of dining at this top-name restaurant, but it's well worth the effort. You'll have to give your credit-card number when booking and be prepared to pay £50 ($93) if you don't show. Every dish, from the fish and lighter Mediterranean-style choices to *assiette* of pork on creamed savoy cabbage and bacon, is a culinary achievement of the highest order, winning two Michelin stars. And the celebrated cappuccino of white beans with grated truffle makes a perfect ending to a superb dining experience. The service is polished and efficient.

See map p. 152. 11 Park Walk, SW10. ☎ 020/7352-3449. Reservations essential. Tube: Sloane Square (then a ten-minute walk southwest on King's Road to Park Walk; or bus 11, 19, 22, or 211 southwest on King's Road from the Tube station). Fixed-price menu: Lunch £32 ($59); dinner £55–£72 ($102–$133). AE, DC, MC, V. Open: Mon–Fri noon to 2:15 p.m., Mon–Sat 7–10:15 p.m.

The skinny on the beef

Sirloin, so the story goes, got its name from James I when he was a guest at Houghton Tower in Lancashire. When a succulent leg of beef was placed before him, he knighted it with his dagger, crying, "Arise, Sir Loin!"

Restaurants in and around the City

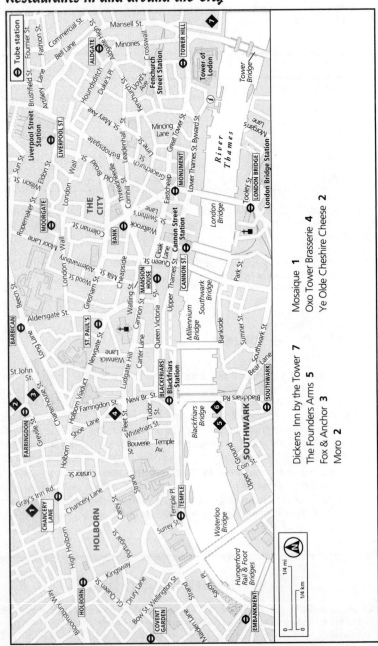

Dickens Inn by the Tower **7**
The Founders Arms **5**
Fox & Anchor **3**
Moro **2**

Mosaique **1**
Oxo Tower Brasserie **4**
Ye Olde Cheshire Cheese **2**

Restaurants in Westminster and Victoria

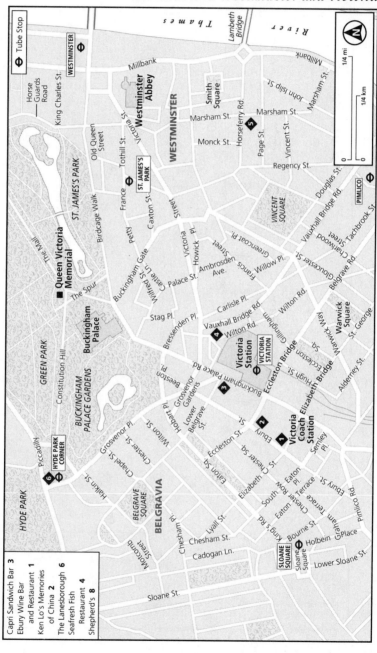

Capri Sandwich Bar **3**
Ebury Wine Bar
  and Restaurant **1**
Ken Lo's Memories
  of China **2**
The Lanesborough **6**
Seafresh Fish
  Restaurant **4**
Shepherd's **8**

Restaurants in the West End

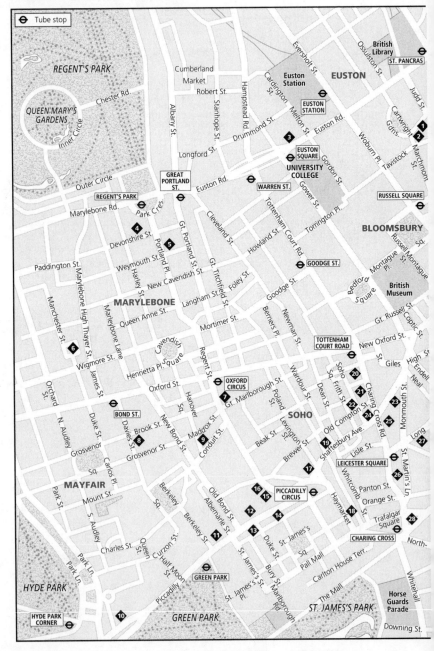

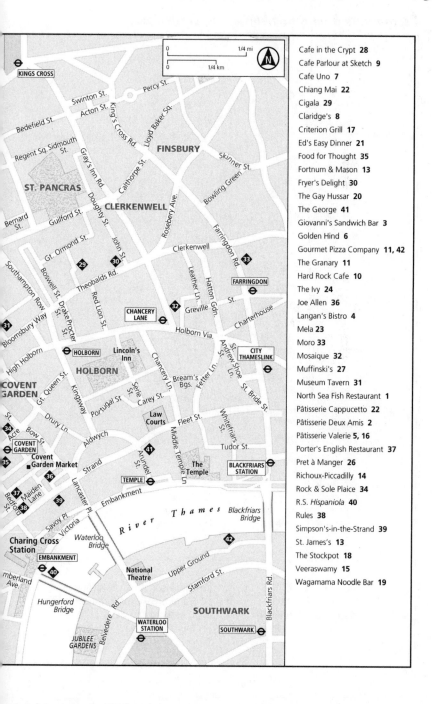

Cafe in the Crypt **28**
Cafe Parlour at Sketch **9**
Cafe Uno **7**
Chiang Mai **22**
Cigala **29**
Claridge's **8**
Criterion Grill **17**
Ed's Easy Dinner **21**
Food for Thought **35**
Fortnum & Mason **13**
Fryer's Delight **30**
The Gay Hussar **20**
The George **41**
Giovanni's Sandwich Bar **3**
Golden Hind **6**
Gourmet Pizza Company **11, 42**
The Granary **11**
Hard Rock Cafe **10**
The Ivy **24**
Joe Allen **36**
Langan's Bistro **4**
Mela **23**
Moro **33**
Mosaique **32**
Muffinski's **27**
Museum Tavern **31**
North Sea Fish Restaurant **1**
Pâtisserie Cappucetto **22**
Pâtisserie Deux Amis **2**
Pâtisserie Valerie **5, 16**
Porter's English Restaurant **37**
Pret à Manger **26**
Richoux-Piccadilly **14**
Rock & Sole Plaice **34**
R.S. *Hispaniola* **40**
Rules **38**
Simpson's-in-the-Strand **39**
St. James's **13**
The Stockpot **18**
Veeraswamy **15**
Wagamama Noodle Bar **19**

Restaurants from Knightsbridge to Earl's Court

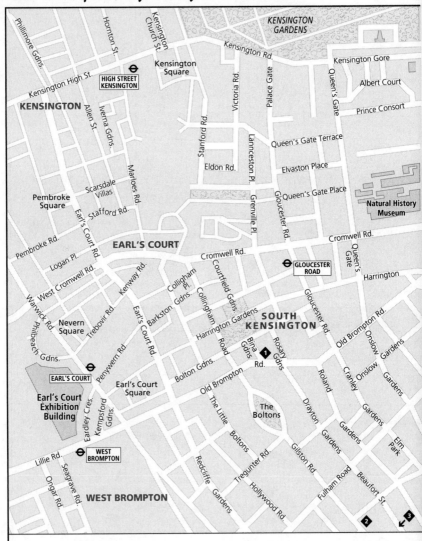

Aubergine **4**
Boxwood Cafe **11**
Brasserie St. Quentin **9**
Chelsea Kitchen **18**

Fifth Floor at Harvey Nichols **9**
Harrods Georgian Restaurant **13**
Lanesborough **12**
Mona Lisa **3**

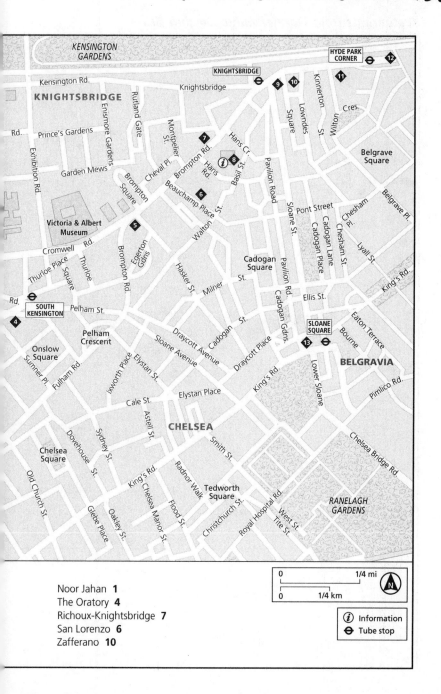

Noor Jahan **1**
The Oratory **4**
Richoux-Knightsbridge **7**
San Lorenzo **6**
Zafferano **10**

0   1/4 mi
0   1/4 km

(i) Information
⊖ Tube stop

Restaurants from Marylebone to Notting Hill

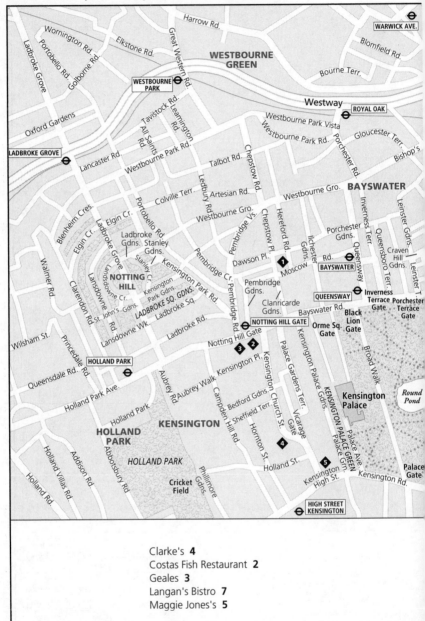

Clarke's **4**
Costas Fish Restaurant **2**
Geales **3**
Langan's Bistro **7**
Maggie Jones's **5**

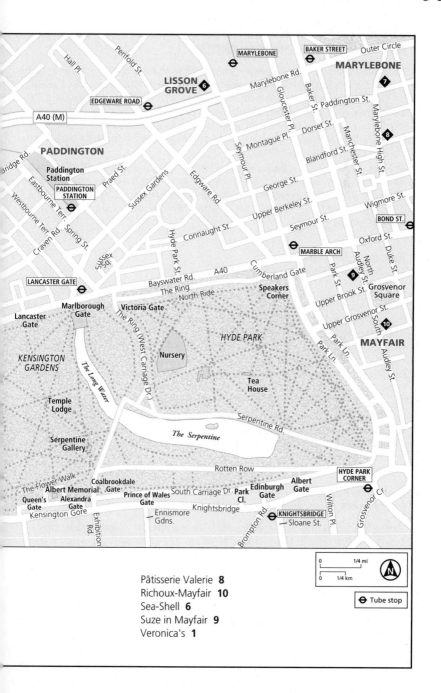

Pâtisserie Valerie **8**
Richoux-Mayfair **10**
Sea-Shell **6**
Suze in Mayfair **9**
Veronica's **1**

Boxwood Café
$$$ **Knightsbridge** **MODERN BRITISH**

This may be the most stylish kid-friendly restaurant in London, but grownups will find plenty of comforting delights on the menu, too. Created by Gordon Ramsay, Boxwood Café is chic without being fussy, and the same goes for the food, which emphasizes fresh and healthy dishes ranging from a baked macaroni of wild mushrooms and parmesan to fresh steamed fish, grilled calf's liver, roast chicken salad, veal, and steaks. The entire restaurant is nonsmoking.

See map p. 152. In the Berkeley Hotel, Wilton Place, SW1. ☎ *020/7235-1010. Reservations recommended. Tube: Knightsbridge (then a five-minute walk east on Brompton Road). Main courses: £14–£25 ($26–$46); fixed-price lunch: £21 ($39); children's menu: £7.50 ($14). AE, DISC, MC, V. Open: Mon–Fri noon–3 p.m.; Sat–Sun noon to 4 p.m.; daily 6–11 p.m.*

Brasserie St. Quentin
$$ **South Kensington** **FRENCH**

London's most authentic-looking French brasserie, St. Quentin attracts many people in the city's French community (a positive sign for a French restaurant outside of France). Mirrors and crystal chandeliers add a touch of elegance. The brasserie has excellent-value fixed-price meals, two or three courses, both at lunch and pre-theater. These menus offer a blend of classic and updated French fare, from shoulder of lamb with root vegetables to roast monkfish. Vegetarian options include artichoke fondant with seasonal vegetables, spinach ravioli, and warm leek salad.

See map p. 152. 243 Brompton Rd., SW3. ☎ *020/7589-8005. Reservations required. Tube: South Kensington (then a five-minute walk east on Brompton Road). Main courses: £11–£24 ($19–$44); fixed-price lunch and pre-theater (6:30–7:30 p.m.) menus: £15–£17 ($28–$31). AE, DC, MC, V. Open: Daily noon to 3 p.m.; Mon–Sat 6–11:30 p.m., Sun 6:30–10:30 p.m.*

Cafe in the Crypt
$ **Piccadilly Circus and Leicester Square** **BRITISH**

Eating in a crypt may not be everyone's idea of fun, but eating in this crypt — below St. Martin's-in-the-Fields church on Trafalgar Square — is an inexpensive London dining experience that you won't forget. The food is basic but good, served cafeteria-style. Choose from a big salad bar; traditional main courses, such as shepherd's pie; filled rolls; and delicious soups. One fixture is that most traditional of British desserts, bread-and-butter pudding (bread soaked in eggs and milk with currants or sultanas and then oven-baked). The cavernous, candlelit room with its great stone pillars is wonderfully atmospheric.

See map p. 150. St. Martin-in-the-Fields, Duncannon St., WC2. ☎ *020/7839-4342. Tube: Charing Cross (then a three-minute walk west to Trafalgar Square). Main courses: £5.95–£7.50 ($11–$14); fixed-price meal: £5.25 ($9.70). No credit cards. Open: Mon–Wed 10 a.m.–7:30 p.m.; Thurs–Sat 10 a.m.–10:15 p.m.*

Chelsea Kitchen
$ Chelsea INTERNATIONAL

A London institution, Chelsea Kitchen has been feeding locals and drop-ins since 1961. At this simple place with a dinerlike atmosphere, both the plates and the crowds move fast. Menu staples include leek-and-potato soup, chicken parmigiana, spaghetti Bolognese, omelets, burgers, goulash, and lamb chops. Kids enjoy the casual atmosphere and simple foods.

See map p. 152. 98 King's Rd. (off Sloane Square), SW3. ☎ 020/7589-1330. Reservations recommended. Tube: Sloane Square (the restaurant is at the beginning of King's Road just west of the square). Main courses: £3–£6.50 ($5.55–$12); fixed-price menu: £6–£7 ($11–$13). No credit cards. Open: Mon–Sat 7:30 a.m.–11:45 p.m.

Chiang Mai
$$ Soho THAI

Chiang Mai is next door to Ronnie Scott's, the most famous jazz club in England (see Chapter 16), so it's a good stop for an early dinner before a night on the town. Named after the ancient northern capital of Thailand (known for its rich, spicy foods), this unpretentious but pleasant place is good for green curry noodles, hot-and-sour beef, fish and chicken dishes, pad thai noodles with various toppings, and vegetarian meals. I suggest that you order a couple of different courses and share. Children's specials are available.

See map p. 150. 48 Frith St. (off Soho Square), W1. ☎ 020/7437-7444. Tube: Tottenham Court Road (then a five-minute walk west on Oxford Street and south on Soho Street; Frith Street is at the southwest corner of Soho Square). Main courses: £4.50–£7.50 ($8.35–$14); fixed-price lunch: £7.50 ($14); fixed-price pre-theater (5:30–7 p.m.) menu: £8.50 ($16). AE, DC, MC, V. Open: Mon–Sat 12:30–3 p.m. and 4:30–11 p.m., Sun 5:30–10:30 p.m.

Cigala
$$ Bloomsbury SPANISH

This hip restaurant has attracted its share of celebs, in part because it serves great tapas. Order two or three tapas per person and then share. Some possibilities include chorizo (sausage with hot paprika sauce), oak-smoked cured beef, marinated sardines, wind-dried tuna, olives, and scrambled eggs with artichokes. At lunch or dinner, you may prefer to begin with something like spicy chorizo and lentil soup, and follow up with an entree of pork loin with potatoes. The vegetarian stew is bland and not particularly memorable, but the dish of scallops with pancetta, sherry vinegar, and lentils is delectable, and so is the paella, which requires 30 minutes of preparation.

See map p. 150. 54 Lamb's Conduit St., WC1N 3LW. ☎ 020/7405-1717. Tube: Holborn (then a seven-minute walk east on High Holborn and north on Red Lion Street, which becomes Lamb's Conduit when you cross Theobald's Road). Main courses: £12–£18 ($22–$33); tapas: £3–£5.50 ($5.55–$10); fixed-price lunch (Mon–Fri): £16–£19 ($30–$35). AE, MC, V. Open: Mon–Fri noon to 3 p.m. and 6–10:45 p.m., Sat 12:30–3:30 p.m. and 6–10:45 p.m., Sun 12:30–9:30 p.m.

Clarke's
$$$ **Notting Hill** **MODERN EUROPEAN**

This bright modern restaurant, owned by chef Sally Clarke, is among the hottest in town. There's a four-course fixed-price dinner menu as well as a two-course lunch and a Saturday brunch. The menu changes daily but always emphasizes British produce and Mediterranean-style charcoal-grilled foods with herbs and organically grown vegetables. A typical meal may include an appetizer of grilled goat cheese *crostini* with fresh tomato chutney; an entree of wild sea bass roasted with tarragon and lemon hollandaise; followed by an assortment of cheeses with oatmeal biscuits and celery, plus warm bitter chocolate pudding with whipped cream and raspberries.

See map p. 154. 124 Kensington Church St., W8. ☎ *020/7221-9225. Reservations essential. Tube: Notting Hill Gate (then a five-minute walk south on Kensington Church Street). Fixed-price menus: two-course lunch £9.50–£15 ($18–$28), 4-course dinner £50 ($93). AE, DC, MC, V. Open: Mon–Fri 12:30–2 p.m., Sat 11 a.m.–2 p.m., Tues–Sun 7–10 p.m.*

Criterion Grill
$$–$$$ **Piccadilly Circus and Leicester Square** **BRITISH/FRENCH**

It's almost worth coming to the Criterion just to see its Byzantine palace interior with gold vaulted ceiling. The food — a mixture of modern French and British standards — doesn't quite match the grandeur of the décor, but it's generally quite good. You can order Brit faves like haddock or sausages, or French faves like slow-roast duck with apple sauce or steak au poivre. This place is smack-dab on Piccadilly Circus, so it's wonderfully convenient. The fixed-price lunches and dinners are a great deal.

See map p. 155. 224 Piccadilly, W1. ☎ *020/7930-0488. Reservations recommended. Tube: Piccadilly Circus (the restaurant is right on Piccadilly Circus). Main courses: £11–£23 ($20–$43); fixed-price lunch and pre-theater dinner (5:30–7 p.m.): £15–£18 ($28–$33). AE, DC, MC, V. Open: Daily noon–2:30 p.m., Mon–Sat 5:30–11:30 p.m.*

Dickens Inn by the Tower
$–$$ **The City** **TRADITIONAL/MODERN BRITISH**

This former spice warehouse is now a three-story restaurant with sweeping Thames and Tower Bridge views. The ground-floor Tavern Bar serves a variety of traditional pub food. Pizza on the Dock, a floor above and a good spot for families, offers four sizes of pizza. Grill on the Dock, on the top floor, is a relatively formal dining room serving Modern British cuisine; specials include steaks and a variety of charcoal-grilled dishes.

See map p. 148. St. Katharine's Way (near the Tower of London), E1. ☎ *020/7488-2208. Reservations recommended. Tube: Tower Hill (then a ten-minute walk east on Tower Hill East and south on St. Katherine's Street to St. Katherine's Way). Main courses: Grill on the Dock £13–£20 ($24–$37); Tavern Bar £5–£7.50 ($9.25–$14); Pizza on the Dock £9–£15 ($17–$28). AE, DC, MC, V. Open: Grill on the Dock daily noon to 3 p.m. and 6:30–10:30 p.m.; Tavern Bar daily 11 a.m.–3 p.m.; Pizza on the Dock daily noon to 10 p.m.*

Ebury Wine Bar & Restaurant
$$ Westminster and Victoria   MODERN BRITISH/INTERNATIONAL

This popular wine bar offers a surprisingly good and varied menu and excellent wines. The narrow, woodsy, attractive interior is reminiscent of a Paris bistro. In addition to steaks, the oft-changing menu features traditional dishes and specials such as chicken-and-bacon terrine with red onion marmalade or rich mushroom-y sausages with mash and onion gravy.

See map p. 149. 139 Ebury St., SW1. ☎ *020/7730-5447. Reservations recommended. Tube: Victoria (then a ten-minute walk west on Belgrave Street and south on Ebury Street). Main courses: £10–£20 ($19–$37); fixed-price lunch and pre-theater dinner: £13 ($24). Cover £2 ($3.70). AE, DC, MC, V. Open: Daily noon–2:45 p.m. and 6–10 p.m.*

Ed's Easy Diner
$ Soho   NORTH AMERICAN

It may seem strange to go to London to visit this replica of an old American diner, where customers perch on stools at a wraparound counter and listen to old songs blaring from the jukebox, but it's a safe bet for the kids. A bit more authentic than the version at the Pepsi Trocadero in Piccadilly Circus, this Ed's still attracts a fair share of teens. If you've a yen for the cholesterol-laden food that you're supposed to avoid, chow down with Ed's big burgers with fries or onion rings, or giant kosher weenies slathered with cheddar cheese. On the lighter side, you can get a veggie burger, tuna salad, or a chicken Caesar salad.

See map p. 150. 12 Moor St. (off Cambridge Circus), W1. ☎ *020/7439-1955. Tube: Leicester Square (then a five-minute walk north on Charing Cross Road and west on Moor Street). Main courses: £5–£6.50 ($9.25–$12). MC, V. Open: Mon–Thurs 11:30 a.m. to midnight, Fri and Sat 11:30 a.m.–1:00 a.m., Sun 11:30 a.m.–11:30 p.m.*

Food for Thought
$ Covent Garden   VEGETARIAN

Covent Garden offers a plethora of expensive restaurants for meat-eaters, so this basement hole-in-the-wall with cafeteria-style service is a pleasant and welcome alternative. The menu changes constantly, but the daily soup is always a treat (such as carrot and fresh coriander), and the main courses can include a sweet and tangy Jamaican curry, Italian bean casserole, and cannelloni *ripieni* (stuffed with eggplant), as well as daily quiche and salad specials. The desserts generally include simple fare, such as apple-and-rhubarb crumble and fruit with yogurt.

See map p. 150. 31 Neal St., WC2. ☎ *020/7836-0239. Reservations not accepted. Tube: Covent Garden (then a two-minute walk north on Neal Street). Main courses: £4–£6.50 ($7.40–$12). No credit cards. Open: Mon–Sat 9:30 a.m.–8:30 p.m., Sun noon to 5 p.m.*

Fortnum & Mason
$$ St. James's TRADITIONAL BRITISH

Fortnum & Mason, a posh, legendary London store that's a "purveyor to the Queen" and famous for its food section (see Chapter 12), also has three restaurants. The mezzanine-level **Patio** is a good lunch spot, with a menu that offers an assortment of pricey sandwiches and main courses, including hot and cold pies (steak and kidney, curried fish and banana, chicken, and game) and *Welsh rarebit* (thick melted cheese poured over toast) prepared with Guinness stout. The lower-level **Fountain** offers breakfast and lunch, and the fourth-floor **St. James's** serves lunch and afternoon tea. The more well heeled dine at St. James's, where the menu is traditionally British: For starters, try the *kipper* (smoked herring) mousse or potato and Stilton brûlée; main courses include pies and roast rib of Scottish beef. Although crowded with tourists, these three establishments remain pleasant places where you can get a good meal and a glimpse of the fading Empire. The Fountain and Patio are good places to dine with a family.

See map p. 150. 181 Piccadilly, W1. ☎ *020/7734-8040. Reservations accepted for St. James's only. Tube: Piccadilly Circus (then a five-minute walk west on Piccadilly). Main courses: Lunch £9–£24 ($17–$44); fixed-price menus £20–£23 ($37–$43). AE, DC, MC, V. Open: St. James's and the Patio Tues–Sat 9:30 a.m.–5:30 p.m.; the Fountain Mon–Sat 8:30 a.m.–7:45 p.m.*

The Founders Arms
$ South Bank MODERN BRITISH

This modern pub/restaurant sits right on the Thames, a few minutes' walk east from the South Bank Centre or west from the new Tate Modern and Shakespeare's Globe. You can sit inside or out by the water. Although some British pub favorites such as *bangers and mash* (sausages and mashed potatoes), game pie, and fish and chips are available, other dishes are more ambitious. Pasta, fresh fish, and other daily specials are listed on a chalkboard. Or you can just get a sandwich.

See map p. 148. 52 Hopton St., SE1. ☎ *020/7928-1899. Tube: Waterloo (then a ten-minute walk north along the Thames Path in front of the National Theatre). Main courses: £7.50–£12 ($14–$22). AE, MC, V. Open: Mon–Sat noon to 8:30 p.m., Sun noon to 7 p.m.*

Fox & Anchor
$ The City TRADITIONAL BRITISH

This unique pub is one of the best places in town for a big English breakfast. Butchers from the nearby Smithfield meat market, nurses coming off of their night shifts, clerks from the City, and tycoons have been eating enormous breakfasts here since 1898. The full house breakfast plate comes with at least eight items, including sausage, bacon, kidneys, eggs, beans, black pudding, and a fried slice of bread, along with unlimited tea or coffee, toast, and jam. You can order breakfast until 3 p.m., and breakfast is the meal to go for. If you'd rather have lunch, try a steak or the steak-and-kidney pie. Meat is what the Fox & Anchor does best.

See map p. 148. 115 Charterhouse St., EC1. ☎ *020/7253-5075. Reservations recommended. Tube: Barbican (then a five-minute walk north on Aldersgate and west on Charterhouse Street). Breakfast: £7.50–£9.95 ($14–$18); main courses: £4.50–£15 ($8.35–$28). AE, DC, MC, V. Open: Mon–Fri 7 a.m.–9 p.m., food served 7 a.m.–3 p.m.*

The Gay Hussar
$–$$ Soho   HUNGARIAN

The Gay Hussar is considered to be one of the best Hungarian restaurants outside Hungary. *Gay* in the cheery old "ha-ha" sense of the word, the restaurant serves undeniably authentic Hungarian comfort food: chilled wild-cherry soup, caraway potatoes, cabbage stuffed with minced veal and rice, tender chicken served in mild paprika sauce with cucumber salad and noodles, and, of course, veal goulash with egg dumplings. The portions are large, but try to save room for the poppyseed strudel or the walnut pancakes for dessert.

See map p. 150. 2 Greek St. (off Soho Square), W1. ☎ *020/7437-0973. Reservations recommended. Tube: Tottenham Court (then a two-minute walk west on Oxford Street and south on Soho Street; Greek Street is at the southeast corner of Soho Square). Main courses: £9.50–£17 ($18–$31); fixed-price lunch menus: £17–£19 ($31–$35). AE, DC, MC, V. Open: Mon–Sat 12:15–2:30 p.m. and 5:30–10:45 p.m.*

The George
$ The Strand   TRADITIONAL BRITISH

Beware: A headless cavalier is rumored to haunt these premises, evidently looking for his noggin *and* a drink. A favorite pub for barristers, the George is opposite the Royal Courts of Justice and dates back to 1723, with much of the original structure still standing. Hot and cold meals, including bangers and mash, fish and chips, sandwiches, and steak-and-ale pie are served from a counter at the back.

See map p. 150. 213 The Strand, WC2. ☎ *020/7427-0941. Tube: Temple (then a five-minute walk north on Arundel Street and east on The Strand). Main courses: £5.95–£7 ($11–$13). AE, DC, V. Open: Pub Mon–Fri 11 a.m.–11 p.m., Sat noon to 5 p.m.; food served Mon–Fri noon to 7 p.m., Sat noon to 2:30 p.m.*

Gourmet Pizza Company
$ St. James's   PIZZA/PASTA

This large, bright eatery, frequented by workers in the area's shops and offices, provides an economical meal if you're in the West End — and a good choice if you need to please some pizza-loving kids. You can choose from 20 varieties of pizza — everything from a B.L.T. to one with Cajun chicken and prawns. About half the choices are vegetarian. The crusts are light and crispy, and the toppings are fresh and flavorful. If you don't want pizza, try the tortellini with cream, ham, and tomato. *Delicioso!* The new branch at Upper Ground, Gabriel's Wharf, SE7 (☎ 020/7928-3188) is right on the river.

See map p. 150. 7–9 Swallow St. (off Piccadilly), W1. ☎ *020/7734-5182. Tube: Piccadilly Circus (then a five-minute walk west on Piccadilly and north on Swallow Street). Pizzas: £6–£9 ($11–$17); pastas: £7.75–£9.25 ($14–$17). AE, DC, MC, V. Open: Daily noon10:30 p.m.*

The Granary
$ Piccadilly Circus and Leicester Square TRADITIONAL BRITISH

The newly refurbished Granary serves a simple but flavorful array of home-cooked dishes, listed daily on a chalkboard. Menu favorites include lamb casserole with mint and lemon; pan-fried cod; or avocado stuffed with prawns, spinach, and cheese. Common vegetarian meals include meatless versions of *paella* (a Spanish rice dish), lasagna, and *korma* (curried vegetables with Greek yogurt). This reliable restaurant also offers such traditional but tempting desserts as bread-and-butter pudding and Brown Betty (both served hot).

See map p. 150. 39 Albemarle St., W1. ☎ *020/7493-2978. Tube: Green Park (then a five-minute walk east on Piccadilly to Albermarle) or Piccadilly Circus (then a five-minute walk west on Piccadilly). Main courses: £9–£11 ($17–$20). MC, V. Open: Mon–Fri 11:30 a.m.–7:30 p.m., Sat 11:30 a.m.–3:30 p.m.*

Hard Rock Cafe
$$ Mayfair NORTH AMERICAN

This restaurant is one of a worldwide chain of rock-'n'-roll/American-road-side-diner-themed restaurants. Teens enjoy the rock memorabilia and loud music as well as the burgers and shakes. Tasty vegetarian dishes are available, too. The portions are generous, and main dishes include salad and fries or baked potato. Consider the homemade apple pie if you have room for dessert. Be prepared to stand in line on weekend evenings.

See map p. 150. 150 Old Park Lane, W1. ☎ *020/7629-0382. Tube: Hyde Park Corner (take the Park Lane exit; Old Park Lane is just to the east of Park Lane). Main courses: £7.50–£14 ($14–$26). AE, MC, V. Open: Sun–Thurs 11:30 a.m. to midnight, Fri–Sat 11:30 a.m.–1 a.m.*

The Ivy
$$ Soho BRITISH/FRENCH

Are you looking for a hip place to dine after enjoying the theater? The Ivy, with its 1930s look, tiny bar, glamour-scene crowd, and later-than-usual hours, fits the bill. The cooking features skillful preparations of fresh ingredients, with such popular dishes as white asparagus with sea kale and truffle butter, roast chicken and stuffing, and roast beef and potatoes. You can also enjoy Mediterranean fish soup, salmon fish cakes, shepherd's pie, and traditional English desserts, such as sticky toffee and caramelized bread-and-butter pudding. You need to book as far in advance as possible for this top dining spot.

See map p. 150. 1–5 West St., WC2. ☎ *020/7836-4751. Reservations required. Tube: Leicester Square (then a five-minute walk north on Charing Cross Road; West Street is at the southeastern end of Cambridge Circus). Main courses: £9.50–£35 ($18–$65); fixed-price menu (Sat–Sun lunch): £20–£22 ($37–$41). AE, DC, MC, V. Open: Daily noon–3 p.m. and 5:30 p.m.–midnight.*

Joe Allen
$$ Covent Garden   NORTH AMERICAN

Joe Allen is a low-profile place on a back street in Covent Garden. Its crowded dining room with checkered tablecloths is the sort of place where actors like to come after a performance to scarf down chili con carne or gnaw on barbecued ribs. The dependable food includes American classics with some international twists, and the set menu is a real value: After a starter (maybe *smoked haddock vichyssoise,* a cold soup with fish), you can choose main courses such as pan-fried Parmesan-crusted lemon sole, Cajun chicken breast, and grilled spicy Italian sausages. If you're a tad homesick, try a burger, a brownie, and a Coke for consolation. Come before the show for the best prices, come after for potential star-gazing.

See map p. 150. 13 Exeter St., WC2. ☎ *020/7836-0651. Reservations recommended. Tube: Covent Garden (then a five-minute walk south past the Market to Burleigh Street on the southeast corner of the Piazza and west on Exeter Street). Main courses: £9–£15 ($17–$28); fixed-price menus: Lunch and pre-theater dinner Mon–Fri £14–£16 ($26–$30), Sun brunch £18–£20 ($33–$37). AE, MC, V. Open: Mon–Fri noon–12:45 a.m., Sat 11:30 a.m.–12:45 a.m., Sun 11:30 a.m.–11:30 p.m.*

Ken Lo's Memories of China
$$$$ Westminster and Victoria   CHINESE

Founded by the late Ken Lo, author of more than 30 cookbooks and once the host of a TV cooking show, this restaurant is one of the better (and certainly one of the more expensive) pan-Chinese restaurants in London. The interior decor is appealingly minimalist, and the service is impeccable. Spanning broadly divergent regions of China, the ambitious menu features Cantonese quick-fried beef in oyster sauce, lobster with Szechuan pepper sauce, and "bang-bang chicken" (a Szechuan dish), among many others.

See map p. 149. 65–69 Ebury St. (near Victoria Station), SW1. ☎ *020/7730-7734. Reservations recommended. Tube: Victoria Station (then a ten-minute walk west on Belgrave Street and south on Ebury Street). Main courses: £4.50–£27 ($8.35–$50); fixed-price menus: Lunch £19–£22 ($35–$41), dinner £30–£48 ($56–$89). AE, DC, MC, V. Open: Mon–Sat noon to 2:30 p.m., daily 7–11:15 p.m.*

Langan's Bistro
$$ Marylebone BRITISH/FRENCH

The menu for this bistro is English with an underplayed (some may say underdeveloped) French influence. Behind a brightly colored storefront, the dining room is covered with clusters of Japanese parasols, rococo mirrors, paintings, and old photographs. Depending on the season, the fixed-price menu may start with smoked mackerel pâté or leek and Stilton tart and move on to grilled plaice with parsley butter or lamb kebab with polenta. The dessert extravaganza known as "Mrs. Langan's Chocolate Pudding" is a must for chocoholics.

See map p. 154. 26 Devonshire St., W1. ☎ *020/7935-4531. Reservations recommended three days in advance. Tube: Regent's Park (then a five-minute walk south on Portland Place and west on Devonshire Street). Fixed-price menus: £19–£22 ($35–$41). AE, DC, MC, V. Open: Mon–Fri 12:30–2:30 p.m., Mon–Sat 6:30–11 p.m.*

Maggie Jones's
$$ Kensington TRADITIONAL BRITISH

At this tri-level restaurant with pine tables, the menu is all British, including such traditional favorites as grilled leg of lamb chop with rosemary, grilled trout with almonds, steak-and-kidney and chicken-and-artichoke pies, and Maggie's famous fish. For dessert, try the bread-and-butter pudding. Everything tastes good and is reliably cooked, but don't expect anything exceptional. By the way, the place was named for the late Princess Margaret, who used to eat here.

See map p. 154. 6 Old Court Place (off Kensington Church Street), W8. ☎ *020/ 7937-6462. Reservations recommended. Tube: High Street Kensington (then a five-minute walk east on Kensington High Street, north on Kensington Church Street, and east on Old Court Place). Main courses: £5–£20 ($9.25–$37); fixed-price Sun lunch: £16 ($30). AE, DC, MC, V. Open: Daily 12:30–2:30 p.m. and 6:30–11 p.m.*

Mela
$ Covent Garden INDIAN

Winner of Moët & Chandon's 2001 award for best Indian restaurant in London, Mela claims to take its inspiration from a food stall favored by workers in Delhi. Lunch here is a fantastic deal: curry or dahl of the day, with bread, pickle, and chutney for under £2 ($3.70). Pay a little more, and you can build your own version of the meal with different breads and toppings. This is a great, inexpensive way for curry novices to have a try — and to see it being made in the open kitchen. But do come back in the evening for a proper go at the innovative Indian country cuisine. Early birds get three courses. Fixed-price sharers have ten dishes and accompaniments between them. The word *mela* means "fair," and Mela the restaurant does its best to create a festive atmosphere.

See map p. 150. 152–156 Shaftesbury Ave., WC2. ☎ *020/7836-8635. Tube: Leicester Square (then a three-minute walk east on Shaftesbury Avenue). Main courses: £4.95–£19*

($9.15–$35); fixed-price lunch: £1.95–£4.95 ($3.60–$9.15); pre-theater (5:30–7 p.m.) menu: £11 ($20). AE, MC, V. Open: Mon–Sat noon to 11:30 p.m., Sun noon to 10:30 p.m.

Mona Lisa
$ **Chelsea ITALIAN**

Make Mona Lisa your destination for lunch or dinner after walking the length of King's Road, one of London's great shopping streets (from Sloane Square, the walk takes about 40 minutes, or you can hop on a bus). A popular cafe by day, the place becomes a restaurant at night, although they serve many of the same dishes for lunch and dinner. Everything is homemade and fresh, and the ambience is informal and fun. The menu includes many fish dishes, including sea bass and Dover sole. *Pasta da Vinci,* a house specialty, is pasta cooked in a paper bag with a sauce of squid, mussels, and prawns. Salad lovers can try the Mona Lisa salad with mozzarella, tomatoes, crispy bacon, avocado, and basil.

See map p. 152. 417 King's Rd. (near Millman's Street, just south of Beauford Street), SW10. ☎ 020/7376-5447. Tube: Sloane Square (then bus no. 11, 22, or 211; or a 40-minute walk south on King's Road). Main courses: £4.50–£16 ($8.35–$30). MC, V. Open: Mon–Sat 7 a.m.–11 p.m., Sun 9 a.m.–5:30 p.m.

Moro
$$ **Clerkenwell SPANISH/NORTH AFRICAN**

Clerkenwell, on the fringes of the City, has become a very hip neighborhood in recent years, and award-winning Moro has become this unpretentious area's best haute spot. The décor is modern and minimalist, and the North African cuisine is earthy and powerful. The kitchen uses only the best ingredients, organic whenever possible, in its daily-changing menu. Highly recommended are the quail baked in flatbread with pistachio sauce and the tender wood-roasted pork, marinated in sherry. For dessert, try one of the yummy house-specialty desserts: Yogurt cake with pistachios or rosewater and cardamom ice cream.

See map p. 150. 34–36 Exmouth Market, EC1. ☎ 020/7833-8336. Reservations recommended. Tube: Farringdon (then a five-minute walk north on Farringdon to Exmouth Market). Main courses: £14–£18 ($26–$33); tapas: £3–£5 ($5.55–$9.25). AE, DC, MC, V. Open: Mon–Fri 12:30–2:30 p.m., Mon–Sat 7–10:30 p.m.

Mosaique
$$ **Holborn MEDITERRANEAN**

Tourists staying on the beaten track never find this wonderful restaurant, but the people who work in the area know it well. The interior is bright and cheerful, with yellow walls and white tablecloths glowing under skylights. The menu choices feature dishes from all across the Mediterranean region, prepared with an assured hand. You can dine here on the *mezes* (small plates), such as grilled *halloumi* or *tabbouleh,* or feast on a lamb or chicken "shish" (as in "kebab"), served with vegetables and rice. Vegetarian choices include risotto primavera and vegetable moussaka. At night, a jazz pianist adds to the ambience.

See map p. 150. 73 Gray's Inn Rd., WC1. ☎ *020/7404-7553. Tube: Chancery Lane (then a five-minute walk north on Gray's Inn Road). Main courses: £7.50–£15 ($14–$28); mezes: £2.95–£3.95 ($5.45–$7.30). AE, MC, V. Open: Mon–Fri noon to midnight; Sat 5 p.m. to midnight.*

The Museum Tavern
$ Bloomsbury   TRADITIONAL BRITISH

Across from the British Museum's front entrance, this ornate Victorian pub is a convenient spot for a hearty lunch after perusing the Parthenon sculptures. You order food at the counter and drinks at the bar and bring them to your table. Most of the main courses are traditional pub staples: meat pies (chicken and ham; steak and kidney; cottage), bangers and mash, fish and chips, salads, and lasagna. Traditional roasts are also served.

See map p. 150. 49 Great Russell St., WC1. ☎ *020/7242-8987. Tube: Russell Square (then a five-minute walk south on Montgomery Street, along the west side of Russell Square, to Great Russell Street). Main courses: £3.95–£9.50 ($7.30–$18). AE, MC, V. Open: Mon–Sat 11 a.m.–11 p.m., Sun 11 a.m.–10:30 p.m. (food served daily to half an hour before closing).*

Noor Jahan
$$ South Kensington   INDIAN

Noor Jahan is a neighborhood favorite in South Ken. The restaurant is small and unpretentious. The reliably good food includes moist and flavorful marinated chicken and lamb dishes cooked tandoori-style in a clay oven. If you want to try one of their tasty specialties, consider chicken *tikka,* a staple of northern India, or the *biriani* dishes — where chicken, lamb, or prawns are mixed with basmati rice, fried in *ghee* (thick, clarified butter), and served with a mixed vegetable curry. If you're unfamiliar with Indian food, the waiters will gladly explain the dishes.

See map p. 152. 2A Bina Gardens (off Old Brompton Road), SW5. ☎ *020/7373-6522. Reservations recommended. Tube: Gloucester Road (then a five-minute walk south on Gloucester Road, west on Brompton Road, and north on Bina Gardens). Main courses: £3.50–£15 ($6.50–$28); fixed-price menu: £19 ($35). AE, DC, MC, V. Open: Daily noon to 2:45 p.m. and 6–11:45 p.m.*

North Sea Fish Restaurant
$$ Bloomsbury   SEAFOOD

When they go to London, many people want to experience *real* fish and chips — not the generic frozen stuff that often passes for this traditional dish. Definitely try this unassuming chippie where the fish is *always* fresh. This restaurant, with its sepia prints and red velvet seats, is pleasant, comfortable, and popular with adults and kids. You may want to start with grilled fresh sardines or a fish cake before digging into a main course of cod or haddock. The fish is most often served battered and deep-fried, but you can also order it grilled. The chips are almost as good as the fish.

See map p. 150. 7–8 Leigh St. (off Cartwright Gardens), WC1. ☎ 020/7387-5892. Reservations recommended. Tube: Russell Square (then a ten-minute walk north on Marchmont Place and east on Leigh Street). Main courses: £8–£17 ($15–$31). AE, DC, MC, V. Open: Mon–Sat noon to 2:30 p.m. and 5:30–10:30 p.m.

The Oratory
$$ South Kensington   MODERN BRITISH

Named for the nearby Brompton Oratory, a famous late-19th-century Catholic church, and close to the Victoria & Albert Museum and Harrods shopping, this funky bistro serves some of the best and least expensive food in posh South Ken. The high-ceilinged room is decorated in what I call Modern Rococo, with enormous glass chandeliers, patterned walls and ceiling, and wooden tables with wrought-iron chairs. Note the daily specials on the chalkboard, especially any pasta dishes. The homemade fish cakes, roasted field mushroom risotto, and grilled calf's liver with bacon and deep-fried sage are all noteworthy. For dessert, the sticky toffee pudding with ice cream is a melt-in-the-mouth delight.

See map p. 152. 232 Brompton Rd., SW3. ☎ 020/7584-3493. Tube: South Kensington (then a five-minute walk north on Brompton Road). Main courses: £7–£15 ($13–$28); fixed-price lunch specials: £3.50–£6.95 ($6.50–$13). MC, V. Open: Daily noon to 11 p.m.

Oxo Tower Brasserie
$$$ South Bank   FRENCH/INTERNATIONAL

This stylish brasserie sits atop the landmark Oxo Tower on the South Bank. Although the brasserie is less elegant than the adjacent Oxo Tower Restaurant, its food is marvelous and costs about half of what you pay to dine on tablecloths. The superlative river-and-city views are just as sublime, so book in advance and insist on a window table. The food has taken on more fusion elements but remains as good as ever. Order such tasty dishes as roasted halibut with fried sweet potato or twice-cooked pork with coriander and chilis. The fixed-price lunch and pre-theater menu make this brasserie an affordable extravagance.

See map p. 148. Oxo Tower Wharf, Barge House St., SE1. ☎ 020/7803-3888. Reservations essential at least one or two weeks in advance. Tube: Waterloo (the easiest foot route is to head north to the South Bank Centre and then follow the Thames pathway east to the Oxo Tower, about a ten-minute walk). Main courses: £11–£17 ($20–$31); fixed-price lunch and pre-theater menu (Mon–Fri): £17–£22 ($31–$41). AE, DC, MC, V. Open: Daily noon to 3:15 p.m.; Mon–Sat 5:30–11 p.m., Sun 6–10 p.m.

Porter's English Restaurant
$$ Covent Garden   TRADITIONAL BRITISH

This comfortably informal restaurant specializes in English pies, including Old English fish pie; lamb and apricot; and steak, mushroom, and

Guinness stout. Forgo appetizers because the main courses, accompanied by vegetables and side dishes, are generous. If pie isn't your thing, try the bangers and mash, grilled sirloin, or lamb steak. The desserts, including bread-and-butter pudding and spotted dick (suet with raisins), are served hot or cold, with whipped cream or custard. The casual atmosphere makes this a good spot for families.

See map p. 150. 17 Henrietta St., WC2. ☎ 020/7836-6466. Reservations recommended. Tube: Covent Garden (then a five-minute walk south on James Street; Henrietta Street is at the southwest corner behind Covent Garden Market). Main courses: £8.95–£14 ($17–$26); fixed-price menu: £20 ($37). AE, DC, MC, V. Open: Mon–Sat noon to 11:30 p.m., Sun noon to 10:30 p.m.

R.S. Hispaniola
$$$ The Strand BRITISH/FRENCH

This former passenger boat is permanently moored in the Thames and provides good food and spectacular views of the river traffic. The menu changes often, with a variety of sturdy and generally well-prepared dishes, such as calf's liver with olive mash, beef stroganoff with wild rice, rack of lamb marinated in honey, and several vegetarian dishes. The place can be fun and romantic — live music is played most nights.

See map p. 150. River Thames, Victoria Embankment, Charing Cross, WC2. ☎ 020/7839-3011. Reservations recommended. Tube: Embankment (the restaurant is a few steps from the station). Main courses: £13–£18 ($24–$33); fixed-price lunch and dinner: £25–£45 ($46–$83). AE, DC, MC, V. Open: Daily noon–3 p.m. and 6:30–11 p.m. Closed Dec 24–Jan 4.

Rules
$$ Covent Garden TRADITIONAL BRITISH

If you want to eat classic British cuisine in a memorable (nay, venerable) setting, put on something dressy and head for Maiden Lane. Founded in 1798, Rules is London's oldest restaurant, with two centuries worth of prints, cartoons, and paintings decorating its walls. If you're game for game, go for it because that's what Rules is famous for. On the menu, you may find lobster and asparagus salad with mango dressing, or fallow deer with spiced red cabbage, blueberries, and bitter chocolate sauce. The food is delicious: traditional yet innovative, until you get to the puddings (desserts), which are a mix of nursery and dinner-dance classics. In recent years, the restaurant has added fish and a few vegetarian dishes. The restaurant is completely nonsmoking.

See map p. 150. 35 Maiden Lane, WC2. ☎ 020/7836-5314. Reservations recommended. Tube: Covent Garden (then a five-minute walk south on James Street to Southampton Street behind Covent Garden Market and west on Maiden Lane). Main courses: £16–£21 ($30–$39); fixed-price post-theater menu (Mon–Thurs 10–11:30 p.m.): £18 ($33). AE, DC, MC, V. Open: Mon–Sat noon to 11:30 p.m., Sun noon to 10:30 p.m.

San Lorenzo
$$$ Knightsbridge ITALIAN

This fashionable restaurant was once a favorite of Princess Diana. Italian cuisine from all the regions of Italy, with a special nod toward Tuscany and the Piedmont, is the specialty. Seasonal fish, game, and vegetables appear in such dishes as risotto with fresh asparagus, partridge in white-wine sauce, and *tagliate di bue* (filet steak with arugula and balsamic vinegar). The fettuccine, gnocchi, and penne are all homemade. The food is reliably good, but some diners complain that too much attitude accompanies it. Dining here is mostly about people-watching.

See map p. 152. 22 Beauchamp Place, SW3. ☎ 020/7584-1074. Reservations required on weekends. Tube: Knightsbridge (then a five-minute walk southwest on Brompton Road and south on Beauchamp Place). Main courses: £18–£29 ($33–$54). No credit cards. Open: Mon–Sat 12:30–3 p.m. and 7:30–11:30 p.m.

Shepherd's
$$$ Westminster and Victoria TRADITIONAL BRITISH

This popular restaurant sits between Tate Britain and Parliament. Regulars include a loyal crowd of barristers and MPs (a bell rings in the dining room to let them know it's time to go back to the House of Commons for a vote). Amid a nook-and-cranny setting of leather banquettes, sober 19th-century accessories, and English portraits and landscapes, you can dine on rib of Scottish beef with Yorkshire pudding, hot salmon and potato salad with dill dressing, cheese and onion tart, filet of lemon sole, or steak-and-kidney pie. You choose everything from a fixed-price menu but are given an impressive number of options.

See map p. 149. Marsham Court, Marsham Street (at the corner of Page Street), SW1. ☎ 020/7834-9552. Reservations recommended. Tube: Westminster (then a ten-minute walk south on St. Margaret Place and Millbank and west on Westminster Street to Page and Marsham streets; or Pimlico, then north on Bessboro Street, John Islip Street, and Marsham Street). Fixed-price menus: £26–£29 ($48–$54). AE, DC, MC, V. Open: Mon–Fri 12:30–2:45 p.m. and 6:30–11 p.m.

Simpson's-in-the-Strand
$$$ The Strand TRADITIONAL/MODERN BRITISH

Open since 1828, Simpson's offers an array of the best roasts in London — sirloin of beef, saddle of mutton with red-currant jelly, and Aylesbury duckling — served by a veritable army of formal waiters. (Remember to tip the tailcoated carver.) For a pudding, try the treacle roll and custard or Stilton with vintage port. You'll find these food options downstairs, where the atmosphere is formal and dressy; **Simply Simpson,** a more relaxed, brighter, lighter dining area on the second floor, is actually (gasp!) nouvelle. You can also come downstairs for a great real English breakfast.

See map p. 150. 100 The Strand (next to the Savoy Hotel), WC2. ☎ 020/7836-9112. Reservations recommended. Tube: Charing Cross (then a five-minute walk east along The Strand). Main courses: Downstairs £20–£24 ($37–$44), Simply Simpson £10–£16

($19–$30); fixed-price menus: £16–£19 ($30–$35); breakfast: £16–£18 ($30–$33). AE, DC, MC, V. Open: Mon–Sat 7:15–10:30 a.m., 12:15–2:30 p.m., and 5–10:45 p.m.; Sun 6–8:30 p.m.

The Stockpot

$ Piccadilly Circus and Leicester Square   BRITISH/CONTINENTAL

Now here's a dining bargain! This simple bi-level restaurant in the heart of the West End doesn't offer refined cooking, but the food is filling and the price is right — making it a good spot for families. You can find such fare as minestrone soup, spaghetti Bolognese (the eternal favorite), braised lamb, and apple crumble on the fixed-price daily menu. (During peak dining hours, you may have to share a table with other guests.)

See map p. 150. 38 Panton St. (off Haymarket, opposite the Comedy Theatre), SW1. ☎ 020/7839-5142. Tube: Piccadilly Circus (then a five-minute walk south on Haymarket and east on Panton Street). Main courses: £3.40–£5.50 ($6.30–$10); fixed-price menu: £5.95 ($11). No credit cards. Open: Mon–Sat 7 a.m.–11 p.m., Sun 7 a.m.–10 p.m.

Suze in Mayfair

$–$$ Mayfair   PACIFIC RIM/INTERNATIONAL

For relaxed, charming, bistrolike ambience in Mayfair, check out Suze. The food is Australasian with some international crossovers and is always simple and well prepared. Try the succulent New Zealand green-tipped mussels, a house specialty, or a New Zealand meat or fish pie. You can also get New Zealand rack of lamb. You can choose from several sharing platters: Italian antipasti, vegetarian, Greek, seafood, and cheese. A must-have dessert is Pavlova, a light meringue covered with kiwi, strawberries, passion fruit, and mangoes. And, of course, you can get a fine glass of Australian wine.

See map p. 154. 41 North Audley St., W1. ☎ 020/7491-3237. Reservations recommended. Tube: Marble Arch (then a five-minute walk east on Oxford Street and south on North Audley Street). Main courses: £6.25–£15 ($12–$28); platters to share: £4.95–£11 ($9.15–$20). AE, DC, MC, V. Open: Mon–Sat 11 a.m.–11 p.m.

Veeraswamy

$$ Piccadilly Circus & Leicester Square   INDIAN

Established in 1926 by a general and an Indian princess, Veeraswamy claims to be the oldest Indian restaurant in London. Over the years, it's been the haunt of princes and potentates, from the Prince of Wales to King Hussein and Indira Gandhi. Nowadays, it's very hip, painted in vibrant colors, with frosted-glass panels dividing up the sections and ultramodern furniture. For starters, the stir-fried mussels with coconut and Kerala spices are sublime. For an exotic and only mildly hot choice, try the shanks of lamb curried in bone stock and spices. Unless you're in the mood to splurge, this isn't the place to sample lots of different dishes. Go for a great-value fixed-price menu and enjoy the best of new Indian cuisine.

See map p. 150. 99–101 Regent St., W1. ☎ 020/7734-1401. Tube: Piccadilly Circus (then a two-minute walk along Regent Street to the restaurant, just off Swallow

Street). Reservations recommended. Main courses: £10–£18 ($19–$33); fixed-price meals: Lunch and pre-/post-theater menu £14–£16 ($26–$30), Sun menu £16 ($30). AE, DC, MC, V. Open: Mon–Sat noon to 2:30 p.m. and 5:30–11:30 p.m.; Sun 12:30–3 p.m. and 5:30–10:30 p.m.

Veronica's
$$ Bayswater   TRADITIONAL/MODERN BRITISH

The food here is an intriguing mix of historical and modern British cuisine. One dining room has a Victorian theme, and the other is avant-garde. Diners choose their meals from the "In the Present" contemporary menu and/or the "From the Past" menu. The historic dishes are creative spins on medieval, Tudor, and Victorian recipes. Your appetizer may be an Elizabethan salad called salmagundy, made with crunchy pickled vegetables, followed by twice-roasted duck or a filet steak. Many dishes are vegetarian, and desserts from the past include such temptations as Lord John Russell's frozen pudding with butterscotch sauce.

See map p. 154. 3 Hereford Rd., W2. ☎ 020/7229-5079. Reservations required. Tube: Bayswater (then a five-minute walk west on Moscow Road and north on Hereford Road). Main courses: £12–£15 ($22–$28). AE, DC, MC, V. Open: Mon–Fri noon to 3 p.m. Mon–Sat 5:30–11 p.m.

Wagamama Noodle Bar
$ Soho   JAPANESE

Try this trendsetting noodle bar, modeled after the ramen shops of Japan, if you're exploring Soho and want a delicious, nutritious, smoke-free meal. You enter along a stark, glowing hall with a busy open kitchen and descend to a large open room with communal tables. The specialties are *ramen,* Chinese-style thread noodles served in soups with various toppings, and the fat white noodles called *udon.* You can also order various rice dishes, vegetarian dishes, dumplings, vegetable and chicken skewers, and tempura. Your order is sent via radio signal to the kitchen and arrives the moment it's ready, which means that not everyone in a group is served at the same time. You may have to stand in line to get in, but it's worth the wait. Teens especially love the loud, hip, casual atmosphere. Several other Wagamamas are scattered around London.

See map p. 150. 10A Lexington St., W1. ☎ 020/7292-0990. Reservations not accepted. Tube: Piccadilly Circus (then a five-minute walk north on Shaftesbury Avenue and Windmill Street, which becomes Lexington Street). Main courses: £5.50–9.25 ($10–$17). MC, V. Open: Mon–Thurs noon to 11 p.m., Fri–Sat noon to midnight, Sun 12:30–10 p.m.

Ye Olde Cheshire Cheese
$$ The City   TRADITIONAL BRITISH

Opened in 1667 and a one-time haunt of Samuel Johnson, Charles Dickens, and Fleet Street newspaper scandalmongers, Ye Olde Cheshire Cheese is London's most famous chophouse. The place contains six bars and two dining rooms and is perennially popular with families and tourists looking for some Olde London atmosphere. The house specialties include "ye famous pudding" (steak, kidney, mushrooms, and game), Scottish roast beef with Yorkshire pudding and horseradish sauce, and fish and chips. If those choices repulse the kids, they can choose sandwiches or salads.

See map p. 148. Wine Office Court, 145 Fleet St., EC4. ☎ 020/7353-6170. Tube: Blackfriars (then a ten-minute walk north on New Bridge Street and west on Fleet Street). Main courses: £7.25–£14 ($13–$26). AE, DC, MC, V. Open: Mon–Sat noon to 11 p.m., Sun noon to 3 p.m.; drinks and bar snacks daily noon to 10 p.m.

Zafferano
$$$$ Knightsbridge   ITALIAN

At Zafferano, you find the best Italian food in London, served in a quietly elegant, attitude-free restaurant. The semolina pastas are perfectly cooked and come with various additions. The main courses, such as roast rabbit with Parma ham and polenta, charcoal-grilled chicken, and tuna with arugula and tomato salad, are deliciously simple and tender. For dessert, try the sublime ricotta and lemon cake.

See map p. 152. 15 Lowndes St., SW1. ☎ 020/7235-5800. Reservations required. Tube: Knightsbridge (then a five-minute walk south on Lowndes Street, two streets east of Sloane Street). Fixed-price menus: Lunch £24–£33 ($44–$61); dinner £30–£42 ($56–$78). AE, MC, V. Open: Daily noon to 2:30 p.m. and 7–11 p.m.

Dining and Snacking on the Go

Londoners have a much less casual attitude toward food than Americans have. You won't see many adults in London eating on the street or having a bite while traveling the Tube. It's mostly tourists carrying those Starbucks cups. And you don't find street vendors peddling hot dogs and other foods from carts (although you may see a fast-food van or two near major attractions). Even the most frenetic Londoner likes to eat a proper, civilized "sit-down" meal. So what's a too-rushed tourist to do? To help you enjoy snacks and light meals the London way, I offer some interesting alternatives to fast-food restaurants.

Sandwich bars

Sandwiches are an English invention (supposedly of the Earl of Sandwich), and sandwich bars are a faster and cheaper alternative to sit-down restaurants and pubs. Most open early for breakfast and close in the afternoon. You can usually eat at a counter or in booths, or you can take your sandwich and go to the nearest park for an alfresco lunch. The bars sell coffee, tea, and nonalcoholic beverages.

Americans are sometimes confused by the way the English name their sandwiches. In general, the Brits use the word *mayonnaise* the way that Americans use *salad*. Tuna mayonnaise or egg mayonnaise simply means "tuna salad" or "egg salad." The word *salad* is used in Britain to denote that lettuce and tomato have been added to a sandwich, as in "chicken with salad."

The following sandwich bars are worth a bite:

✔ Near Victoria Station, **Capri Sandwich Bar** (See map p. 149; 16 Belgrave Rd., NW1; ☎ 020/7834-1989; Tube: Victoria) serves an imaginative variety of sandwiches. The bar is open Monday through Friday 7:30 a.m. to 3:30 p.m.

✔ If you're in the vicinity of Euston Station, try the unpretentious but cheerful **Giovanni's Sandwich Bar** (See map p. 150; 152 North Gower St., at Euston Road; ☎ 020/7383-0531; Tube: Euston), open Monday through Friday 7 a.m. to 3 p.m.

The best sandwich shops in Central London are the **Pret à Manger** chain stores, which offer fresh, inventive, healthy sandwiches and fast counter service. A convenient West End branch is located at 77–78 St. Martin's Lane, WC2 (See map p. 150; ☎ 020/7379-5335; Tube: Leicester Square). It's open Monday through Thursday 7:30 a.m. to 9 p.m., Friday 7:30 a.m. to 11 p.m., Saturday 9 a.m. to 11 p.m., and Sunday 9 a.m. to 9 p.m. You'll find Pret à Manger all over the city.

Fish and chips

The English call a fish and chips place a *chippie.* At some chippies, the food is wonderful; at others, it's hideous. At the good places (the only ones that I recommend), the fish (usually cod, haddock, or plaice) is fresh, the batter crisp, and the fries *(chips)* hand-cut. You can get tartar sauce, but the British also like to splash their fish and chips with malt vinegar.

The following restaurants all have sit-down and *takeaway* (what the Brits call *takeout*) service and welcome families with kids. Also see the North Sea Fish Restaurant in the section "London's Best Restaurants," earlier in this chapter.

✔ **Costas Fish Restaurant** (See map p. 154; 18 Hillgate St., W8; ☎ 020/7727-4310; Tube: Notting Hill Gate) is open Tuesday through Saturday noon to 2:30 p.m. and 5:30 to 10:30 p.m.

✔ **Fryer's Delight** (See map p. 150; 19 Theobald's Rd., WC1; ☎ 020/7405-4114; Tube: Chancery Lane or Holborn) is across from the Holborn Police Station. A plate of cod and chips costs $4.95 ($9.15); takeaway is also available. The Formica-clad chippie is open Monday through Saturday noon to 10 p.m. The fish is fried in beef fat here; other options include pastries and pies.

✔ **Geales** (See map p. 154; 2 Farmer St., W8; ☎ 020/7727-7969; Tube: Notting Hill Gate) is open Tuesday through Saturday noon to 3 p.m. and 6 to 10:30 p.m.

✔ **Golden Hind** (See map p. 150; 73 Marylebone Lane, W1; ☎ 020/ 7486-3644; Tube: Baker Street or Bond Street) is a few blocks south of Madame Tussaud's. This bargain chippie has an average meal cost of £6 ($11); hours are Monday through Friday noon to 3 p.m. and Monday through Saturday 6 to 10 p.m.

✔ **Rock & Sole Plaice** (See map p. 150; 47 Endell St., WC2; ☎ 020/ 7836-3785; Tube: Covent Garden) offers all-day takeaway service, as well as a place to sit down and eat amid the bustle of the Covent Garden Piazza (you can get a table on the lower level). Because of its location, this chippie crowds with theatergoers in the evening. You pay at least £8 ($15) for a meal. It's open Monday through Saturday 11:30 a.m. to 10:30 p.m. and Sunday noon to 10 p.m.

✔ **Seafresh Fish Restaurant** (See map p. 159; 80–81 Wilton Rd., SW1; ☎ 020/7828-0747; Tube: Victoria) offers a good cod filet and great chips for about £8.50 ($16). It's open Monday through Friday noon to 3 p.m. and 5 to 10:30 p.m.

✔ **Sea-Shell** (See map p. 154; 49–51 Lisson Grove, NW1; ☎ 020/7723-8703; Tube: Marylebone) is within easy walking distance west of Madame Tussaud's and is considered one of the best chippies in London. Main courses range from £7 ($13) to £16 ($26); average cost for fish and chips is about £9 ($17). It's open Monday through Friday noon to 2:30 p.m. and 5 to 10:30 p.m., Saturday noon to 10:30 p.m.

Costas Fish Restaurant and **Geales** are both good choices if you've been poking around the antiques and whatnot stands along Portobello Road.

Department-store restaurants

If you're in the midst of a shopping spree and don't want to be distracted, you can easily grab a bite at one of the many department-store restaurants. These eateries are convenient, but they aren't necessarily cheap; see the restaurant entry for Fortnum & Mason in the section "London's Best Restaurants," earlier in this chapter.

Here are some more department-store possibilities:

✔ **Harrods** (87–135 Brompton Rd., SW1; ☎ 020/7730-1234; Tube: Knightsbridge), in addition to its ice-cream parlor and awe-inspiring Food Hall, offers its **Famous Deli Counter,** where you can perch on stools (no reservations) and pay too much for what's called "traditional Jewish food" but often isn't. It's open Monday through Saturday 10 a.m. to 6 p.m.

✔ **Harvey Nichols** (109–125 Knightsbridge, SW7; ☎ 020/7235-5250; Tube: Knightsbridge) is another Knightsbridge emporium with a restaurant, the **Fifth Floor at Harvey Nichols** (See map p. 152). It's open Monday through Friday noon to 3 p.m. and 5:30 to 10 p.m., but eating here is pretty expensive. A better bet is the cafe, also on the fifth floor, where you can get a cup of tea and a salad or light

meal; it's open Monday through Saturday 10 a.m. to 11 p.m. and
Sunday 10 a.m. to 6 p.m. Like Harrods, Harvey Nichols has a fabulous food emporium where you can buy now and eat later.

Treating Yourself to Tea

The stereotype is true: Brits do drink tea. In fact, they drink 171 million
cups per day (give or take a cup), though consumption is dropping
because of the new emphasis on coffee. Teatime is traditionally from
about 3:30 to 5 p.m. Your afternoon tea can be a lavish affair served by
a black-coated waiter in a posh hotel lobby, or a quick "cuppa" with a
slice of cake or a sandwich at a corner tea shop or *pâtisserie* (a bakery
where you can sit down or get pastries to take away). Tea may be served
fast-food style in paper cups, home-style in mugs, or more elegantly on
bone china.

So what exactly, you ask, is the difference between afternoon tea and
high tea?

- ✔ **Afternoon tea** is tea with cakes, scones, sandwiches, or all of them,
  served between 3 and 5 p.m. It's a pre-dinner ritual.

- ✔ **High tea,** served from about 5 to 6 p.m., is a more elaborate affair,
  including a light supper with a hot dish, followed by dessert and
  tea. It often is the evening meal.

Casual tea rooms and pâtisseries

In the following comfortable neighborhood tearooms and pâtisseries,
you can get a good cup of tea, along with a scone or other pastry or a
plate of tea sandwiches, for about £4 to £10 ($7.40–$19):

- ✔ **Café Parlour at Sketch** (See map p. 150; 9 Conduit St., W1; ☎ 0870/
  777-4488; Tube: Oxford Circus): Offers superb pastries and cakes in
  a room that makes up the patisserie component of the ultrahip
  Sketch, a gastro-empire founded by Pierre Gagnaire. You can also get
  breakfast and lunch. Worth a visit just to see the loos. Hours are
  Monday through Friday 8 a.m. to 11 p.m., Saturday 10 a.m. to 11 p.m.

Never too latte: London's coffee bars

It had to happen sooner or later, and frankly I'm glad it did because finding a good cup
of coffee in London wasn't always the easiest thing to do. But now **Starbucks** has
opened branches all over the city, offering nice places to sit down and have a latte,
cappuccino, or "regular" cup of joe. They also sell pastries and sandwiches.

✔ **Muffinski's** (See map p. 150; 5 King St., WC2; ☎ **020/7379-1525;** Tube: Leicester Square) offers great homemade muffins, including low-fat and vegetarian. Hours are Monday through Friday 8 a.m. to 7 p.m., Saturday 9 a.m. to 7 p.m., and Sunday 10 a.m. to 6 p.m.

✔ **Pâtisserie Cappucetto** (See map p. 150; 8 Moor St., W1; ☎ **020/ 7437-9472;** Tube: Leicester Square) serves breakfast, sandwiches, soups, and superb desserts Monday through Thursday 8 a.m. to 11:30 p.m. and Friday and Saturday 8 a.m. to 12:30 a.m.

✔ **Pâtisserie Deux Amis** (See map p. 150; 63 Judd St., WC1; ☎ **020/ 7383-7029;** Tube: Russell Square) is a good choice for a quick bite. Hours are Monday through Saturday 9 a.m. to 5:30 p.m. and Sunday 9 a.m. to 1:30 p.m.

✔ **Pâtisserie Valerie** (See map p. 150; 44 Old Compton St., W1; ☎ **020/ 7437-3466;** Tube: Leicester Square or Tottenham Court Road) has been around since 1926 and serves a mouthwatering array of pastries, but expect to stand in line night or day. Hours are Monday through Friday 7:30 a.m. to 8 p.m., Saturday 8 a.m. to 6:30 p.m., and Sunday 9 a.m. to 6 p.m.

Pâtisserie Valerie also has two branches in Marylebone. One is at 105 Marylebone High St., W1 (☎ **020/7935-6240;** Tube: Bond Street or Baker Street); the other is near Regent's Park at 66 Portland Place, W1 (☎ **020/7631-0467;** Tube: Regent's Park). The Marylebone branch is open Monday through Saturday 7:30 a.m. to 6 p.m., and Sunday 9 a.m. to 6 p.m. The Regent's Park branch stays open until 7 p.m. and opens at 8 a.m. on Sundays.

✔ **Richoux** has three old-fashioned tearooms in choice London locations. They serve food all day long, and they're kind to your budget. **Richoux-Knightsbridge** (See map p. 152; 215 Brompton Rd., SW3; ☎ **020/7823-9971;** Tube: Knightsbridge), **Richoux-Mayfair** (See map p. 154; 41a South Audley St., W1; ☎ **020/7629-5228;** Tube: Bond St. or Green Park), and **Richoux-Piccadilly** (See map p. 150; 172 Piccadilly, W1; ☎ **020/7493-2204;** Tube: Piccadilly Circus). All keep the same hours: Monday through Friday 7 a.m. to 7 p.m., Saturday 7:30 a.m. to 7 p.m., and Sunday 8 a.m. to 6 p.m.

Elegant spots for high tea

A traditional afternoon English tea has cakes, sandwiches, and scones with clotted cream and jam, and is "taken" in a posh hotel or restaurant. These rather lavish affairs are expensive but memorable. At any one of the following places, you can get a proper traditional afternoon or high tea (a smart-casual dress code is in effect — tennis shoes and jeans are inappropriate):

✔ **Claridge's** (See map p. 150; Brook St., W1; ☎ **020/7629-8860;** Tube: Bond Street) serves a glamorous and expensive tea daily from 3 to 5:30 p.m. for £30 ($56). Reservations are a good idea.

✔ **Fortnum & Mason** (181 Piccadilly, W1; ☎ **020/7734-8040;** Tube: Piccadilly Circus) serves tea in the **St. James's Restaurant** Monday through Saturday from 3 to 5:30 p.m. for £20 ($37). Reservations aren't necessary.

✔ **Georgian Restaurant,** on the fourth floor of Harrods (See map p. 152; 87–135 Brompton Rd., SW1; ☎ **020/7225-6800;** Tube: Knightsbridge), serves high tea Monday through Saturday from 3:45 to 5:30 p.m. It costs £19 ($35) per person, and you don't need reservations.

✔ **The Lanesborough Hotel** (See map p. 152; Hyde Park Corner, SW1; ☎ **020/72595-599;** Tube: Hyde Park Corner) requires reservations for high tea daily 3:30 to 6 p.m. The cost is £26 ($48); the price goes up to £34 ($63) if you add strawberries and champagne.

✔ **Palm Court** at the Le Meridien Waldorf Hotel (Aldwych, WC2; ☎ **020/78362-400;** Tube: Covent Garden) serves afternoon tea Monday through Friday from 3 to 5:30 p.m. at a cost of £18 to £21 ($33–$39); reservations are required.

Planning a Picnic

London may not be the perfect city for picnics. Rain can quickly put a damper on a picnic hamper, and nothing is quite as unappetizing as a wet sandwich. But on days when the weather cooperates, nothing is more enjoyable than packing up some sandwiches and heading to a special spot to eat outdoors.

Glean your picnic pickings from delis and sandwich shops (see "Sandwich bars," earlier in this chapter), or drop in at the legendary and far more expensive food halls at **Fortnum & Mason** or **Harrods.** In neighborhoods outside the West End (South Kensington or Marylebone, for example), you can go into any supermarket and generally find packaged sandwiches, crisps (potato chips), fresh fruit, and drinks.

In the West End, the **Embankment Gardens** is a pretty picnic spot, looking out on the Thames. This flower-filled strip of green is next to the Embankment Tube station, below The Savoy hotel. You have to sit on benches instead of the grass, and the traffic noise along the Embankment can be annoying, but it's still a nice place to know about. Sandwich shops and takeaway food shops are clustered around the Embankment Tube station.

Kensington Gardens (see Chapter 11) offers vast green lawns, frolicsome fountains, Kensington Palace, and the famous statue of Peter Pan. This spot is a favorite with children of all ages. The park is close to all the great museums in South Ken. Adjacent **Hyde Park** is another lovely picnic site, particularly along the shores of Serpentine Lake. You can buy sandwiches and snacks at the Dell Restaurant (described under "Hyde Park" in Chapter 11) at the east end of the lake. In summer, bandstand concerts are given in the park.

The royal parks — **Green Park** and **St. James's Park** — are more sedate. You can choose to picnic on a lovely knoll and gaze upon Buckingham Palace.

Looking for an urban space that's good for people-watching and has great views across the river? Picnic on the **South Bank** of the Thames, along the riverside promenade close to Royal Festival Hall and the National Theatre.

Index of Restaurants by Neighborhood

Bayswater
Veronica's (Traditional/Modern British, $$)

Bloomsbury
Cigala (Spanish, $$)
Giovanni's Sandwich Bar (Sandwich Bars, $)
The Museum Tavern (Traditional British, $)
North Sea Fish Restaurant (Fish and Chips/Seafood, $$)

Chelsea
Aubergine (French, $$$$)
Chelsea Kitchen (International, $)
Harvey Nichols (Food Halls, $$)
Mona Lisa (Italian, $)

The City
Dickens Inn by the Tower (Traditional/Modern British, $–$$)
Fox & Anchor (Traditional British, $)
Ye Olde Cheshire Cheese (Traditional British, $$)

Clerkenwell
Moro (Spanish/North African, $$)

Covent Garden
Food for Thought (Vegetarian, $)
Joe Allen (North American, $$)
Mela (Indian, $)
Porter's English Restaurant

(Traditional British, $$)
Rules (Traditional British, $$)

Holborn
Fryer's Delight (Fish and Chips, $)
Mosaique (Mediterranean, $$)

Kensington
Maggie Jones's (Traditional British, $$)

Knightsbridge
Boxwood Café (Modern British, $$$)
Harrods (Food Halls/Tea/Pâtisseries/Traditional British, $$)
Richoux (Tea/Pâtisseries, $)
San Lorenzo (Italian, $$$)
Zafferano (Italian, $$$$)

Marylebone
Golden Hind (Fish and Chips, $)
Langan's Bistro (British/French, $$)
Pâtisserie Valerie (Tea/Pâtisseries, $)
Sea-Shell (Fish and Chips, $)

Mayfair
Café Parlour at Sketch (Tea/Pâtisseries, $)
Claridge's (Tea/Pâtisseries, $$$)
Hard Rock Cafe (North American, $$)
The Lanesborough (Tea/Pâtisseries, $$$–$$$$)
Richoux (Tea/Pâtisseries, $)
Suze in Mayfair (Pacific Rim/International, $–$$)

Notting Hill

Clarke's (Modern European, $$$)
Costas Fish Restaurant (Fish and Chips, $)
Geales (Fish and Chips, $)
Seafresh Fish Restaurant (Fish and Chips, $)

Piccadilly Circus and Leicester Square

Cafe in the Crypt (Traditional British, $)
Criterion Grill (British/French, $$–$$$)
The Granary (Traditional British, $)
Pret à Manger (Sandwich Bars, $)
Richoux (Tea/Pâtisseries, $)
The Stockpot (British/Continental, $)
Veeraswamy (Indian, $$)

Soho

Chiang Mai (Thai, $$)
Ed's Easy Diner (North American, $)
The Gay Hussar (Hungarian, $–$$)
The Ivy (British/French, $$)
Muffinski's (Tea/Pâtisseries, $)
Pâtisserie Cappucetto (Soho, $)
Pâtisserie Deux Amis (Tea/Pâtisseries, $)
Rock & Sole Plaice (Fish and Chips, $)
Wagamama Noodle Bar (Japanese, $)

South Bank

The Founders Arms (Modern British, $)
Oxo Tower Brasserie (French/International, $$$)

South Kensington

Brasserie St. Quentin (French, $$)
Noor Jahan (Indian, $$)
The Oratory (Modern British, $$)

St. James's

Fortnum & Mason (Food Halls/Tea/Pâtisseries/Traditional British, $$)
Gourmet Pizza Company (Pizza/Pasta, $)

The Strand

Le Meridien Waldorf Hotel (Tea/Pâtisseries, $$)
The George (Traditional British, $)
R.S. *Hispaniola* (British/French, $$$)
Simpson's-in-the-Strand (Traditional/Modern British, $$$)

Westminster and Victoria

Capri Sandwich Bar (Sandwich Bar, $)
Ebury Wine Bar & Restaurant (British/International, $$)
Ken Lo's Memories of China (Chinese, $$$$)
Shepherd's (Traditional British, $$$)

Index of Restaurants by Cuisine

British/Continental

The Stockpot (Piccadilly Circus and Leicester Square, $)

British/French

Criterion Grill (Piccadilly Circus and Leicester Square, $$–$$$)
The Ivy (Soho, $$)
Langan's Bistro (Marylebone, $$)
R.S. *Hispaniola* (The Strand, $$$)

British (Modern)

Boxwood Café (Knightsbridge, $$$)
Dickens Inn by the Tower (The City, $–$$)
Ebury Wine Bar & Restaurant (Westminster and Victoria, $$)
The Founders Arms (South Bank, $)
The Oratory (South Kensington, $$)
Simpson's-in-the-Strand (The Strand, $$$)
Veronica's (Bayswater, $$)

British (Traditional)

Cafe in the Crypt (Piccadilly Circus and Leicester Square, $)
Dickens Inn by the Tower (The City, $–$$)
Fortnum & Mason (St. James's, $$)
Fox & Anchor (The City, $)
The George (The Strand, $)
The Granary (Piccadilly Circus and Leicester Square, $)
Harrods (Knightsbridge, $$)
Maggie Jones's (Kensington, $$)
The Museum Tavern (Bloomsbury, $)
Porter's English Restaurant (Covent Garden, $$)
Rules (Covent Garden, $$)
Shepherd's (Westminster and Victoria, $$$)
Simpson's-in-the-Strand (The Strand, $$$)
Veronica's (Bayswater, $$)
Ye Olde Cheshire Cheese (The City, $$)

Chinese

Ken Lo's Memories of China (Westminster and Victoria, $$$$)

Fish and Chips

Costas Fish Restaurant (Notting Hill, $)
Fryer's Delight (Holborn, $)
Geales (Notting Hill, $)
Golden Hind (Marylebone, $)
North Sea Fish Restaurant (Bloomsbury, $$)
Rock & Sole Plaice (Soho, $)
Seafresh Fish Restaurant (Notting Hill, $)
Sea-Shell (Marylebone, $)

Food Halls

Fortnum & Mason (St. James's, $$)
Harrods (Knightsbridge, $$)
Harvey Nichols (Chelsea, $$)

French

Aubergine (Chelsea, $$$$)
Brasserie St. Quentin (South Kensington, $$)
Oxo Tower Brasserie (South Bank, $$$)

Hungarian

The Gay Hussar (Soho, $–$$)

Indian

Mela (Covent Garden, $)
Noor Jahan (South Kensington, $$)
Veeraswamy (Piccadilly Circus and Leicester Square, $$)

International

Chelsea Kitchen (Chelsea, $)
Ebury Wine Bar & Restaurant (Westminster and Victoria, $$)
Oxo Tower Brasserie (South Bank, $$$)

Italian

Mona Lisa (Chelsea, $)
San Lorenzo (Knightsbridge, $$$)
Zafferano (Knightsbridge, $$$$)

Japanese

Wagamama Noodle Bar (Soho, $)

Mediterranean

Mosaique (Holborn, $$)

Modern European

Clarke's (Notting Hill, $$$)

North African

Moro (Clerkenwell, $$)

North American

Ed's Easy Diner (Soho, $)
Hard Rock Cafe (Mayfair, $$)
Joe Allen (Covent Garden, $$)

Pacific Rim/International

Suze in Mayfair (Mayfair, $–$$)

Pizza/Pasta

Gourmet Pizza Company (St. James's, $)

Sandwich Bars
Capri Sandwich Bar (Westminster and Victoria, $)
Giovanni's Sandwich Bar (Bloomsbury, $)
Pret à Manger (Piccadilly Circus and Leicester Square, $)

Seafood
North Sea Fish Restaurant (Bloomsbury, $$)

Spanish
Cigala (Bloomsbury, $$)
Moro (Clerkenwell, $$)

Tea/Pâtisseries
Café Parlour at Sketch (Mayfair, $)
Claridge's (Mayfair, $$$)

Fortnum & Mason (St. James's, $$)
Harrods (Knightsbridge, $$)
The Lanesborough (Mayfair, $$$–$$$$)
Le Meridien Waldorf Hotel (The Strand, $$)
Muffinski's (Soho, $)
Pâtisserie Cappucetto (Soho, $)
Pâtisserie Deux Amis (Soho, $)
Pâtisserie Valerie (Marylebone, $)
Richoux (Knightsbridge, Mayfair, Piccadilly Circus and Leicester Square, $)

Thai
Chiang Mai (Soho, $$)

Vegetarian
Food for Thought (Covent Garden, $)

Index of Restaurants by Price

$

Cafe in the Crypt (Traditional British, Piccadilly Circus and Leicester Square)
Café Parlour at Sketch (Tea/Pâtisseries, Mayfair)
Capri Sandwich Bar (Sandwich Bar, Westminster and Victoria)
Chelsea Kitchen (International, Chelsea)
Costas Fish Restaurant (Fish and Chips, Notting Hill)
Dickens Inn by the Tower (Traditional/Modern British, The City)
Ed's Easy Diner (North American, Soho)
Food for Thought (Vegetarian, Covent Garden)
The Founders Arms (Modern British, South Bank)
Fox & Anchor (Traditional British, The City)
Fryer's Delight (Fish and Chips, Holborn)
The Gay Hussar (Hungarian, Soho)

Geales (Fish and Chips, Notting Hill)
The George (Traditional British, The Strand)
Giovanni's Sandwich Bar (Sandwich Bars, Bloomsbury)
Golden Hind (Fish and Chips, Marylebone)
Gourmet Pizza Company (Pizza/Pasta, St. James's)
The Granary (Traditional British, Piccadilly Circus and Leicester Square)
Mela (Indian, Covent Garden)
Mona Lisa (Italian, Chelsea)
Muffinski's (Tea/Pâtisseries, Soho)
The Museum Tavern (Traditional British, Bloomsbury)
Pâtisserie Cappucetto (Tea/Pâtisseries, Soho)
Pâtisserie Deux Amis (Tea/Pâtisseries, Soho)
Pâtisserie Valerie (Tea/Pâtisseries, Marylebone)
Pret à Manger (Sandwich Bars, Piccadilly Circus and Leicester Square)

Richoux (Tea/Pâtisseries, Knightsbridge, Mayfair, Piccadilly Circus and Leicester Square)
Rock & Sole Plaice (Fish and Chips, Soho)
Seafresh Fish Restaurant (Fish and Chips, Notting Hill)
Sea-Shell (Fish and Chips, Marylebone)
The Stockpot (British/Continental, Piccadilly Circus and Leicester Square)
Suze in Mayfair (Pacific Rim/International, Mayfair)
Wagamama Noodle Bar (Japanese, Soho)

$$

Brasserie St. Quentin (French, South Kensington)
Chiang Mai (Thai, Soho)
Cigala (Spanish, Bloomsbury)
Criterion Grill (British/French, Piccadilly Circus and Leicester Square)
Dickens Inn by the Tower (Traditional/Modern British, The City)
Ebury Wine Bar & Restaurant (Modern British/International, Westminster and Victoria)
Fortnum & Mason (Food Halls/Tea/Pâtisseries/Traditional British, St. James's)
The Gay Hussar (Hungarian, Soho)
Hard Rock Cafe (North American, Mayfair)
Harrods (Food Halls/Tea/Pâtisseries/Traditional British, Knightsbridge)
Harvey Nichols (Food Halls, Chelsea)
The Ivy (British/French, Soho)
Joe Allen (North American, Covent Garden)
Langan's Bistro (British/French, Marylebone)
Le Meridien Waldorf Hotel (Tea/Pâtisseries, The Strand)
Maggie Jones's (Traditional British, Kensington)
Moro (North African/Spanish, Clerkenwell)
Mosaique (Mediterranean, Holborn)
Noor Jahan (Indian, South Kensington)

North Sea Fish Restaurant (Fish and Chips/Seafood, Bloomsbury)
The Oratory (Modern British, South Kensington)
Porter's English Restaurant (Traditional British, Covent Garden)
Rules (Traditional British, Covent Garden)
Suze in Mayfair (Pacific Rim/International, Mayfair)
Veeraswamy (Indian, Piccadilly Circus and Leicester Square)
Veronica's (Traditional/Modern British, Bayswater)
Ye Olde Cheshire Cheese (Traditional British, The City)

$$$

Boxwood Café (Modern British, Knightsbridge)
Claridge's (Tea/Pâtisseries, Mayfair)
Clarke's (Modern European, Notting Hill)
Criterion Grill (British/French, Piccadilly Circus and Leicester Square)
The Gay Hussar (Hungarian, Soho)
The Lanesborough (Tea/Pâtisseries, Mayfair)
Oxo Tower Brasserie (French/International, South Bank)
R.S. *Hispaniola* (British/French, The Strand)
San Lorenzo (Italian, Knightsbridge)
Shepherd's (Traditional British, Westminster and Victoria)
Simpson's-in-the-Strand (Traditional/Modern British, The Strand)

$$$$

Aubergine (French, Chelsea)
Ken Lo's Memories of China (Chinese, Westminster and Victoria)
The Lanesborough (Tea/Pâtisseries, Mayfair)
Zafferano (Italian, Knightsbridge)

Part IV
Exploring London

The 5th Wave   By Rich Tennant

"Now T_H_A_T was a great meal! Beautiful presentation, an imaginative use of ingredients, and a sauce with nuance and depth. The British really know how to make a 'Happy Meal'."

In this part . . .

Ready to hit the streets? Raring to go? Turn to Chapter 11 for descriptions of London's top sights — along with directions, open hours, and admission prices; you can also find my rundown of additional sights to see, all of them intriguing and worth exploring. I also tell you about the best options for guided tours of London by bus, by boat, and on foot.

Check out Chapter 12 for some great tips on how to make the most of your shopping in London, as well as specific stores to visit. Chapter 13 gives you four suggested London itineraries — sightseeing strategies to help you enjoy the city on a *realistic* schedule. Finally, in Chapter 14, I send you on your way to five fascinating places that you can explore on day trips. I think you'll love each and every one of them.

Chapter 11

Discovering London's Top Attractions

- -

In This Chapter

▶ Reviewing London's top attractions

▶ Finding sights and activities for history buffs, art lovers, bookworms, kids, gardeners, and others

▶ Visiting royal palaces and castles

▶ Focusing on Greenwich, home of the prime meridian

▶ Listing London's sights by neighborhood and type

- -

*H*ere's the big question: What do you want to see and enjoy while you're in London? The possibilities are endless: fabulous museums, royal palaces, important historic sites, beautiful parks and gardens, and grand churches. In this chapter, I give you the information that you need to make your itinerary fit your interests, time, and energy level.

To help you find your way around London, you may want to go beyond my directions in this chapter and get yourself a *London A to Z* map. Even Londoners use this comprehensive street gazette, which comes in many different formats and can be found at just about every bookstore in London.

I arranged the top sights in this chapter alphabetically. Following the must-see list are more top attractions grouped together by type. For locations, see the "London's Top Sights" map on p. 186. To help you pull together your itinerary, see the end of this chapter, where I index all the top attractions by neighborhood and type. For useful information about planning workable itineraries based on the length of your trip, turn to Chapter 13.

London's top museums are spectacular treasure troves — and they're all absolutely free. To save money on transportation costs, buy one of the single- or multiday Travelcards I describe in Chapter 8.

London's Top Sights

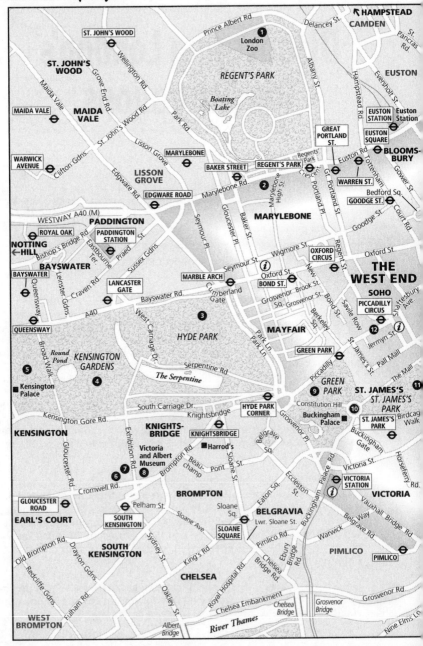

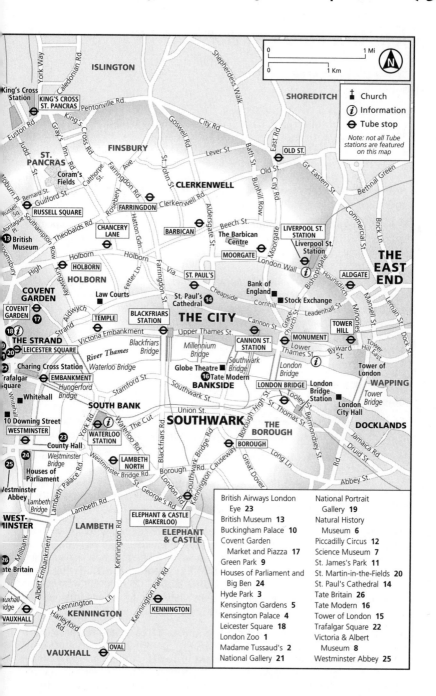

British Airways London Eye **23**
British Museum **13**
Buckingham Palace **10**
Covent Garden Market and Piazza **17**
Green Park **9**
Houses of Parliament and Big Ben **24**
Hyde Park **3**
Kensington Gardens **5**
Kensington Palace **4**
Leicester Square **18**
London Zoo **1**
Madame Tussaud's **2**
National Gallery **21**
National Portrait Gallery **19**
Natural History Museum **6**
Piccadilly Circus **12**
Science Museum **7**
St. James's Park **11**
St. Martin-in-the-Fields **20**
St. Paul's Cathedral **14**
Tate Britain **26**
Tate Modern **16**
Tower of London **15**
Trafalgar Square **22**
Victoria & Albert Museum **8**
Westminster Abbey **25**

The Top Attractions from A to Z

British Airways London Eye
South Bank

As a piece of fast-track engineering, the 400-foot-high London Eye observation wheel is impressive. Each glass-sided elliptical module holds about 25 passengers, with enough space so you can move about freely. Although most people stand the entire time, you can sit on the available bench if you prefer. Lasting about 30 minutes (equivalent to one rotation), the ride (or *flight*, as they call it) is remarkably smooth — even on windy days riders don't feel any nerve-twittering shakes. As long as the weather is good, the wheel provides unrivaled views of London.

For the London Eye, you may want to reserve your place (with a specific entry time) before you arrive; if you're ticketless, you can line up for a ticket at the office right behind the wheel, but you may have to wait an hour or more before you can get on the wheel.

See map p. 190. Bridge Road, SE1 (beside Westminster Bridge). ☎ *0870/500-0600 (advance credit-card booking; 50p/95¢ booking fee added). Tube: Westminster (then a five-minute walk south across Westminster Bridge) or Waterloo (then a three-minute walk west along the riverside promenade). Admission: £13 ($24) adults, £10 ($19) seniors, £6.50 ($12) children under 16. Open: Daily 9:30 a.m.; last admission varies seasonally.*

British Museum
Bloomsbury

The British Museum ranks as the most visited attraction in London, with a splendid, wide-ranging collection of treasures from around the world.

Wandering through the museum's 94 galleries (see the "British Museum" map on p. 190), you can't help but be struck by humanity's enduring creative spirit. Permanent displays of antiquities from Egypt, Western Asia, Greece, and Rome are on view, as well as prehistoric and Romano-British, Medieval, Renaissance, Modern, and Oriental collections.

In November 2000, the museum's **Great Court** reopened with a glass-and-steel roof designed by Lord Norman Foster. Inaccessible to the general public for 150 years, the Great Court is now the museum's new central axis. In the center, you find a circular building completed in 1857 that once served as the museum's famous **Reading Room**. Completely restored, it now houses computer terminals where visitors can access images and information about the museum's vast collections.

The most famous of the museum's countless treasures are the superb **Parthenon Sculptures** brought to England in 1801 by the seventh Lord Elgin. These marble sculptures once adorned the Parthenon in Athens, and Greece desperately wants them returned. Other famous treasures include the **Rosetta Stone**, which enabled archaeologists to decipher

Egyptian hieroglyphics; the **Sutton Hoo Treasure,** an Anglo-Saxon burial ship, believed to be the tomb of a 7th-century East Anglian king; and **Lindow Man,** a well-preserved ancient corpse found in a bog. The museum's ethnography collections are filled with marvelous curiosities: everything from a pair of polar-bear slacks worn by Eskimos to a Hawaiian god with a Mohawk haircut, found by Captain Cook and shipped back to London.

 To enhance your enjoyment and understanding of the Parthenon Sculptures, pick up one of the sound guides available right outside Room 18 on the first floor, where the sculptures are exhibited; the guide costs £3.50 ($6.50).

 I suggest you give yourself at least three unhurried hours in the museum. You can avoid big crowds by going on a weekday morning. If you have only limited time for the British Museum, consider taking one of the 90-minute highlight tours offered daily at 10:30 a.m. and 1 and 3 p.m.; these tours cost £8 ($15). You can rent audio tours, which also cover museum highlights, for £3.50 ($6.50). You can get tickets and information for guided tours and audio tours at the information desk in the Great Court.

See map p. 186. Great Russell Street, WC1, between Bloomsbury Street and Montgomery Street. ☎ *020/7323-8000. Tube: Russell Square (then a five-minute walk south on Montgomery Street, along the west side of Russell Square, to the museum entrance on Great Russell Street). Admission: Free. Open: Sat–Wed 10 a.m.–5:30 p.m., Thurs–Fri 10 a.m.–8:30 p.m.; closed Jan 1, Good Fri, and Dec 24–26. Most of the museum has wheelchair access via elevators; call for entrance information.*

 Buckingham Palace
St. James's

Since 1837, when Victoria ascended the throne, all the majesty, scandal, intrigue, triumph, tragedy, power, wealth, and tradition associated with the British monarchy has been hidden behind the monumental facade of Buckingham Palace, the reigning monarch's London residence.

An impressive early-18th-century pile, the palace was rebuilt in 1825 and further modified in 1913. From August through September, when the royal family isn't in residence, you can buy a ticket to get a glimpse of the impressive staterooms used by Elizabeth II and the other royals. You don't get a guided palace tour; instead, you can wander at your own pace through 19 rooms (including the Throne Room and the vast ballroom built by Queen Victoria), most of them baroque, filled with some fine artwork. In these rooms, the queen receives guests on official occasions. You leave through the gardens where the queen holds her famous garden parties each summer. Budget about two hours for your visit.

Throughout the year, you can visit the **Royal Mews,** one of the finest working stables in existence, where the magnificent Gold State Coach, used in every coronation since 1831, and other royal conveyances are housed (and horses stabled). The **Queen's Gallery,** which features changing exhibits of works from the Royal Collection, went through a refurbishment and reopened for the queen's Golden Jubilee in June 2002.

The British Museum

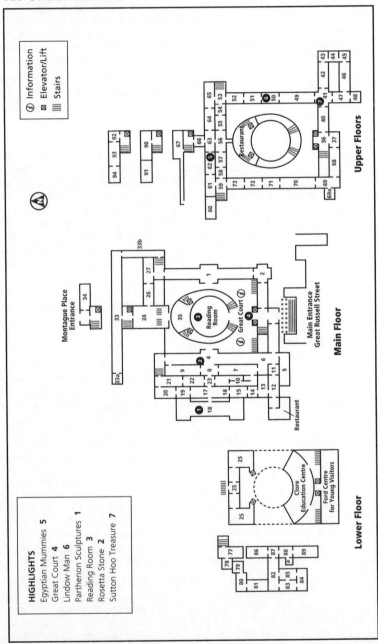

HIGHLIGHTS

Egyptian Mummies **5**
Great Court **4**
Lindow Man **6**
Parthenon Sculptures **1**
Reading Room **3**
Rosetta Stone **2**
Sutton Hoo Treasure **7**

ⓘ Information
⊠ Elevator/Lift
▦ Stairs

Upper Floors

Main Floor

Lower Floor

Montague Place Entrance

Main Entrance
Great Russell Street

Reading Room

Great Court

Restaurant

Restaurant

Clore Education Centre

Ford Centre for Young Visitors

You can charge admission tickets for Buckingham Palace by calling ☎ **020/7766-7300**. Green Park also houses a ticket office, open daily July 29 to October 1; the office opens at 9 a.m. and closes at 4 p.m. or when the last ticket has been sold. Keep in mind that every visitor gets a specific time for entry into the palace, which is why phoning ahead for tickets is smart. All phone-charged tickets cost an additional £1 ($1.85); at the ticket booth, special rates are available for seniors, kids under 17, and families.

See map p. 186. Buckingham Palace Road, SW1. Palace Visitor Office, Royal Mews, and Queen's Gallery ☎ 020/7839-1377 (9:30 a.m.–5:30 p.m.) or 020/7799-2331 (24-hour recorded info). Tube: St. James's Park (then a ten-minute walk north on Queen Anne's Gate and west on Birdcage Walk to Buckingham Gate) or Green Park (walk directly south through the park). Admission: Palace £14 ($26) adults, £12 ($22) seniors, £7 ($13) children under 17, £34 ($63) families (two adults and three children under 17); Royal Mews £6 ($11) adults, £5 ($9.25) seniors, £3.50 ($6.50) children, £14 ($26) families; Queen's Gallery £7.50 ($14) adults, £6 ($11) seniors, £4 ($7.40) children. Open: Palace Aug–Oct daily 9:30 a.m.–6:30 p.m. (last admittance 5:30 p.m.); Royal Mews Mar–July Sat–Thurs 11 a.m.–4 p.m. (last admission 3:15 p.m.), Aug–Sept daily 10 a.m.–5 p.m. (last admission 4:15 p.m.); Queen's Gallery daily 10 a.m.–5:30 p.m. (last admittance 4:30 p.m.). Royal Mews and Queen's Gallery closed Dec 25–26. Visitors with disabilities must prebook for palace visits; Royal Mews and Queen's Gallery are wheelchair accessible.

For a round-up of the latest Royal scandals, see Chapter 2.

Changing of the Guard at Buckingham Palace
St. James's

Free of charge, you can stand outside Buckingham Palace and watch the Changing of the Guard. The Foot Guards of the Household Division of the Army, the queen's personal guard, carry out the ritual. The Old Guard forms in the palace forecourt before going off duty and handing everything over to the New Guard, which leaves Wellington Barracks at precisely 11:27 a.m. and marches to the palace via Birdcage Walk, usually accompanied by a band. The Guard consists of 3 officers and 40 men, but this number decreases when the queen is away. The entire ceremony takes around 40 minutes. If you can't find a spot at the front of the railings of Buckingham Palace, you can see pretty well from the Victoria Memorial in front of the palace.

The pageantry of the Changing of the Guard is no longer a daily occurrence. The event takes place at 11:30 a.m. daily April 1 to early June but only on alternate days at other times of the year. To avoid disappointment, make sure to call ahead or check the Web site listed in the following paragraph.

Buckingham Palace Road, SW1. ☎ 020/7321-2233. www.royal.gov.uk. Tube: St. James's Park (then a ten-minute walk north on Queen Anne's Gate and west on Birdcage Walk to Buckingham Gate); or Green Park (walk directly south through the park). Admission: Free.

More guard changing

If you miss the Changing of the Guard or the event doesn't take place on the day of your visit, you can still get an eyeful of London pageantry by attending the **Mounted Guard Changing Ceremony** at the Horse Guards Building in Whitehall. The ceremony takes place daily Monday through Saturday at 11 a.m. and Sunday at 10 a.m. You don't need a ticket, but arrive early for a good view. To get there, take the tube to Charing Cross and walk south from Trafalgar Square along Whitehall (about a five-minute walk); the Horse Guards Building will be on your right.

Covent Garden Market and Piazza
Covent Garden

In 1970, the old market — the noisy, bustling public market where vendors hawked everything under the sun — moved out of Covent Garden, and the area became the site of London's earliest and most successful urban recycling effort. The market buildings now house dozens of enticing shops and eating and drinking places. The wrought-iron stalls in the former Flower Market are loaded with vendors. The piazza in front may be the most popular public gathering place outside of Trafalgar Square; the space is always "heaving," as the Brits say. Covent Garden is also the home of the **Royal Opera House** (see Chapter 15) and two museums: the excellent **Transport Museum** (see the section "Places that please kids," later in this chapter) and the so-so **Theatre Museum** (see "All manner of intriguing museums," later in this chapter).

Tube: Covent Garden (when you come out of the Tube stop, you're in Covent Garden; the Market and piazza is a one-minute walk south in a pedestrian-only zone).

Houses of Parliament and Big Ben
Westminster

The **Houses of Parliament,** situated along the Thames, house the landmark clock tower containing **Big Ben,** the biggest bell in the booming hourly chime that Londoners have been hearing for nearly 150 years. Designed by Sir Charles Barry and A.W.N. Pugin, the impressive Victorian buildings were completed in 1857. Covering approximately 8 acres, they occupy the site of an 11th-century palace of Edward the Confessor.

At one end (Old Palace Yard) you find the **Jewel House,** built in 1366 and once the treasury house of Edward III, who reigned from 1327 to 1377. The best overall view of the Houses of Parliament is from Westminster Bridge, but if you prefer, you can sit in the **Stranger's Gallery** to hear Parliamentary debate.

Previously, overseas visitors had to go through an elaborate procedure weeks in advance of their trip in order to tour the Houses of Parliament. Now, however, 75-minute guided tours are available Monday through Saturday from the last week in July until early October. The tours cost £6 ($11), and you probably want to book your ticket in advance. The London ticket office in Westminster Hall (at the Houses of Parliament) opens in mid-July. You can reserve by phone at ☎ 0870/906-3773 or order tickets online at www.firstcalltickets.com. For the rest of the year, the procedure for getting a tour is much more difficult. If you're interested, you can find details on the Web at www.parliament.uk.

See map p. 186. Bridge Street and Parliament Square, SW1. ☎ 020/7219-4272. Tube: Westminster (you can see the clock tower with Big Ben directly across Bridge Street when you exit the Tube). Admission: Free; for tickets, join the line at St. Stephen's entrance. Open: Stranger's Gallery House of Commons Mon 2:30–10:30 p.m., Tues–Wed 11:30 a.m.–7:30 p.m., Thurs 11:30 a.m.–6:30 p.m., most Fri 9:30 a.m.–3 p.m.; House of Lords Mon–Wed 2:30–10 p.m., Thurs 10 a.m.–7:30 p.m. Parliament isn't in session late July to mid-Oct or on weekends.

Hyde Park
Westminster

Once the private hunting domain of the royals, including Henry VIII, Hyde Park is now open to everyone and is one of the largest urban free parks in the world. With adjoining Kensington Gardens, it offers 630 acres of lushly landscaped lawns, magnificent flower beds, avenues of trees, and a 41-acre lake known as the **Serpentine,** where you can row and sail model boats. **Rotten Row,** the park's famous 300-year-old riding track, was the country's first public road to be lit at night. At the northeastern tip, near Marble Arch, is **Speakers' Corner,** a famous Sunday-morning venting spot for anyone who wants to climb up on a soapbox. Free band concerts are held in the park's band-shell on Sundays and Bank Holidays May to August, and the **Dell Restaurant** (☎ 020/7706-0464), at the east end of the Serpentine, offers cafeteria-style food and drinks Monday through Friday 10 a.m. to 4 p.m. in winter (to 5 p.m. on weekends) and 10 a.m. to 6 p.m. in summer (to 7 p.m. on weekends). The park is a pleasant place for an hour's stroll, but staying longer is always tempting.

See map p. 186. Bounded by Knightsbridge to the south, Bayswater Road to the north, and Park Lane to the east. ☎ 020/7298-2100. Tube: Marble Arch or Lancaster Gate on the north side (the park is directly across Bayswater Road) or Hyde Park Corner in the southeast corner of the park. Open: Daily dawn–midnight.

Big Ben tolls for thee

"Big Ben" isn't the name of the clock tower or its clock. It's the name of the largest bell that you hear booming in that famous hourly chime. Some believe that the bell was named after Sir Benjamin Hall, the commissioner of works when the bell was hung in 1859. Others maintain that Big Ben was named for a champion prizefighter of the time, Ben Gaunt.

The 5-ton clock mechanism housed in the 316-foot tower kept ticking until 1976, when it succumbed to "metal fatigue" and had to be repaired. At night, new energy-efficient lighting now gives the illuminated clock faces a greenish tinge. The light at the very top is lit when Parliament is in session.

Trivia buffs will be interested to know that the minute hands on each of the tower's four clocks are as large as a double-decker bus. For information on touring the tower holding Big Ben, which you can do only if you write for tickets three months in advance, go to the Web site www.parliament.uk.

Kensington Gardens
Kensington

Kensington Gardens adjoins Hyde Park west of the lake known as the Serpentine. Children especially love the famous bronze statue of **Peter Pan,** located north of the Serpentine Bridge. Commissioned in 1912 by Peter Pan's creator, J.M. Barrie, the statue marks the spot where Peter Pan in the book *Peter Pan in Kensington Gardens* entered the gardens to get to his home on Serpentine island.

The park is also home to the **Albert Memorial,** an ornate neo-Gothic memorial honoring Queen Victoria's husband, Prince Albert; the lovely **Italian Gardens;** and the free **Serpentine Gallery** (☎ 020/7298-1515), which has a reputation for showing cutting-edge art and is open daily (except Dec 24–27 and Jan 1) 10 a.m. to 6 p.m. The **Princess Diana Memorial Playground** is in the northwest corner of the park. If the weather is fine, give yourself enough time for a leisurely stroll — at least a couple of hours.

See map p. 186. Bounded by Kensington Palace Gardens and Palace Green on the west, Bayswater Road on the north, Kensington Road and Kensington Gore on the south. ☎ 020/7298-2100. Tube: High Street Kensington (then a ten-minute walk east on Kensington High Street) or Queensway (which is directly across from the northwest corner of the park). Open: Daily dawn–midnight.

Kensington Palace
Kensington Gardens

Kensington Palace was used as a royal residence until 1760. Victoria was born in this palace, and it was here, in 1837 when she was 18 years old, that she was awakened from her slumbers and informed that she was the new queen of England (and could move to the grander Buckingham Palace). One wing of Kensington Palace was Princess Diana's London home after her divorce from Prince Charles.

The palace was home to Princess Margaret, who died in 2002, and remains the home of the duke and duchess of Kent, so portions of it are closed off to visitors. But you can see the **State Apartments** and the **Royal Ceremonial Dress Collection's** "Dressing for Royalty" exhibit, which takes visitors through the process of being presented at court, from the first visit to the tailor/dressmaker to the final bow or curtsy. Dresses worn by Queen Victoria, Queen Elizabeth II, and Princess Diana are on display. The freshly restored **King's Apartment** features a magnificent collection of Old Masters. Give yourself about one and a half hours to view the palace.

For a pleasant and not-too-expensive tea or snack after visiting Kensington Palace, stop in at **The Orangery** (☎ **020/7376-0239**) in the gardens adjacent to the palace. The restaurant is open daily noon to 6 p.m. Lunches cost about £10 ($19); from 3 p.m., you can get a good tea for £7.50 to £15 ($14–$28).

See map p. 186. The Broad Walk, Kensington Gardens, W8. ☎ *0870/751-5170. Tube: Queensway on the north side (then a ten-minute walk south through the park) or High Street Kensington on the southwest side (then a ten-minute walk through the park). Open: Daily Nov–Feb 10 a.m.–4 p.m., Mar–Oct 10 a.m.–5 p.m. Admission: £11 ($20) adults, £8.20 ($15) seniors and students, £7 ($13) children 5–15, £32 ($59) family (two adults and two children). Wheelchair accessible, despite some stairs; call first.*

Leicester Square
Leicester Square

Leicester (pronounced *Les*-ter) Square is a crowded place with a big-city buzz. Mimes, singers, and street entertainers of all kinds vie for attention. Once a dueling ground, the square is now a pedestrian zone and the heart of West End entertainment. You can find a half-price ticket booth (no phone) for theater, opera, and dance at the south end of the square (see Chapter 15). In the square's center, surrounded by movie theaters and restaurants, is **Leicester Square Gardens,** a small grassy park with four corner gates named for William Hogarth, Sir Joshua Reynolds, John Hunter, and Sir Isaac Newton, all of whom once lived or worked in the area. You also find statues of William Shakespeare and Charlie Chaplin, a bow to theater and cinema. You probably won't want to linger long, but just walking through the square can be fun. If you're traveling with kids, keep in mind this area is one place with a restroom (coin-operated).

See map p. 186. Tube: Leicester Square (take the Leicester Square exit and you're in the pedestrian-only zone that leads to the square).

London Zoo
Marylebone

The 36-acre London Zoo is Britain's largest, with about 8,000 animals in various species-specific houses. The best attractions are the **Insect House** (bird-eating spiders), the **Reptile House** (huge monitor lizards and a 15-foot python), the **Sobell Pavilion for Apes and Monkeys,** and the **Lion Terraces.** In the **Moonlight World,** special lighting effects simulate night for the nocturnal creatures, so you can see them in action. The newest exhibit, Web of Life, in the **Millennium Conservatory,** brings together special animal displays with interactive activities to show the interconnectedness and diversity of different life forms. The **Children's Zoo,** with interactive exhibits placed at low height, is designed for 4- to 8-year-olds. Many families budget almost an entire day for the zoo; I recommend that you give it at least three hours.

A fun way to arrive at the London Zoo is by water. The **London Waterbus Co.** (☎ 020/7482-2660; www.londonwaterbus.com) operates single and return trips in snug converted canal boats along the Regent's Canal from Warwick Crescent in Little Venice to Camden Lock Market. Take the Tube to Warwick Avenue and walk south across Regent's Canal, and then you can see the moorings. Trips from both locks depart daily 10 a.m. to 5 p.m. The round-trip fare costs £4 ($7.40).

At the north end of Regent's Park, NW1. ☎ 020/7722-3333. www.londonzoo.co.uk. *Tube: Regent's Park (then bus C2 north on Albany Street to Delaney Street, ten-minute or a half-hour walk north through the park) or Camden Town (then a 12-minute walk south on Parkway, following the signs). Admission: £14 ($26) adults; £12 ($22) seniors, students, and the disabled; £11 ($20) children 3–15; £45 ($83) families (two adults and two children). Open: Mar 10–Oct 26 daily 10 a.m.–5:30 p.m.; Oct 27–Feb 10 daily 10 a.m.–4 p.m.; Feb 11–Mar 9 daily 10 a.m.–4:30 p.m.; closed Dec 25.*

Madame Tussaud's
Marylebone

Madame Tussaud's wax museum is a world-famous tourist attraction and a fun spot for older kids. The question is: Do you want to pay the exorbitant admission and devote time to see a collection of lifelike figures? (If you do go in, you need at least one and a half hours to see everything.) The original moldings of members of the French court, to whom Madame Tussaud had direct access (literally because she made molds of their heads after they were guillotined during the French Revolution), are undeniably fascinating. And animatronic gadgetry makes the **Spirit of London** theme ride fun. But the **Chamber of Horrors** is definitely for the ghoulish. (Parents with younger kids may want to think twice about wandering in here.) This exhibit allows you to see one of Jack the Ripper's victims lying in a pool of (wax?) blood and likenesses of mass murderers, such as Gary Gilmore and Charles Manson. You can see better stars next door, at the **London Planetarium** (see "Places that please kids," later in this chapter). The new **Superstars** exhibit features Hollywood faves like Nicolas Cage and Samuel L. Jackson.

Go early to beat the crowds; better still, reserve tickets one day in advance, then go straight to the head of the line. You can order tickets by phone or online.

See map p. 186. Marylebone Road, NW1. ☎ *020/7935-6861 or 0870/400-3000 for advance reservations with credit card.* www.madame-tussauds.com. *Tube: Baker Street (then a two-minute walk east on Marylebone Road). Admission: £20 ($37) adults, £17 ($31) seniors and children under 16; children under 4 not admitted. Combination tickets (including the planetarium): £22 ($41) adults, £19 ($35) seniors, £18 ($33) children under 16. Open: Daily 9 a.m.–5:30 p.m. Wheelchair accessible via elevators, but call first because only three chair-users are allowed in at a time.*

National Gallery
St. James's

If you're passionate about great art, you'll think that the National Gallery is paradise. This museum houses one of the world's most comprehensive collections of British and European paintings. All the major schools from the 13th to the 20th century are represented, but the Italians get the lion's share of wall space, with works by artists such as Botticelli, Leonardo da Vinci, and Raphael. The French Impressionist and post-Impressionist works by Cézanne, Degas, Manet, Monet, Seurat, and van Gogh are splendid. And because you're on English soil, check out at least a few of Turner's stunning seascapes, Constable's landscapes, and Reynolds' society portraits. And you won't want to miss the Rembrandts. Budget at least two hours to enjoy the gallery. The second floor has a good restaurant for lunch, tea, or snacks.

Use the free computer information center to make the most of your time at the gallery. The center allows you to design a tour based on your preferences (a maximum of 10 paintings from the 2,200 entries) and prints out a customized tour map. You can also rent a portable audio tour guide for £3 ($5.55). Every painting has a reference number. Punch in the appropriate number to hear information about any work that interests you.

See map p. 186. Trafalgar Square, WC2. ☎ *020/7747-2885. Tube: Charing Cross (then a two-minute walk north across Trafalgar Square). Admission: Free, but special exhibits may require paying a fee, usually around £5 ($9.25). Open: Thurs–Tues 10 a.m.–6 p.m., Wed 10 a.m.–9 p.m.; closed Jan 1, Dec 24–26. The entire museum is wheelchair accessible.*

National Portrait Gallery
St. James's

What do these people all have in common: Sir Walter Raleigh, Shakespeare (wearing a gold earring), Queen Elizabeth I, the Brontë sisters, Winston Churchill, Oscar Wilde, Noël Coward, Mick Jagger, and Princess Di? You can find lifelike portraits of them, as well as nearly every other famous English face, at the National Portrait Gallery. The portraits are arranged in chronological order. The earliest portraits are in the **Tudor Gallery;** portraits from the 1960s to the 1980s are displayed in the **Balcony Gallery.**

Plan on spending at least two hours, but getting sidetracked here is easy, so you may want more time. On the top floor, the **Portrait Restaurant & Bar** looks out over the rooftops of the West End.

See map p. 186. St. Martin's Place (off Trafalgar Square behind the National Gallery), WC2. ☎ *020/7306-0055. Tube: Leicester Square (then a two-minute walk south on Charing Cross Road). Admission: Free; audio tour £3 ($5.55). Open: Sat–Wed 10 a.m.–6 p.m., Thurs–Fri 10 a.m.–9 p.m. All but the landing galleries are wheelchair accessible; call first for entry instructions.*

Natural History Museum
South Kensington

Filled with magnificent specimens and exciting displays relating to natural history, this museum houses the national collections of living and fossil plants, animals, and minerals. The most popular attraction in this enormous Victorian-era museum is the huge **Dinosaurs** exhibit, with 14 complete skeletons, two creepy animatronic raptors, and a full-size, robotic T. Rex guarding a fresh kill. Kids also love the bug-filled **Creepy Crawlies.** The sparkling gems and crystals in the **Mineral Gallery** literally dazzle, and in the **Meteorite Pavilion,** you can see fragments of rock that crashed into the earth from the farthest reaches of the galaxy. The newest addition is the intriguing new **Darwin Centre,** which showcases the private collection of Charles Darwin, father of evolutionary theory, and houses the museum's huge collection of preserved specimens. The museum offers enough to keep you occupied for at least two hours.

See map p. 186. Cromwell Road, SW7. ☎ *020/7942-5000. Tube: South Kensington (the Tube station is on the corner of Cromwell Road and Exhibition Road, at the corner of the museum). Admission: Free. Open: Mon–Sat 10 a.m.–5:50 p.m., Sun 11 a.m.–5:50 p.m. Nearly all the galleries are flat or ramped for wheelchair users; call for instructions on entering the building.*

Piccadilly Circus
Piccadilly Circus

Nearly everyone who visits London wants to see Piccadilly Circus, which lies at the beginning of the West End. Piccadilly Circus, along with neighboring Leicester Square, is London's equivalent to New York's Times Square. Around the landmark statue of Eros, jostling crowds pack the pavements and an international group of teens heads for the **Pepsi Trocadero,** the area's mega-entertainment center (see "Activities for teens," later in this chapter). Regent Street at the west side of the circus and Piccadilly at the south end are major shopping streets (see Chapter 12). Piccadilly, traditionally the western road out of town, was named for the *picadil,* a ruffled collar created by a 17th-century tailor named Robert Baker.

See map p. 186. Tube: Piccadilly Circus.

Picture-perfect Queen Mum

The Royal Family portrait commissioned by the National Portrait Gallery to celebrate the Queen Mother's 100th birthday in 2000 (she died in 2002) is the newest royal addition to go on display in the National Portrait Gallery. Artist John Wonnacott painted the canvas that portrays Queen Elizabeth, Prince Phillip, Prince Charles, and Princes William and Harry in conversation with the Queen Mother in the White Drawing Room in Buckingham Palace. Interestingly, Prince William — Charles' firstborn and thus the second in line to the throne — dominates the picture.

Science Museum
South Kensington

The Science Museum is a popular tourist attraction that showcases the history and development of science, medicine, and technology. The state-of-the-art, interactive displays tickle the brains of 7- to 12-year-olds, and the **Garden Galleries** provide construction areas, sound-and-light shows, and games for younger kids. The fascinating displays include the Apollo 10 space module, an 1813 steam locomotive, Fox Talbot's first camera, and Edison's original phonograph. The **Wellcome Wing,** which opened in summer 2000, is devoted to contemporary science and has an **IMAX 3-D film theater.** Give yourself at least two hours, more if you're going to see the film.

See map p. 186. Exhibition Road, London SW7. ☎ 020/7942-4454. Tube: South Kensington (a signposted exit in the Underground station goes directly to the museum). Admission: Museum free; IMAX £7.50 ($14) adults, £6 ($11) seniors and children 5–15. To book IMAX tickets in advance, call ☎ 0870/870-4868. Open: Daily 10 a.m.–6 p.m.; closed Dec 24–26. All galleries are wheelchair accessible.

St. James's Park and Green Park
St. James's

Henry VIII acquired these two adjoining royal parks in the early 16th century. St James's Park, the prettier of the two, was landscaped in 1827 by John Nash in a picturesque English style with an ornamental lake and promenades. **The Mall,** the processional route between Buckingham Palace and Whitehall and Horse Guards Parade, is the route used for major ceremonial occasions. Prince Charles and his sons reside at **St. James's Palace,** and the late Queen Mum lived at **Clarence House** next door. The residences — closed to visitors — are between the Mall and **Pall Mall** (pronounced *Pell Mell*), a broad avenue running from Trafalgar Square to St. James's Palace.

See map p. 186. Bounded by Piccadilly to the north, Regent Street to the east, Birdcage Walk and Buckingham Palace Road to the south, and Grosvenor Place to the west. ☎ 020/7930-1793. Tube: Green Park (the Tube station is right at the northeast corner of Green Park) or St. James's Park (then a five-minute walk north on Queen Anne's Gate to Birdcage Walk, the southern perimeter of St. James's Park). Open: Daily dawn to dusk.

Green with envy

Green Park is called Green Park because it's the only royal park without any flower beds. Why? A popular story has it that one day, as Charles II was walking through the park with his entourage, he announced that he was going to pick a flower and give it to the most beautiful lady present. This lady happened to be a milkmaid and not Queen Catherine, his wife. The queen was livid and ordered that all flowers be removed from the park (a horticultural version of "Off with their heads!").

St. Paul's Cathedral
The City

After the Great Fire of 1666 destroyed the city's old cathedral, the great architect Christopher Wren was called upon to design St. Paul's, a huge and harmonious Renaissance-leaning-toward-baroque building (see the "St. Paul's Cathedral" map on p. 201). During World War II, Nazi bombing raids wiped out the surrounding area but spared the cathedral, so Wren's masterpiece, capped by the most-famous dome in London, rises majestically above a crowded sea of undistinguished office buildings. Grinling Gibbons carved the exceptionally beautiful choir stalls, which are the only impressive artwork inside.

Christopher Wren is buried in the **crypt,** and his epitaph, on the floor below the dome, reads LECTOR, SI MONUMENTUM REQUIRIS, CIRCUMSPICE ("Reader, if you seek his monument, look around you"). His companions in the crypt include two of Britain's famed national heroes: the duke of Wellington, who defeated Napoleon at Waterloo, and Admiral Lord Nelson, who took down the French at Trafalgar during the same war. But many people want to see St. Paul's simply because Lady Diana Spencer wed Prince Charles here in what was billed as "the fairy-tale wedding of the century."

You can climb up to the **Whispering Gallery** for a bit of acoustical fun or gasp your way up to the very top for a breathtaking view of London. You can see the entire cathedral in an hour or less.

St. Paul's is now linked to the Tate Modern on the South Bank by the pedestrian-only **Millennium Bridge,** designed by Lord Norman Foster.

See map p. 186. St. Paul's Churchyard, Ludgate Hill, EC4. ☎ 020/7246-8348. Tube: St. Paul's (then a five-minute walk west on Ludgate to the cathedral entrance on St. Paul's Churchyard). Admission: £8 ($15) adults, £7 ($13) seniors and students, £3.50 ($6.50) children. Tours: Guided tours (11, 11:30 a.m., 1:30, and 2 p.m.) £2.50 ($4.65) adults, £2 ($3.70) seniors, £1 ($1.85) children under 10; audio tours (available 8:30 a.m.–3 p.m.) £3.50 ($6.50) adults, £3 ($5.55) seniors and students. Open: Mon–Sat 8:30 a.m.–4 p.m.; no sightseeing on Sun (services only). The cathedral is wheelchair accessible by the service entrance near the South Transept; ring the bell for assistance.

St. Paul's Cathedral

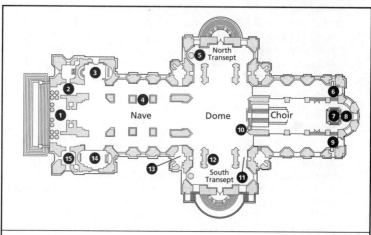

All Souls' Chapel **2**
American Memorial Chapter **8**
Anglican Martyr's Chapel **6**
Chapel of St. Michael
    & St. George **14**
Dean's Staircase **15**
Entrance to Crypt
    (Wren's grave) **11**
Font **5**

High Altar **7**
Lady Chapel **9**
Nelson Monument **12**
Pulpit **10**
St. Dunstan's Chapel **3**
Staircase to Library, Whispering
    Gallery & Dome **13**
Wellington Monument **4**
West Doorway **1**

Tate Britain
Pimlico

The Tate Gallery took this name to distinguish it from its new counterpart, Tate Modern, which opened in May 2000 and is devoted to International Modernism. Tate Britain retains the older (pre-20th century) collections of exclusively British art plus works by major British stars like David Hockney and experimental works by Brits and foreigners living in Britain. Among the masterpieces on display in a host of newly refurbished galleries are dreamy works by the British pre-Raphaelites, the celestial visions of William Blake, bawdy satirical works by William Hogarth, genteel portraits by Sir Joshua Reynolds, pastoral landscapes by John Constable, and the shimmering seascapes of J.M.W. Turner. The collection is hung thematically rather than chronologically. Plan on spending at least two hours here. The gallery has a restaurant and a cafe on the lower level.

See map p. 186. Millbank, Pimlico SW1. ☎ *020/7887-8000. Tube: Pimlico (then a ten-minute walk south on Vauxhall Bridge Road to the river and north on Millbank to the museum entrance). Bus: For a more scenic route, take bus 77A, which runs south along The Strand and Whitehall to the museum entrance on Millbank. Admission: Free; varying admission fees for special exhibits. Tours: Audio tours £3 ($5.55). Open: Daily 10 a.m.–5:50 p.m. Most of the galleries are wheelchair accessible, but call first for details on entry.*

Tate Modern
South Bank

The former Bankside Power Station is the setting for the fabulous Tate Modern, which opened in May 2000. Considered one of the three or four top modern art museums in the world, it houses the Tate's collection of international 20th-century art, displaying major works by some of the most influential artists of this century: Frances Bacon, Salvador Dalí, Marcel Duchamp, Henri Matisse, Henry Moore, and Pablo Picasso among them. A gallery for the 21st-century collection exhibits contemporary art. Fans of contemporary art and architecture shouldn't miss this new star on the London art scene. Plan on spending at least two hours. The museum is now linked to St. Paul's Cathedral by the pedestrian-only **Millennium Bridge,** designed by Lord Norman Foster.

See map p. 186. 25 Sumner Street, SE1. ☎ *020/7887-8000. Tube: Southwark (then a ten-minute walk north along Blackfriars Road and east along the riverside promenade) or Blackfriars (then a ten-minute walk south across Blackfriars Bridge). Admission: Free; varying admission fees for special exhibits. Tours: Free, hourly 11 a.m.–3 p.m. Open: Sun–Thurs 10 a.m.–6 p.m., Fri–Sat 10 a.m.–10 p.m.; closed Dec 24–26 and Jan 1.*

Inter-Tate travel

From Millbank Pier, on the river just outside Tate Britain, a ferry service links the Tate Britain and the Tate Modern. Vessels operated by Thames Clippers make the run between Millbank Pier and Bankside Pier, with one additional stop at Waterloo Pier, in case you want to take a spin on the British Airways London Eye or check out the new Saatchi Gallery. A one-way fare costs £2.50 ($4.65) for adults, £1.25 ($2.30) for children; if you have a Travelcard, you get one-third off the price. For more information, contact **Transport for London** (☎ 020/7222-1234; www.tfl.gov.uk).

That's the way the bridge bounces

Lord Norman Foster's $28-million **Millennium Bridge** linking Tate Modern to St. Paul's got off to a very wobbly start on its opening day, June 10, 2000. This much publicized, highly visible, high-tech pedestrian span had one slight problem: It swayed and bounced so much that people couldn't walk on it. Seems that the "untraditional" suspension system of aluminum and stainless steel wasn't doing in real life what it had done on paper. The bridge had to be closed immediately to determine whether major repairs were needed. When Foster's bridge reopened, the same problem occurred, and it was closed for a second time. In fall 2001, however, the bridge was deemed safe and opened to the public.

 Tower of London
The City

The Tower of London offers enough to keep you captivated for a good three to four hours, but make sure that you save time for the **Crown Jewels,** which include the largest diamond in the world (the 530-carat Star of Africa) and other breathtaking gems set into royal robes, swords, scepters, and crowns.

The Tower of London (see the "Tower of London" map on p. 205) is the city's best-known and oldest historic site. In 1066, William the Conqueror built the tower, which served as his fortress and later as a prison, holding famous captives, such as Sir Walter Raleigh and Princess Elizabeth I. Anne Boleyn and Catherine Howard (two of the eight wives of Henry VIII), the nine-day queen Lady Jane Grey, and Sir Thomas More were among those unlucky souls who got their heads chopped off on **Tower Green.** According to Shakespeare, the two little princes (the sons of Edward IV) were murdered in the **Bloody Tower** by henchmen of Richard III — but the story is controversial among modern historians.

You can attend the nightly **Ceremony of the Keys,** the ceremonial locking-up of the Tower by the Yeoman Warders. For free tickets, write to the Ceremony of the Keys, Queen's House, HM Tower of London, London EC3N 4AB, and request a specific date, but also list three alternate dates. At least six weeks' notice is required. You must enclose an International Reply Coupon and a self-addressed stamped envelope (British stamps only), or two International Reply Coupons with all requests and list the names and addresses for all visitors. If you have a ticket, a Yeoman Warder will admit you at 9:35 p.m.

 Huge black ravens hop around the grounds of the Tower of London. An old legend says that the British Commonwealth will end when the ravens leave the tower. Their wings have been clipped as a precaution.

In the bad old days, important prisoners often arrived at the tower by boat. You can, too. **Catamaran Cruisers** (☎ 020/7925-2215; www. catamarancruisers.co.uk) provides daily ferry service between Embankment Pier (Tube: Embankment) and Tower Pier. A one-way ticket for the 30-minute trip is £5.50 ($10) adults and £2.75 ($5.10) children under 16. **City Cruises** (☎ 020/7740-0400; www.citycruises.com) makes the journey to the Tower of London from Wesminster Pier approximately every 40 minutes from 10:10 a.m. to 5:50 p.m. for £5.60 ($10).

See map p. 186. Tower Hill, EC3. ☎ *020/7709-0765. Tube: Tower Hill (then a five-minute walk west and south on Tower Hill). Bus: You can take the eastbound bus 25 from Marble Arch, Oxford Circus, or St. Paul's; it stops at Tower Hill, north of the entrance. Admission: £15 ($28) adults, £11 ($20) seniors and students, £9.50 ($18) children 5–15, £42 ($78) families (two adults and three children). Tours: The Yeoman Warders (also known as Beefeaters) give free one-hour guided tours of the entire compound every half hour, starting at 9:30 a.m. (Sun 10 a.m.) from the Middle Tower near the main entrance. The last guided walk starts about 3:30 p.m. in summer or 2:30 p.m. in winter; weather permitting. Open: Mar–Oct Mon–Sat 9 a.m.–6 p.m., Sun 10 a.m.–5 p.m.; Nov–Feb Tues–Sat 9 a.m.–4 p.m., Sun–Mon 10 a.m.–5 p.m. (last admission one hour before closing); closed Jan 1 and Dec 24–26. Wheelchair access onto the grounds is available, but many of the historic buildings can't accommodate wheelchairs.*

Trafalgar Square
St. James's

Until very recently, Trafalgar Square was an island in the midst of a roaringly busy traffic interchange surrounded by historic buildings, such as St. Martin-in-the-Fields church and the National Gallery. Then, after a major urban redesign, it reopened in 2003 with one side attached to the steps of the National Gallery, so visitors can easily get to the square without crossing any streets at all. Besides being a major tourist attraction, Trafalgar Square is the site of many large gatherings, such as political demonstrations and holiday celebrations. The square honors military hero Horatio Viscount Nelson (1758–1805), who lost his life at the 1805 Battle of Trafalgar against the French. **Nelson's Column,** with fountains and four bronze lions at its base, rises 145 feet above the square. At the top, a 14-foot-high statue of Nelson (5'4" tall in real life) looks commandingly toward **Admiralty Arch,** passed through by state and royal processions between Buckingham Palace and St. Paul's Cathedral. You don't need more than a few minutes to take in the square.

The neoclassical church on the northeast corner of Trafalgar Square was the precursor for dozens of similar-looking churches throughout colonial New England. Designed by James Gibbs, a disciple of Christopher Wren, **St. Martin-in-the-Fields** (see the map on p. 186; ☎ 020/7930-0089) was completed in 1726; the 185-foot spire was added about 100 years later. The **Academy of St. Martin-in-the-Fields,** a famous music ensemble, frequently performs here. Lunchtime concerts are held on Monday, Tuesday, and Friday at 1 p.m., and evening concerts are held Thursday through Saturday at 7:30 p.m. Concert tickets cost £6 to £15 ($11–$28). For reservations by credit card, call ☎ 020/7839-8362. The church is open Monday through Saturday 10 a.m. to 6 p.m. and Sunday noon to 6 p.m.; admission is free.

The Tower of London

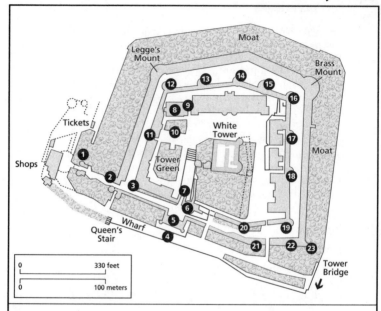

Moat

Legge's Mount

Brass Mount

Tickets

White Tower

Shops

Tower Green

Moat

Wharf

Queen's Stair

0 — 330 feet
0 — 100 meters

Tower Bridge

Beauchamp Tower **11**	Flint Tower **13**
Bell Tower **3**	Jewel House (entrance) **9**
Bloody Tower **7**	Lanthorn Tower **20**
Bowyer Tower (torture chamber) **14**	Martin Tower **16**
Brick Tower **15**	Middle Tower **1**
Broad Arrow Tower **18**	Salt Tower **19**
Byward Tower **2**	Site of Scaffold **10**
Chapel Royal of St. Peter ad Vincula **8**	St. Thomas's Tower **5**
Constable Tower **17**	Traitor's Gate **4**
Cradle Tower **21**	Wakefield Tower **6**
Develin Tower **23**	Well Tower **22**
Devereux Tower **12**	

Café-in-the-Crypt (☎ 020/7839-4342), one of the West End's most pleasant restaurants, is in the crypt of St. Martin-in-the-Fields (see Chapter 10 for the restaurant review). The busy crypt also contains the **London Brass Rubbing Centre** (☎ 020/7437-6023), which provides paper, metallic waxes, and instructions on how to rub your own replica of historic brasses. Prices range from £3 to £15 ($5.55–$28). This activity is a great diversion for kids 10 and up. The center is open Monday through Saturday 10 a.m. to 6 p.m. and Sunday noon to 6 p.m.

See map p. 186. Bounded on the north by Trafalgar, on the west by Cockspur Street, and on the east by Whitehall. Tube: Charing Cross (the Underground station has an exit to the square).

Victoria & Albert Museum
South Kensington

The Victoria & Albert (known as the V&A) is the national museum of art and design. In the 145 galleries, filled with fine and decorative arts from around the world, you find superbly decorated period rooms, a fashion collection spanning 400 years of European designs, Raphael's designs for tapestries in the Sistine Chapel, the Silver Galleries, and the largest assemblages of Renaissance sculpture outside Italy and of Indian art outside India. The Canon Photography Gallery shows works by celebrated photographers. In November 2001, the museum opened its spectacular new British Galleries. Allow at least two hours just to cover the basics.

See map p. 186. Cromwell Road, SW7. ☎ *020/7942-2000. Tube: South Kensington (the museum is across from the Underground station). Admission: Free. Open: Thurs–Tues 10 a.m.–5:45 p.m., Wed 10 a.m.–10 p.m.; closed Dec 24–26. The museum is wheelchair accessible (only about five percent of the exhibits include steps).*

Westminster Abbey
Westminster

The Gothic and grand Westminster Abbey is one of London's most important historic sites. (See the "Westminster Abbey" map on p. 207.) The present abbey dates mostly from the 13th and 14th centuries, but a church has been on this site for more than a thousand years. Since 1066, when William the Conqueror became the first English monarch to be crowned here, every successive British sovereign except for two (Edward V and Edward VIII) has sat on the **Coronation Chair** to receive the crown and scepter. In the **Royal Chapels,** you can see the **chapel of Henry VII,** with its delicate fan vaulting, and the **tomb of Queen Elizabeth I,** who was buried in the same vault as her Catholic half-sister, Mary I, and not far from her rival, Mary Queen of Scots. In **Poets' Corner,** some of England's greatest writers (including Chaucer, Dickens, and Thomas Hardy) are interred or memorialized. Other points of interest include the College Garden, cloisters, chapter house, and the Undercroft Museum, which contains the Pyx Chamber with its display of church plate, the silver owned by the church. In September 1997, the abbey served as the site of Princess Diana's funeral, and in 2002, the funeral service for the Queen Mother was held there. The abbey is within walking distance of the Houses of Parliament.

See map p. 186. Broad Sanctuary, SW1. ☎ *020/7222-7110. Tube: Westminster (then a three-minute walk west following Parliament Square to Broad Sanctuary). Bus: The 77A going south along The Strand, Whitehall, and Millbank stops near the Houses of Parliament, near the Abbey. Admission: £8 ($15) adults; £6 ($11) seniors, students, and children 11–16; £18 ($33) families (two adults and two children). Guided tours: Led by an Abbey Verger £4 ($7.40) (call for times); tickets for tours at Enquiry Desk in the Abbey; audio tours £3 ($5.55). Open: Cathedral Mon–Fri 9 a.m.–3:45 p.m., Sat 9 a.m.–1:45 p.m., no sightseeing on Sun (services only); College Garden Apr–Sept 10 a.m.–6 p.m., Oct–Mar 10 a.m.–4 p.m. You can use ramped wheelchair access through the Cloisters; ring the bell for assistance.*

Westminster Abbey

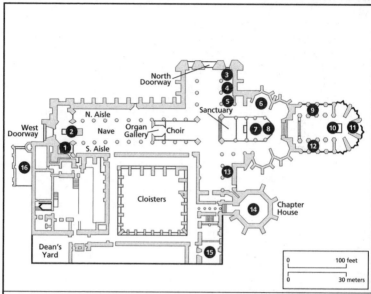

Bookshop **16**

Chapel of St. John the Baptist **6**

Chapel of St. John the Evangelist **5**

Chapter House **14**

Henry V's Chantry **8**

Poets' Corner **13**

Royal Air Force Chapel **11**

St. Andrew's Chapel **3**

St. Edward's Chapel
(Coronation Chair) **7**

St. George's Chapel **1**

St. Michael's Chapel **4**

Tomb of Mary I &
Elizabeth I **9**

Tomb of Henry VII **10**

Tomb of Mary,
Queen of Scots **12**

Tomb of the Unknown Warrior/
Memorial to Churchill **2**

Undercroft Museum and
Pyx Chamber **15**

Oscar Wilde's window

In 1995, 100 years after Oscar Wilde was tried for "gross indecency" and sentenced to two years hard labor in Reading Gaol, the Church of England finally recognized his immortal genius with a memorial window at Westminster Abbey. But because his name is nowhere to be seen in the abbey, the blue window with its abstract design is the kind of dubious honor that would no doubt provoke a witty quip from the great playwright. Maybe something like, "Clear glass wasn't good enough for me; it had to be stained."

Finding More Cool Things to See and Do

If you think you've done London because you've marveled at Westminster Abbey, seen where the queen lives, wandered through St. Paul's Cathedral, toured the Tower of London, and feasted your eyes on the masterpieces in the British Museum, think again. London is teeming with more sightseeing possibilities: glorious gardens, magnificent mansions, singular museums, ancient corners, historic churches, and many themed attractions that fill you in on the history and flavor of majestic London Town. In the following sections, I highlight a few more of the many activities that may tickle your fancy. For locations, see the "More London Sights" map on p. 210.

In the following sections, I also cover four major attractions just outside Central London and easily accessible by Tube or train — **Hampstead Heath, Hampton Court Palace, Royal Botanic Gardens,** and **Windsor Castle.** You can spend the better part of a day visiting any one of these sights — all trips well worth your time — before returning to Central London in time for a play or concert in the evening.

The following sights are fully or partially wheelchair accessible; visitors with disabilities should call the attraction to find out about special entrances, ramps, and elevator locations:

- ✔ Bank of England Museum
- ✔ British Library Exhibition Galleries
- ✔ Chelsea Physic Garden
- ✔ Courtauld Gallery
- ✔ Design Museum
- ✔ Hampton Court
- ✔ Imperial War Museum
- ✔ London Aquarium
- ✔ London Dungeon
- ✔ London Planetarium
- ✔ London Transport Museum
- ✔ Museum of Childhood
- ✔ Museum of London
- ✔ Regent's Park

✔ Royal Academy of Arts

✔ Royal Botanic Gardens (Kew Gardens)

✔ Theatre Museum

✔ Tower Bridge Experience

✔ Wallace Collection

Sights for history buffs

You can't escape history in London. The past is woven into the very fabric of the city, and it's why many visitors want to come here. The "history" contained in the sights in this section is as old as Rome, as new as the current prime minister, and as dramatic as the events of World War II.

Cabinet War Rooms
Westminster

You can almost hear the air-raid sirens. In this 21-room underground bunker, Prime Minister Winston Churchill and his War Cabinet planned out the military campaigns of World War II. The site has been meticulously preserved, right down to the nightshirt and cigar waiting by Churchill's bed. Give yourself an hour to explore the site.

See map p. 210. Clive Steps, King Charles Street, SW1. ☎ *020/7930-6961. Tube: Westminster (then a ten-minute walk west, staying on the north side of the street, to Parliament Street; turn right to reach King Charles Street). Admission: £10 ($19) adults, £8 ($15) seniors and students, free for children under 16; a free self-guided audio tour comes with your ticket. Open: Apr–Sept 9:30 a.m.–6 p.m., Oct–Mar 10 a.m.–6 p.m. (last admission 5:15 p.m.).*

Imperial War Museum
Lambeth

The former insane asylum known as Bedlam is now devoted to the insanity of war. You can see a wide range of weapons and equipment, including a Battle of Britain Spitfire, a German one-man submarine, a Mark V tank, and a rifle once carried by Lawrence of Arabia. Other exhibits include coded messages, forged documents, espionage equipment from World War I to the present, and multimedia presentations about the Blitz and trench warfare. The Holocaust Gallery documents one of history's darkest episodes through film, photos, and artifacts, many shown for the first time. Enough history is on display to keep you occupied for a couple of hours.

See map p. 210. Lambeth Road, SE1. ☎ *020/7416-5320. Tube: Lambeth North (then a ten-minute walk south on Kennington, south of Westminster Bridge Road, and east on Lambeth Road). Admission: Free. Open: Daily 10 a.m.–6 p.m. Closed Dec 24–26.*

More London Sights

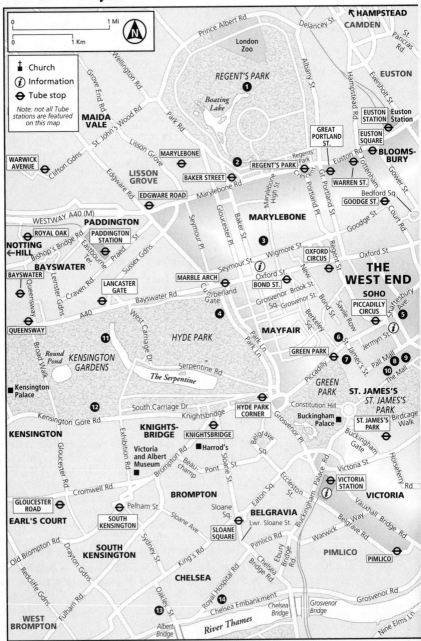

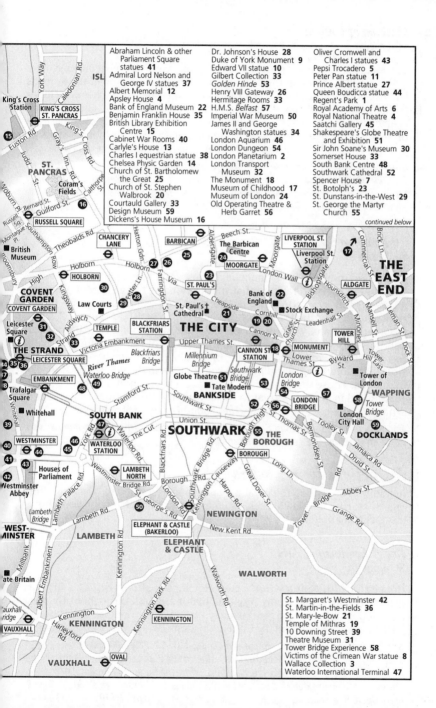

Abraham Lincoln & other
    Parliament Square
    statues **41**
Admiral Lord Nelson and
    George IV statues **37**
Albert Memorial **12**
Apsley House **4**
Bank of England Museum **22**
Benjamin Franklin House **35**
British Library Exhibition
    Centre **15**
Cabinet War Rooms **40**
Carlyle's House **13**
Charles I equestrian statue **38**
Chelsea Physic Garden **14**
Church of St. Bartholomew
    the Great **25**
Church of St. Stephen
    Walbrook **20**
Courtauld Gallery **33**
Design Museum **59**
Dickens's House Museum **16**

Dr. Johnson's House **28**
Duke of York Monument **9**
Edward VII statue **10**
Gilbert Collection **33**
Golden Hinde **53**
Henry VIII Gateway **26**
Hermitage Rooms **33**
H.M.S. *Belfast* **57**
Imperial War Museum **50**
James II and George
    Washington statues **34**
London Aquarium **46**
London Dungeon **54**
London Planetarium **2**
London Transport
    Museum **32**
The Monument **18**
Museum of Childhood **17**
Museum of London **24**
Old Operating Theatre &
    Herb Garret **56**

Oliver Cromwell and
    Charles I statues **43**
Pepsi Trocadero **5**
Peter Pan statue **11**
Prince Albert statue **27**
Queen Boudicca statue **44**
Regent's Park **1**
Royal Academy of Arts **6**
Royal National Theatre **4**
Saatchi Gallery **45**
Shakespeare's Globe Theatre
    and Exhibition **51**
Sir John Soane's Museum **30**
Somerset House **33**
South Bank Centre **48**
Southwark Cathedral **52**
Spencer House **7**
St. Botolph's **23**
St. Dunstans-in-the-West **29**
St. George the Martyr
    Church **55**

continued below

St. Margaret's Westminster **42**
St. Martin-in-the-Fields **36**
St. Mary-le-Bow **21**
Temple of Mithras **19**
10 Downing Street **39**
Theatre Museum **31**
Tower Bridge Experience **58**
Victims of the Crimean War statue **8**
Wallace Collection **3**
Waterloo International Terminal **47**

Museum of London
The City

The Museum of London is the most comprehensive city museum anywhere in the world. Located in the original square-mile Londinium of the Romans and overlooking the city's Roman and medieval walls, the museum includes archaeological finds; paintings and prints; social, industrial, and historical artifacts; and costumes, maps, and models to recount the city's history from prehistoric times to today. Give yourself at least an hour to skim through the engaging collections; although, spending more time than that is easy.

See map p. 210. 150 London Wall (in the Barbican district near St. Paul's Cathedral), EC2. ☎ *0870/444-3853. Tube: St. Paul's (then a ten-minute walk north on St. Martin Le Grand and Aldersgate). Admission: Free. Open: Mon–Sat 10 a.m.–5:50 p.m., Sun noon–5:50 p.m. Closed Dec 24–26 and Jan 1.*

10 Downing Street
St. James's

The prime minister's residence is a place on many visitors' "must-see" lists, so I'm sorry to tell you that there's nothing to see except a heavily guarded gate. By peering through the gate, you can get a glimpse, on the right side, of No. 10, the official residence of the British PM since 1732. The sizeable Blair family (Tony, Cherie, and four kids) found No. 10 too small and moved into No. 11, where the Chancellor of the Exchequer usually resides. No. 12 serves as the office of the chief government whip, responsible for maintaining discipline and cooperation in the vociferous House of Commons. These three small brick terrace houses, built on a cul-de-sac in 1680, stand in sharp contrast to the enormous 19th-century offices lining Whitehall, the government quarter around Downing Street.

See map p. 210. 10 Downing St., SW1. Tube: Westminster (then a five-minute walk north on Parliament Street and Whitehall).

Attractions for art lovers

In addition to visiting the great art museums described in "London's Top Sights," earlier in this chapter, you may want to check out some of the city's smaller galleries.

Royal Academy of Arts
St. James's

Housed in 18th-century Burlington House, the site of Britain's first art school, the Royal Academy presents major exhibits throughout the year and mounts a renowned (and usually jam-packed) Summer Exhibition of juried works from around the United Kingdom. Give yourself about an hour.

See map p. 210. Burlington House, Piccadilly, W1. ☎ *020/7300-8000.* www.royal academy.org.uk. *Tube: Piccadilly Circus (then a five-minute walk down Piccadilly; the Academy is on the north side of the street just before the Burlington Arcade). Admission: Varies according to exhibit but usually £10 ($19) adults, £8 ($15) seniors, £2.50 ($4.65) children. Open: Sat–Thurs 10 a.m.–6 p.m. (last admission 5:30 p.m.), Fri 10 a.m.–8:30 p.m.*

Prime-time prime minister

Of course, London gossip swirls around 10 Downing Street, just as it does around Buckingham Palace. In 1999, Cherie Blair, wife of poll-sensitive Prime Minister Tony Blair and a high-powered lawyer specializing in employment law, announced that she was pregnant with the couple's fourth child and thought her husband should take advantage of the 13-week unpaid paternity leave policy his Labour government had incorporated into law. Mr. Blair, a seasoned spin-meister, was uncharacteristically tongue-tied by his wife's suggestion. In the end, he took only a week off when their son, Leo, was born.

Gossip swirled again in July 2000, when the Blair's 16-year-old son, Euan, was arrested in Leicester Square for drunkenness. And again in 2001, when Cherie Blair outpolled the queen as "Britain's most powerful woman." Cherie Blair is the first prime minister's wife to hold a full-time job and reputedly earns three times the $175,000 annual salary of her prime minister husband. But Superwoman Cherie was forced to eat humble pie in 2003 when it was discovered that she had participated in some rather shady real-estate transactions, purchasing property on the advice of a convicted criminal. She went so far as to issue a tearful public apology. After Tony Blair's position on the Iraq war cost his New Labour Party one-third of their seats in 2005, he announced that he would not run for a fourth term.

Saatchi Gallery
South Bank

Ex-adman Charles Saatchi has amassed one of the largest independent collections of contemporary British and international art in the world. His gallery shows pieces from the permanent collection, as well as changing international exhibits. Regardless of what you think of the sometimes controversial works on display — many of them vapid, self-serving, and silly — the gallery remains a showcase for the art trends of the second.

See map p. 211. County Hall, Southbank, SE1. ☎ *020/7825-2363.* www.saatchi-gallery.co.uk. *Tube: Westminster (then a five-minute walk across Westminster Bridge to County Hall). Admission: £9 ($17) adults, £6.75 ($12) seniors and students. Open: Sun–Thurs 10 a.m.–8 p.m., Fri–Sat 10 a.m.–10 p.m.*

Somerset House
The Strand

The late Queen Mother once remarked how sad it was that the courtyard at Somerset House had become an Inland Revenue car park. It was just the spur that the long-running campaign needed to open up the 1,000-room civil service palace, designed by Sir William Chambers (1724–1796), to the public. The government moved its workers out and the Heritage Lottery Fund coughed up the millions needed to restore the buildings, the courtyard with its dancing fountains, and the river terrace that's now the home of a great summer cafe. A heady mix of high culture and street entertainment, the "new" Somerset House houses three noteworthy art collections. Each gallery charges an admission fee of £5 ($9.25) for adults, £4 ($7.40) for seniors; children under 18 enter free. The three galleries are all open daily from 10 a.m. to 6 p.m.

The **Courtauld Gallery** (☎ 020/7848-2526) has been in Somerset House since 1989. Impressionist and post-Impressionist paintings are still the gallery's main strength. Major works include Manet's *Bar at the Folies Bergères;* Monet's *Banks of the Seine at Argenteuil; Lady with Parasol* by Degas; *La Loge* by Renoir; Van Gogh's *Self-Portrait with Bandaged Ear;* and several Cézannes, including *The Card Players.* But you'll find work by most great names (many by Rubens), right up to modern greats Ben Nicholson, Graham Sutherland, and Larry Rivers.

The **Gilbert Collection** (☎ 020/7420-9400), in the South Building, showcases the glittering gold, silver, and mosaics that were valued at £75 million when Arthur Gilbert donated the 800-piece collection to the nation in 1996. Some objects came from Princess Diana's old home, Althorp.

The last and perhaps most extraordinary of the treasures of Somerset House are the **Hermitage Rooms** (☎ 020/7845-4630). This offshoot of the State Hermitage Museum in St. Petersburg exhibits pieces from the Russian Imperial collections in changing shows.

See map p. 210. Strand, WC2. ☎ 020/7845-4600. www.somerset-house.org.uk. *Tube: Temple (then a five-minute walk north on Arundel Street and west on The Strand). Admission: Somerset House free; separate admissions for the galleries. Open: Courtyard 7:30 a.m.–11 p.m. (7 p.m. in winter); galleries daily 10 a.m.–6 p.m. (last admittance 45 minutes to one hour earlier). Closed Jan 1 and Dec 24–26.*

Wallace Collection
Marylebone

The palatial townhouse of the late Lady Wallace is the setting for a spectacular collection of art, ornaments, and armaments. You can enjoy outstanding French works by the likes of Watteau and Fragonard, as well as masterpieces from the Dutch (Frans Hals and Rembrandt), English, Spanish, and Italian schools. Decorative art from 18th-century France and European and Asian weapons are also on display. Give yourself at least an hour. The courtyard, with its new glass roof, is a pleasant spot for tea.

See map p. 210. Hertford House, Manchester Square, W1. ☎ 020/7563-9500. Tube: Baker Street (then a ten-minute walk south on Baker Street to the museum entrance on the north side of Manchester Square). Admission: Free. Open: Mon–Sat 10 a.m.– 5 p.m., Sun noon–5 p.m.

Literary landmarks

Writers have been drawn to London for centuries and have left their literary imprints all over this vast metropolis. Listed in this section are some of the unique places associated with writers who lived in London, as well as one of the world's great storehouses of literary treasures.

British Library Exhibition Centre
Marylebone

The venerable British Library moved to this new building in 1998 and displays some of the world's most famous books, maps, manuscripts, and documents in a series of special galleries. This is where you can see a copy of the Magna Carta, Shakespeare's first folio, and handwritten manuscripts by authors such as Jane Austen, Charlotte Brontë, and Thomas Hardy. Just as fascinating are the audio recordings that let you hear the voices of Virginia Woolf and William Butler Yeats among others reading from their own works. Give this sight at least an hour; allow more time if you love literature or literary history.

See map p. 210. Euston Road, NW1. ☎ *020/7412-7332. Tube: King's Cross/St. Pancras (then a five-minute walk west on Euston; the museum entrance is just beyond Midland Road). Admission: Free. Tours: Mon, Wed, Fri 3 p.m., Sat 10:30 a.m. and 3 p.m., Sun 11:30 a.m. and 3 p.m.; £6 ($11) adults, £4.50 ($8.35) seniors, students, and children. Open: Mon and Wed–Fri 9:30 a.m.–6 p.m., Tues 9:30 a.m.–8 p.m., Sat 9:30 a.m.–5 p.m., Sun 11 a.m.–5 p.m.*

Carlyle's House
Chelsea

Thomas Carlyle (author of *The French Revolution* and many other rarely read books) and his witty wife, Jane (a noted letter writer), lived in this pretty 1708 Queen Anne terrace house from 1834 to 1881. Furnished as it was during their residence, the house is an accurate representation of middle-class Victorian domestic life. Carlyle's "soundproof" study in the skylit attic is filled with memorabilia — his books, a letter from Benjamin Disraeli, personal effects, a writing chair, and even his death mask. You can browse through the house in about a half-hour.

See map p. 210. 24 Cheyne Row, SW3. ☎ *020/7352-7087. Tube: Sloane Square (then a 20-minute walk south on Lower Sloane Street and Hospital Road to Cheyne Walk and north on Cheyne Row; or from Sloane Square, take bus 11, 19, or 22). Admission: £3.70 ($6.85) adults, £1.80 ($3.35) children. Open: Apr–Oct Wed–Fri 2–5 p.m., Sat–Sun 11 a.m.–5 p.m.*

Dickens's House Museum
Bloomsbury

Charles Dickens lived in many places, but he and his family called this Bloomsbury house home from 1837 to 1839. Here, the great author penned *The Pickwick Papers, Oliver Twist,* and *Nicholas Nickleby,* the poignant and famous portrayals of Victorian England. The museum contains the world's most comprehensive Dickens library, portraits, illustrations, and rooms furnished exactly as they were in Dickens's time. You can see everything in a half-hour, but allow more time if you're a Dickens fanatic.

See map p. 210. 48 Doughty St., WC1. ☎ *020/7405-2127. Tube: Russell Square (then a ten-minute walk up Guilford Street and turn right on Doughty Street; the museum is on the east side of the street). Admission: £5 ($9.25) adults, £4 ($7.40) seniors, £3 ($5.55) children. Open: Mon–Sat 10 a.m.–5 p.m.*

Benjamin Franklin's London abode

A signer of the Declaration of Independence, Benjamin Franklin (1706–1790) was as American as they come. As a writer, he coined such famous aphorisms as "A penny saved is a penny earned." Franklin was also an inventor, and St. Paul's Cathedral in London was the first public building in the world to get one of his new lightning rods. Franklin the statesman resided in London between 1757 and 1775, and his "genteel lodgings," on Craven Street near Charing Cross Station, served as the first de facto American embassy after Independence. The **Benjamin Franklin House** (see the map on p. 210; 36 Craven St., WC2N; ☎ **020/7930-9121**), the only Franklin house remaining in the world today, is scheduled to open to the public in early 2006. Opening times and admissions weren't available at press time, but you can find more information at www.rsa.org.uk/franklin.

Dr. Johnson's House
Holborn

Hidden away in a tiny square north of Fleet Street is the Queen Anne house where Dr. Samuel Johnson, best known as the lexicographer who compiled one of the first dictionaries of the English language, lived (quite humbly) from 1748 to 1759. A copy of the original dictionary is on display, along with Johnson memorabilia. The restored 17th-century house is close to Ye Olde Cheshire Cheese pub (see Chapter 10), a favorite haunt of the good doctor, who was celebrated as a storyteller of the first order. You can see everything on view here in less than half an hour.

See map p. 210. 17 Gough Square, EC4. ☎ 020/7353-3745. Tube: Temple (then a ten-minute walk north on Arundel Street to Fleet Street and east on Fleet Street to Dunstan's Court; Gough Square is to one side of Dunstan's Court). Admission: £4 ($7.40) adults, £3 ($5.55) seniors and students. Open: May–Sept Mon–Sat 11 a.m.–5:30 p.m., Oct–Apr Mon–Sat 11 a.m.–5 p.m.

All manner of intriguing museums

London's museums are surprisingly varied in their scope and substance. In addition to all the great art museums that you can read about in the section "Attractions for art lovers," earlier in this chapter, the city has museums dedicated to theater, architecture, design, medicine, and money.

Bank of England Museum
The City

Devoted capitalists enjoy the Bank of England Museum, housed in the enormous Bank of England building. The museum chronicles changes in the banking industry since the Bank of England's beginnings in 1694, when funds were needed to finance the war against France's Louis XIV. On display are documents from famous customers (including George Washington), gold bullion, bank notes (forged and real), and coins. Interactive video displays present information about today's high-tech world of finance and a reconstructed 18th-century Banking Hall. You can see it all in less than an hour. *See map p. 210. Bartholomew Lane, EC2.* ☎ *020/7601-5545. Tube: Bank (then a five-minute walk east on Threadneedle Street; turn left on Bartholomew's Lane for the museum entrance). Admission: Free. Open: Mon–Fri 10 a.m.–5 p.m.*

Design Museum
South Bank

If you're a design enthusiast — or want to see how commercial design affects our everyday lives — check out this museum in the hot "new" Butler's Wharf area east of Tower Bridge. You can find classical, kitsch, modern, surreal, and innovative — from Corbusier chairs to the Coke bottle — all chronicled here. Plus, you get to see some great river views. Plan to spend at least an hour.

See map p. 210. Butlers Wharf, Shad Thames, SE1. ☎ *020/7403-6933. Tube: Tower Hill (then a ten-minute walk across Tower Bridge to Butler's Wharf east of the bridge on the South Bank; or London Bridge, then a ten-minute walk east along The Queen's Walk beside the Thames). Admission: £6 ($11) adults, £4 ($7.40) seniors and children, £16 ($30) families (two adults and two children). Open: Daily 10 a.m.–5:45 p.m.*

Old Operating Theatre & Herb Garret
South Bank

The Old Operating Theatre isn't for the faint of heart. The roof garret of the church of St. Thomas, once attached to St. Thomas's Hospital, contains Britain's oldest operating theater (from 1822), where students could witness surgical procedures on poor (literally and figuratively) patients. You'll shudder over the collection of mid-19th-century "state-of-the-art" medical instruments, including amputation saws. The theater was in use long before the advent of anesthesia in 1846. Prior to that time, if a patient had a limb amputated, only a blindfold and a bottle of liquor were provided (and you thought your HMO was bad). The herb garret was used for the storage and curing of medicinal herbs.

See map p. 210. 9A St. Thomas St., SE1. ☎ *020/7955-4791. Tube: London Bridge (then a five-minute walk east on St. Thomas Street). Admission: £4.75 ($8.80) adults, £3.75 ($6.95) seniors, £2.75 ($5.10) children. Open: Daily 10:30 a.m.–5 p.m.; closed Dec 15–Jan 5.*

Sir John Soane's Museum
Holborn

The house of Sir John Soane (1753–1837), architect of the Bank of England, is an eccentric cache of ancient sculpture, artifacts, and art mixed in with odd architectural perspectives, fool-the-eye mirrors, flying arches, and domes. This captivating Holborn attraction is rarely crowded, which makes spending an hour even more of a treat. The oldest piece in the house is the 3,300-year-old sarcophagus of Pharaoh Seti I. Top prize in the picture gallery goes to William Hogarth's satirical and sometimes bawdy series from *The Rake's Progress*. On the first Tuesday of every month, the house is open in the evening and illuminated by candlelight.

See map p. 210. 13 Lincoln's Inn Fields, WC2. ☎ 020/7405-2107. Tube: Holborn (then a five-minute walk south on Kingsway to Lincoln's Inn Fields; the museum entrance is on the north side of the street). Admission: Free. Guided tours (Sat 2:30 p.m.): £3 ($5.55). Open: Tues–Sat 10 a.m.–5 p.m., first Tues of every month 6–9 p.m.

Theatre Museum
Covent Garden

The National Collections of the Performing Arts are housed at this branch of the Victoria & Albert Museum. Oddly enough, it's kind of dull for a museum devoted to performing arts, but you can spend a half-hour or so checking out the collections related to British theater, ballet, opera, music-hall pantomime, puppets, circus, and rock and pop music (both past and present). Kids love the daily stage make-up demonstrations. The costume workshops use costumes from the Royal Shakespeare Company and the Royal National Theatre.

See map p. 210. Russell Street, WC2. ☎ 020/7945-4700. Tube: Covent Garden (then a three-minute walk south to Russell Street on the east side of Covent Garden Piazza). Admission: Free. Open: Tues–Sun 10 a.m.–6 p.m.

Activities for teens

If you have teens in tow, you may wonder where to take them so that they won't feel as though their interests are being completely ignored. The choices in this section — all places where teens hang out — provide a few screams, a wonderland of games, and some really loud music.

London Dungeon
South Bank

Don't bring young children here unless you want to pay for therapy, but teens seem to love the grisly re-creations of medieval torture and executions presented at this house of horrors. You find a scream (literally) around every corner. Amid the tolling bells, dripping water, and caged rats, you can face Jack the Ripper or witness a simulated burning at the stake. It's ghoulishly expensive, but some think it's more fun than Madame Tussaud's.

See map p. 210. 28–34 Tooley St., SE1. ☎ 020/7403-7221. www.thedungeons.com. *Tube: London Bridge (the exhibit is across from the station). Admission: £15 ($28) adults, £13 ($24) students, £12 ($22) seniors and children under 15; children 14 and under must be accompanied by an adult (not recommended for young children). Open: Apr–Sept daily 10 a.m.–6:30 p.m. (last admission 5:30 p.m.); Oct–Mar daily 10 a.m.–5:30 p.m. (last admission 4:30 p.m.). Closed Dec 25.*

Pepsi Trocadero
Piccadilly Circus

This "total entertainment complex" is right on Piccadilly Circus. The lead attraction is **Segaworld,** which offers various rides, including Max Drop, the world's first indoor freefall ride (don't eat for at least an hour before), and 400 ear-splitting, eye-popping video games and simulators. Theme restaurants include the ersatz **Rainforest Café** (which doesn't pretend its proceeds go to support the rain forests and has what may be the worst food in London) and the 1950s-style **Ed's Easy Diner.** Plan to spend some time, because the Pepsi Trocadero is designed and packaged in such a way that after you're in, finding your way out again seems to take forever.

See map p. 210. Piccadilly Circus. ☎ 09068/881100. Tube: Piccadilly Circus (then a one-minute walk to the northeast side). Admission: Segaworld is free, but games and rides cost £1–£3 (£1.85–$5.55). Open: Sun–Thurs 10 a.m.–midnight, Fri–Sat 10 a.m.–1 a.m.

Places that please kids

The little(r) ones probably won't have much interest in London's art museums and historic buildings. But the city offers all kinds of diversions for pre-teens, including a museum crammed with antique toys and attractions related to the sea, the stars, and the subway (Tube).

London Aquarium
South Bank

London's subterranean aquarium, located right beside the British Airways London Eye, may be a bit disappointing if you've been to any of the great aquariums in the United States. Nevertheless, children enjoy observing its more than 350 species of fish and aquatic invertebrates, including sharks, graceful stingrays, man-eating piranhas, and sea scorpions. Exhibits, a couple with floor-to-ceiling tanks, re-create marine habitats from around the world. Plan on spending at least an hour here — more if you can't pull the kids away.

See map p. 210. Bridge Road (beside Westminster Bridge), SE1. ☎ 020/7967-8000. Tube: Waterloo (then a five-minute walk west along the river). Admission: £9.75 ($18) adults, £7.50 ($14) seniors, £6.25 ($12) children, £29 ($54) families (two adults and two children). Open: Daily 10 a.m.–6 p.m. (last admission 5 p.m.). Closed Dec 25.

London Planetarium
Marylebone

Partnered with Madame Tussaud's wax museum (see the listing earlier in this chapter), the planetarium takes you on a journey to very different stars from the ones cast in wax next door. The planetarium offers many kid-friendly hands-on exhibits (including one that lets you see what shape or weight you'd be on other planets). You can also hear Stephen Hawking talk about mysterious black holes. You get to visit the major landmarks of the solar system and witness spectacular cosmic activity, all from the comfort of the planetarium's auditorium. Give this sight at least an hour.

See map p. 210. Marylebone Road, NW1. ☎ 0870/400-3000. Tube: Baker Street (then a one-minute walk east on Marylebone Road). Admission: £8.75 ($16) adults, £5.75 ($11) children under 16. Children under 5 not admitted. Combination ticket for Planetarium and Madame Tussaud's: £22 ($41) adults, £19 ($35) seniors, £18 ($33) children under 16. Open: Daily 10 a.m.–5:30 p.m. Half-hour shows begin at 10 a.m. or 10:30 a.m., depending on season, and run until closing.

London Transport Museum
Covent Garden

Housed in a splendid Victorian building (once the Flower Market at Covent Garden), this museum chronicles the development of the city's famous Underground and double-decker red bus system. A fabulous collection of historic vehicles, including an 1829 omnibus, a horse-drawn bus, and London's first trolley bus, are on display. Several KidZones offer interactive exhibits that enable younger visitors to operate the controls of a Tube train, get their tickets punched, and play with touch-screen technology. After two hours, you may have to drag them away.

See map p. 210. The Piazza, WC2. ☎ 020/7379-6344. Tube: Covent Garden (then a two-minute walk west to the Piazza; the museum is in the southeast corner). Admission: £5.95 ($11) adults, £4.50 ($8.35) seniors, free for children under 16. Open: Sat–Thurs 10 a.m.–6 p.m., Fri 11 a.m.–6 p.m. (last admission at 5:15 p.m.).

Museum of Childhood
Bethnal Green

A branch of the Victoria & Albert Museum, this museum specializes in toys from the past and present. You can find a staggering collection of dolls, many with elaborate period costumes, and fully furnished dollhouses ranging from simple cottages to miniature mansions. Optical toys, marionettes, puppets, tin soldiers, war toys, toy trains and aircraft, and a display of clothing and furniture relating to the social history of childhood make this museum an enchanting place to invest a couple of hours. Oh, how times — and toys — have changed.

See map p. 210. Cambridge Heath Road, E2. ☎ 020/8980-2415. Tube: Bethnal Green (then a five-minute walk north on Cambridge Heath Road to the museum entrance on the east side of the street). Admission: Free. Open: Sat–Thurs 10 a.m.–5:50 p.m.

To see or not to see: Shakespeare sights

If you don't have time to visit Stratford-upon-Avon (see Chapter 14), where the great poet and dramatist William Shakespeare was born and died, you can visit two Shakespeare-associated sights on London's South Bank.

Shakespeare's Globe Theatre & Exhibition
South Bank

At this full-size replica of Shakespeare's Globe Theatre, just east of its original site, you can take guided tours through the theater and its workshops. You can find out about the days of Shakespeare and Elizabethan theater: what audiences were like, the rivalry among the theaters, the cruel bear-baiting shows, and the notorious Southwark Stews (a nearby area where prostitutes plied their trade). Watching a Shakespeare play from one of the benches in this roofless "wooden O" is a memorable experience, though the hard benches can be rough on the backside. See Chapter 15 for details on obtaining tickets for one of the performances, presented May through September.

If you plan to see a Shakespeare play at the Globe, you can have a snack, tea, or a full meal in the theater itself. You don't need to make reservations at **The Globe Café**; it's open daily May through September 10 a.m. to 11 p.m. and October through April 10 a.m. to 6 p.m. Make reservations ahead for lunch or dinner at **The Globe Restaurant** (☎ 020/7928-9444), open daily noon to 2:30 p.m. and 6 to 11 p.m.

See map p. 210. New Globe Walk (just west of Southwark Bridge), SE1. ☎ 020/ 7902-1500. Tube: Mansion House (then a ten-minute walk across Southwark Bridge; the theater is visible on the west side along the river). Tours: £8 ($15) adults, £6.50 ($12) seniors and students, £5.50 ($10) children, £24 ($44) family. Open: Oct–Apr daily 10 a.m.–5 p.m., May–Sept (performance season) daily 9 a.m.–noon.

Southwark Cathedral
South Bank

Chaucer and Shakespeare both worshiped at Southwark Cathedral. London's second-oldest church after Westminster Abbey, Southwark (pronounced *Suth*-ick) Cathedral is in what was London's first theater district (as well as a church-sanctioned center of prostitution). Although the cathedral was partially rebuilt in 1890, a great deal of history is associated with this 15th-century church. In under 30 minutes, you can see the entire site, including the Shakespeare memorial window and a 13th-century wooden effigy of a knight. Lunchtime concerts are regularly given on Monday and Tuesday; call for exact times and schedules.

See map p. 210. Montague Close (just west of London Bridge), SE1. ☎ 020/7367-6700. Tube: London Bridge (then a five-minute walk across London Bridge Road to Cathedral Street). Admission: Free, but a £2 ($3.70) donation is suggested. Open: Mon–Fri 7:30 a.m.–6 p.m., Sat–Sun 8:30 a.m.–6 p.m.

Ships ahoy! Nautical London

The river Thames, London's watery artery to the English Channel, is full of all kinds of watercraft. This section details two intriguing ships that you can visit. I tell you about touring the Thames by boat in the "Seeing London by Guided Tour" section, later in this chapter.

Golden Hinde
South Bank

A full-scale reconstruction of Sir Francis Drake's 16th-century flagship, complete with a crew dressed in Tudor costumes, the *Golden Hinde* was built in Devon but launched in San Francisco in 1973 to commemorate Drake's claiming of California for Queen Elizabeth I. Like the original, this ship circumnavigated the globe, sailing more than 140,000 miles before becoming a permanent floating museum in 1996. A self-guided tour of the fully rigged ship, once the home to 20 officers and gentlemen and between 40 to 60 crew members, takes about a half-hour.

See map p. 210. St. Mary Overie Dock, Cathedral Street (west of London Bridge), SE1. ☎ *08700/118-700. Tube: London Bridge (then a five-minute walk west on Bedale and Cathedral streets). Admission: £3.50 ($6.50) adults, £3 ($5.55) seniors, £2.50 ($4.65) children, £15 ($28) families (two adults and two children). Open: Daily, but call for times.*

H.M.S. Belfast
South Bank

The *Belfast*, a huge Royal Navy cruiser built in 1938 and used in World War II, is now moored in the Thames near London Bridge, opposite the Tower of London. Tours of this floating 10,500-ton museum allow visitors to see all seven decks. On-ship exhibits are devoted to the history of the ship and the Royal Navy. You and your kids can witness a re-created surface battle. Plan to spend about 90 minutes.

See map p. 210. Morgan's Lane, Tooley Street (between Tower Bridge and London Bridge), SE1. ☎ *020/7940-6300. Tube: London Bridge (then a ten-minute walk north across Tooley Street and north on Hays Lane toward the entrance on the river). Admission: £7 ($13) adults, £5 ($9.25) seniors and students, free for children under 16. Open: Mar–Oct daily 10 a.m.–6 p.m.; Nov–Feb daily 10 a.m.–5 p.m. (last admission 45 minutes before closing).*

Architectural highlights and stately homes

Stepping into one of London's great mansions, you can see what life lived on a grand scale was really like. The capital is also full of intriguing monuments, including one called, simply, The Monument, and famous bridges, such as Tower Bridge, which you can visit high above the Thames.

Apsley House
St. James's

Once known as Number One London because it was the first house past the tollgate into London, this magnificent neoclassical mansion, designed by Robert Adam and built between 1771 and 1778, was the London residence of the first duke of Wellington. The last great London townhouse, Apsley contains original collections that are mostly intact. After his phenomenal military career, which included defeating Napoleon at Waterloo in 1815, the duke was one of the most popular men in England. Apsley House, with its sumptuous interiors and treasure trove of paintings, china, swords, and military honors, reflects the first duke's position as the most powerful commander in Europe. A free audio guide explains it all on a self-guided tour that lasts about an hour. The family is still in residence, although you never see them.

See map p. 210. Hyde Park Corner, W1. ☎ 020/7499-5676. Tube: Hyde Park Corner (Exit 3 brings you up next to the house). Admission: £4.50 ($8.35) adults, £3 ($5.55) seniors, free for children under 16. Open: Tues–Sun 11 a.m.–5 p.m. Closed Dec 24–26, Jan 1, Good Friday, and May 1.

The Monument
The City

This 202-foot-high Doric column was designed by Sir Christopher Wren and commemorates the Great Fire of 1662, which allegedly began in nearby Pudding Lane and swept through London. The Monument is the tallest isolated stone column in the world — you'll know just how tall if you climb the 311 steps to the viewing platform at the top.

See map p. 210. Monument Street (just north of London Bridge), EC3. ☎ 020/ 7626-2717. Tube: Monument (you get out right across the street). Admission: £2 ($3.70) adults, £1 ($1.85) children. Open: Daily 10 a.m.–5:40 p.m.

Spencer House
St. James's

The late Princess Diana is probably the most famous member of the Spencer family, but she never lived in her family's ancestral London home, built for the first Earl Spencer in 1766. The house, one of London's most beautiful private palaces, hasn't been a private residence since 1927. Brilliantly restored and opened as a museum in 1990, its rooms are filled with period furniture and art loans from Queen Elizabeth, the Tate Britain, and the Victoria & Albert Museum. Guided tours (the only way to see the place) take about an hour.

See map p. 210. 27 St. James's Place, SW1. ☎ 020/7499-8620. Tube: Green Park (then a five-minute walk south on Queen's Walk to St. James's Place on your left). Admission: £9 ($17) adults, £7 ($13) seniors and students. Children under 10 not admitted. Open: Sun 10:30 a.m.–4:45 p.m. Closed Jan and Aug.

Tower Bridge Experience
South Bank

The "experience" lets you get inside one of the world's most famous bridges to find out why, how, and when it was built. Harry, a Victorian bridge worker brought to life by animatronics, tells you the story of this famous drawbridge with its pinnacled towers and how the mechanism for raising the bridge for ship traffic actually works. You also meet the architect's ghost and visit a miniature music hall. The experience takes about

90 minutes. The spectacular views up and down the Thames from the bridge's glass-enclosed walkways double the value of this attraction.

See map p. 210. North Pier, Tower Bridge, SE1. ☎ 020/7378-1928. Tube: Tower Hill (then a ten-minute walk south to the north pier of Tower Bridge). Admission: £5.50 ($10) adults, £4.25 ($7.85) seniors and students, £3 ($5.55) children 5–15. Open: Daily Nov–Mar 9:30 a.m.–6 p.m., Apr–Oct 10 a.m.–6:30 p.m. (last admission 75 minutes before closing). Closed Dec 25–26.

Parks and gardens

Part of London's charm comes from its giant green parks, small neighborhood squares, and special gardens. You never have to feel oppressed by too much brick and concrete in this city. If the mood strikes, you may want to visit one of the lovely spots in this section.

Chelsea Physic Garden
Chelsea

Hidden behind high brick walls, the Chelsea Physic Garden is the second-oldest surviving botanical garden in England and one of London's most beautiful places. The garden, containing more than 7,000 exotic herbs, shrubs, trees, and flowers, plus England's earliest rock garden, was founded in 1673 by the Worshipful Society of Apothecaries to develop medicinal and commercial plant species. Cotton seeds from this garden launched an industry in the new colony of Georgia. The garden is small enough (3½ acres) to wander through in an hour, but budget some more time if you love plants.

See map p. 210. Swan Walk, 66 Royal Hospital Rd., SW3. ☎ 020/7352-5646. Tube: Sloane Square (then a 15-minute walk south on Lower Sloane Street and west to the end of Royal Hospital Road). Bus: Southbound bus 11, 19, or 22 from Sloane Square. Admission: £5 ($9.25) adults, £3 ($5.55) students and children 5–15. Open: Apr–Oct Wed 2–5 p.m., Sun 2–6 p.m.; during the Chelsea Flower Show in May daily 2–5 p.m.

For fans of Princess Di

If you're a true Princess Diana fan, note that she's buried on a picturesque island on the Oval Lake at **Althorp,** the Spencer family estate in Northamptonshire. The grounds are open for a limited time each year from July through September, but you can view the island from across the lake only. Admission costs £12 ($22) adults, £10 ($19) seniors, £6 ($11) children, and £30 ($56) families (two adults and two children). The charge includes admission to the Diana Museum set up by her brother, Earl Spencer. The museum contains an exhibit celebrating Diana's childhood, her royal wedding (including her famous wedding gown), and her charitable works. You can book your tickets in advance by calling ☎ **0870/167-9000.** You can also buy day-of tickets at the Gate House or online at www.althorp.com.

Regent's Park
Marylebone

Regent's Park spans 400 acres of green, mostly open parkland fringed by imposing Regency terraces. The park is the home of the **London Zoo** (described under "London's Top Sights," earlier in this chapter). People come here to play soccer, cricket, tennis, and softball; boat on the lake; visit **Queen Mary's Rose Garden** (which includes an outdoor theater — see Chapter 15); and let their kids have fun at the many playgrounds. The park offers summer lunch and evening bandstand concerts, as well as puppet shows and other children's activities on weekdays throughout August. The northernmost section of the park rises to the summit of **Primrose Hill,** which provides fine views of Westminster and the City. The restrooms by Chester Gate, on the east side of the park, offer facilities for persons with disabilities.

See map p. 210. Just north of Marylebone Road and surrounded by the Outer Circle road. ☎ *020/7486-7905, or 020/7486-2431 for advance booking for Open Air Theatre (operating late May to early Sept).* www.openairtheatre.org. *Tube: Regent's Park or Baker Street (then a five-minute walk north to the south end of the park). Open: Daily 5 a.m.–dusk.*

Royal Botanic Gardens
Kew

Located 9 miles southwest of Central London, the **Royal Botanic Gardens at Kew** — more familiarly known as Kew Gardens — are a gift to garden lovers. A trip to Kew takes the better part of a day to allow for travel time and garden strolling, but the enjoyment that you receive is well worth the time investment. On display in the 300-acre gardens is a marvelous array of specimens first planted in the 17th and 18th centuries. Orchids and palms are nurtured in the Victorian glass pavilion hothouse. The site contains a lake, aquatic gardens, a Chinese pagoda, and even a royal palace. **Kew Palace,** the smallest and most lovely of the former royal compounds, is where King George III went insane. **Queen Charlotte's Cottage** served as the mad king's summer retreat (unfortunately, the palace and cottage are not open to the public).

Tired of the Tube? Why not take a boat to Kew Gardens? April to late September, vessels operated by the **Westminster Passenger Service Association** (☎ **020/7930-4721;** www.wpsa.co.uk) leave from Westminster Pier daily at 10:15, 11:15 a.m., noon, and 2 p.m. Round-trip fare for the 90-minute journey costs £17 ($31) adults, £11 ($20) seniors, £8.25 ($15) children, and £41 ($76) families. The last boat from Kew usually departs around 5.30 p.m. (depending on the tide).

Kew. ☎ *020/8332-5622. Tube: Kew Gardens (then a ten-minute walk west on Broomfield Street to the Victoria Gate entrance on Kew Road). Admission: £10 ($19) adults, free for children 5–16. Tours: Mar–Nov free one-hour tours daily at 11 a.m. and 2 p.m. Open: Gardens daily 9:30 a.m.–dusk; glass pavilion closes one hour before gardens. Closed Dec 25 and Jan 1.*

A quaint village just a Tube ride away

The London that you see today was once a series of separate villages. The nearby village of Hampstead, with its adjacent heath land, still retains its rural charm and makes for an excellent mini–day trip.

Hampstead and Hampstead Heath

Although only 15 minutes by Tube from Central London, **Hampstead** maintains its old-world charm. It's filled with Regency and Georgian houses (many set in lovely gardens) favored by artists and writers, from Keats to John Le Carré. **Flask Walk,** the village's pedestrian mall, provides an eclectic assemblage of historic pubs, shops, and chic boutiques. The village itself has a lot of old alleys, steps, courts, and groves just begging to be explored.

Adjacent **Hampstead Heath** is 800 acres of high parkland offering an opportunity for picnicking, swimming, and fishing. On a clear day, you can see St. Paul's Cathedral and even the hills of Kent. An excursion here takes up at least a half-day or more.

See map p. 227. Tube: Hampstead (the Tube stop is a minute from Flask Walk) or Hampstead Heath (Parliament Hill, right behind the Tube stop, leads up into to the park itself).

Kenwood House

This lovely neoclassical villa sits on the shore of Kenwood Lake in the northern section of Hampstead Heath. The villa was remodeled in the 1760s by Robert Adam. Inside, you find a small but impressive collection of paintings (with works by Gainsborough, Rembrandt, Reynolds, Turner, and Vermeer) and jewelry. You can get something to eat in the cafeteria in the former coach house. For a remarkable summer outdoor concert experience, visit the Kenwood Lakeside concert. (See Chapter 15 for information.)

Hampstead Lane (Hampstead), NW3. ☎ 020/8348-1286. Tube: Archway (then bus 210 west along Highgate and Hampstead Lane). Admission: Free. Open: Apr–Oct daily 10 a.m.–6 p.m., Nov–Mar daily 10 a.m.–4 p.m. (opens year-round at 10:30 a.m. Wed and Fri).

Royal castles and palaces

Everyone wants to see Buckingham Palace, the queen's London residence. But another royal residence, accessible year-round, awaits in nearby Windsor. Just as memorable is Hampton Court, another great royal compound from the time of Henry VIII.

Hampton Court Palace

In 1514, Cardinal Wolsey began building the splendid Tudor Hampton Court in East Moseley, Surrey, 13 miles west of London on the north side of the Thames. Henry VIII nabbed Hampton Court for himself and made it

Hampstead

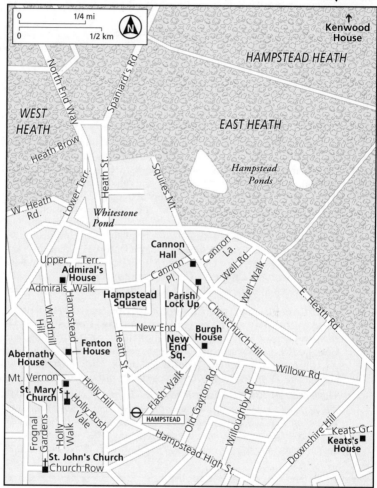

a royal residence, which it remained until 1760. The **Anne Boleyn Gate,** with its 16th-century astronomical clock, and the **Great Hall,** with its hammer-beam ceiling, are remnants from Hampton Court's Tudor days. Later, the palace was much altered by Sir Christopher Wren for William and Mary. Wren also designed the famous **Maze,** where visitors can wander in dizzy confusion. Inside the enormous palace are various state apartments and private rooms, including the **King's Dressing Room** and Tudor kitchens, and containing wooden carvings by Grinling Gibbons, Italian paintings, and guides dressed in period costumes. The manicured Thames-side gardens are lovely. You find a cafe and restaurant on the grounds. You need a full day for this excursion.

Hampton Court, East Moseley, Surrey. ☎ *0870/752-7777. Train: Frequent trains from Waterloo Station make the half-hour trip to Hampton Court Station; the round-trip fare costs about £5 ($9.25). Admission: £12 ($22) adults, £8.70 ($16) seniors and students, £7.70 ($14) children 5–15. Open: Apr–Oct daily 10 a.m.–6 p.m.; Nov–Feb Tues–Sun 9:30 a.m.–4:30 p.m., Mon 10:15 a.m.–4:30 p.m. Closed Jan 1 and Dec 24–26.*

Windsor Castle

Windsor is one of the queen's official residences. The castle, with its imposing skyline of towers and battlements rising from the center of the 4,800-acre Great Park, is located in Windsor, Berkshire, 20 miles from the center of London. Royals have used the castle as a residence since its construction by William the Conqueror approximately 900 years ago. The **State Apartments** that are open to visitors range from the intimate chambers of Charles II to the enormous Waterloo Chamber, built to commemorate the victory over Napoléon in 1815. All apartments are furnished with important works of art from the Royal Collection. **Queen Mary's Dollhouse,** designed by Sir Edwin Lutyens as a present for Queen Mary in 1921, is a marvelous palace in miniature. **St. George's Chapel,** a Gothic masterpiece of the 14th century, is the burial place of ten monarchs and the home of the Order of the Garter.

April through June, the **Changing of the Guard** takes place Monday through Saturday at 11 a.m. (on alternate days the rest of the year). From the ramparts of Windsor, you can look down on the playing fields of **Eton College,** where aristocrats have been sending their boys for generations. All the royals attend the famous school in the charming town of **Eton** across the Thames Bridge. Give yourself a full day for this excursion.

Windsor. ☎ *01753/831118. Train: Trains leave every half-hour from Waterloo Station for the 50-minute trip (the stop is Windsor and Eton); the round-trip fare costs £7 ($13). Admission: £13 ($24) adults, £11 ($20) seniors and students, £6.50 ($12) children under 17, £32 ($59) families. Open: Mar–Oct daily 9:45 a.m.–5:30 p.m. (last entry 4 p.m.), Nov–Feb daily 9:45 a.m.–4:15 p.m. (last entry 3 p.m.); closed Jan 1, Mar 28, June 16, and Dec 25–26.*

Ghost palace

So many people, from staff to visitors, have reported encounters with Catherine Howard's ghost in the "haunted gallery" at Hampton Court that psychologists from the University of Hertfordshire conducted an investigation to see if they could find a scientific explanation for the phenomenon — not surprisingly, the results were inconclusive. Catherine, the fifth wife of King Henry VIII, was locked up in Hampton Court prior to her beheading for adultery in 1542. One day, she supposedly escaped and in desperation ran along the 40-foot gallery to pound on the King's door and beg for mercy. Sightings in this gallery of a running, screaming apparition have been reported for centuries.

Greenwich: The center of time and space

Time is of the essence in Greenwich, a town and borough of Greater London, about 4 miles east of the City. The world's clocks are set according to Greenwich mean time, and visitors from around the globe flock here to stand on the **prime meridian,** the line from which the world's longitude is measured. The historic buildings in Greenwich are important enough that UNESCO has listed them as a World Heritage Site. Greenwich offers enough to keep you fully occupied for a full day, and it makes a great outing for kids.

The most interesting route to get to Greenwich is by Docklands Light Rail from Tower Hill Gateway, which takes you past Canary Wharf and all the new Docklands development. The one-way fare costs £2 ($3.70). Take the train to Island Gardens, the last stop, and then walk through the foot tunnel beneath the Thames to Greenwich. You come out next to the *Cutty Sark.* You can also take the Jubilee Underground line to Greenwich North and then bus no. 188 to the *Cutty Sark.* **Thames River Services (☎ 020/ 7930-4097)** runs a year-round fleet of boats from Westminster Pier to Greenwich Pier. A round-trip ticket costs £8.60 ($16) adults, £22 ($41) for families (two adults and two children).

All the attractions in Greenwich are clearly signposted, and you can reach them on foot. The Greenwich Tourist Information Centre (Pepys House, Cutty Sark Gardens; ☎ 0870/608-2000) is open daily 10 a.m. to 5 p.m. The center offers one-and-a-half-hour to two-hour walking tours (at 12:15 and 2:15 p.m.) of the town's major sights for £4 ($7.40). Reservations aren't necessary, but you may want to call first to make certain that the schedule hasn't changed.

Cutty Sark

The majestic *Cutty Sark,* berthed on the river Thames, is the last of the tea-clipper sailing ships. It was launched in 1869 and first used for the lucrative China Sea tea trade. Later, the ship carried wool from Australia and after that (up until the end of World War II) served as a training ship. Today, the hold contains a rich collection of nautical instruments and paraphernalia. You can visit the ship on a self-guided tour and see everything in under an hour. Kids enjoy the experience of being aboard the old ship as much as adults.

King William Walk. ☎ *020/8858-3445. Admission: £4.50 ($8.35) adults, £3.75 ($6.95) seniors and students, £3.30 ($6.10) children, £12 ($22) families (two adults and two children). Open: Daily 10 a.m.–5 p.m; closed Dec 24–26.*

National Maritime Museum

The paintings of ships are boring, but the National Maritime Museum also displays sailing crafts and models and an extensive exhibit on Lord Nelson, which includes hundreds of his personal artifacts (including the coat that he was wearing when he was shot at the Battle of Trafalgar). New galleries with interactive technology explore modern maritime issues. You can sail through in about a half-hour. There's a nice café for lunch or a snack.

In Greenwich Park. ☎ *020/8312-6608. Admission: Free. Open: Daily 10 a.m.–5 p.m. (June–Sept until 6 p.m.).*

Queen's House

Adjacent to the National Maritime Museum, you can find the splendidly restored Queen's House, designed by Inigo Jones in 1616 and later used as a model for the White House. The house, the first classical building in England, was commissioned by Anne of Denmark, the wife of James I, and completed in 1635 (with later modifications). You can visit the royal apartments on a self-guided tour that takes about a half-hour. You may catch a special exhibit being held here.

In Greenwich Park. ☎ *020/8312-6608. Admission: Free. Open: Daily 10 a.m.–5 p.m.*

Royal Naval College

Near the *Cutty Sark,* the Royal Naval College occupies the site of Greenwich Palace, which stood here from 1422 to 1620 and was the birthplace of Henry VIII, Mary I, and Elizabeth I. Badly damaged by Cromwell's troops during the English Civil War, the palace was later torn down, and in 1696, a naval hospital for retired seamen was erected in its place. The Thames-side buildings, designed by Sir Christopher Wren, became the Naval College in 1873 and are today a UNESCO-designated World Heritage Site. The only rooms open to visitors are the chapel and the imposing **Great Hall** with its dazzling painted ceiling. The body of Lord Nelson lay in state here in 1805.

King William Walk. ☎ *020/8858-2154. Admission: Free. Open: Daily 10 a.m.–5 p.m.*

Royal Observatory Greenwich

You can huff your way up the hill from Queen's House (see listing earlier in this section) in Greenwich Great Park to explore the Royal Observatory, where you can straddle the **prime meridian** (longitude 0 degrees), the center of time and space. Of particular interest inside the observatory is the collection of original 18th-century *chronometers* (marked H1, H2, H3, and H4), beautiful instruments that were developed to help mariners chart longitude by time instead of by the stars. The prime meridian line and the various astronomical gadgets in the observatory appeal to the imaginations of older kids.

In Greenwich Park. ☎ *020/8312-6608. Admission: Free. Open: Daily 10 a.m.–5 p.m. (June–Sept until 6 p.m.).*

Seeing London by Guided Tour

When it comes to London sightseeing tours, you're limited only by your imagination, stamina, and budget. You can tour London with an experienced guide by bus, by boat, or on foot.

Bus tours

Original London Sightseeing Tours (☎ 020/8877-1722; www.the
originaltour.com) maintains a fleet of double-decker buses (many of
them open on top) and offers hop-on/hop-off service at more than 90
boarding points around the city. You can choose from four tour routes.
The **Original London Sightseeing Tour** lasts 90 minutes and passes every
major sight in Central London and the South Bank; the tour starts from
Piccadilly Circus (Tube: Piccadilly Circus) outside the Planet Hollywood
restaurant on Coventry Street and departs every few minutes daily from
9 a.m. to 6 p.m. (to 9 p.m. in summer). You don't have to book any of the
sightseeing tours in advance; you can pay on the bus. A ticket good for
24 hours on all routes costs £16 ($30) for adults and £10 ($19) for children
under 16. For more information or to book online, check out the Web site.

The **Big Bus Company** (☎ 020/7233-9533; www.bigbus.co.uk) leaves
from Green Park, Victoria, and Marble Arch daily, from 8:30 a.m. to 7 p.m.
(4:30 p.m. in winter) on three different routes that take anywhere from
one and a half to two and a half hours. Tickets include a river cruise and
walking tours, and cost £18 ($33) for adults and £8 ($15) for children
ages 5 to 15. Valid for 24 hours, they let you hop on and off at 54 locations. Big Bus often has special offers, too, throwing in cheap theater
tickets, fast-entry to popular attractions, and so on.

Another tour company with many guided excursions is **Golden Tours**
(4 Fountain Square, 123–151 Buckingham Palace Rd.; ☎ **800-456-6303**
in the U.S. or 020/7233-7030; www.goldentours.co.uk). Its buses are
comfy and have restrooms, and the certified guides have a certifiable
sense of humor. The daily **Historic & Modern London** tour is a full-day
outing that includes the West End, Westminster Abbey, the Changing of
the Guard (at Buckingham Palace or Horse Guards Parade), the City of
London, St. Paul's Cathedral, the Tower of London, and a cruise from the
Tower down to Charing Cross Pier; the price includes a pub lunch and
all admissions. This tour costs £64 ($118) for adults and £54 ($100) for
kids under 16. Tours depart from the office at Buckingham Palace Road
(Tube: Victoria) and other points in Central London. You can book your
tickets directly or online, or you can ask your hotel concierge to do it
two days in advance.

Boat tours

A cruise down the majestic Thames is a marvelous way to take in the
city's sights. Sightseeing boats regularly ply the river between Westminster
and the Tower of London; some continue downstream to Greenwich
(site of the prime meridian, *Cutty Sark,* and Old Royal Observatory) and
upstream to Kew Gardens and Hampton Court. The main departure
points along the Thames are at **Westminster Pier** (Tube: Westminster),
Waterloo Pier (Tube: Waterloo), **Embankment Pier** (Tube: Embankment),
Tower Pier (Tube: Tower Hill), and **Greenwich Pier** (Tube: Greenwich).

Evan Evans (☎ 020/7950-1777; www.evanevans.co.uk) offers three cruises. A **daily lunch cruise** departs at 12:15 p.m. from Embankment Pier aboard the *Silver Bonito;* this cruise costs £20 ($37) for adults, £12 ($22) for children. Another daily offering starts with a guided boat tour of the Thames, includes a tour of the Tower of London, and continues by bus to the City and St. Paul's; this cruise costs £37 ($68) for adults and £32 ($59) for children 3 to 16. A **full-day tour,** offered Monday through Saturday, takes in Westminster Abbey, and continues to Buckingham Palace (or Horse Guards Parade) for the Changing of the Guard, St. Paul's Cathedral, and the Tower of London. This tour, which includes a pub lunch and a river cruise, costs £63 ($117) adults and £53 ($98) children.

Transport for London (☎ 020/7222-1234; www.tfl.gov.uk) runs a fleet of commuter and sightseeing boats on the Thames. A round-trip ticket from Westminster Pier to Greenwich costs £8.60 ($16) adults, £22 ($41) for families (two adults and two children).

Daily from March through November and on weekends the rest of the year, **Catamaran Cruisers** (☎ 020/7987-1185; www.catamarancruisers.co.uk) offers a one-hour circular cruise from Westminster Pier (Tube: Westminster) that passes most of London's major monuments and stops at Festival Pier, Bankside Pier, London Bridge City Pier, and St. Katharine's Pier (hop-on/hop-off service). All the boats provide live commentary and have a fully licensed bar. The cruise costs £8 ($15) for adults, £6 ($11) for children, and £22 ($41) for families (two adults and three children).

Bateaux London (☎ 020/7925-2215; www.catamarancruisers.co.uk) offers a **nightly dinner cruise** that leaves Embankment Pier (Tube: Embankment) at 7:15 p.m. and returns at 9:45 p.m. The cruise, which includes a two- to four-course dinner with live music and after-dinner dancing, costs £65 to £95 ($120–$176) per person, depending on the various add-ons that you choose. A one-hour **lunch cruise** with a multi-course set menu and live commentary is offered Monday to Saturday for £20 to £30 ($37–$56) per person; the boat departs from Embankment Pier at 12:15 p.m. A two-hour **Sunday lunch cruise** departs from Embankment Pier at 12:15 p.m. and costs £38 to £45 ($70–$83) per person. Advance reservations are required for all tours, and a smart-casual dress code applies (no sweatpants or running shoes).

An amphibious tour

London Duck Tours (☎ 020/7928-3132; www.londonducktours.co.uk) has adapted several World War II amphibious troop carriers, known as DUKWs, to civilian comfort levels and painted them bright yellow. It runs 80-minute road-and-river trips. Tours start behind County Hall (site of the British Airways London Eye giant observation wheel). It picks up passengers on Chicheley Street (Tube: Westminster, then walk across Westminster Bridge), then rumbles through Westminster and up to Piccadilly, gathering bemused stares as it passes many of London's major tourist sites. Then the vehicle splashes into the Thames at Vauxhall for a 30-minute cruise as far as the Houses of Parliament. The tours cost £18 ($33) for adults, £14 ($26) for seniors, and £12 ($22) for children.

Walking tours

A walking tour is an affordable way to see London from street level in the company of a knowledgeable guide. This type of tour is great for history, literature, and architecture buffs, and older kids generally have a good time, as well. The weekly events listings in *Time Out* magazine, available at every news agent in London, include dozens of intriguing walks; a walk happens every day.

The Original London Walks, P.O. Box 1708, London NW6 4LW (☎ **020/ 7624-3978;** www.walks.com), offers a terrific array of tours, including **Jack the Ripper's London, Christopher Wren's London, Oscar Wilde's London,** and **The Beatles' Magical Mystery Tour.** Guides lead different walks every day of the week, rain or shine; tours last about two hours and end near an Underground station. You don't need to make advance reservations. Call for schedules and departure points. A London Walk costs £5.50 ($10) for adults and £4.50 ($8.35) for students with ID; kids can tour for free if accompanied by a parent.

If you want to follow detailed strolls on your own, check out the 11 tours offered in *Frommer's Memorable Walks in London,* by Richard Jones (Wiley).

Index of Top Attractions by Neighborhood

Bethnal Green
Museum of Childhood

Bloomsbury
British Museum
Dickens's House Museum

Chelsea
Carlyle's House
Chelsea Physic Garden

The City
Bank of England Museum
The Monument
Museum of London
St. Paul's Cathedral
Tower of London

Covent Garden
Covent Garden Market and Piazza
London Transport Museum
Theatre Museum

Greenwich
Cutty Sark
National Maritime Museum
Prime Meridian
Queen's House
Royal Naval College
Royal Observatory Greenwich

Hampstead
Hampstead Heath
Kenwood House

Hampton Court
Hampton Court Palace

Holborn

Dr. Johnson's House
Sir John Soane's Museum

Kensington and South Kensington

Kensington Gardens
Kensington Palace
Natural History Museum
Science Museum
Victoria & Albert Museum

Lambeth

Imperial War Museum

Kew

Royal Botanic Gardens

Marylebone

British Library Exhibition Centre
London Planetarium
London Zoo
Madame Tussaud's
Regent's Park
Wallace Collection

Piccadilly Circus and Leicester Square

Leicester Square
Pepsi Trocadero
Piccadilly Circus

Pimlico

Tate Britain

South Bank

British Airways London Eye
Design Museum
Golden Hinde

H.M.S. *Belfast*
London Aquarium
London Dungeon
Old Operating Theatre & Herb Garret
Saatchi Gallery
Shakespeare's Globe Theatre &
Exhibition
Southwark Cathedral
Tate Modern
Tower Bridge Experience

St. James's

Apsley House
Buckingham Palace
Changing of the Guard at Buckingham
Palace
National Gallery
National Portrait Gallery
Royal Academy of Arts
Spencer House
St. James's Park and Green Park
St. Martin-in-the-Fields
10 Downing Street
Trafalgar Square

The Strand

Benjamin Franklin House
Somerset House (Courtauld Gallery,
Gilbert Collection, and Hermitage
Rooms)

Westminster

Cabinet War Rooms
Houses of Parliament and Big Ben
Hyde Park
Westminster Abbey

Windsor

Windsor Castle

Index of Attractions by Type

Art Galleries

Kenwood House
National Gallery
National Portrait Gallery
Royal Academy of Arts

Saatchi Gallery
Somerset House (Courtauld Gallery,
Gilbert Collection, and Hermitage
Rooms)
Tate Britain

Tate Modern
Wallace Collection

Churches

St. Martin-in-the-Fields
St. Paul's Cathedral
Southwark Cathedral
Westminster Abbey

Entertainment Venues and Themed Attractions

British Airways London Eye
Cutty Sark
Golden Hinde
H.M.S. *Belfast*
London Aquarium
London Dungeon
London Planetarium
Madame Tussaud's
Pepsi Trocadero
Shakespeare's Globe Theatre & Exhibition
Tower Bridge Experience

Historic Houses and Buildings

Apsley House
Benjamin Franklin House
Cabinet War Rooms
Carlyle's House
Dickens's House Museum
Dr. Johnson's House
Houses of Parliament and Big Ben
Kenwood House
The Monument
Old Operating Theatre & Herb Garret
Queen's House
Royal Naval College
Royal Observatory Greenwich
Sir John Soane's Museum
Spencer House
10 Downing Street
Tower of London

Museums

Bank of England Museum
British Library Exhibition Centre
British Museum
Design Museum
Imperial War Museum
London Transport Museum
Madame Tussaud's
Museum of Childhood
Museum of London
National Maritime Museum
Natural History Museum
Science Museum
Theatre Museum
Victoria & Albert Museum

Palaces and Castles

Buckingham Palace
Changing of the Guard at Buckingham Palace
Hampton Court Palace
Kensington Palace
Queen's House
Tower of London
Windsor Castle

Parks, Gardens, and the Zoo

Chelsea Physic Garden
Hampstead Heath
Hyde Park
Kensington Gardens
London Zoo
Regent's Park
Royal Botanic Gardens
St. James's Park and Green Park

Squares

Covent Garden Market and Piazza
Leicester Square
Piccadilly Circus
Trafalgar Square

Chapter 12

Shopping the Local Stores

In This Chapter
▶ Getting your VAT refund
▶ Taking your purchases through Customs
▶ Visiting the big department stores
▶ Shopping Knightsbridge and the West End

*L*ondon is one of the world's great shopping meccas. If shopping is on your agenda, you can find any item that you're looking for. But you won't find many bargains, except during the department stores' big sales in January and July (see the "Saving on the London sales" sidebar).

Surveying the Shopping Scene

You get the best values on goods that are manufactured in England. Items from the Body Shop, Filofax, or Dr. Martens cost less than they do in the United States. Other potentially good values include woolens and cashmeres, English brands of bone china, English toiletries, antiques, used silver, old maps and engravings, and rare books. You can also do well with French products; the prices are almost as good as in Paris.

You may be surprised — and perhaps disappointed — at the number of big U.S. chains that have opened stores in London. But in addition to the familiar chains and mega-stores, London is still the home of hundreds of small, unique specialty shops and boutiques to delight the eye and empty the wallet.

Normal shopping hours are Monday through Saturday 10 a.m. to 5:30 p.m., with a late closing (7 or 8 p.m.) on Wednesday or Thursday. The law allows stores to be open for six hours on Sunday, usually 11 a.m. to 5 p.m.

Table 12-1 lists conversions for U.S. and U.K. sizes.

Saving on the London sales

Traditionally, London stores hold sales in January and July. In recent times, the July sales have begun in June or earlier. The January sale is the main event, and it generally starts after the first week (when round-trip airfares are low).

The January sale at Harrods is the most world famous, but nearly every other store has a big sale at the same time. Discounts usually range from 25 to 50 percent at the major stores, such as Harrods and Selfridges. At Harrods, you can find the best buys on the store's logo souvenirs, English china, and English designer brands, such as Jaeger.

Table 12-1		The Right Fit: Size Conversions	
U.S.	**U.K.**	**U.S.**	**U.K.**
Women's Clothes		**Women's Shoes**	
8	10	4½	3
10	12	5½	4
12	14	6½	5
14	16	7½	6
16	18	8½	7
18	20	9½	8
Men's Clothes/Shirts		**Men's Shoes**	
Sizes are the same		7	6
		8	7
		9	8
		10	9
		11	10
		12	11

Getting the VAT back

You have to pay a 17.5-percent *VAT* (value-added tax) in London and throughout the United Kingdom on every retail item except books and children's clothing. Anyone who isn't a resident of the European Union can get a VAT refund, but every store requires a minimum purchase to qualify. The exact amount varies from store to store, but the minimum amount is never less than £50 ($93) and may be as high as £100 ($185) at a store like Harrods. But qualifying for a tax refund is far easier in Britain than in almost any other country in the European Union.

VAT isn't charged on goods shipped out of the country, no matter how much you spend. You can avoid VAT and the hassle of lugging large packages back with you by having London stores ship your purchases for you; many are happy to do so. However, shipping charges can *double* the cost of your purchase, and you may also have to pay U.S. duties when the goods arrive. Rather than using this costly strategy, consider paying for excess baggage (rates vary with the airlines) when you fly home.

To get a VAT refund, you must get a VAT refund form from the retailer, and the retailer must complete the form at the time of purchase. Don't leave the store without a completed refund form. Don't let any merchant tell you that you can get refund forms at the airport.

You can get back about 15 percent of the 17.5 percent VAT that you pay on your purchases. (You can't get back the entire amount.) To obtain your refund, follow these steps:

1. **Ask the store whether it does VAT refunds and how much the minimum purchase is.**

2. **If you've spent the minimum amount, ask for the VAT refund paperwork.**

   The retailer must fill out a portion.

3. **Fill out your portion of the form (name and address).**

4. **Present the form — along with the goods — at the VAT Refunds counter at the airport.**

You may be required to show the goods at your time of departure, so don't pack them in your checked luggage; put them in your carryon instead.

After the paperwork is stamped, you have two choices:

 ✔ You can mail in the papers and receive your refund in a British check (no!) or a credit-card refund (yes!).

 ✔ You can go directly to the Cash VAT Refund desk at the airport and get your refund in cash.

If you're traveling from London to other countries in the European Union, don't apply for your VAT refund at the London airport. Apply for all your VAT refunds at one time at your final destination, prior to departure from the European Union.

Getting your goodies through Customs

The Customs authority doesn't impose limits on how much loot U.S. citizens can bring home from a trip abroad, but it does put limits on how much they can bring back for free. You may bring home $800 worth of goods duty-free if you've been out of the country at least 48 hours and haven't used the exemption in the past 30 days. Here's some additional information about the limit and Customs law:

✔ You can bring back not more than 1 liter of an alcoholic beverage (you must be over 21 to carry any alcohol).

✔ You can carry not more than 200 cigarettes and 100 cigars.

✔ Antiques more than 100 years old and works of art are exempt from the $800 limit, as is anything that you mail home from abroad.

✔ You may mail up to $200 worth of goods to yourself (marked "For Personal Use") and up to $100 worth to others (marked "Unsolicited Gift") once each day, as long as the package doesn't include alcohol or tobacco products.

✔ You have to pay an import duty on anything over these limits — a flat rate of 10 percent duty on the next $1,000 worth of purchases.

✔ You have to show proof of ownership for any expensive items, such as cameras or laptop computers, that you take with you to the United Kingdom. If you don't have proof (such as sales receipts or insurance forms), you can register the items before your trip by using Custom Form 4457, available through the U.S. Customs Service.

Be sure to have your receipts with you. For more specific guidance, contact the **U.S. Customs Service** (P.O. Box 7407, Washington, DC 20044; ☎ **202/927-6724**) and request the free pamphlet *Know Before You Go*. Or check out the details and order online at the Customs Department Web site, www.customs.ustreas.gov.

Returning Canadian citizens are allowed a C$300 exemption and can bring back, free of duty, 200 cigarettes, 2.2 pounds of tobacco, 40 imperial ounces (1.2 quarts) of liquor, and 50 cigars. Declare all valuables that you're taking with you to the United Kingdom, such as expensive cameras, on the Y-38 Form before you leave Canada. For a clear summary of Canadian rules, write for the booklet *I Declare,* issued by Revenue Canada (2265 St. Laurent Blvd., Ottawa K1G 4KE; ☎ **800/461-9999** or 613-993-0534).

Returning Australian citizens have a duty-free allowance of A$400 (A$200 for children under 18). Citizens can bring home, free of duty, 250 cigarettes or 250 grams of loose tobacco, and 1.125 liters of alcohol. Australian citizens who plan to return home with valuable goods that they already own (for example, foreign-made cameras) need to file Form B263 before leaving Australia. For more information, contact Australian Customs Services (GPO Box 8, Sydney NSW 2001; ☎ 02/9213-2000).

The duty-free allowance for New Zealand citizens is NZ$700. Citizens over 17 can bring in 200 cigarettes, 50 cigars, or 250 grams of tobacco, or a mix of all three if the combined weight doesn't exceed 250 grams; plus 4.5 liters of beer and wine, or 1.125 liters of liquor. To avoid paying duty on goods that you already own (cameras and the like), fill out a certificate of export before you leave New Zealand, listing the valuables that you're taking out of the country. For more information, contact New Zealand Customs (50 Anzac Ave., P.O. Box 29, Auckland; ☎ 09/359-6655).

Checking Out the Big Names

London is full of department stores. Some, like world-famous Harrods, may be familiar to you. Others, like Harvey Nichols, may be pleasant surprises. All these established department stores have their own style and personality. For store locations, see the "Shopping in Knightsbridge and Chelsea" map on p. 246 and the "Shopping in the West End" map on p. 248.

Fenwick of Bond Street
Mayfair

Fenwick of Bond Street is a high-style women's fashion store. Fenwick (pronounced *Fen*-ick) was founded in 1891 and offers an impressive collection of designer women's wear, ranging from moderately priced ready-to-wear items to more expensive designer fashions. Fenwick also sells an array of lingerie in all price ranges.

See map p. 248. 63 New Bond St., W1. ☎ *020/7629-9161. Tube: Bond Street. Open: Mon–Tues and Thurs–Sat 10 a.m.–6:30 p.m. and Wed 10 a.m.–8 p.m.*

Fortnum & Mason
St. James's

Fortnum & Mason, down the street from the Ritz hotel, holds two *royal warrants* (a form of official patronage that the store can use in its advertising) and is the queen's London grocer. Amid a setting of deep-red carpets and crystal chandeliers, you can find everything from pâté de foie gras to Campbell's soup. The grocery department carries the finest foods from around the world, and on the other floors, you can find bone china, crystal, leather, antiques, and stationery departments. Dining choices include **Patio, St. James's,** and **The Fountain** (see Chapter 10).

See map p. 248. 181 Piccadilly, W1. ☎ *020/7734-8040. Tube: Piccadilly Circus. Open: Mon–Sat 10 a.m.–6:30 p.m.*

Harrods loses royal warrant

The London gossip columns were ablaze early in 2000 when Prince Philip withdrew his *royal warrant* (a sign of official royal patronage) from Harrods, claiming that the royal household just didn't use the store as much as it used to. Harrods just happens to be owned by Mohamed Al Fayed, father of Dodi Al Fayed, who was killed with Princess Diana in that famous car crash. The elder Mr. Al Fayed, an Egyptian who's been denied U.K. citizenship, has made some startling allegations against the House of Windsor, claiming that the deaths of Diana and his son were not accidental. Could that be the real reason that Harrods is now warrant-less?

Harrods
Knightsbridge

Harrods may be the most famous department store in the world, but I've always found its merchandise to be pretty dull stuff. Carrying one of the coveted green plastic Harrods bags that you get with your purchase can provide you with a sense of accomplishment, though. The store's 300 departments offer an enormous range and variety of merchandise. Best of all are the Food Halls, stocked with a huge variety of foods and several cafes. Believe it or not, you may not be admitted if you're wearing inappropriate clothing or your belly button is showing.

See map p. 246. 87–135 Brompton Rd., SW1. ☎ 020/7730-1234. Tube: Knightsbridge. Open: Mon–Sat 10 a.m.–7 p.m.

Harvey Nichols
Knightsbridge

Harvey Nichols, the late Princess Diana's favorite store, has its own gourmet food hall and fancy restaurant, the **Fifth Floor,** and is crammed with designer home furnishings, gifts, and fashions. Women's clothing is the largest segment of its business, a familiar fact to those fans of the British TV series *Absolutely Fabulous*. Harvey Nicks, as it's called, doesn't compete with Harrods because the former features a much more upmarket, fashionable image.

See map p. 246. 109–125 Knightsbridge, SW1. ☎ 020/7235-5000. Tube: Knightsbridge. Open: Mon, Tues, and Sat 10 a.m.–7 p.m., Wed–Fri 10 a.m.–8 p.m., and Sun noon–6 p.m.

Liberty
Mayfair

Liberty provides six floors of fashion, china, home furnishings, upholstery fabrics, scarves, ties, luggage, and gifts. The store is best known for its

Liberty Prints — fine quality fabrics, typically in floral patterns. These distinctive fabrics are highly sought after by interior decorators because they add an unmistakable touch of England to any room décor. A Liberty tie makes a great gift for your guy back home.

See map p. 248. 214–220 Regent St., W1. ☎ 020/7734-1234. Tube: Oxford Circus. Open: Mon–Wed 10 a.m.–6:30 p.m, Thurs 10 a.m.–8 p.m., Fri–Sat 10 a.m.–7 p.m., Sun noon to 6 p.m.

Marks & Spencer
Mayfair

Marks & Spencer is a private-label department store that offers basics of all kinds. The merchandise at both locations is high quality, if a bit conservative.

See map p. 248. 458 Oxford St., W1 (☎ 020/7935-7954; Tube: Marble Arch) and 173 Oxford St., W1 (☎ 020/7437-7722; Tube: Oxford Circus). Open: Mon–Fri 9 a.m.–8 p.m., Sat 9 a.m.–7:30 p.m., and Sun noon–6 p.m.

Selfridges
Mayfair

Selfridges is one of the largest department stores in Europe. The store has been redone to attract upscale customers, but the vast size of the store provides room for less-expensive, mass-marketed lines, as well. More than 500 divisions sell everything, from artificial flowers to groceries. The Miss Selfridge boutique, on one side of the store near the cosmetics department, features teen fashions, hotshot clothes, accessories, makeup, and moderately priced, cutting-edge fashions. While on this side of the store, you can visit the cafe.

See map p. 248. 400 Oxford St., W1. ☎ 020/7629-1234. Tube: Bond Street or Marble Arch. Open: Mon–Wed 10 a.m.–7 p.m., Thurs–Fri 10 a.m.–8 p.m., Sat 9:30 a.m.–7 p.m., and Sun 11:30 a.m.–6 p.m.

Finding a drugstore

The English refer to a drugstore as a *chemist's shop*. All over London, you can find **Boots the Chemist** stores. In terms of size and convenience, the best one is just across from Harrods (at 72 Brompton Rd., SW3; ☎ 020/7589-6557; Tube: Knightsbridge). In addition to medicine, Boots sells film, pantyhose (called *tights*), sandwiches, and all of life's little necessities. The store is open Monday through Friday 8:30 a.m. to 7 p.m. and Saturday 9 a.m. to 7 p.m. One of the most centrally located chemists is **Bliss the Chemist** (5 Marble Arch, W1; ☎ 020/7723-6116; Tube: Marble Arch), open daily 9 a.m. to midnight. **Zafash Pharmacy** (233–235 Old Brompton Rd., SW5 ☎ 020/7373-2798; Tube: Earl's Court) is London's only 24-hour pharmacy.

Shopping the Street Markets

Markets make for fun shopping because you never know what you may find. Adventurous shoppers who like to browse and dawdle can really enjoy themselves at the places listed in this section.

Chelsea and Antiquarius

In a rambling old building, the **Chelsea Antiques Market** (253 King's Rd., SW3; ☎ 020/7352-5686; Tube: Sloane Square; see the map on p. 246) offers endless bric-a-brac browsing possibilities. You can search out old or rare books at this market. You'll probably run across Staffordshire dogs, shaving mugs, Edwardian buckles and clasps, ivory-handled razors, old velours, lace gowns, and wooden tea caddies; and that's just the beginning. The market is closed on Sunday.

Another good market is **Antiquarius** (131–141 King's Rd., SW3; ☎ 020/7351-5353; Tube: Sloane Square; see the map on p. 246), where more than 120 dealers offer specialized merchandise — usually of the small, domestic variety, such as antique and period jewelry, porcelain, silver, first-edition books, boxes, clocks, prints, and paintings. The shops and booths are generally open Monday through Saturday from 10 a.m. to 6 p.m.

Covent Garden

The **Covent Garden Market** (☎ 020/7836-9136; Tube: Covent Garden; see the map on p. 248) includes retail stores and two different markets (the kind with open-air stalls), open daily 9 a.m. to 5 p.m. Traders sell all kinds of goods at the busy **Apple Market.** Much of the merchandise is what the English call *collectible nostalgia,* which includes glassware and ceramics, leather goods, toys, clothes, hats, and jewelry. Antiques dealers predominate on Mondays. You can find **Jubilee Market** (☎ 020/7836-2139), a bit more downscale market where you can find cheap clothes and books, at the backside of Covent Garden. You can find some of London's best shopping at the restored hall on The Piazza and at specialty shops in the area.

Portobello Road

Kensington Church Street dead-ends at the Notting Hill Gate Tube station, which is the jumping-off point for **Portobello Market** (no phone; Tube: Notting Hill Gate), the famous London street market along Portobello Road. Portobello (market and road) is a magnet for collectors of virtually anything from precious junk to precious antiques. The market is generally open Saturday 6 a.m. to 5 p.m. You may find that perfect Regency commode that you've always wanted or a piece of Art Deco jewelry. But mixed in with the good stuff is an abundance of overpriced junk. Now that everything's been discovered and designated *collectible,* the prices are often too high.

The Portobello Market on a busy Saturday is prime pickpocketing territory. Keep an eye or a hand on your wallet or purse.

If you want to check out the shops along Portobello Road, you may want to visit during the week. Approximately 90 antiques and art shops are open here during the week when the street market is closed. Weekdays are a better time for serious collectors to shop, because they get more attention from dealers and aren't distracted by the throngs of shoppers.

Discovering the Best Shopping Neighborhoods

London's two major shopping areas are Knightsbridge and the West End. You can find some of London's most famous and most impressive stores along several key streets in these two areas. You also can find all the department stores listed in the "Checking Out the Big Names" section, earlier in this chapter.

Knightsbridge: Home of Harrods

The home of department stores Harrods and Harvey Nichols, Knightsbridge is the second-most-famous of London's retail districts. (See the map "Shopping in Knightsbridge and Chelsea" on p. 246.)

Brompton Road (home to Harrods) runs southwest from the Knightsbridge Tube stop. Beauchamp Place (pronounced *Beech*-um), one of the streets running south from Brompton Road, is only 1 block long, but it's full of the kinds of trendy, upscale shops where young British aristocrats buy their clothing for "the season." In the 1980s, the future Princess Diana and other young bluebloods and yuppies were dubbed "the Sloane Rangers" because this area near Sloane Square was their favorite shopping grounds (and Range Rovers were their favorite cars). Cheval Place, running parallel to Brompton Road to the north, is lined with designer resale shops. Sloane Street, where you can find plenty of fashion boutiques, runs south from the Knightsbridge Tube stop to Sloane Square and the beginning of Chelsea.

The **Map House of London** (54 Beauchamp Place, SW3; ☎ 020/7589-4325; Tube: Knightsbridge) is an ideal place to find a sophisticated souvenir, maybe an antique map, an engraving, or an old print of London; a century-old original engraving can cost as little as £15 ($28).

Chelsea: The young and the antique

Chelsea is famous for King's Road (Tube: Sloane Square). This is the area's main street and, along with Carnaby Street, is branded in Londoner's minds (those over 40, that is) as the street of the Swinging Sixties. It's still swinging today, especially on a Saturday, when you can hardly find room to walk. About one-third of King's Road is devoted to antiques markets and *multi-stores* (large or small groups of indoor stands, stalls, and booths within one enclosure); another third houses design trade showrooms and stores of household wares; and the remaining third remains faithful to the area's teenybopper roots. King's Road begins on the west side of the Sloane Square Tube stop.

Shopping in Knightsbridge and Chelsea

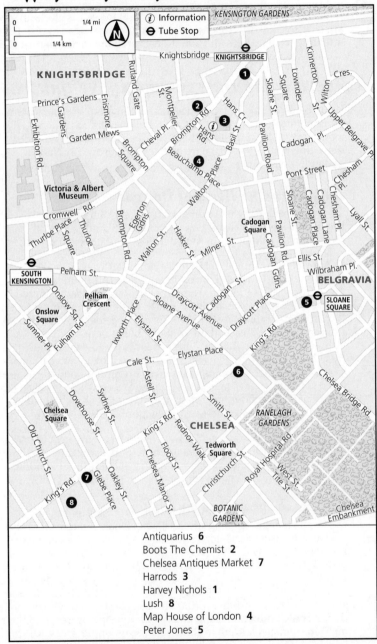

Antiquarius **6**
Boots The Chemist **2**
Chelsea Antiques Market **7**
Harrods **3**
Harvey Nichols **1**
Lush **8**
Map House of London **4**
Peter Jones **5**

A Chelsea emporium founded in 1877, **Peter Jones** (Sloane Square, SW1; ☎ **020/7730-3434;** Tube: Sloane Square; see the map on p. 246) is known for household goods, household fabrics and trims, china, glass, soft furnishings, and linens. The linen department is one of the best in London. **Lush** (123 King's Rd., SW3; Tube: Sloane Square; see the map on p. 246) is an aromatherapy bath and body shop where handmade soaps are cut from blocks, like cheese, and potential gifts include fizzing bath bombs. The other branches are in Covent Garden, Oxford Street, Kensington High Street, and Carnaby Street. You may also want to check out the **Chelsea Antiques Market** and **Antiquarius.** (See the section "Shopping the Street Markets," earlier in this chapter.)

Kensington: Street chic

You can reach Kensington, west of Knightsbridge, by taking the Tube to High Street Kensington, the area's preeminent shopping street. Many of this neighborhood's retail shops cater to street-chic teens. Several chain stores are here as well.

Kensington Church Street, running north to Notting Hill, is one of the city's main shopping avenues for antiques, selling everything from antique furniture to Impressionist paintings.

The **Children's Book Centre** (237 Kensington High St., W8; ☎ **020/7937-7497;** Tube: High Street Kensington) is the best place in London to go for children's books. Fiction is arranged according to age, up to 16. The center also sells videos and toys for kids.

Holborn: Heigh-ho, Silver!

Don't let the slightly out-of-the-way Holborn location, or the facade's lack of charm, put you off visiting the **London Silver Vaults** (Chancery House, 53–63 Chancery Lane, WC2; ☎ **020/7242-3248;** Tube: Chancery Lane; see the map on p. 248). Downstairs are the real vaults — 40 in all — filled with a staggering collection of old and new silver and silver plate, plus a collection of jewelry.

The West End: More famous shopping streets and stores

See the "Shopping in the West End" map on p. 248 for locations of the West End stores that I describe in the following sections. The key shopping areas in the West End are

- ✔ **Oxford Street** for affordable shopping

- ✔ **Regent Street** for fancier shops and more upscale department stores and specialty dealers

- ✔ **Piccadilly** for older, established department stores

- ✔ **Jermyn Street** for traditional English luxury goods

Shopping in the West End

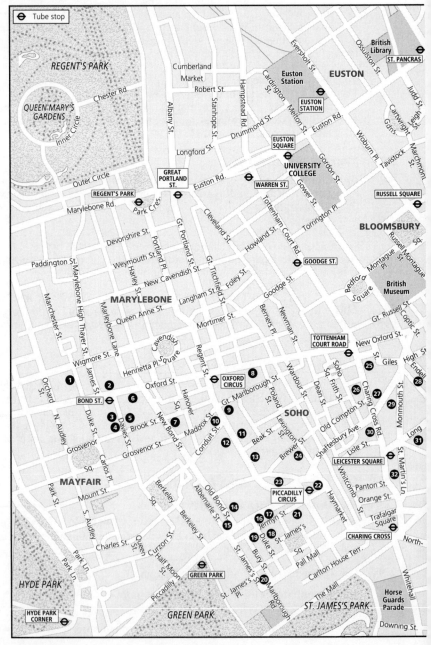

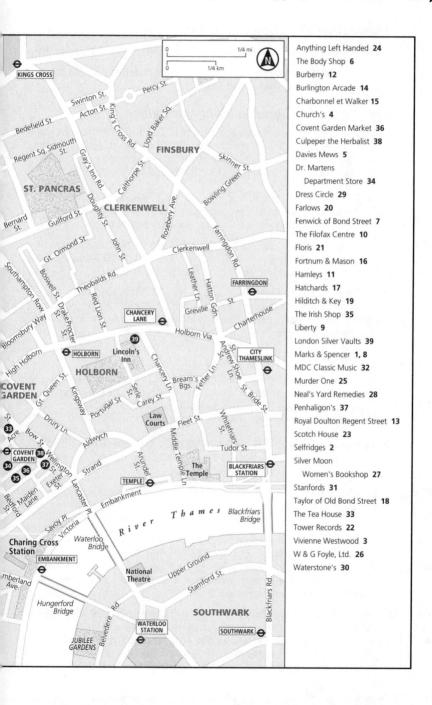

Anything Left Handed **24**
The Body Shop **6**
Burberry **12**
Burlington Arcade **14**
Charbonnel et Walker **15**
Church's **4**
Covent Garden Market **36**
Culpeper the Herbalist **38**
Davies Mews **5**
Dr. Martens
    Department Store **34**
Dress Circle **29**
Farlows **20**
Fenwick of Bond Street **7**
The Filofax Centre **10**
Floris **21**
Fortnum & Mason **16**
Hamleys **11**
Hatchards **17**
Hilditch & Key **19**
The Irish Shop **35**
Liberty **9**
London Silver Vaults **39**
Marks & Spencer **1, 8**
MDC Classic Music **32**
Murder One **25**
Neal's Yard Remedies **28**
Penhaligon's **37**
Royal Doulton Regent Street **13**
Scotch House **23**
Selfridges **2**
Silver Moon
    Women's Bookshop **27**
Stanfords **31**
Taylor of Old Bond Street **18**
The Tea House **33**
Tower Records **22**
Vivienne Westwood **3**
W & G Foyle, Ltd. **26**
Waterstone's **30**

✔ **Bond Street** for chic, upscale fashion boutiques

✔ **Covent Garden** for all-purpose shopping, often with a hipper edge

✔ **St. Martin's Court** (between Charing Cross Road and St. Martin's Lane) for prints, posters, and books

Around Piccadilly Circus: A bit of everything

Many consider Piccadilly Circus the center of London. For the best shopping in this area, head south from the Piccadilly Tube stop along Piccadilly (the street) or northwest along Regent Street. The following list gives you some of the most renowned stores around Piccadilly Circus:

✔ **Burberry** (18–22 Haymarket, SW1; ☎ **020/7930-3343**; Tube: Piccadilly Circus) sells those famous raincoats, plus top-quality men's shirts, sportswear, knitwear, and accessories.

✔ **Hatchards** (187 Piccadilly, W1; ☎ **020/7439-9921**; Tube: Piccadilly Circus; see the map on p. 248) was established in 1797 and is London's most historic and atmospheric bookstore.

✔ **Tower Records** (1 Piccadilly Circus, W1; ☎ **020/7439-2500**; Tube: Piccadilly Circus; see the map on p. 248) is one of the largest tape and CD stores in Europe. This store is practically a tourist attraction in its own right.

Jermyn Street: Traditional luxury

Two-block-long Jermyn Street lies a block south of Piccadilly between St. James's Street and Duke Street. Many of the posh men's haberdashers and toiletry shops along this street have been doing business for centuries and cater to the Royals. They include the following shops:

✔ **Farlows** (5 Pall Mall, SW1; ☎ **020/7839-2423**; Tube: Piccadilly Circus; see the map on p. 248) is famous for fishing and shooting equipment and classic country clothing.

✔ **Floris** (89 Jermyn St., SW1; ☎ **020/7930-2885**; Tube: Piccadilly Circus; see the map on p. 248) is a small mahogany-clad store that's been selling its own line of soaps and perfumes since 1851.

✔ **Hilditch & Key** (73 Jermyn St., SW1; ☎ **020/7930-5336**; Tube: Piccadilly Circus; see the map on p. 248) has been selling perhaps the finest men's shirts in the world for more than a century. These quality goods are 100-percent cotton, cut by hand, and sport buttons fashioned from real shell.

✔ **Taylor of Old Bond Street** (74 Jermyn St., SW1; ☎ **020/7930-5544**; Tube: Piccadilly Circus; see the map on p. 248) was established in 1954 and is devoted to the shaving and personal hygiene needs of men. The store offers the world's finest collection of shaving brushes, razors, and combs, plus soaps and hair lotions.

Regent Street: Upscale specialties

Regent Street begins in a grand sweeping curve on the west side of Piccadilly Circus and heads north to intersect with Oxford Street. This majestic thoroughfare is lined with upscale department stores and specialty boutiques. The **Burlington Arcade** is a must-see if you're in this area. This famous glass-roofed Regency passage, running from Piccadilly to Burlington Gardens, is lit by wrought-iron lamps and decorated with clusters of ferns and flowers. The arcade is lined with intriguing shops and boutiques. (See the "Shopping in the West End" map on p. 248 for locations of all the stores that I describe in this section.)

Savile Row, synonymous with hand-tailored men's suits, lies a block west of Regent Street. Its once-countercultural counterpart — in the early Beatles years — is **Carnaby Street,** now making a comeback after years as a depressing street of souvenir shops; Carnaby Street is a block east of Regent Street. **Royal Doulton Regent Street** (154 Regent St., W1; ☎ 020/7734-3184; Tube: Piccadilly Circus or Oxford Circus) carries English bone china, including Minton, Royal Crown Derby, and Royal Doulton. (The Jan and July sales are excellent.) **Scotch House** (84–86 Regent St., W1; ☎ 020/7734-0203; Tube: Piccadilly Circus) is known globally for its selection of cashmere and wool knitwear for men, women, and children; the store also sells tartan garments and accessories, as well as Scottish tweed classics.

If you're left-handed, you're in luck at **Anything Left Handed** (57 Brewer St., off Regent Street, W1; ☎ 020/7437-3910; Tube: Piccadilly Circus). This unique store sells practical items — everything from scissors to corkscrews — for the southpaws in the world.

Hamleys (188–196 Regent St., W1; ☎ 020/7494-2000; Tube: Piccadilly Circus), the finest toy shop in the world, stocks more than 35,000 toys and games on seven floors of fun and magic. You can get everything, from cuddly stuffed animals and dolls to radio-controlled cars, train sets, model kits, board games, outdoor toys, and computer games.

Oxford Street: Affordable big names

You may want to begin your shopping adventure at Oxford Street, getting out at the Oxford Circus, Bond Street, or Tottenham Court Road Tube stop. Oxford Street is more affordable than Regent Street (which you can read about in the preceding section) — not as grand, but offering a good variety and quantity of stylish merchandise. (See the "Shopping in the West End" map on p. 248 for the locations of all the stores that I describe in this section.)

If you're a chronic organizer who can't live without your Filofax, head immediately for **The Filofax Centre** (21 Conduit St., W1; ☎ 020/7499-0457; Tube: Oxford Circus). At this store on Conduit Street, which leads west from Regency Street, you can find the entire range of inserts and books at prices that are about half of what they are in the States. **The Body Shop** stores are based in the United Kingdom but are now all over the States;

however, prices at the London branches are much lower. You can stock up on their politically and environmentally correct beauty, bath, and aromatherapy products (375 Oxford St., W1; ☎ 020/7409-7868; Tube: Bond Street). You can find other branches in every shopping zone in London.

Bond Street: Designer chic

Bond Street, running parallel to Regent Street on the west and connecting Piccadilly with Oxford Street, is home to all the hot international designers and is London's answer to New York's Fifth Avenue. Bond Street is divided into New (northern section) and Old (southern section). Very expensive fashion boutiques line Bond Street and the adjacent streets. **Davies Street,** running south from outside the Bond Street Tube station, is just one of the area's choicer streets; **Davies Mews** is an upscale shopping zone noted for its antiques dealers. You can access the area from the north by the Bond Street Tube stop and from the south by Green Park. (See the "Shopping in the West End" map on p. 248 for the locations of the stores that I describe in this section.)

Vivienne Westwood (6 Davies St., W1; ☎ 020/7629-3757; Tube: Bond Street) is one of the hottest British designers for women. This flagship store carries a full range of jackets, skirts, trousers, blouses, dresses, and evening dresses. **Church's** (133 New Bond St., W1; ☎ 020/7493-1474; Tube: Bond Street) sells classy shoes easily recognized by the fashion elite. Chocolate connoisseurs should visit **Charbonnel et Walker** (1 The Royal Arcade, 28 Old Bond St., W1; ☎ 020/7491-0939; Tube: Green Park), famous for its hot chocolate (buy it by the tin) and strawberries-and-cream chocolates.

Around Leicester Square: Music and memorabilia

Leicester Square itself boasts only giant movie palaces and touristy restaurants (and a reduced-price ticket booth). But the streets around Leicester Square are filled with shops selling rare books, prints, and posters, some relating to the performing arts. (See the "Shopping in the West End" map on p. 248 for the locations of the stores that I describe in this section.)

The Leicester Square shops include the following:

- ✔ **Dress Circle** (57–59 Monmouth St., WC2; ☎ 020/7240-2227; Tube: Leicester Square) specializes in show-business memorabilia for all West End and Broadway shows.

- ✔ **MDC Classic Music** (31–32 St. Martin's Lane, WC2; ☎ 020/7240-0270; Tube: Leicester Square), sitting right next to the English National Opera, specializes in opera recordings; you receive expert knowledge and personal service from the staff.

- ✔ **Stanfords** (12–14 Long Acre, WC2; ☎ 020/7836-1321; Tube: Leicester Square) was established in 1852, and is the world's largest map shop (many of its maps, which include worldwide touring and survey maps, are unavailable elsewhere). Stanfords is also London's best travel bookstore.

Charing Cross Road: A book lover's delight

Charing Cross Road is a book lover's paradise because of its vast number of bookstores, selling both new and old volumes. Many of these places sell maps and guides, too, including the tourist's necessity, *London A to Z.* **Remember:** There is no added 17.5 percent VAT charge on books. Some of the most fascinating bookstores include the following (for locations, see the "Shopping in the West End" map on p. 248):

- **Murder One** (71–73 Charing Cross Rd., WC2; ☎ 020/7734-3483; Tube: Leicester Square) specializes in crime, romance, science-fiction, and horror books. Crime and science-fiction magazines, some obscure, are also available.

- **Silver Moon Women's Bookshop** (64–68 Charing Cross Rd.; ☎ 020/7836-7906; Tube: Tottenham Court Road) stocks thousands of titles by and about women, including a large selection of lesbian-related books. Plus the shop offers videos and jewelry.

- **W & G Foyle, Ltd.** (113–119 Charing Cross Rd., WC2; ☎ 020/7440-3225; Tube: Tottenham Court Road) claims to be the world's largest bookstore, with an impressive array of hardcovers and paperbacks, as well as travel maps, records, videotapes, and sheet music.

- **Waterstone's** (121 Charing Cross Rd.; ☎ 020/7434-4291; Tube: Tottenham Court Road) is a U.K. chain with branches all over London. You can find the latest releases and well-stocked sections of books currently in print.

Covent Garden: Something for everyone

Try to save some of your shopping energy for Covent Garden, home of what may be the most famous "market" in all of England: the **Covent Garden Market.** (See the section "Shopping the Street Markets," earlier in this chapter.)

Excellent English soaps, toiletries, and aromatherapy goods, as well as herbal goods, are available throughout the market and surrounding streets, including at the following shops (for locations, see the "Shopping in the West End" map on p. 248):

- **Culpeper the Herbalist** (8 The Market, Covent Garden, WC2; ☎ 020/7379-6698; Tube: Covent Garden) sells food, bath, and aromatherapy products, as well as dream pillows, candles, sachets, and that popular favorite: the battery-operated aromatherapy fan.

- **Neal's Yard Remedies** (15 Neal's Yard, off Shorts Garden, WC2; ☎ 020/7379-7222; Tube: Covent Garden) is noted the world over for its all-natural, herbal-based bath, beauty, and aromatherapy products in cobalt-blue bottles.

✔ **Penhaligon's** (41 Wellington St., WC2; ☎ 020/7836-2150; Tube: Covent Garden) is an exclusive-line Victorian perfumery dedicated to good grooming. Choose from a large selection of perfumes, after-shaves, soaps, candles, and bath oils for women and men.

Also in Covent Garden, you can find **Dr. Martens Department Store** (1–4 King St., WC2; ☎ 020/7497-1460; Tube: Covent Garden), the flagship for internationally famous "Doc Marts" shoes. Prices are far better here than they are in the States.

Farther along, at 14 King St., is **The Irish Shop** (☎ 020/7379-3625; Tube: Covent Garden), which sells a wide variety of articles shipped directly from Ireland, including colorful knitwear, traditional Irish linens, hand-knitted Aran fisherman's sweaters, and Celtic jewelry.

And you can finish off at **The Tea House** (15A Neal St., WC2; ☎ 020/7240-7539; Tube: Covent Garden), which sells everything associated with tea, tea drinking, and teatime.

Index of Stores by Merchandise

Antiques
Antiquarius (Chelsea)
Chelsea Antiques Market (Chelsea)
Map House of London (Knightsbridge)

Bath and hygiene products
The Body Shop (Mayfair)
Culpeper the Herbalist (Covent Garden)
Floris (St. James's)
Lush (Chelsea)
Neal's Yard Remedies (Covent Garden)
Penhaligon's (Covent Garden)
Taylor of Old Bond Street (St. James's)

Books and maps
Children's Book Centre (Kensington)
Hatchards (St. James's)
Murder One (Soho)
Silver Moon Women's Bookshop (Soho)
Stanfords (Covent Garden)
W & G Foyle, Ltd. (Soho)
Waterstone's (Soho)

Candy
Charbonnel et Walker (Mayfair)

Clothing
Burberry (St. James's)
Hilditch & Key (St. James's)
Scotch House (St. James's)
Vivienne Westwood (Mayfair)

Department stores
Fenwick of Bond Street (Mayfair)
Fortnum & Mason (St. James's)
Harrods (Knightsbridge)
Harvey Nichols (Knightsbridge)
Liberty (Mayfair)
Marks & Spencer (Mayfair)
Selfridges (Mayfair)

Drug stores (chemists)
Bliss the Chemist (Bayswater)
Boots the Chemist (Knightsbridge)
Zafash Pharmacy (South Kensington)

Housewares and china

Peter Jones (Chelsea)
Royal Doulton Regent Street (St. James's)

Markets

Antiquarius (Chelsea)
Chelsea Antiques Market (Chelsea)
Covent Garden Market (Covent Garden)
Portobello Market (Notting Hill)

Miscellaneous

Anything Left Handed (Soho)
Dress Circle (Soho)
The Filofax Centre (Covent Garden)
The Irish Shop (Covent Garden)
The Tea House (Covent Garden)

Music

MDC Classic Music (Covent Garden)
Tower Records (St. James's)

Shoes

Church's (Bond Street)
Dr. Martens Department Store (Covent Garden)

Silver

London Silver Vaults (Holborn)

Sporting goods

Farlows (St. James's)

Toys

Hamleys (St. James's)

Chapter 13

Following an Itinerary: Four Great Options

In This Chapter

▶ Seeing London on a reasonable schedule
▶ Planning fun itineraries for trips lasting three to seven days
▶ Visiting London with kids

*E*very London visitor has to face one problem: how to see as much as possible in a limited amount of time. You're lucky if you have an entire week or even more. But what if you have only three or five days at your disposal? What if you're bringing the family along? These questions are what this chapter is all about. If you budget your time wisely and choose your sights carefully, you can make the most of a limited schedule or a trip with the kids.

This chapter offers four easy-to-do suggested daily itineraries. The first itinerary covers the big sights. The next two are a little more adventurous. The itinerary for families first addresses the top spots and then heads to family-friendly destinations just outside the city.

The itineraries are common-sense, limited-time suggestions only. You may want to spend your days doing something else entirely. Maybe you'd really rather spend an entire day, rather than just a couple of hours, in the British Museum. Maybe shopping in Chelsea and cafe hopping in Soho is more appealing to you than watching the Changing of the Guard at Buckingham Palace. Go for it! London can be enjoyed in countless ways that have nothing to do with traditional sightseeing.

For complete descriptions of the sights, plus exact street addresses, open hours, and admission prices, see Chapter 11, unless I give you a different chapter to check out.

London in Three Days

Three days doesn't seem like a very long time. But in that short period, you can hit most of the key sights in London and enjoy a memorable trip.

Start **Day One** with a visit to majestic **Westminster Abbey,** visiting the Royal Tombs and Poets' Corner. Afterward, because they're right next door, stroll around the **Houses of Parliament.** Unless you queue up to hear a debate or take one of the guided tours, available from August through September (see Chapter 11 for details), you won't be able to get inside, but you can enjoy a great riverside view from Westminster Bridge. On the opposite side of the Thames is the **British Airways London Eye,** a 450-foot-high observation wheel. Reserve in advance for the trip up and over London; otherwise, you may spend at least a half-hour in line for a ticket and another hour before your scheduled "flight." You're not far from **Tate Britain,** so if you're in the mood to look at great English art, head over to Pimlico. Renting a self-guided audio tour will add to your enjoyment. Later in the afternoon, explore **Piccadilly Circus,** the teeming epicenter of London's West End. You find great shopping on Regent Street, Piccadilly, and Jermyn Street (see Chapter 12 for shopping). If you haven't already reserved a seat for a **West End show,** you may want to stop by the half-price ticket booth in **Leicester Square** to see what's available (see Chapter 15 for info on theaters). Have dinner in Soho before the show (see Chapter 10 for restaurants).

Greet **Day Two** with a walk through **Green Park.** You're on your way to **Buckingham Palace** to witness the pageantry of the **Changing of the Guard** (check beforehand to make sure that it's taking place that day). For details on touring the State Rooms of Buckingham Palace during August and September, see Chapter 11. Reserve tickets in advance, so you know your specific entry time; otherwise, you may have to wait in line for an hour or more to get in. If you're not touring the palace itself, visit the **Royal Mews.** From Buckingham Palace, you can stroll down the Mall, through **St. James's Park,** passing **Clarence House,** where the Queen Mother lived until her death in 2002, and **St. James's Palace,** once the London home of Prince Charles and his two sons, William and Harry.

Trafalgar Square, London's grandest and certainly most famous plaza, is your next stop. You can have lunch or tea at the **National Gallery's restaurant** or at **Café-in-the-Crypt** in St. Martin-in-the-Fields church on the east side of the square (see Chapter 10 for more on these restaurants). Spend your afternoon viewing the treasures of the **National Gallery.** Renting one of the self-guided audio tours will help you to home in on the most important paintings in the collection. After dinner in the Covent Garden area or on the Thames (see Chapter 11 for cruises), head to one of the bars, pubs, or clubs that I describe in Chapter 16.

On **Day Three,** arrive as early as you can at the **Tower of London** and immediately join one of the one-hour guided tours led by the Beefeaters. Later, you can explore the precincts on your own, making certain you allot enough time to see the **Crown Jewels.** From the Tower, head over to nearby **St. Paul's Cathedral,** which you can see in about a half-hour.

The **British Museum,** your next stop, has enough to keep you occupied for several days; if you want to see only the highlights, allow yourself a minimum of two hours. Finish off your afternoon in Knightsbridge at

Harrods (see Chapter 12), the most famous department store in London, and perhaps the world. Knightsbridge and adjacent South Kensington offer innumerable dining options (see Chapter 10).

London in Five Days

This section assumes that you've already followed the suggested itineraries (see the preceding section) for your first three days.

Day Four begins at the **National Portrait Gallery,** where you can find the likeness of just about every famous British person you've ever heard of. Renting one of the self-guided audio tours is a good idea. From the portrait gallery, you can easily walk to **Covent Garden Market** (see Chapter 12). Scores of interesting shops are in and around the market, and **Covent Garden Piazza,** a lively hub filled with restaurants, makes a perfect spot for lunch. Spend your afternoon strolling in **Kensington Gardens** and visiting **Kensington Palace,** once the London home of Princess Diana. Then go for a traditional English dinner at **Rules,** London's oldest restaurant, or **Simpson's-in-the-Strand** (see Chapter 10). Are you up for a play or a concert tonight? If so, check your theater options in Chapter 15.

Day Five begins with a morning at the museum of your choice. Choosing among the three major South Kensington museums — the **Natural History Museum,** the **Science Museum,** and the **Victoria & Albert Museum** — is entirely a matter of taste. If you like modern art, the new **Tate Modern** on the South Bank is the place to spend your morning. (See Chapter 11 for descriptions of all the museums.) In the afternoon, expand your horizon with a short trip outside the city. Chapter 11 offers descriptions of the **Royal Botanic Gardens** at Kew, **Hampton Court, Windsor Palace, Hampstead Heath,** and **Greenwich.** None of these places is terribly far away; the trips to reach them take anywhere from 20 minutes to an hour. You can be back in London in time for dinner.

London in Seven Days

How time flies! By now, if you follow the suggested itineraries for the last five days (see the preceding two sections), you've seen most of the major sights in London.

On **Day Six,** you're ready for a day trip. Riding in one of Britain's sleek new trains is terrific fun. The only problem is that you have to decide where you want to go. In Chapter 14, I give you the lowdown on five places, each remarkable in its own way. Do you want to see Shakespeare's birthplace in **Stratford-upon-Avon** or the famous prehistoric stone circle called **Stonehenge?** Do you want to spend a day by the seaside in **Brighton** or strolling around ancient **Canterbury** with its mighty cathedral? Or perhaps head to **Bath** to discover its splendid Georgian crescents. You can reach most of these places in 90 minutes or less.

Day Seven is your last day in London, and you'll want it to be special. In the morning, visit **Madame Tussaud's** wax museum or one of the museums that you haven't yet seen. Afterward, stroll through **Hyde Park** and stop at **Apsley House,** the London home of the first Duke of Wellington. This house gives you a glimpse of what life was like inside one of London's great private palaces. If it's Sunday, you may instead want to visit **Spencer House,** the family home of the late Princess Diana. (See Chapter 11 for descriptions of all these attractions.) You can also do some last-minute shopping, if you prefer. Check out London's various shopping neighborhoods in Chapter 12, and then make your way to the major shopping arteries: Knightsbridge, Oxford Street, Bond Street, King's Road in Chelsea, or Regent Street. A traditional afternoon tea at one of London's great hotels (see Chapter 10) makes a delightful end to the afternoon. After that? You've booked theater tickets, haven't you?

London with Kids

So you want to spend five days in London and bring along your kids? No problem. I have a few suggestions to keep you *and* your kids excited and entertained. (For tips on traveling with kids, see Chapter 6.)

Don't schedule too much on **Day One.** Exercise helps ward off jet lag. After sitting in a plane for several hours, the best option may be to take smaller children to one of London's great parks, so they can run and let off steam. Depending on where your hotel is located, your destination may be **Hyde Park, Kensington Gardens, Green Park, St. James's Park,** or **Regent's Park.** If you're traveling with teens, you may want to introduce them to the city by taking a stroll through London's four royal parks, following the **Princess Diana Commemorative Walk.** (All these possibilities are described in Chapter 11.)

You can begin more focused sightseeing on **Day Two.** Consider a guided bus tour that helps orient everyone and gives you at least a glimpse of all the major sights (see Chapter 11). Several outfits provide tours on double-decker buses — always a treat for kids — and one outfit offers a wonderful road and river trip on amphibious vehicles. After the tour, make the **British Airways London Eye** your first stop. Reserve your ticket beforehand to avoid waiting in a long line. Afterward, cross Westminster Bridge and stroll over to view the **Houses of Parliament** and **Big Ben** (if you're lucky, the clock will strike the hour while you're in the vicinity). And because it's close at hand, use this opportunity to visit **Westminster Abbey.** Younger children may not get much out of the place, but you will. Later in the afternoon, take a boat ride down the Thames to the **Tower of London;** you can board the boat at Westminster Pier near the Houses of Parliament. When you're inside the Tower, hook up with one of the Beefeater tours. (All the attractions suggested here are described in Chapter 11.) If you're with a kid ages 10 to 17, you may want to have dinner at the **Hard Rock Café** in Mayfair (see Chapter 10).

Organizing your time

You can make the most of your visit to London if you organize your days efficiently and with common sense. Disorganized travelers waste a lot of time, show up at the museum on the day it's closed, and end up in the nether regions of Tooting Bec because they hopped on the wrong Underground line. Don't assume that every museum or site is open every day, all day. Take a moment to look at the details that I provide for each attraction in Chapter 11. And carry a copy of *London A to Z*.

An average top sight takes about two hours to visit, after you're actually inside. Some (Buckingham Palace and the Royal Mews) take more; others (Westminster Abbey and St. Paul's) take less. But other variables enter in: whether you're taking a guided tour (usually about an hour to an hour and a half, no matter where), whether you have kids in tow, or whether lines move slowly due to the crowds of visitors. Predicting how much time you'll spend at a major attraction, such as the British Museum and the National Gallery, is difficult. But as a general rule, you can do about three or four sights in a day if you're pushing yourself, fewer if you're not.

Many of London's major sights are concentrated in specific areas, so walking is the best way to see several sights in a short period of time. To cover larger areas, I recommend that you take the fast and convenient Underground.

Try to hit the very top sights on your list early in the day, preferably when they open, or late in the afternoon. Visit the places that are really important to you when you're feeling fresh and when they're less crowded. I mean, in particular, Buckingham Palace (when it's open to the public during Aug and Sept), the Tower of London, Westminster Abbey, and Madame Tussaud's. Westminster Abbey, to cite just one example, can receive upwards of 15,000 visitors per day!

Unless you have adrenaline to spare, try to unwind a little before you begin your round of after-dark diversions. You may need some downtime between the end of your sightseeing day and the beginning of your evening activities. I suggest that you head back to your hotel to take a shower or bath, to curl up with a novel or the evening paper for an hour, or maybe to catch a quick snooze to recharge your batteries. Then it's back to those perennially fascinating London streets.

Begin **Day Three** at the **Natural History Museum** in South Kensington, where the dinosaur exhibit with a ferocious animatronic T. Rex captures the imaginations of both young and old(er). If your child's a budding Einstein, the **Science Museum** with its many hands-on, interactive exhibits may be a better choice. Afterward, if you have small children in tow, stroll over to **Kensington Gardens** for a look at the famous statue of Peter Pan. The new **Princess Diana Memorial Playground** in the northwest corner of Kensington Gardens enchants little ones. You can have lunch in **The Orangery** of adjacent Kensington Palace (see Chapter 11) or make your way to **Café-in-the-Crypt** (see Chapter 10) in St. Martin-in-the-Fields church in Trafalgar Square; you find a brass-rubbing center in the church, too. If you're with a teen, you may want to spend the morning or afternoon in **Madame Tussaud's wax museum** or the **London Dungeon;** just keep in mind that young children may find some of the gorier exhibits frightening. In the evening, older kids and teens may also enjoy one of the West End's razzmatazz musicals. If dinner and a play for just the grown-ups sounds good, you can get a babysitter for the little ones (see the Quick Concierge, at the end of this book, for a reputable service).

Make **Day Four** a day trip to **Brighton** on the Sussex coast (see Chapter 14). The quick trip takes less than an hour. After you arrive, you can visit the **Royal Pavilion** and take the kids over to **Palace Pier,** a spot filled with games and souvenir stands. If the weather's warm, you can rent a deck chair and sit on the beach. Brighton is a fun place just to stroll around, with plenty to keep you and the family entertained.

On **Day Five,** head out to **Hampton Court Palace,** another quick train ride of less than an hour (see Chapter 11). Hampton Court offers much to explore, so give yourself at least four hours. Small children may not get much out of the visit, but they'll probably be intrigued by the staff wearing period costumes. You can eat on the premises. Save the best part for last: The famous maze in the gardens brings out the kid in everyone. Finally, return to London for a good night's rest before flying out the next morning.

Chapter 14

Going Beyond London: Five Great Day Trips

● ●

In This Chapter

▶ Taking the best day trips from London

▶ Getting there and back

▶ Deciding what to see and do after you arrive

▶ Choosing where to eat and where to stay

● ●

*I*n comparison to the United States, England is a small country. You can visit countless places on one-day side trips from London.

In Chapter 11, I describe the easiest side trips from London: **Kew Gardens, Hampton Court Palace, Windsor Palace,** and **Greenwich.** In this chapter, I venture out to some of England's most popular, impressive, and famous places: Bath, Brighton, Canterbury, Stratford-upon-Avon, and Stonehenge. By train, you can get to all these sites in less than two hours from London (see the "Day Trips from London" map on p. 264).

By Train or by Car: Weighing the Options

Because of England's small size and easy-access train and road networks, this country is a joy to explore.

For all the trips in this chapter, you may want to take the train instead of renting and driving a car. From London, you can reach Bath, Brighton, and Canterbury in 90 minutes or less by train. The train trip to Stratford-upon-Avon or to Salisbury (the closest large town to Stonehenge) takes about two hours. At each of these places, the attractions are within walking distance of the train station. The one exception is Stonehenge, which you can reach by public bus from Salisbury. If you get an early start, you can explore any one of these places, have lunch, and still get back to London in time for dinner.

The following sections help you decide whether train travel or automotion is for you.

Day Trips from London

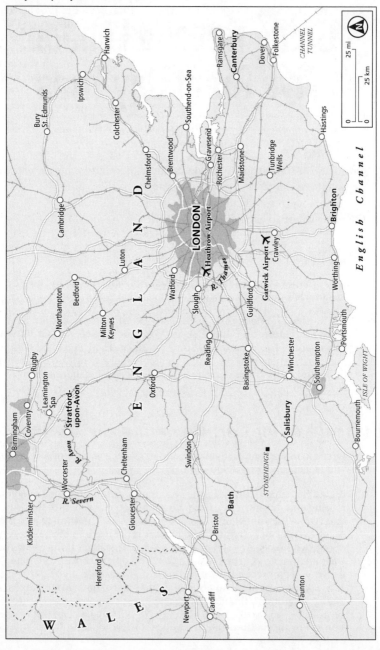

Taking the train

If you plan to travel around England by train, get a **BritRail pass** *before* you arrive (they're not available in the U.K.) from **RailEurope** (☎ **877/ 272-7245** in the U.S. or 800-361-7245 in Canada; www.raileurope.com). The **London Plus Pass** gets you to three of the towns in this chapter — Brighton, Canterbury, and Salisbury (plus Windsor, which you can read about in Chapter 11, but not to Bath or Stratford-upon-Avon). Trains offer first- and standard-class seating — first-class cars are less crowded, and the seats are roomier and more comfy. Because the train trips to the destinations in this chapter aren't very long, standard-class may be fine for most travelers. For 2 days of travel in an 8-day period, the pass costs $91 first class, $69 standard class; for 4 days in an 8-day period, it costs $169 first class, $129 standard class; and for 7 days of travel in a 15-day period, it costs $225 first class, $169 standard class. See RailEurope's Web site for more information on the London Plus and other BritRail passes.

Taking a car: Driving on the left, passing on the right

I always suggest that people visiting London travel by train instead of driving. Much of your car trip will be on motorways without much scenery, so what's the point? Then, when you arrive, you have to find parking (generally outside the historic city center); if you arrive by train, however, you can easily walk to the center of town from the train station (or take a cab if you have mobility issues). The historic towns of England aren't laid out like American cities or suburbs, where you need a car to get from point A to point B.

Before you even consider renting a car, ask yourself whether you're comfortable driving with a steering wheel on the right-hand side of the vehicle while shifting with your left hand (you can get an automatic, but it costs considerably more). *Remember:* You must drive on the left and pass on the right.

Although the car-rental market in Britain is highly competitive, renting a car here costs more than in the United States — unless you can find a special promotional offer from an airline or a car-rental agency. Most U.K. car-rental agencies accept U.S. driver's licenses. In most cases, you must be 23 years old (21 in some instances), no older than 70, and have had your U.S. license for more than a year.

You can often get a discount on car-rental rates if you reserve 48 hours in advance through the toll-free reservations offices. Weekly rentals are almost always less expensive than daily rates. And the rate, of course, depends on the size of the vehicle.

When you make your reservation, ask whether the quoted price includes the 17.5 percent VAT and unlimited mileage. Then find out whether personal accident insurance (PAI), collision-damage waiver (CDW), and any other insurance options are included. If they aren't a part of the deal, which they usually aren't, be sure to ask how much they cost. When you drive in any foreign country (or anywhere, for that matter), arrange for as much coverage as possible.

 Some credit-card companies offer the collision-damage waiver and other types of insurance for free if you use that card to pay for the rental. If you're planning to rent a car, check with your credit-card company to see what's covered, or you may end up paying for coverage you already have.

Bath: Hot Mineral Springs and Cool Georgian Magnificence

Bath, 115 miles west of London, is a beautiful spa town on the Avon River (see the "Bath" map on p. 267). Since the days of the ancient Celts — and later the Romans — Bath has been famous for its hot mineral springs. In 1702, Queen Anne frequented the soothing, sulfurous waters and transformed Bath into a spa for the elite. Aristocrats, socialites, social climbers, and flamboyant dandies, such as Beau Nash, have added to the spa's fashionable and fascinating history. The great author Jane Austen used Bath as an upwardly genteel setting for her class-conscious plots.

Today, the spa is a grand legacy from the Georgian era, boasting beautiful curving *crescents* (a row of houses built in a long curving line) and classically inspired buildings of honey-colored stone. Must-sees are the **Roman Baths Museum** and adjoining **Pump Room** (where visitors can continue the long tradition of sipping water while listening to music), the adjacent **Abbey,** and the **Assembly Rooms** (once used for balls and gaming).

Getting there

Trains for Bath leave from London's Paddington Station every hour; the trip takes about 90 minutes. The standard return (round-trip) fare costs £35 ($65). By car, take the M4 to Junction 18 and then drive a few miles south on A46.

Finding information and taking a tour

Bath's Tourist Information Centre (☎ 01225/477-761; www.visitbath.co.uk), located in the center of town on the square in front of Bath Abbey, is open Monday through Saturday 9:30 a.m. to 5 p.m. and Sunday 10 a.m. to 4 p.m. The Centre provides **free guided walks** that leave from outside the **Pump Room** Sunday through Friday at 10:30 a.m. and 2 p.m. and Saturday at 10:30 a.m. Additional walks are offered at 7 p.m. on Tuesday, Friday, and Saturday from May through September.

Bath

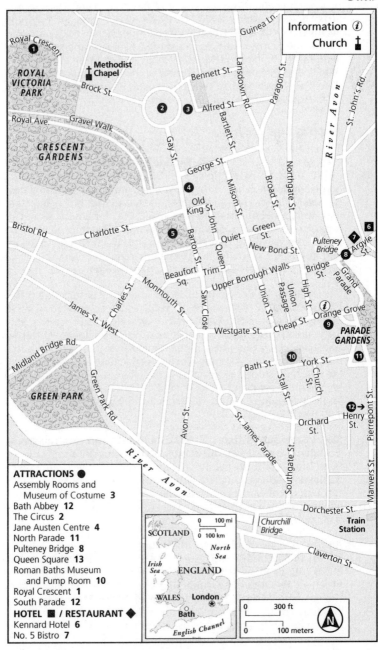

Information ⓘ
Church ✝

Guinea Ln.

Royal Crescent ❶

ROYAL VICTORIA PARK

✝ Methodist Chapel

Bennett St.

Lansdown Rd.

Paragon St.

River Avon

St. John's Rd.

Brock St.

❷ ❸ Alfred St.

Bartlett St.

Royal Ave.

Gravel Walk

Gay St.

CRESCENT GARDENS

George St.

Milsom St.

Northgate St.

Broad St.

Bristol Rd.

Charlotte St.

❹ Old King St.

John St.

Green St.

❻

Pulteney Bridge ❼

❺

Barton St.

Quiet

New Bond St.

Argyle St.

❽

Beaufort Sq.

Trim

Queen

Upper Borough Walls

Union Passage

Bridge St.

Grand Parade

Charles St.

Monmouth St.

Saw Close

High St.

James St. West

Union St.

ⓘ

Orange Grove ❾

PARADE GARDENS

Midland Bridge Rd.

Westgate St.

Cheap St.

Bath St. ❿

York St.

Church St.

⓫

Green Park Rd.

GREEN PARK

Stall St.

Avon St.

St. James Parade

⓬➜ Henry St.

Orchard St.

Pierrepont St.

Manvers St.

River Avon

Southgate St.

Dorchester St.

Train Station

Churchill Bridge

Claverton St.

ATTRACTIONS ●
Assembly Rooms and
    Museum of Costume **3**
Bath Abbey **12**
The Circus **2**
Jane Austen Centre **4**
North Parade **11**
Pulteney Bridge **8**
Queen Square **13**
Roman Baths Museum
    and Pump Room **10**
Royal Crescent **1**
South Parade **12**
HOTEL ■ / RESTAURANT ◆
Kennard Hotel **6**
No. 5 Bistro **7**

SCOTLAND
North Sea
Irish Sea
ENGLAND
WALES   London ✪
Bath
English Channel

0   100 mi
0   100 km

0   300 ft
0   100 meters

N

One-hour, open-top **bus tours** with live guides and plenty of commentary are presented by **City Tour** (☎ **07721/559-686**). The tour costs £6.50 ($12) for adults, £4.50 ($8.35) for seniors and students. **City Sightseeing** (☎ **01871/666-0000**) offers basically the same tour, but with audio commentary, at a cost of £9 ($17) for adults, £6.50 ($12) for seniors and students, and £4.50 ($8.35) for children. Tours for both companies depart from the bus station every 15 minutes in summer; otherwise, they leave hourly. Tickets are valid all day, and you can get off and on to explore places along the route.

Seeing the sights

The Romans — who arrived in A.D. 75 — built the huge bath-and-temple complex at the center of the **Roman Baths Museum** (☎ **01225/477-785**) beside Bath Abbey. When visitors enter, they receive a portable self-guided audio tour keyed to everything on display, including the original Roman baths and heating system; the audio tour is fun, informative, and very well done. Admission costs £9.50 ($18) for adults, with discounts for seniors, students, children, and families. The museum is open daily March through June, September, and October 9:30 a.m. to 5 p.m.; July and August 9 a.m. to 9 p.m.; January through February and November through December 9:30 a.m. to 4:30 p.m. (See map p. 267.)

Overlooking the Roman baths is the late-18th-century **Pump Room** (☎ **01225/477-7785**), where the fashionable assembled to sip the vile-tasting but reputedly health-promoting water. You're welcome to taste it for yourself (your ticket to the Roman Baths Museum entitles you to one free glass of mineral water in the Pump Room). Admission is free. In the Pump Room, you can enjoy *elevenses* (morning tea), lunch, or afternoon tea to a background of live music. Main courses cost £9 to £12 ($17–$22); afternoon tea goes for £7 to £9 ($13–$17). The Pump Room is open Monday through Saturday 9:30 a.m. to 4:40 p.m. and Sunday 10:30 a.m. to 4:30 p.m. (See map p. 267.)

Step inside **Bath Abbey** (☎ **01225/422-462**) and view the graceful fan vaulting, the great East Window, and the ironically simple memorial to Beau Nash, the most flamboyant of the dandies who frequented Bath in its heyday. Admission is by a suggested donation of £2.50 ($4.65). April through October, the abbey is open Monday through Saturday 9 a.m. to 6 p.m. (to 4:30 p.m. Nov–Mar); year-round, it's open Sunday 1 to 2:30 p.m. and 4:30 to 5:30 p.m. (See map p. 267.)

Another classic building worth visiting is the **Assembly Rooms** (Bennett Street; ☎ **01225/477-789**), the site of all the grand balls and social climbing in 18th-century Bath. Entrance is free unless you want to visit the excellent **Museum of Costume** that's part of the complex. Admission for the museum costs £6.25 ($12) adults; £5.25 ($9.70) seniors, students, and children 6 to 18. The museum is open daily 10 a.m. to 5 p.m.; the Assembly Rooms are open when not in use. (See map p. 267.)

Bath's newest attraction, the **Jane Austen Centre** (40 Gay St.; ☎ **01225/ 443-000**), is located in a Georgian townhouse on an elegant street where Austen once lived. Exhibits and a video convey a sense of what life in Bath was like during the Regency period; all in all, though, this museum is a bit of a bore to all but the most avid Austen fans. Admission costs £5.95 ($11). The center is open daily 10 a.m. to 5 p.m. (Sun from 10:30 a.m.). (See map p. 267.)

Bath is a wonderful walking town, filled with beautiful squares and sweeping residential crescents. Stroll along the **North Parade** and the **South Parade, Queen Square,** and **The Circus** and be sure to have a look at the **Royal Crescent,** a magnificent curving row of 30 townhouses designed in 1767 by John Wood the Younger. Regarded as the epitome of England's *Palladian style* (a classical style incorporating elements from ancient Greek and Roman buildings), the Royal Crescent is now designated a UNESCO World Heritage site. **No. 1 Royal Crescent** (☎ **01225/ 428-126**) is a gorgeously restored 18th-century house with period furnishings. Admission costs £4 ($7.40). The house is open mid-February through October, Tuesday through Sunday 10:30 a.m. to 5 p.m. (to 4 p.m. in Nov).

Pulteney Bridge, built in 1770, spans the River Avon a few blocks south of the Assembly Rooms. The bridge is one of the few in Europe lined with shops and restaurants.

Dining locally

A popular French eatery in Bath's city center is **No. 5 Bistro** (5 Argyle St.; ☎ **01225/444-499**). The chef at this pleasant, smoke-free restaurant produces mouth-watering dishes that may include choices such as baked ricotta with olive, spinach, and sun-dried tomato soufflé; Provençal fish soup; char-grilled loin of lamb; or vegetarian dishes, such as roasted stuffed peppers and vegetable gratin. Main courses cost £14 to £16 ($26–$30). The bistro is open daily noon to 2:30 p.m. and 6:30 to 10:30 p.m. The bistro accepts American Express, MasterCard, and Visa. (See the "Bath" map on p. 267.)

Spending the night

If you want to spend the night in Bath, try the **Kennard Hotel** (11 Henrietta St.; ☎ **01225/310-472;** Fax: 01225/460-054; www.kennard. co.uk). On the east side of Pulteney Bridge, within walking distance of everything in Bath, this elegant hotel with 13 guest rooms occupies a beautifully restored 1794 Georgian townhouse. The rates cost £98 to £118 ($181–$218) for a double, breakfast included. The hotel accepts American Express, MasterCard, and Visa. (See map p. 267.)

Brighton: Fun beside the Seaside

On the Sussex coast, a mere 50 miles south of London, Brighton is England's most famous, and probably most popular, seaside town (see the "Brighton" map on p. 271). Brighton was a small fishing village until the Prince Regent, who would become George IV, became enamored with the place and had the incredible Royal Pavilion built. Where royalty moves, fashion follows, and Brighton eventually became one of Europe's most fashionable towns. The lovely Georgian terraces that you see everywhere date from this period. Later in the 19th century, when breathing sea air was prescribed as a cure-all for everything from depression to tuberculosis, the Victorians descended in hordes. Today, Brighton is a commuter suburb of London and a popular place for conventions and romantic weekend getaways. Gays and lesbians are very much a part of the local and visitor scene.

Brighton is a compact town, and the easiest way to get around is on foot. Forget about that frantic need for sightseeing and relax. Relaxation is what Brighton is all about. This place is for leisurely strolling, either in the town or along the seaside promenades. The town is small enough so you won't get lost and large enough to offer some good cultural diversions.

Getting there

More than 40 trains a day leave from London's Victoria Station for Brighton. The trip takes about an hour. If you travel off-peak (after 9:30 a.m.), a *cheap day-return* (round-trip) ticket costs £17 ($31). If you're driving, the M23 from central London leads to Brighton. The drive typically takes about an hour, but if roads are clogged, it may take twice as long.

Finding information

Brighton's **Visitor Information Centre** (10 Bartholomew Square; ☎ 0906/ 711-2255; www.visitbrighton.com) opposite the town hall, about a ten-minute walk south from the train station. The center is a good place to pick up info on current events and a Gay Information Sheet listing gay guesthouses, pubs, and clubs. If you fall in love with Brighton and decide to stay overnight, you can reserve a room here. The center is open Monday through Friday 9 a.m. to 5 p.m., Saturday 10 a.m. to 5 p.m., and Sundays during summer from 10 a.m. to 4 p.m. (See map p. 271.)

Seeing the sights

Brighton's one must-see attraction is the **Royal Pavilion** (☎ 01273/ 290-900), set in a small landscaped park bounded by North Street, Church Street, Olde Steine, and New Road. The pavilion is one of the most extraordinary palaces in Europe. John Nash redesigned the original farmhouse and villa on this site for George IV (when the king was still Prince Regent), who lived here with his mistress, Lady Conyngham, until 1827.

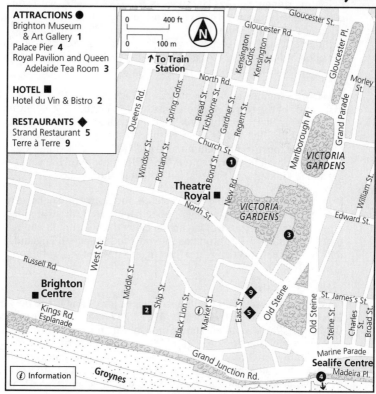

Brighton

ATTRACTIONS ●
Brighton Museum
  & Art Gallery **1**
Palace Pier **4**
Royal Pavilion and Queen
  Adelaide Tea Room **3**

HOTEL ■
Hotel du Vin & Bistro **2**

RESTAURANTS ◆
Strand Restaurant **5**
Terre à Terre **9**

The exterior, as crazily wonderful as anything King Ludwig of Bavaria dreamed up, is an Indian fantasy of turrets and minarets. The interior, decorated in a Chinese style, is fantastically extravagant. The king's brother, William IV, and Queen Victoria later used the pavilion. Admission costs £6.10 ($11) adults, £4.30 ($7.95) seniors and students, £3.60 ($6.65) children under 16, and £16 ($30) for families (two adults and up to four children). The pavilion is open daily October through May 10 a.m. to 5 p.m. and June through September 10 a.m. to 6 p.m. (See map above.)

Before you leave the pavilion, consider having lunch or a *cream tea* (tea and scones served with clotted cream and strawberry preserves) in the restored **Queen Adelaide Tea Room** (☎ 01723/292-736), open daily 10:30 a.m. to 4:30 p.m. (to 5 p.m. in summer). Queen Adelaide, who used this suite in 1830, didn't appreciate the epicurean tastes of her husband, George IV. Dismissing his renowned French chefs, she reverted back to British cuisine so dreary that Lord Dudley complained "you now get cold pâté and hot champagne." The lunch selections and cream teas range from £6 to £12 ($11–$22).

Close to the Royal Pavilion, on Church Street, you find the small **Brighton Museum & Art Gallery** (☎ 01273/290-900), with some interesting collections of Art Nouveau and Art Deco furniture, glass, and ceramics, plus a Fashion Gallery. Reopened in 2002 after a major refurbishment, it's a good place to while away an hour. Admission is free, and it's open Monday, Tuesday, and Thursday through Saturday from 10 a.m. to 7 p.m., Sunday 2 to 5 p.m. (See map p. 271.)

The town's famous amusement area, **Palace Pier,** jutting out into the sea just south of the Royal Pavilion, was built in the late 19th century. Today the pier is rather tacky but worth visiting nonetheless. At night, all lit up with twinkling lights, this place is almost irresistible. Spend half an hour, but don't expect to find much more than junk food, kiddie rides, and arcade games. The more famous West Pier, now over 130 years old and gradually sinking into the sea, isn't open to the public.

Brighton and neighboring Hove stretch out along the English Channel. The entire **seafront** is a pebbly public beach used for swimming and sunning. Promenades for strolling are all along the seafront. If you're into sunbathing *au naturel,* Brighton has the only nude beach in England, about a mile west of Brighton Pier. You'll recognize it when you get there.

Dining locally

One of the hippest (and friendliest) places for dining is the bow-fronted **Strand Restaurant** (6 East St.; ☎ 01273/747-096), which serves Modern British cuisine with an emphasis on fish. The ever-changing menu may include herby homemade vegetable soup, followed by chicken breast with creamy mushrooms, smoked haddock lasagna, lamb *en croute,* or pan-fried filet steak with potatoes. Main courses cost £13 to £18 ($24–$33). The restaurant is open daily noon to 10 p.m. It accepts American Express, Diners Club, MasterCard, and Visa. (See map p. 271.)

For a new outlook on vegetarian food, try **Terre à Terre** (71 Little East St.; ☎ 01273/729-051). Considered the best vegetarian restaurant in England, perhaps in all Europe, this place elevates meatless cuisine to an art form. The food is impeccably fresh and beautifully presented. You can eat your way through the menu with the Terre à Tapas, a superb selection of all their best dishes, big enough for two. Main courses cost £12 to £13 ($22–$24). The restaurant is open Tuesday through Saturday noon to 10:30 p.m., Sunday 10 a.m. to 10 p.m. (brunch 10 a.m.–1 p.m.). Reservations are essential on weekends. The restaurant accepts Diners Club, MasterCard, and Visa. (See map p. 271.)

Spending the night

A sophisticated new addition to Brighton's hotel scene, the ultrastylish **Hotel du Vin & Bistro** (Ship Street; ☎ 01273/718-588; Fax: 01273/718-599; www.hotelduvin.com) occupies a set of Mock Tudor and Gothic Revival buildings a stone's throw from the seafront. This is Brighton's most unique contemporary hotel, with an impressive three-story lobby, a signature French bistro, and 37 cool, uncluttered, and very comfortable bedrooms featuring marvelous beds with fine Egyptian linens, deep soaker tubs, and power showers. Rack rates for a double room with breakfast range from £130 to £230 ($241–$426). The hotel accepts all major credit cards. (See map p. 271.)

Canterbury: Tales from the Great Cathedral

Magnificent **Canterbury Cathedral** is one of the glories of England. Spinning the yarns found in *The Canterbury Tales,* Chaucer's pilgrims made their way here. For nearly 400 years, the devout, in search of miracles, salvation, and a bit of adventure, trekked to the cathedral's shrine of Thomas à Becket, Archbishop of Canterbury, who was murdered in 1170 by henchmen of Henry II. (The pilgrims didn't stop coming until Henry VIII had the shrine destroyed in 1538.) Modern pilgrims, today called *day-trippers,* continue to pour into the Kentish city of Canterbury on the river Stour, 62 miles east of London (see the "Canterbury" map on p. 274). They come to see the cathedral, of course, but also to visit the host of small museums and to enjoy the picturesque town surrounding it.

Getting there

Canterbury has two train stations, Canterbury East and Canterbury West, and you can easily walk to the city center from either one. From London's Victoria Station, trains run about every half-hour to Canterbury East. Hourly trains from London's Charing Cross stop at Canterbury West. The journey takes one and a half hours and costs £18 ($33) for a *cheap day-return* (round-trip) ticket. For schedules and information, call ☎ 0845/ 484-950. To drive from London, take the A2 and then the M2; Canterbury is signposted all the way. The city center is closed to cars, but you find several parking areas close to the cathedral.

Finding information and taking a tour

The **Visitors Information Centre** (12–13 Sun St.; ☎ 01227/378-100; www.canterbury.co.uk), opposite Christchurch Gate at the entrance to the cathedral precincts, is open Easter to October, Monday through Saturday 9:30 a.m. to 5:30 p.m. and Sunday 10 a.m. to 4 p.m.; the rest of the year, the center is open Monday through Saturday from 9:30 a.m. to 5 p.m. At the Centre, you can buy tickets for daily guided-tour walks of the city and cathedral at 2 p.m. (additional walks in July and Aug, Mon–Sat at 11:30 a.m.). The tour costs £4 ($7.40) adults; £3.25 ($6) seniors, students, and children under 12; and £12 ($22) families (two adults and two children). (See map p. 274.)

Canterbury

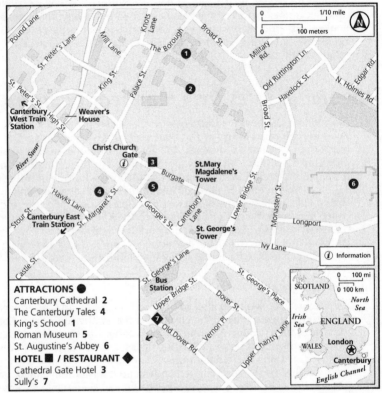

ATTRACTIONS ●
Canterbury Cathedral **2**
The Canterbury Tales **4**
King's School **1**
Roman Museum **5**
St. Augustine's Abbey **6**
HOTEL ■ / RESTAURANT ◆
Cathedral Gate Hotel **3**
Sully's **7**

Canterbury Historic River Tours (Weavers House, 1 St. Peter's St.;
☎ 07790/534-744) offers half-hour boat trips on the Stour River with a
commentary on the history of the buildings that you pass. April through
September, river conditions permitting, boats depart daily each half-
hour from 10 a.m. to 5 p.m. Tickets cost £5 ($9.25) adults, £3.80 ($7.05)
children, and £16 ($30) for families (two adults and two children).
Umbrellas are available in case of rain. The boats leave from behind the
15th-century Weavers House (access via the Weavers restaurant
garden).

Seeing the sights

Make your first stop the imposing **Canterbury Cathedral** (11 The
Precincts; ☎ 01227/762-862), a magnificent structure that was the first
major expression of the Gothic style in England. The crypt dates from
about 1100, and the cathedral itself (rebuilt after a fire) dates from the
13th century, with a bell tower added in the 15th century.

Although Henry VIII destroyed Becket's shrine, its site is still marked in the Trinity Chapel near the high altar. Noteworthy features of the cathedral include a number of panels of rare stained glass and the medieval royal tombs of Henry IV and Edward the Black Prince. Admission costs £5 ($9.25) adults; £4 ($7.40) seniors, students, and children. The cathedral is open Monday through Saturday 9 a.m. to 5 p.m. (until 6 p.m. in summer), and Sunday 12:30 to 2:30 p.m. and 4:30 to 5:30 p.m.; closed to sightseeing during services. (See map p. 274.)

As you stroll the cathedral grounds, you may encounter flocks of well-behaved boys and girls wearing blazers and ties: They attend **King's School,** the oldest public school in England, housed in several fine medieval buildings north of the cathedral.

Off High Street, near the cathedral, is the entertaining exhibition known as **The Canterbury Tales** (23 St. Margaret's St.; ☎ **01227/454-888**), where the pilgrimages of Chaucerian England are recreated in tableaux. On audio headsets, you can hear five of Chaucer's *Canterbury Tales* and the story of the murder of St. Thomas à Becket. Give yourself 45 minutes to an hour to see and hear the entire show. Admission costs £6.95 ($13) adults, £5.95 ($11) seniors and students, £5.25 ($9.70) children 5 to 15. The attraction is open daily from 10 a.m. to 4:30 p.m. (9:30 a.m. to 5 p.m. in summer). (See map p. 274.)

Two millennia ago, the conquering Romans were living in Canterbury, which they called Cantuaria. Their daily lives are chronicled in the small but fascinating **Roman Museum** (☎ **01227/785-575**), in the excavated Roman levels of the city between the cathedral and High Street on Butchery Lane. Admission costs £2.90 ($5.35) adults; £1.80 ($3.35) seniors, students, and children. The museum is open Monday through Saturday 10 a.m. to 5 p.m. (also Sunday 1:30 to 5 p.m. from June through October). (See map p. 274.)

Although the cathedral gets the lion's share of attention in Canterbury, another Christian site predates it by about 600 years. Set in a spacious park, about a ten-minute walk east from the center of town, you find the atmospheric ruins of **St. Augustine's Abbey** (Longport; ☎ **01227/767-345**), founded in A.D. 598 and one of the oldest Anglo-Saxon monastic sites in the country. This UNESCO World Heritage site offers interactive audio tours. Admission costs £3.70 ($6.85) adults, £2.80 ($5.20) seniors and students, and £1.90 ($3.50) children. The site is open daily April through September 10 a.m. to 6 p.m., October through March 10 a.m. to 4 p.m.

Trek another five minutes east from St. Augustine's Abbey to visit the oldest parish church in England. **St. Martin's Church** (North Holmes Road; ☎ **01227/459-482**), founded by Queen Bertha (the French wife of Saxon King Ethelbert), was already in existence when Augustine arrived from Rome to convert the natives in A.D. 597. Admission is free, and the church is open daily 9 a.m. to 5 p.m.

Dining locally

One of the best restaurants in Canterbury is **Sully's,** located in the County Hotel (High Street; ☎ 01227/766-266). You can choose from a selection of traditional English dishes or try one of the more imaginatively conceived platters or seasonal specialties. Reservations are recommended. A fixed-price lunch costs £17 ($31); a fixed-price dinner goes for £23 to £28 ($43–$52). Sully's accepts American Express, Diners Club, MasterCard, and Visa. It's open daily 12:30 to 2:20 p.m. and 7 to 10 p.m.

Spending the night

If you're planning an overnight stay in Canterbury and want, like the pilgrims of yore, to stay near the cathedral, you can't get any closer than the **Cathedral Gate Hotel** (36 Burgate; ☎ 01227/464-381; Fax: 01227/462-800; www.cathgate.co.uk). Dating from 1438, the 27-room hotel adjoins Christchurch Gate and overlooks the Buttermarket. The guest rooms are comfortable and modestly furnished, with sloping floors, massive oak beams, and winding corridors — what else would you expect from a hotel built more than 500 years ago? Rates are £52 to £90 ($96–$167) for a double, continental breakfast included. The hotel accepts American Express, Diners Club, MasterCard, and Visa.

Stratford-upon-Avon: In the Footsteps of the Bard

Stratford-upon-Avon (see the "Stratford-upon-Avon" map on p. 277) is a shrine to the world's greatest playwright, William Shakespeare, who was born, lived much of his life, and is buried in this market town on the Avon River, 91 miles northwest of London. In summer, crowds of international tourists overrun Stratford, which aggressively hustles its Shakespeare connection.

Stratford boasts many Elizabethan and Jacobean buildings, but it's not really a quaint village anymore. If you're arriving by train, your first glimpse will be of a vast parking lot across from the station. Don't let this sight put you off. The charms of Stratford haven't been completely lost — you find lots of lovely corners as you explore. Besides the literary pilgrimage sights, the top draw in Stratford is the **Royal Shakespeare Theatre,** where Britain's foremost actors perform.

Getting there

Direct trains leave frequently from London's Paddington Station; the journey takes two hours and costs £25 ($46) for a standard-class off-peak (after 9:30 a.m.) round-trip ticket. Call ☎ 0845/484-950 for information and schedules. To drive from London, take the M40 toward Oxford and continue to Stratford-upon-Avon on the A34.

Stratford-upon-Avon

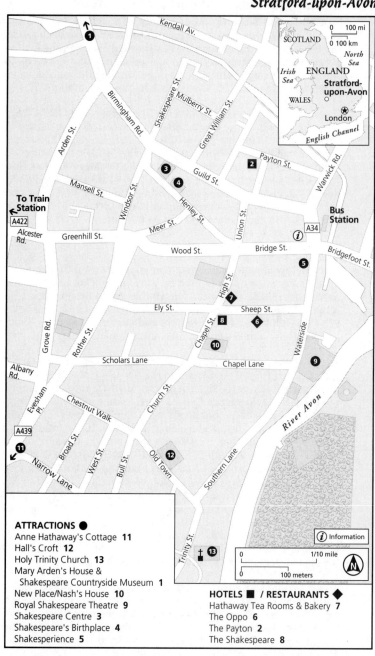

ATTRACTIONS ●
Anne Hathaway's Cottage **11**
Hall's Croft **12**
Holy Trinity Church **13**
Mary Arden's House &
  Shakespeare Countryside Museum **1**
New Place/Nash's House **10**
Royal Shakespeare Theatre **9**
Shakespeare Centre **3**
Shakespeare's Birthplace **4**
Shakesperience **5**

HOTELS ■ / RESTAURANTS ◆
Hathaway Tea Rooms & Bakery **7**
The Oppo **6**
The Payton **2**
The Shakespeare **8**

Finding information and taking a tour

Stratford's **Tourist Information Centre** (Bridgefoot; ☎ 01789/293-127; www.shakespeare-country.co.uk) provides information and maps of the town and its major sites. Easter through October, the center is open Monday through Saturday 9 a.m. to 6 p.m. and Sunday 11 a.m. to 5 p.m.; November through February, it's open Monday through Saturday 9 a.m. to 5 p.m. and Sunday 10:30 a.m. to 4:30 p.m. (See map p. 277.)

Bus tours of Stratford, provided by **City Sightseeing** (☎ 01708/866-000), leave from outside the tourist office. Open-top, double-decker buses depart every 15 minutes daily 9:30 a.m. to 5:30 p.m. in summer. You can take the one-hour ride without stops or get off and on at any or all of the town's five Shakespeare properties, including Mary Arden's House in Wilmcote (see the following section). The tour ticket is valid all day but doesn't include admission into any of the houses. The tours cost £8 ($15) adults, £6 ($11) seniors and students, and £3 ($5.55) children under 12. You can buy your ticket on the bus.

Seeing the sights

You can buy a combination ticket at your first stop that gets you into the five sites administered by the Shakespeare Birthplace Trust: **Shakespeare's Birthplace, Anne Hathaway's Cottage, New Place/ Nash's House, Mary Arden's House,** and **Hall's Croft.** The ticket costs £13 ($24) adults, £12 ($22) seniors and students, £6.50 ($12) children, and £29 ($54) families (two adults and three children).

A logical place to begin your tour is **Shakespeare's Birthplace** (Henley Street; ☎ 01789/204-016), where the Bard, son of a glover and wool merchant, first saw the light of day on April 23, 1564. You enter through the modern **Shakespeare Centre,** where you can spend a few minutes browsing the exhibits that illustrate his life and times. The house, filled with Shakespeare memorabilia, is actually two 16th-century half-timbered houses joined together. His father's shop was on one side, and the family residence was on the other. After visiting the bedroom where wee Willie was (probably) born, the Elizabethan kitchen, and other rooms, you can walk through the garden. Admission costs £6.70 ($12) adults, £5.50 ($10) seniors and students, £2.60 ($4.80) children, and £15 ($28) families (two adults and three children). Shakespeare's Birthplace is open daily April through May and September through October 10 a.m. to 5 p.m. (Sun from 10:30 a.m.); June through August 9 a.m. to 5 p.m. (Sun from 9:30 a.m.); and November through March 10 a.m. to 4 p.m. (Sun from 10:30 a.m.). It's closed December 24 to 26. (See map p. 277.)

To visit **Anne Hathaway's Cottage** (Cottage Lane, Shottery [about a mile south of Stratford]; ☎ 01789/292-100), take a bus from Bridge Street or, better still, walk there along the well-marked country path from Evesham Place. Anne Hathaway, who came from a family of yeomen farmers, lived in this lovely thatched cottage before she married 18-year-old Shakespeare (a May-December marriage in reverse, although Anne was only 25). Many original 16th-century furnishings, including the *courting settle* (a type of bench that courting couples often sat on), are preserved inside the house, which was occupied by Anne's ancestors until 1892. Before leaving, be sure to stroll through the beautiful garden and orchard. Admission costs £5.20 ($9.60) adults, £4 ($7.40) seniors and students, £2 ($3.70) children, and £12 ($22) families (two adults and three children). The cottage is open daily April through May 10 a.m. to 5 p.m. (Sun from 10:30 a.m.); June through August 9 a.m. to 5 p.m. (Sun from 9:30 a.m.); September through October from 9:30 a.m. to 5 p.m. (Sun from 10 a.m.); and November through March from 10 a.m. to 4 p.m. (Sun from 10:30 a.m.). The cottage is closed January 1, Good Friday, and December 24 to 26. (See map p. 277.)

Shakespeare retired in 1610 to **New Place** (Chapel Street; ☎ **01789/ 204-016**). By that time, he was a relatively prosperous man whose plays had been seen by Queen Elizabeth. New Place was a Stratford house that he'd purchased a few years earlier and where he would die in 1616. The house was later torn down and, today, only the gardens remain. To reach the site from his birthplace, walk east on Henley Street and south on High Street, which becomes Chapel Street. Visitors enter through **Nash's House,** which belonged to Thomas Nash, husband of Shakespeare's granddaughter. The house contains 16th-century period rooms and an exhibit illustrating the history of Stratford. Adjoining the house is a knot garden landscaped in an Elizabethan style. Admission costs £3.50 ($6.50) adults, £3 ($5.55) seniors and students, £1.70 ($3.15) children, and £9 ($17) families (two adults and three children). Hours are daily April through May and September through October 11 a.m. to 5 p.m.; June through August 9:30 a.m. to 5 p.m. (Sun from 10 a.m.); and November through March 11 a.m. to 4 p.m. (See map p. 277.)

Shakespeare's daughter, Susanna, probably lived with her husband, Dr. John Hall, in **Hall's Croft** (Old Town; ☎ **01789/292-107**), a magnificent Tudor house with a walled garden. From New Place, continue south on Chapel and Church streets and turn east on Old Town to reach Hall's Croft. The house is furnished in the style of a middle-class 17th-century home. On view are exhibits illustrating the theory and practice of medicine in Dr. Hall's time. Hours and admission are the same as for Nash's House (see the preceding paragraph).

Shakespeare died on his birthday, at age 52, and was buried in **Holy Trinity Church** (Old Town; ☎ **01789/266-316**), a beautiful parish church beside the Avon River. His wife, Anne, his daughter Susanna, and Susanna's husband, John Hall, lie beside him in front of the altar. A bust of the immortal Bard looks down upon the gravesite. I find it a bit odd that the inscription on the tomb of the man who wrote some of the world's most enduring lines is little more than doggerel, ending with "and curst be he who moves my bones." Obviously William Shakespeare didn't want to leave Stratford — ever. Admission to the church is free, but a small donation is requested to see Shakespeare's tomb. March through October, you can visit the church Monday through Saturday 8:30 a.m. to 6 p.m. (to 4 p.m. the rest of the year); year-round, the church is open Sunday 2 to 5 p.m.

About 3½ miles north of Stratford on the A34 (Birmingham) road is **Mary Arden's House & Shakespeare Countryside Museum** (Wilmcote; ☎ **01789/204-016**), the last of the five Shakespeare shrines. For more than 200 years, Palmers Farm, a Tudor farmstead with an old stone dovecote and outbuildings, was identified as the girlhood home of Mary Arden, Shakespeare's mother. Recent evidence revealed, however, that Mary Arden actually lived in the house next door, at Glebe Farm. In 2000, the house at Glebe Farm was officially re-designated as the Mary Arden House. Dating from 1514, the house contains country furniture and domestic utensils; in the barns, stable, cowshed, and farmyard, you find an extensive collection of farming implements illustrating life and work in the local countryside from Shakespeare's time to the present. Admission costs ₤5.70 ($11) adults, ₤5 ($9.25) seniors and students, ₤2.50 ($4.65) children, and ₤14 ($26) families (two adults and three children). Hours are November through March and September through October 10 a.m. to 4 p.m. (Sun from 10:30 a.m.); April through May 10 a.m. to 5 p.m. (Sun from 10:30 a.m.); and June through August 9:30 a.m. to 5 p.m. (Sun from 10 a.m.).

Seeing a play at the Royal Shakespeare Theatre

The **Royal Shakespeare Theatre** (Waterside; ☎ **01789/295-623;** www.rsc.org.uk) is the home of the **Royal Shakespeare Company,** which typically stages five Shakespeare plays during a season, running from November through September (for current offerings, and to book tickets online, visit its Web site). A few tickets are always held for sale on the day of a performance, but if you wait until you arrive in Stratford, you may not be able to get a good seat. The box office is open Monday through Saturday 9:30 a.m. to 8 p.m. but closes at 6 p.m. on days when no performances are on the schedule. Tickets cost ₤8 to ₤46 ($15–$85). (See map p. 277.)

Stratford's newest attraction, **Shakespearience** (Waterside Theatre, Waterside; ☎ **01789/290-111**), presents the life and works of Shakespeare in a unique way, using show technology and special effects. The show includes information about the Bard of Stratford and dramatic highlights from nine of his best-loved plays. Tickets cost ₤7.25 ($13) adults; ₤6.25 ($12) seniors, students, and children under 12; and ₤23 ($43) families (two adults and two children).

Dining locally

If you want to have lunch or afternoon tea in enjoyably old-fashioned surroundings, try **Hathaway Tea Rooms & Bakery** (19 High St.; ☎ **01789/ 292-404**). The tea rooms are on the second floor of a building that dates from 1610. Cream tea comes with homemade fruit scones, clotted cream, and jam, and high tea includes a variety of sandwiches. You can also get an English breakfast and light meals throughout the day. Main courses run from ₤5.50 to ₤7.50 ($10–$14); cream teas cost ₤4.50 ($8.35); and high teas cost ₤6.20 ($11). This place doesn't accept credit cards. The tea rooms are open daily 9 a.m. to 5:30 p.m. (See map p. 277.)

The Oppo (13 Sheep St.; ☎ **01789/269-980**), housed in a 16th-century building in the heart of Stratford, offers a historic setting and a mix of traditional and Modern British cuisine. Reservations are recommended. Main courses run from £9 to £17 ($17–$31). The restaurant accepts MasterCard and Visa, and it's open daily noon to 2 p.m. and 5 to 11 p.m.

Spending the night

During the long theater season, reserve in advance if you're planning to sleep, perchance to dream, in Stratford. However, the **Tourist Information Centre** (Bridgefoot; ☎ **01789/293-127**) can help you find accommodations.

The Shakespeare (Chapel Street; ☎ **0870/400-8182**; Fax: 01789/415-411; www.macdonaldhotels.co.uk) successfully blends old and new. Parts of this centrally located hotel date from 1635 and preserve the original Tudor-era beams and stone floor, but all 76 rooms were completely refurbished in 2005 in a comfortably elegant and traditional style. The rooms come with a host of modern amenities, and all the bathrooms have bathtubs with showers. Rack rates for a double with English breakfast range from £138 to £158 ($255–$292). The hotel accepts all major credit cards. (See map p. 277.)

The Payton (6 St. John St.; ☎/Fax **01789/266-442**; www.payton.co.uk), a Georgian-era townhouse B&B, is located on a quiet side street that's just a three-minute walk from the town center. The five en-suite guest rooms are stylish, comfortable, and charming. A double room with English breakfast costs £68 ($126). The Payton accepts MasterCard and Visa. (See map p. 277.)

Salisbury and Stonehenge: Gothic Splendor and Prehistoric Mysteries

The tall, slender spire of Salisbury Cathedral rises up from the plains of Wiltshire like a finger pointing toward the heavens. Salisbury (see the "Salisbury" map on p. 282), or New Sarum as it was once called, lies in the valley of the Avon River, 90 miles southwest of London. Filled with Tudor inns and tearooms and dominated by its beautiful cathedral, this old market town is often overlooked by visitors eager to see Stonehenge, about 9 miles away.

Getting there

From London's Waterloo Station, trains run hourly to Salisbury; the journey takes about one and a half hours and costs £24 ($44) for an off-peak (after 9:30 a.m.) round-trip ticket. For information and schedules, call ☎ **0845/484950**. If you're driving from London, head west on the M3 to the end of the run, continuing the rest of the way on the A30.

Salisbury

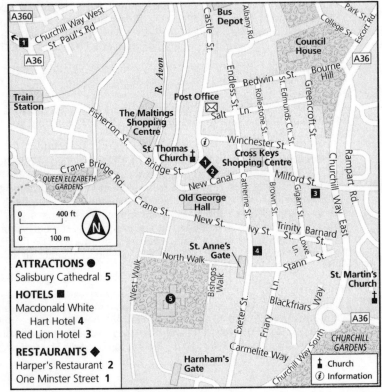

Finding information

Salisbury's **Tourist Information Centre** is on Fish Row (☎ **01722/ 334-956**; www.visitsalisbury.com) and is open Monday through Saturday 9:30 a.m. to 5:30 p.m. (also Sun May–Sept 10:30 a.m.–4:30 p.m.). (See map above.)

Seeing the sights

Visitors eager to see Stonehenge often overlook the lovely old market town of Salisbury, but I suggest that you try to spend a bit of time wandering through Salisbury Cathedral.

Salisbury

Despite an ill-conceived renovation in the 18th century, the **Salisbury Cathedral's** (The Close; ☎ **01722/555-120**) 13th-century structure remains the best example in England of Early English and Perpendicular Gothic style. The 404-foot spire is the tallest in the country. The beautiful

13th-century, octagonal **chapter house** possesses one of the four surviving original texts of the *Magna Carta.* Adding to the serene beauty of the cathedral are the cloisters and an exceptionally large **close,** comprising about 75 buildings. The suggested donation for admission is £4 ($7.40) for adults, £3.50 ($6.50) for children, and £8.50 ($16) for families. The cathedral opens daily September through May at 7:15 a.m. and closes at 6:15 p.m., and June through August, it closes at 7:15 p.m. (See map p. 282.)

Wilton House (☎ 01722/746-720), in the town of Wilton, 3 miles west of Salisbury on the A30, is one of England's great country estates. The home of the earls of Pembroke, the house is noted for its 17th-century staterooms by the celebrated architect Inigo Jones. Shakespeare's troupe is believed to have entertained here. Several centuries later in this house, General Eisenhower and his advisers made preparations for the D-Day landings at Normandy. Beautifully maintained furnishings and paintings by Brueghel, Reynolds, Rubens, and Van Dyck fill the house. You can visit a reconstructed Tudor kitchen and Victorian laundry, plus the "Wareham Bears," a collection of some 200 miniature dressed teddy bears. The 21-acre grounds include rose and water gardens, riverside and woodland walks, and a huge adventure playground for children. Admission costs £9.75 ($18) adults, £8 ($15) seniors, £5.50 ($10) children 5 to 15, and £24 ($44) families (two adults and two children). Mid-April through October, the house and grounds are open Tuesday through Sunday 10:30 a.m. to 5:30 p.m. (last admission 4:30 p.m.). The house is closed July 4 through 6. If you don't have a car, you can take the bus that stops on New Canal, a ten-minute walk north of Salisbury train station; check with the tourist office for schedules.

Stonehenge

About 9 miles north of Salisbury, at the junction of the A303 and the A344/A360, you find one of the world's most renowned prehistoric sites and one of England's most popular attractions, the prehistoric stone circle known as **Stonehenge (☎ 01980/624-715).** If you're not driving, hop on one of the Wilts & Dorset buses that depart from the Salisbury train station daily between 11 a.m. and 2 p.m.; the trip takes about 40 minutes, and the round-trip fare costs about £5 ($9.25). The crowds can be overwhelming as the day wears on, so arrive as early as possible.

Stonehenge is a stone circle of megalithic pillars and lintels built on the flat Salisbury Plain. Experts believe that the site is from 3,500 to 5,000 years old. Many visitors to Stonehenge are disappointed to find that Stonehenge isn't as enormous as they envisioned, and is now surrounded by a fence that keeps sightseers 50 feet from the stones. Keep in mind, however, that many of the stones, which weigh several tons, were mined and moved from distant quarries in a time before forklifts, trucks, and dynamite.

Stonehenge was probably a shrine and/or ceremonial gathering place of some kind. The old belief that Stonehenge was built by the Druids has been discredited (it's probably older than the Celtic Druids). A popular theory is that the site was an astronomical observatory because it's aligned to the summer solstice and can accurately predict eclipses based on the placement of the stones. But in an age when experts think they know everything, Stonehenge still keeps its tantalizing mysteries to itself. Admission costs £5.50 ($10) adults, £4.10 ($7.60) seniors and students, and £2.80 ($5.20) children. The site is open daily from March 16 through May, and September through October 15 9:30 a.m. to 6 p.m.; June through August 9 a.m. to 7 p.m.; and October 16 to March 15 9:30 a.m. to 4 p.m.

Dining locally

Looking for simple, healthy, homemade food? Go to **Harper's Restaurant** (7–9 Ox Row, Market Square; ☎ **01722/333-118**). You can order from two menus, one featuring cost-conscious, bistro-style platters and the other a longer menu with all-vegetarian pasta dishes. Reservations are recommended. Main courses cost £8.50 to £13 ($16–$24), and fixed-price meals are £7.50 ($14) at lunch and £9 ($17) at dinner. The restaurant accepts American Express, MasterCard, and Visa. It's open Monday through Saturday noon to 2 p.m. and 6:30 to 9:30 p.m. (See map p. 282.)

One Minster Street (1 Minster St.; ☎ **01722/322-024**) is the new name for a creaky-timbered, wonderfully atmospheric, 1320 chophouse and pub that used to be called the Haunch of Venison. The trendy new menu at the third-floor restaurant isn't always successful but does feature some good dishes, such as cassoulet with wild mushrooms and shank of pork with foie gras. Main courses go for £7.50 to £15 ($14–$28); a £9.90 ($18) fixed-price menu is served from noon to 1 p.m. and 6 to 7 p.m. Food is served daily noon to 2:30 p.m. and 6 to 9:30 p.m. It accepts American Express, MasterCard, and Visa. Do check out the ancient pub rooms (still called the Haunch of Venison), even if you don't dine here; the pub is open Monday through Saturday 11 a.m. to 11 p.m., Sunday noon to 10:30 p.m. (See map p. 282.)

Spending the night

A Salisbury landmark since Georgian times, the **Macdonald White Hart Hotel** (1 St. John St.; ☎ **01722/327-478**; www.macdonaldhotels.co.uk) was totally renovated in 1995. The hotel offers accommodations in the older section of the building or in a new motel-like section in the rear. A good restaurant is on-site. Rates start at £84 ($155) for a double. The hotel accepts American Express, MasterCard, and Visa. (See map p. 282.)

Atmosphere fills every nook and cranny of the **Red Lion Hotel** (Milford Street; ☎ **01722/323-334**; www.the-redlion.co.uk), founded more than 750 years ago. The cozy lounge is a popular spot for tea, and, in good weather, the vine-covered courtyard is a pleasant place for drinks.

Although now part of the Best Western chain, the hotel has maintained its own venerable identity. Each guest room is uniquely furnished, some with fireplaces and four-poster beds. Double rooms with breakfast cost £88 to £109 ($163–$202). The hotel accepts American Express, Diners Club, MasterCard, and Visa. (See map p. 282.)

Part V
Living It Up after Dark: London Nightlife

The 5th Wave   By Rich Tennant

I love visiting London. There's so much history there - my first boyfriend, my second divorce, my third face lift...

In this part . . .

London, for some people, is synonymous with the performing arts. Planning a night out here isn't the problem — choosing among all the possibilities is where the difficulty lies. In Chapter 15 I give you the scoop on London's world-class performing arts scene, tell you how to find out what's going on and how to get tickets, and provide information on the main venues for theater, music — including opera and symphony concerts — and dance. The performing arts are only part of London's pulsing nightlife, so in Chapter 16 I introduce you to some of the many places where you can rub elbows with Londoners and have a pint or two — pubs, bars, clubs, discos, and jazz spots.

Chapter 15

Applauding the Cultural Scene

. . . .

In This Chapter

▶ Getting the inside scoop on London's theater and performing arts scene

▶ Going to the symphony, listening to chamber music, and hitting rock concerts

▶ Seeing opera and dance performances

▶ Finding out what's on and getting tickets

. . . .

*L*ondon is a mecca of the performing arts, offering world-class theater, a symphony orchestra, rock concerts, operas, modern dance,
and classical ballets. In a city renowned for its theater scene, you can
enjoy every kind of play or musical. Or take your pick from the city's
own **Royal Opera, Royal Ballet, English National Opera,** or **London
Symphony Orchestra.** This chapter gives you the information that you
need to plan your trip to include the performing arts.

Getting the Inside Scoop

In the United States, people think of New York City as *the* theater and
performing arts capital. But from a global perspective, London may hold
that title, based on the number of offerings and the quality of the performances. Of course, London didn't attain this stature overnight. The
city has been building its theatrical reputation since the Elizabethan era,
when Shakespeare, Marlowe, and others were staging their plays in a
South Bank theater district. A strong musical tradition has been in place
since the 18th century.

The performing arts scene, in general, helps to give London such a buzz
for residents and visitors alike. Major British stars with international
screen reputations regularly perform in the West End, although you're
just as likely to see a show starring someone that you've never heard
of but who's well known in England. You can also expect to find a few
American plays and musicals, because the crossover between London
and New York is increasing.

And here's some good news: Tickets are considerably cheaper here than in New York. In London theaters, you rarely pay more than £50 ($93) for the best seats in the house. The price is dramatically less for symphony concerts, too: £5 to £20 ($9.25–$37) for excellent seats at the Barbican, for example. The same goes for that priciest of art forms, opera — you can get special day-of-performance seats for £5 to £20 ($9.25–$37).

Wondering what to wear to the theater? London theater audiences are, generally speaking, pretty well dressed. There are no hard and fast rules here, but if you arrive in a sweat suit and running shoes, you'll be pretty conspicuous. A "smart casual" approach is best.

Plays and performances in London have varying curtain times. Evening performances may begin at 7:30, 8, or 8:30 p.m., and matinees at 1:30, 2, or 2:30 p.m. Check your ticket to be certain, because if you're late, you won't be admitted until the second act or a suitable pause in the action occurs. If you come laden with packages, you can check them in the coatroom. Talking and noisily unwrapping pieces of candy during the performance will be frowned upon — especially if I'm in the audience.

Finding Out What's Playing and Getting Tickets

For the most comprehensive listings of London performances, buy a copy of the weekly magazine *Time Out,* available at London newsstands on Wednesdays. You can find details for all London shows, concerts, and other performances in the daily London newspapers: the *Daily Telegraph,* the *Evening Standard,* the *Guardian,* the *Independent,* and the *Times.* Another good source is the free booklet *London Planner,* available at the British & London Visitor Centre (1 Regent St., SW1), or online or by mail from a VisitBritain travel office (see the Quick Concierge, at the end of this book, for contact info).

To find out the performance schedule for an entire season, check out the Web sites that I list for specific opera, symphony, and ballet groups throughout this chapter.

The Web is one of the best places to search in advance for information on plays and performances currently running in London. You may find the following sites useful:

✔ www.officiallondontheatre.co.uk

✔ www.londontheatre.co.uk

✔ www.keithprowse.com

✔ www.albemarle-london.com

Getting tickets

If you're in London and decide that you want to see a show, you'll probably be able to get a seat. Even if an announcement has been made that a show is sold out, you can usually buy a ticket from the theater's box office, most of which open at 10 a.m. Ticket cancellations occur, and last-minute house seats go on sale the day of the performance or an hour before.

If you don't have time to go to the box office and you have a major credit card handy, call the theater directly. Box-office phone numbers are listed in the papers and in *Time Out*. Many London theaters accept telephone credit-card bookings at regular prices (plus a minimal fee of about £1.50/$2.80). They'll hold your tickets at the box office, where you pick them up any time up to a half-hour before the curtain. By buying directly from the box office, you don't have to pay the commission fee (up to 30 percent) that ticket agencies charge.

Buying a ticket in the stalls doesn't mean that you'll be seated in the ladies' powder room. It means that you may have one of the best seats in the house. *Stalls* is the British term for first-floor orchestra. Most of the West End theaters are fairly old, which means that they may have *boxes* for sale as well; these box seats will be on the sides of the second or third tiers.

Using ticket agencies

Ticket agencies are used for commercial West End plays and musicals, not for opera, ballet, or other performing arts. All over the West End, and particularly around Leicester Square, ticket agencies boldly advertise that they have tickets to the sold-out hit shows. Most of these places are legitimate, but their commission fees vary.

If you choose to use the services of a ticket agency instead of booking directly with the box office (see the preceding section), I recommend that you call, stop in, or book online at one of the following trustworthy agencies:

✔ **Keith Prowse** maintains a counter at the Britain & Visitor Center (1 Regent St., SW1; ☎ 020/7808-3871; www.keithprowse.com; Tube: Piccadilly Circus). The counter is open Monday through Friday 10:15 a.m. to 6:15 p.m. and Saturday and Sunday 10 a.m. to 4 p.m. You pay a variable commission on top of the ticket price.

✔ **The Albemarle Booking Agency** (74 Mortimer St., W1; ☎ 020/7637-9041; www.albemarle-london.com; Tube: Oxford Circus or Goodge Street) is another long-established agency, open Monday through Friday 10 a.m. to 6 p.m. and Saturday 10 a.m. to 5 p.m. Albemarle maintains dedicated theater desks at several of London's ritzier hotels, including the **Savoy,** the **Park Lane Hilton,** the **Dorchester,** and **Claridge's** (see Chapter 9). Its commission fee of 25 percent on top of the ticket price is what you can expect to pay for just about any theater booking made through a hotel concierge.

Before you buy any ticket from any agency, the agent must tell you the face value of the tickets (you can ask to see them). Before you sign the charge receipt, be sure to check the seat numbers, the face value of the tickets, and the agent's booking fee. If you're making a telephone booking, the agent must disclose the face value of the tickets, their locations, and whether you have a restricted view.

Beware of unlicensed ticket agencies that charge far more than the face value of the ticket plus a very hefty commission fee. A commission fee should *never* be more than 30 percent of the regular ticket price. Reputable ticket agencies belong to the Society of Ticket Agents and Retailers (STAR) and always advertise this fact.

The **Society of London Theatres** (☎ **020/7836-0971**) operates a half-price ticket booth in the clock tower building by the gardens in Leicester Square (Tube: Leicester Square). The booth has no telephone info line, so you have to show up in person to see what's on sale that day. The booth is open Monday through Saturday noon to 6:30 p.m. and noon to 2 p.m. for matinees (which may be on Wed, Thurs, Sat, or Sun). Tickets are sold only on the day of the performance; you can pay with cash or by MasterCard or Visa. You pay exactly half the price plus a nominal fee (usually about £3/$5.50). The most popular shows usually won't be available, but you may luck out. Tickets for the English National Opera and other events are sometimes available as well. You may want to stop by, in any case, to pick up a free copy of *The Official London Theatre Guide*, which lists every show with addresses and phone numbers and includes a map of the West End theater district.

Ticket agencies advertising half-price or reduced-price tickets are located around Leicester Square. Keep in mind that the Society of London Theatres operates the only official half-price ticket booth. And wave away those pesky scalpers who hang out in front of mega-hits. They may indeed be selling (for an astronomical price) a valid ticket. But some of these *touts,* as they're called, also forge tickets, which means that you'll be out of cash and out of a show. By law, any tout must disclose the face value of the ticket, so you know exactly what the markup is. The best advice: Don't deal with them.

Raising the Curtain on the Performing Arts

London is famous for the scope and excellence of its theater scene, but this world capital offers visitors a wealth of possibilities for enjoying all the performing arts.

Theater

Plays and musicals are staged all over the city in approximately 100 theaters, but the commercial hits are centered in the **West End theatre** district — also called Theatreland — concentrated in the area around Piccadilly Circus, Leicester Square, and Covent Garden. The theaters at the **Barbican** and the **South Bank Centre** (see the following section) also provide major theater venues. Just like New York, London is the home of many *fringe venues* (the equivalent of off- or off-off-Broadway theaters).

London's theater offerings always include new plays and musicals, long-run favorites, and revivals of the classics, as well as Shakespeare. Some of the shows in the West End — such as Agatha Christie's *Mousetrap* and Andrew Lloyd Webber's *Phantom of the Opera* — have been running for years and show no sign of winding down. The newest long-running musicals are *Mary Poppins* and *Billy Elliott,* both of which opened in 2005. In general, evening performances are Monday through Saturday and, depending on the show, matinees are on Wednesday or Thursday, and Saturday. Some shows have added Sunday performances, too. Matinees are a couple of pounds cheaper than evening performances.

In London, theaters don't hand out play programs free of charge to every patron. If you want a program, you must buy it. They usually cost £2.50 to £3 ($4.65–$5.55).

Major stages beyond the West End

I can't list all the theaters in Theatreland, but I can highlight three standout venues. They're geographically outside London's West End, but they're still considered part of the West End theater community.

- ✔ **The Old Vic** (The Cut, Waterloo, SE1; ☎ 020/7928-7616; www.oldvictheatre.com; Tube: Waterloo), on the South Bank near Waterloo Station, has long been known as "the actors' theatre." Many of England's greatest performers have played on its stage, including Laurence Olivier, Maggie Smith, and Judi Dench. Its adjunct theater, the **Young Vic** (☎ 020/7928-6363; www.youngvic.org), hosts productions of the Royal Shakespeare Company and touring companies. The box office for both venues is open Monday through Saturday 10 a.m. to 7 p.m.

- ✔ **Shakespeare's Globe Theatre** (New Globe Walk, Bankside, SE1; ☎ 020/7401-9919; Tube: Cannon Street or London Bridge) is the newest addition to the South Bank theater scene. The Globe presents a June-through-September season of the Bard's plays in a reconstructed oak-and-thatch, open-air, Elizabethan theater. (Performances may be cancelled because of rain.) The benches can be numbing, but the discomfort is worth the opportunity to see Shakespeare performed not far from the original theater and right beside the Thames. Check out www.shakespeares-globe.org for current performances.

- ✔ **The South Bank Arts Centre** (South Bank, SE1; Tube: Waterloo) is home to the **Royal National Theatre** (☎ 020/7452-3000), which performs in three theaters — the **Olivier** (1,160 seats), **Lyttelton**

(890 seats), and **Cottesloe** (a smaller theater-in-the-round). The Royal National performs Shakespeare, but it also offers revivals of big Broadway musicals. Tickets cost slightly less than at the commercial theaters on the other side of the river, generally £10 to £35 ($19–$65) for evening performances and £9 to £30 ($17–$56) for matinees. You can get unsold seats at even lower prices two hours before curtain. The facility also houses cafes, bars, and a good bookstore. The box office is open Monday through Saturday from 10 a.m. to 8 p.m. For information on performances, call ☎ 020/7452-3400 (Mon–Sat 10 a.m.–11 p.m.). You can find all performances and an online booking form at www.nt-online.org.

The fringe

In many ways, fringe theater is London's real theatrical heartbeat. The *fringe,* London's equivalent of New York's off- or off-off-Broadway, is now commonly called *Off West End.* (When my own play, *Beardsley,* was produced in London, it was on the fringe.) Groups performing on the fringe don't have the big bucks to mount lavish West End productions.

With the overabundance of acting talent in London, the fringe is where you may see tomorrow's stars acting today and next season's hit in its original, bare-bones form. The plays performed on the fringe are sometimes controversial or experimental, but for true theater lovers, they can provide a stimulating alternative to the tradition and glamour of the West End.

The performance spaces for fringe productions are usually smaller than for West End shows (sometimes tiny, sometimes above a pub), and the ticket prices are usually much lower (rarely more than £12/$22). Fringe theaters and spaces adapted to fringe productions are scattered far and wide, so consult a *London A to Z* or *Time Out,* or call the theaters directly for directions on how to find them.

Royal Shakespeare shake-up

The prestigious **Royal Shakespeare Company** (☎ **0870/609-1110;** www.rsc.org.uk), headquartered in Stratford-upon-Avon (see Chapter 14), dropped a theatrical bombshell when it announced in 2002 that it was leaving its long-time London home, the Barbican Centre, and would mount its London productions in West End theaters. The RSC now mounts productions in the **Gielgud Theatre** (Shaftesbury Avenue, W1; ☎ **020/7494-5085;** Tube: Piccadilly Circus) and the **Theatre Royal Haymarket** (Haymarket, SW1; ☎ **0870/901-3356;** Tube: Piccadilly Circus).

Outdoor theater

What could be more fun than watching a good play performed under the stars? The **Regent's Park Open Air Theatre** (Inner Circle, Regent's Park, NW1; ☎ 020/7486-2431; Tube: Baker Street) has a May-to-August season. This large venue offers theater seats but no roof, so rain may cancel the show. You can find the theater on the north side of Queen Mary's Rose Garden. Ticket prices range from £10 to £30 ($19–$56); you can check out the program on the theater's Web site, www.openairtheatre.org. **Shakespeare's Globe** (see the previous section, "Major stages beyond the West End") is another venue that's open to the heavens.

Opera

Two major opera companies call London home. The **Royal Opera** enjoys international prestige, performs operas in the original languages, and boasts the most famous international singers. Its home is the **Royal Opera House** (Covent Garden, WC2E; ☎ 020/7304-4000; Tube: Covent Garden), which recently reopened after a year-long state-of-the-art refurbishment that added two smaller venues — the **Linbury Studio Theatre** and the **Glore Studio Theatre**. Ticket prices for the grand opera run £10 to £150 ($19–$278), but a block of reduced-price tickets go on sale at 10 a.m. on the day of the performance. For a summary of the opera (and ballet) season, check the Web site www.royalopera.org. If you have your heart set on seeing an opera at the Royal Opera, book as far ahead as you possibly can — I'm talking weeks, not days. The season runs September through July.

The **English National Opera** (usually referred to as the ENO) offers more inventive productions than the Royal Opera. It performs at the freshly refurbished **London Coliseum** (St. Martin's Lane, WC2N; ☎ 020/7632-8300; Tube: Leicester Square). All the operas are sung in English. Seats sell for £5 to £70 ($9.25–$130). The opera season runs September through July. You can see the ENO program and book online by going to its Web site at www.eno.org.

The following two venues also offer you the opportunity to see opera during your time in London:

- ✔ **The D'Oyly Carte Opera Company** (☎ 020/7793-7100): For nearly 130 years, this company has been performing the comic operas of Gilbert & Sullivan. Venues change, and the schedule is irregular, so you may want to check out the company's Web site, at www.doylycarte.org.uk, for current information.

- ✔ **The Holland Park Theatre** (Holland Park, W8; ☎ 020/7602-7856; Tube: Holland Park): London's most charming stage uses the ruins of a Jacobean mansion in Holland Park as a backdrop for a mid-June–August season of opera and ballet. Tickets run £21 to £43 ($39–$80). You can view the performance schedule and book tickets online at www.operahollandpark.com.

Symphony

London offers some of the world's finest classical and chamber music. The home base for the **London Symphony Orchestra** (www.lso.co.uk) is the **Barbican Hall** at the Barbican Centre (Silk Street, EC2Y; ☎ 020/ 7638-8891; Tube: Barbican), the concert hall portion of a giant performing arts complex in the City. Seats in this acoustically fabulous hall sell for £5 to £20 ($9.25–$37). You may also catch a performance by the **Royal Philharmonic Orchestra** (www.rpo.co.uk), which plays concerts here and at the Royal Albert Hall, another all-purpose venue for classical music.

The **Royal Albert Hall** (Kensington Gore, SW7; ☎ 020/7589-8212; Tube: High Street Kensington) is an enormous, circular, domed concert hall that has been a landmark in South Kensington since 1871. The box office is open daily 9 a.m. to 9 p.m.; ticket prices vary by event.

The **South Bank Centre** (South Bank, SE1; ☎ 020/7960-4242; Tube: Waterloo) presents approximately 1,200 classical music and dance concerts per year. Performances are held year-round in three separate auditoriums. The **Royal Festival Hall** presents symphonic works performed by a variety of orchestras (some British, some international). The **Queen Elizabeth Hall,** a smaller venue that offers chamber music concerts and dance programs, is closed for refurbishment and will reopen sometime in 2006. The **Purcell Room,** an intimate setting, is ideal for recitals. You can get tickets and information on all three venues at the box office (Level 1, Belvedere Road), open 10 a.m. to 9 p.m., or online at www.sbc.org.uk; prices vary for each event. For credit-card bookings, call ☎ 020/7960-4242.

Wigmore Hall (36 Wigmore St., W1; ☎ 020/7935-2141; Tube: Bond Street) is a beautifully renovated, century-old concert hall used for chamber-music and solo concerts and recitals. You can find performance information on the Web at www.wigmore-hall.org.uk.

Summer Proms

From mid-July through mid-September, fans of classical and pops concerts attend the wildly popular concert series called the *Proms.* Featuring musicians from all over Europe, Proms concerts are held at the **Royal Albert Hall** (see the "Symphony" section, earlier in this chapter), where they began in 1895. For Proms concerts, all seats are removed from the orchestra and gallery levels. Reserved seats are available, but devotees stand for a close look at the orchestras. Starting in July, you can book seats through the Royal Albert Hall box office at ☎ 020/7589-8212. To get one of the 1,000 standing-room places (£4/$7.40), you have to queue up on the day of the performance. You can check out the Proms schedule on the Web at www.bbc.co.uk/proms.

Concerts by candlelight

Evening candlelit concerts of baroque music are performed weekly (usually on Thurs–Sat nights) at 7:30 p.m. in the lovely church of **St. Martin-in-the-Fields** (Trafalgar Square, W1; ☎ 020/7839-8362; Tube: Charing Cross; see Chapter 11). Lunchtime concerts are usually held on Monday, Tuesday, and Friday at 1 p.m. Tickets run £6 to £17 ($11–$31).

Music under the stars

Kenwood House (Hampstead Lane, NW3; ☎ 0870/890-0146; Tube: East Finchley), a picturesque lakeside estate on Hampstead Heath, is the setting for **Kenwood Lakeside Concerts,** a series of outdoor concerts held at 7:30 p.m. on Saturdays in July and August. A free shuttle bus runs between the East Finchley Tube station and the concert bowl. From Central London, you need at least 20 minutes to get to the Tube stop and another 15 minutes for the ride on the shuttle bus. Tickets cost £15 to £20 ($28–$37). You can find more information online at www.picnicconcerts.com.

Dance

The **Royal Ballet** performs at the **Royal Opera House,** and the **English National Ballet** and other visiting companies perform at the **London Coliseum** (see the "Opera" section, earlier in this chapter, for details).

Refurbished in 1998, **Sadler's Wells** (Rosebery Avenue, Islington EC1R; ☎ 020/7863-6000; Tube: Angel) is well known for its contemporary dance, theater, and music productions and as a venue for solo performers. Sadler's Wells also manages the **Peacock Theatre** (Portugal Street, WC2; ☎ 020/7863-8222; Tube: Covent Garden), a home for dance in the West End, and the **Lillian Baylis Theatre** (Arlington Way, EC1; ☎ 020/7713-6000; Tube: Farringdon), a smaller venue for dance and performance. Programs for all three theaters are listed on the Web at www.sadlers-wells.com.

The **Place Theatre** (17 Duke's Rd., WC1; ☎ 020/7387-0161; www.the place.org.uk; Tube: Euston) is the main venue for contemporary dance in the United Kingdom. **Riverside Studios** (Crisp Road, W6; ☎ 020/ 8237-1111; www.riversidestudios.co.uk; Tube: Hammersmith) is an arts center that showcases theater, cinema, and dance.

Rock concerts

When the rock and pop stars play London, they need a *huge* arena to hold their shrieking fans. The two biggest venues are **Wembley Stadium** (Empire Way, Wembley, Middlesex; ☎ 020/8902-8833; Tube: Wembley Park) and the **Earl's Court Exhibition Centre** (Warwick Road, SW5; ☎ 020/7385-1200; Tube: Earl's Court).

Dining before or after the performance

Will you eat dinner before or after going to the theater? Many of the restaurants that I review in Chapter 10 serve pre-theater meals. These places are geared for the theater crowd, so they know your time is limited. Restaurants usually serve their pre-theater menus from 5:30 to 7 p.m. The restaurant limits your choices to a set menu, but you can be done with your meal and out of the restaurant by 7:30 p.m. or earlier. You find post-theater menus less often; they go into effect around 9:30 p.m. You can usually find a good value in pre- and post-theater fixed-price menus.

The following restaurants (all of which you can read more about in Chapter 10) are close to West End theaters and have pre-theater or post-theater menus:

✔ **The Ivy:** 1–5 West St., Soho, WC2; ☎ 020/7836-4751; Tube: Leicester Square

✔ **Joe Allen:** 13 Exeter St., Covent Garden, WC2; ☎ 020/7836-0651; Tube: Covent Garden

✔ **Rules:** 35 Maiden Lane, Covent Garden, WC2; ☎ 020/7836-5314; Tube: Covent Garden

✔ **Simpson's-in-the-Strand:** 100 The Strand (next to the Savoy Hotel), WC2; ☎ 020/7836-9112; Tube: Charing Cross

Just be certain to book a table beforehand. If you're dining outside the West End, allot extra time to order, eat, pay the bill, get your coats, and then hop on the Tube or hail a taxi to make the curtain.

If you're not fussy about what you eat and just want to keep your stomach from growling during the performance, fast-food joints are plentiful in Leicester Square and Piccadilly Circus. And if you're going farther afield — to the **Barbican** or **South Bank Centre** — you can ward off impending hunger pangs with a light meal or a sandwich at one of the cafes or restaurants on the premises.

A much smaller (by that I mean less than 70,000 seats) rock-and-pop venue is the **Brixton Academy** (211 Stockwell Rd., SW9; ☎ 020/7771-3000; Tube: Brixton).

Another big-event hall is **Shepherd's Bush Empire** (Shepherd's Bush Green, W12; ☎ 020/7711-3000; Tube: Shepherd's Bush). And sometimes the old **Royal Albert Hall** (see the "Symphony" section, earlier in this chapter) rocks, too.

Chapter 16

London's Best Pubs, Clubs, and Bars

In This Chapter

▶ Getting the lowdown on the London pubs
▶ Searching out your kind of music and dancing
▶ Getting a dose of British humor
▶ Unwinding over cocktails
▶ Staying up late: The real late-night spots
▶ Finding gay and lesbian nightclubs and bars

*M*aybe your idea of a perfect evening is going to an elegant hotel bar for a cocktail or sitting back in a historic pub and quaffing a pint of ale. In this chapter, I help you find a fun and fitting nightspot. And if you need music to make you happy, this chapter can point you in the direction of your kind of beat. For locations, see the "London Clubs, Pubs, and Bars" map on p. 300.

Enjoying a Pint: London Pubs

A great way to experience real-life London is to do a *pub crawl* — that is, walk from pub to pub and sample the different brews. If you're accustomed to ordering a typical American beer with a rather conventional name, you may be bowled over by the colorful names and vast assortment of British beers on tap in a pub. You can find Brakspears, Courage Best, Friary Meux, Ind Coope Burton, Old Speckled Hen, and Wadworths 6X, to name just a few. Although you can get a hard drink at both bars and pubs, when you're in a pub you're better off confining yourself to beer because pubs don't generally carry all the ingredients necessary for a fancy cocktail. Of course, if you find just the right pub, you can order a pint, get comfortable, and even order a good meal; see Chapter 10 for restaurants that serve pub grub.

London Pubs, Clubs, and Bars

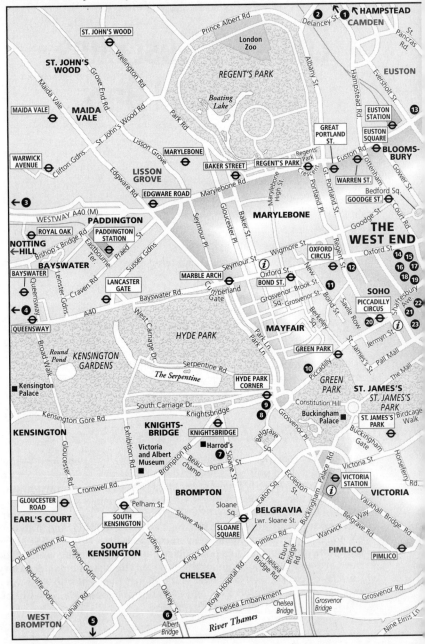

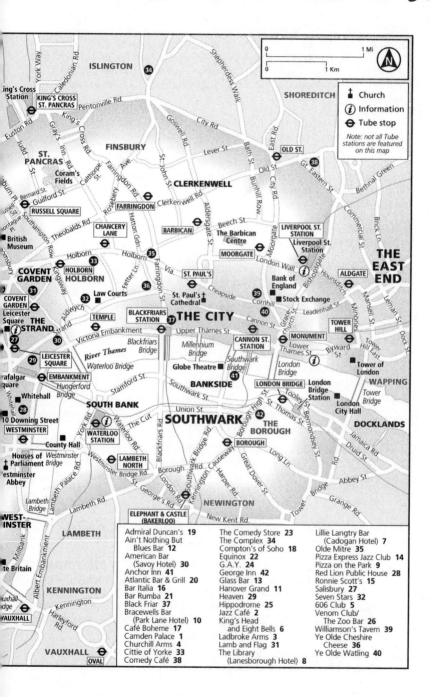

ELEPHANT & CASTLE
(BAKERLOO)

Admiral Duncan's **19**	The Comedy Store **23**	Lillie Langtry Bar
Ain't Nothing But	The Complex **34**	(Cadogan Hotel) **7**
Blues Bar **12**	Compton's of Soho **18**	Olde Mitre **35**
American Bar	Equinox **22**	Pizza Express Jazz Club **14**
(Savoy Hotel) **30**	G.A.Y. **24**	Pizza on the Park **9**
Anchor Inn **41**	George Inn **42**	Red Lion Public House **28**
Atlantic Bar & Grill **20**	Glass Bar **13**	Ronnie Scott's **15**
Bar Italia **16**	Hanover Grand **11**	Salisbury **27**
Bar Rumba **21**	Heaven **29**	Seven Stars **32**
Black Friar **37**	Hippodrome **25**	606 Club **5**
Bracewells Bar	Jazz Café **2**	Venom Club/
(Park Lane Hotel) **10**	King's Head	The Zoo Bar **26**
Café Boheme **17**	and Eight Bells **6**	Williamson's Tavern **39**
Camden Palace **1**	Ladbroke Arms **3**	Ye Olde Cheshire
Churchill Arms **4**	Lamb and Flag **31**	Cheese **36**
Cittie of Yorke **33**	The Library	Ye Olde Watling **40**
Comedy Café **38**	(Lanesborough Hotel) **8**	

Most pubs adhere to strict hours governed by Parliament: Monday through Saturday 11 a.m. to 11 p.m. and Sunday noon to 10:30 p.m. Americans take note: In a pub, you never tip the bartender; the best you can do is offer to buy him or her a drink — a time-honored tradition. Ten minutes before closing, a bell rings, signaling that it's time to order your last round.

A movement is afoot to abolish the strict pub hours throughout the United Kingdom. The laws restricting pub hours were passed during World War I so that munitions workers and others involved in the war effort couldn't spend too much time drinking at their "local." The change requires an Act of Parliament to deregulate pub hours, but the drinkers who want pubs to remain open till the wee hours have a great deal of public support.

When you're in the City, try these pubs (all of which you can see on the "London Pubs, Clubs, and Bars" map on p. 300):

- ✔ **Black Friar** (174 Queen Victoria St., EC4; ☎ 020/7236-5650; Tube: Blackfriars) is an Edwardian wonder made of marble and bronze Art Nouveau. The interior features bas-reliefs of mad monks, a low-vaulted mosaic ceiling, and seating carved out of gold marble recesses.

- ✔ **Cittie of Yorke** (22 High Holborn, WC1; ☎ 020/7242-7670; Tube: Holborn or Chancery Lane) has the longest bar in Britain and looks like a great medieval hall — an appropriate appearance because a pub has existed at this location since 1430.

- ✔ **Olde Mitre** (Ely Place, EC1; ☎ 020/7405-4751; Tube: Chancery Lane), named after an inn built on this site in 1547, is a small pub with an eccentric assortment of customers.

- ✔ **Seven Stars** (53 Carey St., WC2; ☎ 020/7242-8521; Tube: Holborn): This tiny and modest pub has a collection of Toby mugs and law-related art. You can find the pub at the back of the law courts, so a lot of barristers drink here — you can pick up some British legal jargon while having a pint.

When you're in West London, check out these pubs (which appear on the "London Pubs, Clubs, and Bars" map on p. 300):

- ✔ **Churchill Arms** (119 Kensington Church St., W8; ☎ 020/7727-4242; Tube: Notting Hill Gate or High Street Kensington) is loaded with Churchill memorabilia. The pub hosts an entire week of celebration leading up to Sir Winston's birthday on November 30. Visitors are often welcomed like regulars here, and you'll find the overall ambience to be down-to-earth and homey.

- ✔ **Ladbroke Arms** (54 Ladbroke Rd., W11; ☎ 020/7727-6648; Tube: Holland Park) strays a bit from a traditional pub environment with its jazz in the background and rotating art prints, but it makes for a pleasant stop and a good meal. The pub's changing menu may include such items as chicken breast stuffed with avocado and garlic steak in pink peppercorn sauce.

For more information on pubs and British beer, see Chapter 2. If you want to try a truly historic pub, check out my suggestions in Chapter 19.

Focusing on the Music: The Best Jazz and Blues Clubs

Small, smoky jazz clubs are common in London. In Soho, **Ronnie Scott's** (47 Frith St., W1; ☎ 020/7439-0747; Tube: Tottenham Court Road) has been London's preeminent jazz club for years, with dependably high-caliber performances. Bring a full wallet because you have to order food (meals or snacks) on top of the £15 to £25 ($28–$46) admission. (See map p. 300.)

In Earl's Court, the **606 Club** (90 Lots Rd., SW10; ☎ 020/7352-5953; Tube: Earl's Court or Fulham Broadway) is a basement club where young British jazz musicians play. You don't have to pay a cover charge to get in, but you do have to order food. And to pay the musicians, the establishment adds to your bill an additional charge of £5 ($9.25) Sunday through Thursday and about $1 more on Friday and Saturday. You can find good food and diverse music (Afro-Latin jazz to rap) at the **Jazz Café** (5 Parkway, NW1; ☎ 020/7916-6060; Tube: Camden Town). Admission costs £12 to £18 ($22–$33). (See map p. 300.)

In Soho, try the **Pizza Express Jazz Club** (10 Dean St., W1; ☎ 020/7439-8722; Tube: Tottenham Court Road). Big names from the American jazz scene regularly perform in this intimate venue, and you can enjoy pizza, too. The club is open daily 7:45 p.m. to midnight, and the admission is £10 to £20 ($19–$37). In Knightsbridge, you can hear mainstream jazz performed in the basement Jazz Room of **Pizza on the Park** (11 Knightsbridge, SW1; ☎ 020/7235-5273; Tube: Hyde Park Corner). The club is open daily from 7:30 p.m., with sets at 9:15 and 11:15 p.m.; admission is £16 to £18 ($30–$33). Neither club's cover charge includes food. (See map p. 300.)

London's only authentic blues venue is the **Ain't Nothing But Blues Bar** (20 Kingly St., W1; ☎ 020/7287-0514; Tube: Oxford Circus). The club features local acts and touring American bands. Expect long lines on weekends. Hours are Monday through Thursday 6 p.m. to 1 a.m., Friday and Saturday 6 p.m. to 3 a.m., and Sunday 7:30 p.m. to midnight. Free every night except Friday and Saturday after 8:30 p.m.; cover charge varies from £3 to £5 ($5.55–$9.25). (See map p. 300.)

Laughing the Night Away: Comedy Clubs

The **Comedy Store** (1A Oxendon St., off Piccadilly Circus, SW1; ☎ 020/ 7344-0234; Tube: Piccadilly Circus) is London's best showcase for established and rising comic talent. Visitors must be 18 or older. Doors open at 6:30 p.m., and shows start at 8 p.m.; cover charge is £12 to £15 ($22–$28). You can't reserve seats, so arrive early to get a good spot. You can also sample standup, London-style, at the **Comedy Cafe** (66 Rivington St., EC2; ☎ 020/7739-5706; Tube: Old Street). Doors open at 7 p.m., and shows start at 8:30 p.m.; the cover is £3 ($5.55) on Thursday, £10 ($19) on Friday, and £12 ($22) on Saturday. (See map p. 300.)

Shaking Your Groove Thing: The Best Dance Clubs

London is a large, multicultural city, and its music scene reflects its diversity. In the London clubs, you can listen to drum 'n' bass, indie, Asian underground (or *tabla 'n' bass,* as it's called), chemical beats (don't ask), break beats, techno, trance, psychedelic, and many others.

Cover charges vary according to the day of the week and what band is playing. For more options, check out the music and club listings in *Time Out,* a weekly entertainment magazine.

The **Complex,** in Islington (1–5 Parkfield St., N1; ☎ 020/7288-1986; Tube: Angel), frequently books live bands. The club has four floors with different dance vibes on each. Hours are Friday and Saturday 10 p.m. to 7 a.m.; admission is £10 to £12 ($19–$22). (See map p. 300.)

The **Equinox** (Leicester Square, WC2; ☎ 020/7437-1446; Tube: Leicester Square) boasts London's largest dance floor and one of the largest lighting rigs in Europe. A diverse crowd dances to equally diverse music, including dance hall, pop, rock, and Latin. The hours are Monday through Saturday 9 p.m. to 3 a.m., and the cover is £7 to £12 ($13–$22). (See map p. 300.)

The **Hippodrome** (at the corner of Cranbourn Street and Charing Cross Road, WC2; ☎ 020/7437-4311; Tube: Leicester Square) is a cavernous place with a great sound system and lights to match. This club was a favorite of Princess Diana during her early club-hopping days; now the place is tacky, touristy, and packed on weekends. The hours are Monday through Saturday 9 p.m. to 3 a.m., and the cover is £7 to £12 ($13–$22). (See map p. 300.)

Venom Club/The Zoo Bar (13–17 Bear St., WC2; ☎ 020/7839-4188; Tube: Leicester Square) features a trendy Euro-androgynous crowd and music so loud that you have to use sign language. The club boasts the slickest, flashiest, most psychedelic decor in London, and even 35-year-olds come here. The hours are daily 9 p.m. to 3 a.m., and the cover (charged only after 10 p.m.) is £3 to £5 ($5.55–$9.25). (See map p. 300.)

Bar Rumba (36 Shaftesbury Ave., W1; ☎ 020/7287-2715; Tube: Piccadilly Circus) is all over the map, musically. Every night, this club features a different type of music, including jazz fusion, phat funk, hip hop, drum 'n' bass, soul, R&B, and swing. The minimum age for admittance is 21 on Saturday and Sunday and 18 Monday through Friday. Hours are Monday through Thursday 10 p.m. to 3 a.m., Friday 10 p.m. to 4 a.m., Saturday 9 p.m. to 6 a.m., and Sunday 8 p.m. to 1 a.m. The cover is £3 to £12 ($5.55–$22). (See map p. 300.)

The **Hanover Grand** (6 Hanover St., W1; ☎ 020/7499-7977; Tube: Oxford Circus) is funky and down and dirty on Thursday, but otherwise, it's cutting-edge and always crowded. Age and gender are not always easy to distinguish here. Hours are Monday through Saturday 10 p.m. to 4 a.m., and the cover is £10 to £12 ($19–$22). (See map p. 300.)

Housed in a former theater, the **Camden Palace** (1A Camden High St., NW1; ☎ 09062/100-200; Tube: Camden Town) draws a young all-night crowd addicted to trendy, downtown costumes. The music varies from night to night, so call in advance. The club is open Tuesday and Wednesday 9 p.m. to 2 a.m., Friday 10 p.m. to 6 a.m., and Saturday 10 p.m. to 8 a.m. The cover is £5 ($9.25) on Tuesday and Wednesday, and £7 to £20 ($13–$37) on Friday and Saturday. (See map p. 300.)

Unwinding in Elegance: Posh Hotel Bars

Maybe you just want a quiet, romantic spot where you and your significant other can enjoy a cocktail and actually talk to one another. Or perhaps you're looking for a sophisticated place to enjoy a pre- or post-theater drink. The following establishments are just the ticket. They're located in grand hotels and offer a bit of privacy from the crowds. Jackets and ties are required for gents at the American Bar; a "smart casual" dress code is in effect at the others, so leave your jeans and sneakers in the hotel room.

Where's the bartender who's known for his special concoctions, the Savoy Affair and the Prince of Wales, as well as what's reputedly the best martini in town? You can find him at the **American Bar** (in the Savoy Hotel, The Strand, WC2; ☎ 020/7836-4343; Tube: Charing Cross Road or Embankment), one of London's most sophisticated gathering places. (See map p. 300.)

Bracewells Bar (in the Park Lane Hotel, Piccadilly, W1; ☎ 020/7499-6321; Tube: Green Park or Hyde Park) is chic and nostalgic, with a plush décor of Chinese lacquer, comfortable sofas, and soft lighting. (See map p. 300.)

Looking for high ceilings, leather chesterfields, oil paintings, grand windows, and old-world charm? Visit **The Library** (in the Lanesborough Hotel, 1 Lanesborough Place, SW1; ☎ 020/7259-5599; Tube: Hyde Park

Corner), one of London's poshest drinking retreats known for its collection of ancient cognacs. (See map p. 300.)

 At the **Lillie Langtry Bar** (in the Cadogan Hotel, Sloane Street, SW1; ☎ 020/7235-7141; Tube: Sloane Square or Knightsbridge), you can go back in time to the charm and elegance of the Edwardian era, when Lillie Langtry, an actress and a society beauty (and a mistress of Edward VII), lived here. Writer Oscar Wilde — often a guest in Lillie's home and in this hotel — is honored on the drinks menu by his favorite libation, the Hock and Seltzer (see Chapter 9 for a description of the hotel). (See map p. 300.)

Seeking Spots for Night Owls

Except for the die-hards in the all-night discos, Londoners retire to bed fairly early. Restaurants and bars routinely close before midnight. But a few places in restless, nightclub-heavy Soho stay open late to accommodate night owls (you can see these places on the "London Clubs, Pubs, and Bars" map on p. 300):

- ✔ **Atlantic Bar & Grill** (20 Glasshouse St., W1; ☎ 020/7734-4888; Tube: Piccadilly Circus) is open for drinks Monday through Saturday to 3 a.m. You may have to wait in line for a place to sit.

- ✔ **Bar Italia** (22 Frith St., W1; ☎ 020/7437-4520; Tube: Tottenham Court Road) is open 24 hours for coffee and serves a limited snack menu.

- ✔ **Café Boheme** (13–17 Old Compton St., W1; ☎ 020/7734-0623; Tube: Tottenham Court Road or Leicester Square) offers a chance to get a drink Monday through Wednesday until 3 a.m., Sunday until 11:30 p.m., and Thursday through Saturday 24 hours.

Stepping Out: Gay Clubs and Discos

Check the gay listings in *Time Out* for nightclubs that have dedicated gay nights.

To be where it's happenin', stroll along Old Compton Street in Soho (Tube: Leicester Square). You may want to duck into **Admiral Duncan's** (54 Old Compton St., W1; ☎ 020/7437-5300) or the two-floor **Compton's of Soho** (53–55 Old Compton St., W1; ☎ 020/7479-7961). Both of these gay bars/pubs are Soho institutions, open Monday through Saturday noon to 11 p.m. and Sunday noon to 10:30 p.m. (See map p. 300.)

The city's largest women-only bar is the bilevel **Glass Bar** (West Lodge, Euston Square Gardens, 190 Euston Rd., NW10; ☎ 020/7387-6184; Tube: Euston). The bar has a "smart casual" dress code and is open Tuesday through Friday 5 p.m. until "late," Saturday 6 p.m. until "late," and

Sunday 2 to 7 p.m.; you can't get in after 11:30 p.m. Monday through Saturday. (See map p. 300.)

In terms of size, central location, and continued popularity, the best gay (and everyone else) disco in London is **Heaven** (Under the Arches, Craven Street, WC2; ☎ 020/7930-2020; Tube: Charing Cross or Embankment). The place is open Monday and Wednesday 10:30 p.m. to 3 a.m., Friday 10:30 p.m. to 6 a.m., and Saturday 10:30 p.m. to 5 a.m. Admission varies from £3 to £10 ($5.55–19). (See map p. 300.)

G.A.Y. (London Astoria, 157 Charing Cross Rd., Soho, WC2; ☎ 0906/ 100-016; Tube: Tottenham Court Road) is the biggest gay dance venue in Europe. Hours are Saturday 10:30 p.m. to 5 a.m., and admission is £10 ($19). (See map p. 300.)

Part VI

The Part of Tens

The 5th Wave By Rich Tennant

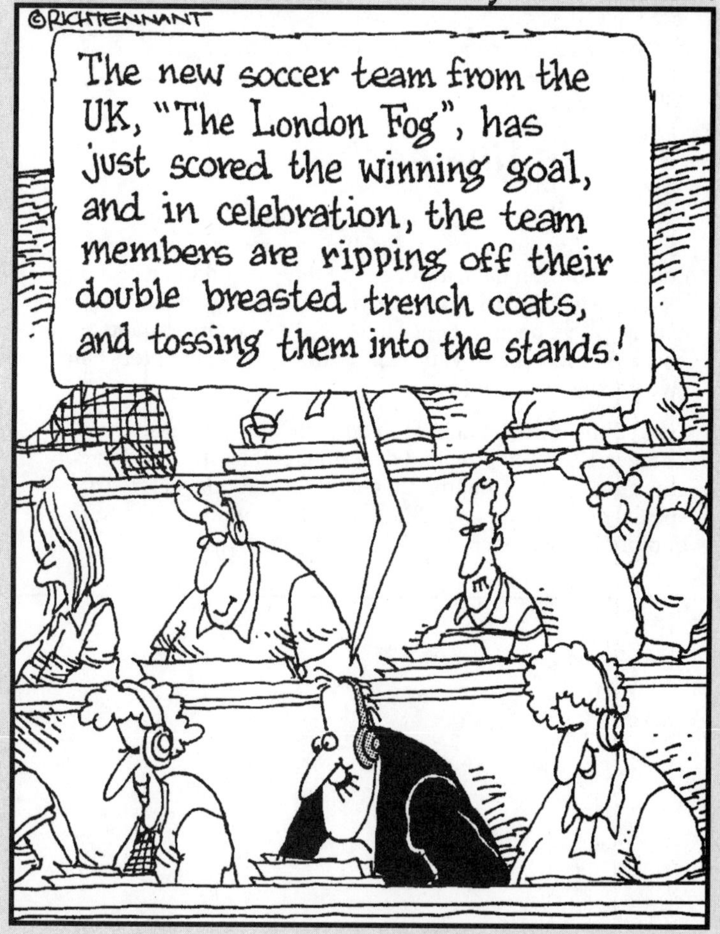

In this part . . .

*T*his part contains plenty of suggestions for having more
fun and delving deeper into the fascinating city of
London. You can have a wonderful time in London without
reading a word of this part, or you can use it to enhance your
trip. If you've been to London once or twice already and are
now ready to expand your explorations, these chapters can
give you a few super ideas.

I unveil the stories behind ten famous London statues in
Chapter 17. In Chapter 18, I describe ten historic London
churches, and in Chapter 19, you get the goods on ten extra-
special London pubs. In Chapter 20, I introduce you to ten
notable royals.

Chapter 17

Striking a Pose: Ten (Or So) Famous London Statues

In This Chapter

▶ Enjoying the statues of royalty: The good, the bad, and the ugly

▶ Checking out London's other statues: From Abraham Lincoln to Queen Boudicca

*U*nlike pigeons, people don't really pay too much attention to statues of public figures anymore. The whole idea of casting a bronze of an important public figure just doesn't fit with the modern worldview. Who'd qualify for such an honor in this day and age? In London, the only person today whom may be considered deserving of such a monument is the late Princess Diana (at least in the general public's opinion). But the city is filled with bronze statues commemorating all sorts of individuals from the past. This chapter offers ten (or so) statues that you may find interesting or that you may run into at some point during your London stay and think "Who *is* that?" (For the location of each statue, see the map "More London Sights," in Chapter 11.)

Admiral Lord Nelson

In Trafalgar Square (Tube: Charing Cross), perched atop the 145-foot Nelson's Column, one of London's most famous monuments, is a statue of (you guessed it) **Admiral Lord Nelson.** Horatio Viscount Nelson defeated the French and Spanish at the 1805 Battle of Trafalgar and is Britain's best-known naval hero. On the column, he's 17 feet high (and had to be hoisted up in three sections), but in real life, he was all of 5'4" tall. (Also in Trafalgar Square, you can see an equestrian statue of **George IV,** who considered himself a gentleman but was nobody's idea of a hero.)

Charles 1

In 1633, French sculptor Hubert Le Sueur completed the equestrian statue of **Charles I** that stands (or rather sits) at the north end of Whitehall, just south of Trafalgar Square (Tube: Charing Cross). For no discernable reason, Royals seem to have elevated egos and think of themselves as larger than life. So Charlie, who came in at just 5 feet tall, had the sculptor tack another foot onto his frame. In real life, alas, the monarch lost whatever symbolic stature the extra foot gave him when Cromwell chopped off his head in 1649.

However, history has many strange twists and turns: This statue was sold to a scrap dealer who was supposed to destroy it but instead shrewdly buried the piece in his garden. In 1660, when the monarchy was restored and Charles II ascended the throne, the scrap dealer was able to sell the new king the undamaged statue. The figure didn't go up in its present spot on Whitehall — with a pedestal by great architect Sir Christopher Wren — until 1765.

Duke of York and Edward VII

Just north of St. James's Park, at the midpoint of Carlton House Terrace (Tube: Charing Cross), you can find the **Duke of York Monument.** So who was the Duke of York (not Prince Andrew), and why did he warrant this massive 7-ton statue? Those are very good questions, and I'm completely unable to answer them. He was the second son of George III (who was on the throne when America gained its independence from Britain), and when he died, he was massively in debt. Sir Richard Westmacott's 1834 sculpture, which rests on a column of pink granite, was funded by withholding a day's pay from every soldier in the Empire. I ask you, was that fair? Some wags have speculated that the duke's statue was placed high up so his creditors couldn't reach him.

The monument looms over Waterloo Place, an enclave of aristocratic elegance and one of London's greatest examples of urban planning. At the entrance of Waterloo Place, you find a statue of **Edward VII,** chiseled by Sir Bertram Mackennal in 1921 to honor the king who gave his name to the Edwardian era. The son of Queen Victoria, "Eddie" had to wait until he was 60 before he could ascend the throne, and he died nine years later.

But not all is royal in Waterloo Place: You also find a **statue dedicated to the victims of the Crimean War.**

Henry VIII

Wouldn't you say that Henry VIII is England's best-known king? You may have "seen" him in plays, movies (such as *Anne of the Thousand Days* and *A Man for All Seasons*), and that great Masterpiece Theatre TV series, *The Six Wives of Henry VIII.* Henry VIII was a huge man, with huge appetites, and he wouldn't take no for an answer. (He didn't have to — he was king.) The much-married monarch has never been considered anyone's idea of a role model, so maybe that explains why London has only one statue of him. You can see it atop the **Henry VIII Gateway** on West Smithfield (Tube: Barbican). In 1702, the stonemasons who built St. Paul's Cathedral built the gateway, which commemorates Henry's giving of St. Bartholomew Hospital to the City — a gift made possible by his dissolution of the monasteries.

James II and George Washington

Two notable statues flank the main entrance of the National Gallery, across from Trafalgar Square (Tube: Charing Cross). On the left, you can see British sculptor Grinling Gibbons's fine statue of **James II,** from 1636, a year after James ascended the throne. Because he immediately levied new taxes and sought to restore Catholicism to England, this monarch never caught on in the public popularity polls. In fact, he was ousted from the throne and spent the rest of his life in exile in France.

The **George Washington** statue on the right is a Jean Antoine Houdon replica of a statue in the capitol building in Richmond, Virginia. A gift from that state, the statue arrived in London with boxes of earth for the base, so the first American president would always stand on American soil.

Oliver Cromwell

The small garden in front of the Houses of Parliament (Tube: Westminster) contains a statue of **Oliver Cromwell,** Lord Protector of England from 1653 to 1658. This fanatical Puritan led the Parliamentary armies during the Civil War that dethroned Charles I. Under Cromwell's "protectorate," at least 30,000 Irish men, women, and children were massacred, and vast tracts of Ireland were handed over to the English. Small wonder that Irish members of Parliament were outraged when Cromwell's statue, by Hamo Thorneycroft, was unveiled in 1899. In fact, Parliament ultimately refused to pay for it, and Lord Rosebery, the prime minister, shelled out the money himself. Cromwell, a sword in one hand and a Bible in the other, appears to be averting his eyes from the bust of **Charles I** (the king that he had beheaded — see "Charles I," earlier in this chapter), which you can see across the street above the doorway of the St. Margaret's Westminster church.

Peter Pan

Children love the famous statue of **Peter Pan,** north of the Serpentine Bridge in Kensington Gardens (Tube: High Street Kensington). Commissioned in 1912 by Peter Pan's creator, J. M. Barrie, the bronze sculpture by George Frampton marks the spot where Peter Pan touched down in the gardens. Of course, this kid could fly — he didn't have to take the Tube like the rest of us. Peter Pan was an adored fantasy hero long before he became a psychological "syndrome" for men who refuse to grow up. He was to children of earlier generations what Harry Potter is to the kids of today. Maybe someday there'll be a Harry Potter statue in Paddington Station.

Prince Albert

Prince Albert of Saxe-Coburg-Gotha (a name that the Royals changed to Windsor at the onset of World War I) was the handsome German consort of Queen Victoria. When he died at age 42 in 1861, the grief-stricken queen donned the black widow's weeds she wore for the rest of her long life. London has two statues of Prince Albert. You can find one at the rejuvenated **Albert Memorial** in Kensington Gardens (see Chapter 11). The other stands in the center of Holborn Circus (Tube: Holborn). The latter has been dubbed "the politest statue in London" because the prince is raising his hat.

Queen Boudicca

Who, you may wonder, is the wild-haired superwoman in the horse-drawn chariot at the north end of Westminster Bridge (Tube: Westminster)? She's **Queen Boudicca** (or Boadicea), that's who, with her fearless warrior-daughters. "Bo" was a fierce Celtic queen who fought back the invading Romans and died in A.D. 60. Thomas Hornicraft created the sculpture in the 1850s; the figure was placed at its current site in 1902.

Winston Churchill and Abraham Lincoln

Parliament Square (Tube: Westminster) boasts more outdoor sculptures than any other place in London. Unless you're a student of British history, most of the bronze gentlemen (**Sir Robert Peel, Benjamin Disraeli, the 14th Earl of Derby,** and **General Jan Smuts**) ranged around the square won't mean anything to you.

But you may recognize two of them. **Sir Winston Churchill,** the prime minister during World War II (you can find info on the Cabinet War Rooms, which Churchill used during the war, in Chapter 11), is at his most bulldoggish in Ivor Roberts-Jones's 1975 sculpture, standing in the square's northeast corner. A statue of **Abraham Lincoln,** by Augustus Saint-Gaudens, stands across the street on the west side of the square. The statue was a gift from the city of Chicago, which has the 1887 original in Lincoln Park.

Chapter 18

Making Amens: Ten Noteworthy London Churches

In This Chapter

▶ Visiting historic churches

▶ Appreciating the architecture of Christopher Wren

▶ Finding the Dickens link

▶ Checking out a Roman ruin

*W*estminster Abbey and St. Paul's Cathedral (both of which you can read about in Chapter 11) are giant repositories of English history and get the lion's share of visitor attention in London. But the city boasts scores of smaller churches also worth visiting. The area known as the City of London is especially rich in neoclassical churches designed by Sir Christopher Wren (1632–1723) after the disastrous Great Fire of 1666. One of England's greatest architects, and certainly its most prolific, Wren designed St. Paul's.

This chapter explores ten London churches that you may want to check out on your ramblings around town. (For their locations, see the map "More London Sights" in Chapter 11.)

Church of St. Bartholomew the Great

On the east side of Smithfield Square, EC1 (Tube: Barbican), you can see a rare 16th-century gatehouse, and perched atop the gatehouse sits an even rarer late-16th-century timber-frame house predating the Great Fire. The gatehouse opens onto the grounds of the **Church of St. Bartholomew the Great,** a little-visited gem that just happens to be the oldest parish church in London. The church was part of an Augustinian priory founded in 1123. Over the centuries, the building has somewhat miraculously escaped major damage — despite being used at various times as stables and a printing office (where Benjamin Franklin worked in 1725). The

15th-century cloisters are to your right as you enter. Inside the church is a "weeping" 17th-century statue of Edward Cooke (the marble condenses moisture from the air); the tomb of Rahere, the priory's founder; and a lovely *oriel* (projecting bay) window.

If you leave the churchyard by using the gate in the far-right corner, you come out on **Cloth Fair,** a street with gabled houses from 1604. Like St. Bartholomew's, they're among the very few surviving buildings predating the disastrous Great Fire that leveled much of London in 1666.

Church of St. Stephen Walbrook

Walbrook, EC4 (Tube: Cannon Street), a lane in the heart of the City, was the site of a brook that was paved over in medieval times. Today, the lane houses the **Church of St. Stephen Walbrook,** one of Sir Christopher Wren's finest works. By the 18th century, the fame of this church had spread throughout Europe, and many still consider it the most beautiful church in London. Its splendid dome served as a model for the one at St. Paul's Cathedral. The altar beneath the dome was sculpted from *travertine* (a porous mineral) in 1956 by British sculptor Henry Moore, who had reservations about tackling the job because he was an agnostic. "Henry, I'm not asking you to take the service," said the rector who offered Moore the commission. "I understand that you're a bit of a chiseler; just do your job."

St. Botolph's

I think it's appropriate to include in this chapter a church dedicated to England's patron saint of travelers: **St. Botolph's** on Aldersgate Street, EC1 (Tube: Barbican), close to the **Museum of London** (see Chapter 11). The church interior has a fine barrel-vaulted roof. Actually, three city churches are dedicated to St. Botolph, and all are located beside now-vanished gates into the city. At one time, instead of being greeted by ATMs and currency-exchange windows, travelers could pause and give thanks to Botolph for their safe journey to London.

St. Dunstan's-in-the-West

The octagonal **St. Dunstan's-in-the-West,** on Fleet Street, EC4 (Tube: Temple), is a fine early example of Gothic Revival architecture. That style was in fashion when an earlier church that survived the Great Fire of 1666 was replaced between 1829 and 1833. The large clock on the tower is something of a historical curiosity: The clock dates from 1671 and was installed by the congregation as an offering of thanks because the church hadn't burned down. Every 15 minutes, two giant clubs strike a bell that has been tolling for more than 330 years. People take clocks, watches, and timepieces for granted nowadays, but this clock was the first in London to have a double face and to have minutes marked on the dial.

St. George the Martyr Church

Also in Southwark, next to the remains of Marshalsea Prison on Borough High Street, SE1 (Tube: Borough), you can find **St. George the Martyr Church.** The church is probably more famous for its literary associations than for any beauty of the structure itself. This church is where Dickens's fictional heroine Little Dorrit is baptized and, at one point, is forced to spend the night when she's locked out of the Marshalsea debtors' prison; later she's married in this church. A stained-glass window in the east wall shows her at prayer.

St. Margaret's Westminster

St. Margaret's Westminster, the parish church of the House of Commons since 1614, is on St. Margaret Street, SW1 (Tube: Westminster), and is often mistaken for Westminster Abbey next door. St. Margaret's is notable for its glorious above-the-altar East Window, the stained glass of which was presented by Ferdinand and Isabella of Spain to commemorate the marriage of their daughter, Catharine of Aragon, to Arthur, the son of Henry VII. By the time the glass arrived, Arthur had died and Henry VIII, his younger brother, had wed Catherine, the first of his eight wives. (He divorced her to marry Anne Boleyn.) The weddings of poet John Milton (1656) and statesman (and future prime minister) Winston Churchill (1908) were held in this church.

St. Martin-in-the-Fields

St. Martin-in-the-Fields, on Trafalgar Square, WC2 (Tube: Charing Cross), was a stylistic prototype for hundreds of churches constructed in 18th-century New England. James Gibbs, who was influenced by the churches of Sir Christopher Wren, designed the church in 1726. Furniture designer Thomas Chippendale, painters Sir Joshua Reynolds and William Hogarth, and Nell Gwynn, mistress of Charles II, are buried within. For details about the concerts held here, see the description of St. Martin in Chapter 11.

St. Mary-le-Bow

Established in the 11th century, **St. Mary-le-Bow,** on Bow Lane, EC4 (Tube: Mansion House), is one of London's most venerable churches. The structure that originally stood here was a casualty of the Great Fire of 1666; the steepled church that you see today is a work by Sir Christopher Wren, who modeled it after Rome's Church of the Basilica of Maxentius. According to tradition, a true *Cockney* (a native of the East End of London) is someone born within hearing distance of the bells of St. Mary-le-Bow. In the churchyard's garden is a statue of Captain John Smith, a one-time parishioner who left London to become one of the first settlers of Jamestown, Virginia. (He's the one who was saved by Pocahontas.)

Southwark Cathedral

Southwark Cathedral, on Montague Close, SE1 (Tube: London Bridge), is one of the oldest buildings in Southwark and also one of the most beautiful (see Chapter 11). A church has occupied this site for at least a thousand years; before that, a Roman villa was located here.

London's second-oldest church, after **Westminster Abbey,** Southwark Cathedral, in the 12th century, was the first Gothic church to be erected in London. Today, you can see the 15th-century cathedral (with Victorian restorations) that once served London's rowdy South Bank theater district. Chaucer and Shakespeare both worshiped here, and Shakespeare's brother Edmund was buried here in 1607.

Besides a memorial to the immortal Bard, the church contains a 13th-century wooden effigy of a knight, one of the oldest surviving wooden effigies in England. John Harvard, founder of Harvard University, was baptized in this church.

Temple of Mithras

Not far from **St. Stephen Walbrook** (see "Church of St. Stephen Walbrook," earlier in this chapter), at the entrance to Temple Court on Queen Victoria Street (Tube: Mansion House), you can find the remains of what's probably London's oldest church site. This church isn't a Christian church, however, but a third-century Roman temple. Unearthed during 1954 excavations and raised to its present level, the **Temple of Mithras** is shaped like a tiny Christian basilica with a central nave and two aisles.

The Mithraic cult, which had its origins in Persia and was brought to London by Roman soldiers in the second century, used this temple. At one time, when the Roman Empire still ruled the Western world, Mithraism was as popular as Christianity. Archaeologists speculate that the pagan temple was destroyed in the fourth century, when Christianity became the official religion of the Empire. Some of the sculptures that were found in the temple are displayed in the **Museum of London** (see Chapter 11).

Chapter 19

Ale's Well that Ends Well: Ten Historic London Pubs

....

In This Chapter
▶ Enjoying some pub history
▶ Finding a pub with character

....

Public houses, better known as pubs, have been a way of life in London and throughout the United Kingdom for centuries. Chapters 2, 10, and 16 offer information about London pubs. But I could write an entire book just on the pubs of London because the city has hundreds of them. Not all these pubs are old, of course, and not all have the kind of character that accumulates over centuries of drinking, talking, smoking, and eating. But dozens upon dozens of these pubs date back anywhere from a century to more than 400 years.

This chapter offers descriptions of ten more pubs. Each of these places has some special story, history, or association attached to it. (For their locations, see the map "London Clubs, Pubs, and Bars," in Chapter 16.) All these pubs are open regular pub hours of Monday through Saturday 11 a.m. to 11:30 p.m.; some are open Sunday noon to 10:30 p.m.

Anchor Inn

Eighteenth-century figures, such as Samuel Johnson, who produced the first *Dictionary of the English Language,* playwright Oliver Goldsmith, whose most famous work is *She Stoops to Conquer,* and painter Sir Joshua Reynolds, the first president of the Royal Academy, frequented the **Anchor Inn** (Park Street, SE1; ☎ **020/7407-1577;** Tube: Southwark). It has a nice riverside terrace.

Coal Hole

Opened in the early 19th century, the **Coal Hole** (91 The Strand, WC2; ☎ **020/7836-7503;** Tube: Covent Garden) got its name from the coal haulers who unloaded their cargo on the Thames nearby. One of Central London's larger pubs, the Coal Hole has many theatrical connections because of its West End location. Famous mid-19th-century Shakespearean actor Edmund Kean used to hire rowdies, get them drunk here, and then send them off to heckle his rivals in other theaters.

George Inn

You can find one of the city's most historically important pubs in the **George Inn** (in George Inn Yard off Borough High Street, SE1; ☎ 020/ 7407-2056; Tube: Borough). It's the last remaining example in London of an old-style coaching inn, with balconies (called *galleries*) around the inner court. The George was doing business during the reign of Henry VIII, and some claim it actually dates back to Chaucer's era.

King's Head and Eight Bells

Chelsea's intimate, clublike **King's Head and Eight Bells** (50 Cheyne Walk, SW3; ☎ 020/7352-1820; Tube: Sloane Square) opened more than 400 years ago, around 1580. Back then, of course, the area was rural; Henry VIII's country house stood nearby. Later, celebrated artists and writers, such as Dante Gabriel Rossetti, Thomas Carlyle (whose house is now a museum; see Chapter 11), Oscar Wilde, Laurence Olivier, and Vivien Leigh made their homes in Chelsea, one of the prettiest (and now one of the most expensive) parts of London. The neighborhood's still filled with literary and other luminaries, so keep your eyes open if you stop in here. You never know who may pop in.

Lamb and Flag

The **Lamb and Flag** (33 Rose St., WC2; ☎ 020/7497-9504; Tube: Leicester Square) was once known by the grisly name "Bucket of Blood" because prizefighters battered one another into a bloody pulp during matches held for betting customers. The pub, a rare survivor of the Great Fire of 1666, has a couple of literary associations to offset its unsavory past. In the 19th century, this place was one of Charles Dickens's favorite taverns. A couple of centuries earlier, poet John Dryden was attacked and beaten just outside, probably because of a lampoon that he directed at the earl of Rochester. Every year on December 16, the pub commemorates the anniversary of the attack with a Dryden Night.

Red Lion Public House

Civil servants and members of Parliament frequent the **Red Lion Public House** (48 Parliament St., SW1; ☎ 020/7930-5826; Tube: Westminster). So many MPs stop in here that the pub rings a special bell before a vote is taken, allowing the lawmakers to get back in time. Charles Dickens stopped in once for a pint of beer — he was 11 years old at the time. (Life was different back then.)

Salisbury

I'm partial to the **Salisbury** (90 St. Martin's Lane, WC2; ☎ 020/7836-5863; Tube: Leicester Square) because I used to hang out there. The pub sits right in the heart of the West End theater district, dates from 1852, and has a beautifully preserved Art Nouveau interior with marble fittings, cut-glass mirrors, and brass statuettes. Like the **Lamb and Flag** noted earlier, the Salisbury was once famous for bare-knuckle prizefights — but that was long before my time.

Williamson's Tavern

Williamson's Tavern (in Groveland Court, off Bow Lane, EC4; ☎ 020/7248-6280; Tube: St. Paul's) was the residence of the Lord Mayor of the City of London before the nearby Mansion House was built. The tavern stands behind a 17th-century gate presented to the Lord Mayor by William and Mary. The building later served as an inn. Inside, you can have a drink and one of its famous steak sandwiches.

Ye Olde Cheshire Cheese

Ye Olde Cheshire Cheese (Wine Office Court, 145 Fleet St., EC4; ☎ 020/7353-6170; Tube: Blackfriars) was established in 1667, but a tavern stood on this site as early as 1590 (see Chapter 11). The earlier tavern burned down in the Great Fire of 1666 and was quickly rebuilt — in fact, Ye Old Cheshire Cheese was the first pub to reopen after the fire. Downstairs, you can see charred wooden beams bearing witness to the massive fire that destroyed a large portion of London. This pub was one of Charles Dickens's favorite hangouts, and he usually sat at a table to the right of the fireplace on the first floor.

Ye Olde Watling

Ye Olde Watling (29 Watling St., EC4; ☎ 020/7248-6252; Tube: Mansion House) is a 17th-century pub that the great architect Sir Christopher Wren used as an office when St. Paul's Cathedral was being constructed. The pub was built from timber taken from dismantled sailing ships.

Chapter 20

Ten Important Royals — Past and Present

In This Chapter

▶ Meeting a few notable Royals

▶ Noting changes in rulers and ruling over two millennia

I am not a royalist, but the kings and queens of England fascinate me. These are people whose lives encapsulated ultimate power and humiliating defeat, people who killed to stay on the throne and were killed by others who wanted it, people who inspired their subjects and treated them like dirt, people who sometimes changed the course of history and sometimes disgraced the nation they ruled.

I had a hard time choosing just ten, but in the thumbnail sketches that follow, you can get at least a glimpse of how the rulers of England — and the rule of England — have changed over the past 2,000 years.

Queen Boudicca (A.D. 30?–60): Braveheart of the Britons

I've always thought Boudicca's story would make a fantastic film, but who would play this fierce Celtic queen who painted her face blue and led 100,000 British troops again the invading Romans in A.D. 60? Angelina Jolie?

Boudicca's story harks back to the earliest period of Britain's recorded history. Historians think that she was born about A.D. 30. In A.D. 48, she married Prasutagus, king of the Iceni, and bore him two daughters. The Iceni were a Celtic tribe that had been made a Roman client-state in A.D. 43. When Prasutagus died, he left his kingdom — as required by Roman law — to the Roman emperor. But hoping to provide for his two daughters, he left a portion of his personal estate to them. For the Romans, that inheritance gave them a perfect excuse to confiscate all of Prasutagus's belongings and punish the Iceni for "disobeying" Roman law. Just days after her husband's death, Boudicca was tripped and publicly whipped, her teenaged daughters raped by Roman soldiers.

The outrages committed by the invading foreigners changed Boudicca's life forever. As more Roman troops arrived to begin the job of conquering all the native Britons, Boudicca managed to raise an army among formerly warring local tribes. The Celts were much feared by the Romans because Celtic women fought alongside the men, painting their faces blue to frighten the enemy and uttering terrifying shrieks as they attacked with swords, axes, and clubs. Boudicca and her army marched to Roman forts and settlements, laid waste to them, and killed their inhabitants. Finally, at a site that was probably somewhere in the West Midlands, Boudicca faced the army of Suetonus Paulinus, the Roman governor of Britannia. She had more troops, but Suetonius and his legionnaires had the discipline that helped Rome conquer the Western world. The Celts under Boudicca were slaughtered. No one knows what happened to Boudicca herself. Some accounts say that she took poison. The alternative, had she lived, would have been worse. She would have been paraded in chains at a public triumph in Rome and then publicly tortured in the Coliseum.

Next time you're crossing Westminster Bridge in London, look up and you can see a bronze statue of Boudicca on the north side. A mid-19th-century work by Thomas Hornicraft, it shows a wild-haired superwoman in a horse-drawn chariot with her two daughters.

Alfred the Great (849–899): A Warrior and a Scholar

If you make a trip to Winchester, the capital of the old Anglo-Saxon kingdom of Wessex, you can see a statue of Alfred the Great on Bridge Street. Alfred is the only English monarch to carry the title "the Great," and that alone makes him an intriguing character. His story goes back to the ninth century A.D. when the Danes, more commonly known as the Vikings, were relentlessly attacking and terrorizing England.

Youngest son of King Æthelwulf, Alfred became King of Wessex in 871. Wessex was an Anglo-Saxon kingdom patched together in southern and southwestern England after the departure of the Romans in A.D. 410. Following a series of attacks led by the Dane Guthorm, Alfred finally defeated the Danes decisively at the Battle of Eddington. As a condition of the peace treaty, Guthorm withdrew his forces from Wessex and Alfred recognized Danish control over East Anglia and parts of Mercia. This partition of England was called the *Danelaw,* and though the English kings soon brought the Danelaw back under their rule, they did not attempt to interfere with the laws and customs of the area, many of which survived until after the Norman Conquest in 1066.

Alfred created a series of fortifications to surround his kingdom and provide security from invasion. You can still find traces of *burh*, the Anglo-Saxon word for these forts, in the common English place-name suffix *–bury*. The reign of Alfred was known for more than military success, however. He promoted better education and helped make learning important in an age when education had gone into a decline because of Danish looting of monasteries and churches, traditional centers of learning. Alfred was also a codifier of law and a patron of the arts. A warrior and a scholar, he translated Latin books into the Anglo-Saxon tongue. With the kind of leadership that he provided, it's no wonder he was proclaimed "the Great."

William the Conqueror (1028–1087): Winner Takes All

The illegitimate son of the Duke of Normandy, William received the duchy of Normandy upon his father's death in 1035. He spent the next several years consolidating his strength on the continent through marriage, diplomacy, war, and savage intimidation. By 1066, Normandy was in a position of virtual independence from William's feudal lord, Henry I of France, and the disputed succession in England offered William an opportunity for invasion.

When Edward the Confessor died childless, the English crown was offered to Harold Godwinson (an Anglo-Saxon), even though Edward had purportedly promised the throne to William, his second cousin. Insisting that Harold had sworn allegiance to him in 1064, William prepared for battle. But as the new King Harold anxiously awaited William's arrival on England's south shores, Harold Hardrada, the King of Norway, invaded England from the north. Harold's forces marched north to defeat the Norse at Stamford Bridge on September 25, 1066. Two days after the battle, William landed unopposed at Pevensey, forcing Harold to move south to a new battle. What has come to be known as the Battle of Hastings took place on October 14, 1066. Harold and his brothers died fighting, thus removing any further organized Anglo-Saxon resistance to the Normans. The Anglo-Saxon earls and bishops soon submitted and crowned him William I on Christmas Day 1066.

William's acquisitive nature never left him. His forces ruthlessly crushed uprisings until, by 1072, the whole of England was conquered and united. William confiscated lands and reallocated them to the Normans. In 1085, William commissioned the *Domesday Book* to survey land ownership, assess property, and establish a tax base. Although he began his invasion with papal support, William refused to let the church dictate policy within English and Norman borders. Ruthless and cruel, the Conqueror exacted a high toll from his subjects, but he also laid the foundation for the economic and political success of England. Buildings from his reign include Windsor Castle and the Tower of London (both of which you can read about in Chapter 11), but you can find perhaps the most atmospheric reminder of William the Conqueror at Battle, where you can visit the battlefield that was William's first conquest in England.

Henry II (1133–1189): Family Plots

Henry II, the first Plantagenet king, was one of the most effective of England's monarchs, refining Norman government and creating a self-standing bureaucracy that could keep the country running even if it had a weak or incompetent monarch. But Henry's personal life was one unending soap opera, with more plots and counterplots than I can possibly detail here.

A grandson of Henry I, Henry was raised in the French province of Anjou. His vast continental possessions more than doubled when he married Eleanor of Aquitane, the ex-wife of King Louis VII of France. Eleanor was 11 years older than Henry and was rumored to have slept with his father. Crowned King of England in October 1154, Henry was technically a feudal vassal of the king of France but, in reality, owned more territory and was more powerful than his French lord.

Throughout his reign, Henry instituted reforms meant to weaken traditional feudal ties and strengthen his position, but in the process of strengthening the royal courts, he became involved in the murder of his best friend, Thomas Beckett. The church courts instituted by William the Conqueror had become a safe haven for criminals, and Henry wanted to transfer sentencing in such cases to the royal courts. Thomas Beckett, named Archbishop of Canterbury in 1162, vehemently opposed the weakening of church courts. He also angered Henry by opposing the coronation of Henry's eldest son. When an exasperated Henry publicly conveyed his desire to be rid of the contentious archbishop, four thuggish knights took the king at his word and murdered Beckett in his own cathedral on December 29, 1170. (You can see the exact spot if you visit Canterbury Cathedral; see Chapter 14.)

Henry's plans for dividing his myriad lands and titles evoked treachery from his sons, who, with the encouragement of their mother, repeatedly rebelled against their father. Eleanor, equally ruthless and scheming, was kept a virtual prison for 16 years. Henry died in 1189, two days after his son Richard, with the assistance of Philip II Augustus of France, attacked and defeated him, forcing Henry to accept a humiliating peace.

Henry VIII (1491–1547): Take My Wife — Please!

The significance of Henry's reign is generally overshadowed by his six marriages, a record topped only by Elizabeth Taylor. There is something scarily pathological about Henry's many marriages, even if they *were* in pursuit of an elusive male heir.

His first wife was Catherine of Aragon (widow of his brother, Arthur), whom he married in 1509 and divorced in 1533; the union produced one daughter, Mary. Henry married the pregnant Anne Boleyn in 1533; she gave him another daughter, Elizabeth, but was executed in 1536 on trumped-up charges of infidelity, a treasonous charge in the king's consort but never for the king. The same month that Anne was beheaded, the monarch married Jane Seymour, who died giving birth to Henry's lone male heir, Edward, in October 1536. After viewing Hans Holbein's beautiful portrait of the German princess Anne of Cleves, Henry arranged a marriage with her early in 1540. When Anne arrived, however, Henry found her so homely that he never consummated the marriage. In 1540, with Anne scratched off the list, he married Catherine Howard, who was executed for infidelity two years later and reputedly haunts Hampton Court Palace to this day. Catherine Parr became Henry's sixth and last wife in 1543, and she provided for the needs of both Henry and his children until his death in 1547.

So what did Henry do besides bed and wed? Most notably, he altered England and the whole of Western Christendom by separating the Church of England from Roman Catholicism. The separation actually happened because of Henry's obsession with producing a male heir. When Catherine of Aragon failed to produce a male, Henry sought an annulment from the pope in order to marry Anne Boleyn. When Cardinal Wolsey failed to secure a legal annulment, Henry summoned the Reformation Parliament, which passed 137 statutes in seven years, influencing political and ecclesiastical affairs in a way previously unknown. By 1536, all ecclesiastical and government officials were required to publicly approve of the break with Rome and take an oath of loyalty. Henry's dissolution of the monasteries filled royal coffers, as revenues from the sale of monastic lands went either to the crown or the nobility. The break with Rome, coupled with an increase in governmental bureaucracy, led to the royal supremacy that lasted until the execution of Charles I and the establishment of the Commonwealth a century after Henry's death.

Elizabeth 1 (1533–1603): Heart and Stomach of a King

In contrast to her much-married father, Henry VIII, Elizabeth I never wed and was known as the Virgin Queen. When she ascended the throne in 1558, dissension between Catholics and Protestants tore at the very foundation of society, and the royal treasury had been bled dry by Mary, Elizabeth's Catholic half-sister, and Mary's advisors.

Instead of being a fanatic like Mary, Elizabeth was strong-willed, tolerant, and intelligent. In religious matters, she devised a compromise that basically reinstated her father's Protestant reforms. Another potentially volatile problem was her cousin, Mary Queen of Scots, who gained the loyalty of Catholic factions and instituted several plots to assassinate or overthrow Elizabeth. After irrefutable evidence of Mary's involvement in such plots came to light, Elizabeth sadly succumbed to the pressure from her advisors and had the Scottish princess executed in 1587.

The persecution of continental Protestants forced Elizabeth into war, a situation which she desperately tried to avoid. She sent an army to aid French Huguenots (Calvinists who had settled in France) after a 1572 massacre in which over 3,000 Huguenots lost their lives, and she assisted Belgium in its bid to gain independence from Spain. After Elizabeth rejected a marriage proposal from Philip II of Spain, the indignant Spanish monarch, incensed by English piracy and forays in the New World, sent his much-feared Armada to raid England. "I know I have but the body of a weak and feeble woman," Elizabeth told her troops, "but I have the heart and stomach of a king." England won the naval battle and emerged as the world's strongest naval power.

In many ways, Elizabeth's reign has come to be regarded as a Golden Age. Literature bloomed through the works of Spenser, Marlowe, and Shakespeare. Francis Drake and Walter Raleigh expanded English influence in the New World. Elizabeth's religious compromise laid many fears to rest and sought to avoid murderous strife. Fashion and education came to the fore because of Elizabeth's penchant for knowledge, courtly behavior, and extravagant dress. Good Queen Bess, as she came to be called, maintained a regal air until the day she died, at 70 years of age and after a very successful 44-year reign. Few English monarchs enjoyed such political power while still maintaining the devotion of the whole of English society.

George III (1738–1820): "My Lords and Peacocks . . . "

George III was in no way an exemplary ruler, but I've long been fascinated by him because he was king at the time of the American Revolution and because he went mad. The only thing he really excelled at was procreation. He married Charlotte of Mecklenburg-Strelitz in 1761, and the prolific couple produced 15 children.

George was descended from the Hanoverian (German) line of succession that first came to the English throne in 1714. Determined to recover royal prerogatives lost to the Whig Party by George I and George II, George III methodically weakened the Whigs through bribery, coercion, and patronage, hand-picking yes-men of mediocre talent and servile minds to serve as Cabinet members.

George's commitment to taxing the American colonies to pay for military protection led to hostilities in 1775. The colonists proclaimed independence in 1776, but George obstinately continued the war until the final American victory at Yorktown in 1781. The Peace of Versailles, signed in 1783, ensured British acknowledgment of the United States of America. Bouts with madness (attributed to a disease called porphyria) and the way he handled the American Revolution eroded his support.

Other major events and people marked George III's reign. The British Army under the Duke of Wellington (whose London residence, Apsley House, you can visit; see Chapter 11) and the British Navy under Lord Horatio Nelson (honored by Nelson's Column in London's Trafalgar Square; see Chapter 11) defeated French forces under Napoleon. England also went to war again with the United States between 1812 and 1814, this time over the British practice of pressing American seamen into service in the British Navy.

It's safe to say that by the time he began an address with "My Lords and Peacocks," it was time for George to step down. Personal rule was given to his son George, the Prince Regent, in 1811. George III died blind, deaf, and mad at Windsor Castle (see Chapter 11) on January 29, 1820. You can see Kew Palace, his favorite residence, on a visit to the Royal Botanic Gardens (also known as Kew Gardens; see Chapter 11).

George IV (1762–1830): A Dandy King for the Regency

George IV, eldest son of George III and Charlotte, was the antithesis of his father (are we starting to see a pattern here?): conservative in his infrequent political involvement and licentious in affairs of the heart. As Prince Regent, he had many mistresses until he secretly married the Catholic widow Maria Fitzherbert in 1785. When George III found out about it, he had the marriage declared illegal because his son would have been ineligible to reign with a Catholic wife. In 1795, George IV married again, this time to his cousin Caroline of Brunswick, who was something of a slob and whom he detested. Caroline took their only child and moved to Italy, returning to England to claim the rights of queen when George succeeded his father in 1820. George created one of the greatest scandals of his reign when he had Caroline barred from his coronation.

Bright, witty, and able on the one hand, indolent, spoiled, and lazy on the other, George was in some ways the psychological forerunner of many modern royals. Although he was scandalous with his mistresses and extravagant in his spending, he was also a patron of the arts and donated his father's immense book collection as the foundation of the British Museum Library. His penchant for building projects inspired the Regency style of architecture, at its most fanciful in the Royal Pavilion in

Brighton (see Chapter 14). But his extravagances came at a time of social distress and general misery, following the Napoleonic Wars and the tremendous changes brought forth by the Industrial Revolution. He was basically a party boy who couldn't transcend his sense of royal entitlement to provide true leadership.

Queen Victoria (1819–1901): Mother of Monarchs

Victoria, who gave her name to an era, was the daughter of Edward, Duke of Kent and Strathearn, and Victoria of Saxe-Coburg-Saalfeld. Her father died when she was an infant, and her mother enacted a strict regimen that turned its back on the scandal-ridden courts of Victoria's uncles, George IV and William IV. Popular respect for the Crown was at a low point at her coronation in 1837, but the modest and straightforward young queen, just 18 years old, eventually won the hearts of her subjects. She refused any further influence from her domineering mother, and though she had no direct input in policy decisions, she wanted to be informed of political matters. (After the Reform Act of 1832, legislative authority resided in the House of Lords, with executive authority resting within a cabinet formed by members of the House of Commons; the monarch was essentially powerless.)

Victoria married Prince Albert of Saxe-Coburg in 1840, a marriage that was apparently happy and certainly fecund: She bore nine children. The public, however, was not fond of Victoria's German prince, and Albert was excluded from holding any official political position, was never granted a title, and was named Prince Consort only after 17 years of marriage. Victoria did nothing without her husband's approval. His interests in art, science, and industry spurred him to organize the Crystal Palace Exhibition in 1851, a highly profitable industrial convention whose proceeds were used to purchase lands in Kensington for the establishment of several museums (one of which is the Victoria & Albert Museum; see Chapter 11). Following his death from typhoid in 1861, Victoria went into seclusion for more than 25 years, not emerging until the Golden Jubilee of 1887. An entire generation had never seen the face of their queen. In that period, she had the Albert Memorial erected in Kensington Gardens (see Chapter 11).

During her reign, the British Empire doubled in size, encompassing Australia, Canada, India, and various locales in Africa and the South Pacific. Victoria was named Empress of India in 1878. England's success in avoiding European conflicts for almost a century (1815 through 1914, the Crimean War of 1853 to 1856 being the major exception) was due, in large part, to the marriages Victoria arranged for her children. Either directly or by marriage, she was related to the royal houses of Belgium, Denmark, Germany, Greece, Norway, Romania, Russia, and Sweden.

Nicholas II of Russia married Victoria's granddaughter Alexandra, and the dreaded Emperor of Germany, Kaiser Wilhelm II, was her grandson "Willy."

The era we now call Victorian England was one in which the queen's rigid ethics and uninspired personal tastes generally reflected those of the middle class. When she died of old age, an entire era died with her.

Queen Elizabeth II (1926–): Monarchy Amidst Media

Elizabeth II, who became queen in 1952, is the best known of the seven remaining monarchs in Europe. The eldest daughter of George VI and Elizabeth Bowes-Lyon, she married a distant cousin, Philip Mountbatten, in 1947 and had four children: Charles, Prince of Wales; Anne; Andrew; and Edward. (For an account of some recent royal scandals involving Elizabeth's kids and grandkids, see Chapter 2.)

In the modern world, where wealth and celebrity have taken the place of actual accomplishment, monarchs are basically privileged show dogs whose pedigrees allow them to amass enormous fortunes, live in a rarified world, and be regarded as newsworthy for no reason other than that they're royal. Seen in the unflattering light of her children, Elizabeth shines like an old-fashioned beacon of virtue and traditional values. She has never embarrassed her nation and she is a hard and disciplined worker, the most widely traveled head of state in the world. She celebrated her Golden Jubilee in 2002 and appears determined to remain on the throne for quite some time — perhaps as long as Victoria.

And yet, overall, the popularity of the English monarchy is in sharp decline. In large part, this is because the disliked and derided Windsor children have tarnished the royal name (Princess Diana was the only recent royal to reach the hearts of the public). But it also has to do with a growing sense that the monarchy is simply irrelevant. The monarchy provides an enormous boost to tourism and sells a lot of books and newspapers, but in a world of democratic models and historical amnesia, how can an elitist monarchy achieve any meaningful relationship to the public it is expected to serve?

It's hard to imagine England without a king or a queen and the traditions associated with royalty. And perhaps the monarchy is worth preserving for that reason alone.

One of my favorite stories about Elizabeth II appeared in a book by Paul Burrell (the queen's butler), *A Royal Duty*. One night, the queen asked if he would like to accompany her as she viewed the latest likeness of herself sent from Madame Tussaud's for her approval. The queen and her butler walked through the hallways and corridors of Buckingham Palace until they came to an enormous, dark drawing room. When the lights were switched on, they saw a lifelike effigy of the queen standing in the center of the room. Elizabeth slowly circled her wax twin, carefully scrutinizing her image, then pronounced herself satisfied, turned off the lights, and left her twin in the dark.

Appendix

Quick Concierge

Fast Facts

American Express

The main Amex office is at 6 Haymarket, SW1 (☎ 020/7930-4411; Tube: Piccadilly Circus). You can get full services Monday through Friday 9 a.m. to 5:30 p.m. and Saturday 9 a.m. to 4 p.m. At other times — Saturday 4 to 6 p.m. and Sunday 10 a.m. to 5 p.m. — you find only the foreign-exchange bureau open. You can find additional Amex offices at 78 Brompton Rd., Knightsbridge SW3 (☎ 020/7584-3431; Tube: Knightsbridge); 84 Kensington High St., Kensington W8 (☎ 020/7795-8703; Tube: Kensington High Street); 51 Great Russell St., Bloomsbury WC1 (☎ 020/7404-8700; Tube: Russell Square); and 1 Savoy Court, Strand WC2 (☎ 020/7240-1521; Tube: Charing Cross).

ATMs

You can access ATMs, also called *cashpoints,* at banks throughout Central London. The most popular networks are Cirrus (☎ 800/424-7787; www.mastercard.com/atm) and Plus (☎ 800/843-7587; www.visa.com/atms).

Babysitters

Universal Aunts (☎ 020/7386-5900) is a trustworthy babysitting agency that's been around for nearly two decades.

Business Hours

Banks are usually open Monday through Friday 9:30 a.m. to 3:30 p.m. Business offices are open Monday through Friday 9 a.m. to 5 p.m. London stores generally stay open 9 a.m. to 6:30 p.m., staying open to 7 p.m. one night a week.

Pubs are allowed to stay open Monday through Saturday 11 a.m. to 11 p.m. and Sunday noon to 10:30 p.m. Some bars stay open past midnight.

Camera Repair

Sendean, 105–109 Oxford St., 1st floor, W1 (☎ 020/7439-8418), gives free estimates and does quick work. It's open weekdays 9:30 a.m. to 5:30 p.m. (Fri until 6 p.m.) and accepts MasterCard and Visa.

Credit Cards

American Express, Diners Club, MasterCard, and Visa are widely accepted in London and throughout the United Kingdom. If your card gets lost or stolen in London, call the following numbers: American Express ☎ 01273/696-933 (☎ 800/221-7282 in the U.S.); Diners Club ☎ 0800/460-800 (☎ 800/525-7376 in the U.S.); MasterCard ☎ 01702/362-988 (☎ 800/307-7309 in the U.S.); Visa ☎ 01604/230-230 (☎ 800/645-6556 in the U.S.).

Currency

Britain's unit of currency is the pound sterling (£). Every pound is divided into 100 pence (p). Coins come in denominations of 1p, 2p, 5p, 10p, 20p, 50p, £1, and £2. You can get notes in £5, £10, £20, and £50 denominations.

Currency Exchange

In London, you can easily exchange cash or traveler's checks by using a currency-exchange service called a *bureau de change*. You can find them at the major London airports, any branch of a major bank (including Barclays, HSBC, Midland Bank, and NatWest), all major rail and Underground stations in Central London, post offices, and American Express or Thomas Cook offices.

Customs

For complete Customs information, see Chapter 12.

Doctors and Dentists

Most hotels have physicians on call. Medical Express, 117A Harley St., W1 (☎ 020/7499-1991; Tube: Oxford Circus), is a private clinic with walk-in medical service (you don't need an appointment) Monday through Friday 9 a.m. to 6 p.m. and Saturday 9:30 a.m. to 2:30 p.m. Dental Emergency Care Service, Guy's Hospital, St. Thomas St., SE8 (☎ 020/7955-2186; Tube: London Bridge), is open Monday through Friday 8:45 a.m. to 3:30 p.m. for walk-in patients.

Electricity

British current is 240 volts, AC cycle, roughly twice the voltage of North American current, which is 115–120 volts, AC cycle. If you're North American, you can't plug the flat pins of your appliance's plugs into the holes of British wall outlets without suitable converters or adapters (which you can get from electrical-supply shops). You can destroy the inner workings of your appliance (and possibly start a fire) if you plug an American appliance directly into a European electrical outlet without a transformer.

Embassies, Consulates, and High Commissions

London is the capital of the United Kingdom and therefore the home of all the embassies, consulates, and high commissions. United States: 24 Grosvenor Sq., W1 (☎ 020/7499-9000; www.usembassy.org.uk; Tube: Bond Street). Canada: MacDonald House, 38 Grosvenor Sq., W1 (☎ 020/7258-6600; www.canada.org.uk; Tube: Bond Street). Ireland: 17 Grosvenor Place, SW1 (☎ 020/7235-2171; www.ireland.embassyhomepage.com; Tube: Hyde Park Corner). Australia: Australia House, Strand, WC2 (☎ 020/7379-4334; www.australia.org.uk; Tube: Charing Cross or Aldwych). New Zealand: New Zealand House, 80 Haymarket at Pall Mall, SW1 (☎ 020/7930-8422; www.new zealandhc.org.uk; Tube: Charing Cross or Piccadilly Circus).

Emergencies

For police, fire, or an ambulance, call ☎ 999.

Holidays

Americans may not know some British holidays, particularly the spring and summer Bank Holidays (the last Mon in May and Aug), when everyone takes off for a long weekend. Most banks and many shops, museums, historic houses, and other places of interest are closed on Bank Holidays, and public-transport services are reduced. The same holds true for other major British holidays: New Year's Day, Good Friday, Easter Monday, May Day (the first Mon in May), Christmas, and Boxing Day (Dec 26). The London crowds swell during school holidays: mid-July to early September, three weeks at Christmas and at Easter, and a week in mid-October and in mid-February (when are those kids *ever* in school?).

Hospitals

The following hospitals offer 24-hour emergency care: Royal Free Hospital, Pond Street, NW3 (☎ 020/7794-0500; Tube: Belsize Park), and University College Hospital, Cecil Fleming House, Grafton Way, WC1 (☎ 020/7387-9300; Tube: Warren Street or Euston Square). Many other London hospitals also have accident and emergency departments.

Hotlines

You can reach the Rape Crisis Line at ☎ 020/7837-1600, which accepts calls after 6 p.m. Samaritans, 46 Marshall St., W1 (☎ 020/7734-2800; Tube: Oxford Circus or Piccadilly Circus), maintains a crisis hotline that helps with all kinds of troubles, even threatened suicides. Doors are open daily 9 a.m. to 9 p.m., but phones are open 24 hours. Alcoholics Anonymous (☎ 020/7833-0022) answers its hotline daily 10 a.m. to 10 p.m. The AIDS 24-hour hotline is ☎ 0800/567-123. If you're in some sort of legal emergency, call Release at ☎ 020/7729-9904, 24 hours a day.

Information

The main Tourist Information Centre, Britain & London Visitor Centre, 1 Regent St., Piccadilly Circus, SW1 (Tube: Piccadilly Circus), provides tourist information to walk-in visitors Monday 9:30 a.m. to 6:30 p.m., Tuesday to Friday 9 a.m. to 6:30 p.m., and Saturday and Sunday 10 a.m. to 4 p.m. You can find another Tourist Information Centre in the Arrivals Hall of the Waterloo International Terminal (open daily 8:30 a.m.–10:30 p.m.). For general London information, call ☎ 020/7234-5800.

Internet Access and Cybercafes

easyEverything (www.easyeverything.co.uk) has cybercafes all over London.

Liquor Laws

No one under 18 can be served alcohol legally. Children under 16 aren't allowed in pubs, except in dining rooms, and then only when accompanied by a parent or guardian. Restaurants are allowed to serve liquor during the same hours as pubs (see "Business Hours," earlier in this appendix, for these hours); however, only people who have a meal on the premises can be served a drink. In hotels, liquor may be served between 11 a.m. and 11 p.m. to both guests and non-guests; after 11 p.m., only guests can get a drink.

Mail

A postcard or airmail letter to North America costs 47p (85¢) for 10 grams and generally takes about five to seven days from London to the U.S. You can send mail within the U.K. first or second class. See "Post Offices," later in this appendix.

Maps

You can get the best all-around street directory, *London A to Z,* at most newsstands and bookstores. You can obtain a bus and Underground map at any Underground station.

Newspapers and Magazines

The *Times, Telegraph, Daily Mail,* and Evening Standard are all dailies carrying the latest news. You can get copies of the *International Herald Tribune,* published in Paris, and an international edition of *USA Today,* beamed via satellite, daily. You can also buy copies of *Newsweek* and *Time* at most newsstands. Magazines such as

City Limits, Time Out, and *Where* contain a lot of useful information about the latest happenings in London. You can pick up a copy of *Gay Times,* a high-quality, news-oriented magazine covering the gay/lesbian community, at most news agents. See "Where to Get More Information," later in this appendix, for more info.

Pharmacies

They're called *chemists* in the United Kingdom. The chain Boots has outlets all over London. Bliss the Chemist, 5 Marble Arch, W1 (☎ 020/7723-6116; Tube: Marble Arch), is open daily 9 a.m. to midnight. Zafash Pharmacy, 233–235 Old Brompton Rd., SW5 (☎ 020/7373-2798; Tube: Earl's Court), is London's only 24-hour pharmacy.

Police

In an emergency, dial ☎ 999.

Post Offices

The Main Post Office, 24 William IV St., WC2 (☎ 020/7930-9580; Tube: Charing Cross), is open Monday through Saturday 8:30 a.m. to 8 p.m. Other post offices and *sub-post offices* (windows in the backs of news-agent stores) are open Monday through Friday 9 a.m. to 5:30 p.m. and Saturday 9 a.m. to 12:30 p.m. Look for red "Post Office" signs outside.

Radio Stations

You can tune into the following FM stations while in London: BBC Greater London Radio (94.9) for rock music; BBC4 (95) for classical music; LBC Crown (97.3) for news and reports of what's happening in London; Capital FM (95.8) for U.S.-style pop and rock music; Choice FM (96.9) for jazz, reggae, or salsa; and Jazz FM (102.2) for jazz, blues, and big-band music.

Restrooms

The English often call toilets *loos.* Loos are marked by "Public Toilets" signs on streets, in parks, and in a few Tube stations. You can also find well-maintained lavatories that anybody can use in all larger public buildings, such as museums and art galleries, large department stores, and rail stations. You can usually use public lavatories for free, but you may need a 20p coin to get in or to use a proper washroom. In some places (like Leicester Square), you can find coin-operated "Super Loos" that are sterilized after each use. If all else fails, duck into the nearest pub.

Safety

Security in the London Underground was dramatically increased following the 2005 terrorist attacks. In general, London is a safe city. Muggings have increased in recent years, however. As in any large metropolis, use common sense and normal caution when you're in a crowded public area or walking alone at night. The area around Euston Station has more purse-snatchings than anywhere else in London.

Smoking

Smoking is forbidden in the Underground (on the cars and the platforms) and on buses. Most restaurants have nonsmoking tables, but they're sometimes separated from the smoking section by very little space. Nonsmoking rooms are available in more and more hotels, and some B&Bs are now entirely smoke-free.

Taxes

The 17.5 percent value-added tax (VAT) is added to all hotel and restaurant bills and is included in the price of many items that you purchase. You can get this tax refunded if you shop at stores that participate in the

Retail Export Scheme (signs are posted in the windows of participating stores).

Taxis

You can hail a cab from the street; if the "For Hire" light is lit, the cab is available. You can phone for a cab at ☎ 020/7272-0272.

Telephone

The country code for the United Kingdom is **44**. London's telephone area code is **020** within the United Kingdom or **20** outside the United Kingdom. If you're calling a London number from outside the city, use 020 followed by the eight-digit number. If you're calling within London, leave off the 020 and dial only the eight-digit number.

For directory assistance in London and the rest of Britain, dial ☎ **192**. To call England from the United States, dial 011-44-20 and then the eight-digit phone number. If you're dialing a London number within London, drop the 020 city code.

You can find three types of public pay phones: those that take only coins (increasingly rare); those that accept only phone cards; and those that take phone cards, credit cards, and coins. You can get phone cards in four values — £3 ($5.55), £5 ($9.25), £10 ($19), and £20 ($37) — and you can reuse them until you use up the total value of the card. You can buy the cards from newsstands and post offices. At coin-operated phones, insert your coins before dialing. The minimum charge is 20p (37¢). The credit-card pay phone operates on credit cards — Access (MasterCard), American Express, Diners Club, and Visa.

To make an international call from London, dial the international access code (00), the country code, the area code, and the local number. Or call through one of the following long-distance access codes: AT&T USA Direct (☎ 0800/890-011), Canada Direct (☎ 0800/890-016), Australia (☎ 0800/890-061), or New Zealand (☎ 0800/890-064). Common country codes are: U.S. and Canada, 1; Australia, 61; New Zealand, 64.

Time Zone

England follows Greenwich mean time (five hours ahead of eastern standard time). Clocks move forward one hour on March 28 and back one hour on October 24. Most of the year, including summer, Britain is five hours ahead of the time observed on the East Coast of the United States. Because the United States and Britain observe daylight saving time at slightly different times of year, for a brief period (about a week) in autumn, London is only four hours ahead of New York, and for a brief period in spring, London is six hours ahead of New York.

Tipping

In restaurants, service charges of 15 to 20 percent are often added to the bill. Sometimes, this tip is clearly marked; at other times, it isn't. When in doubt, ask. If service isn't included, adding 15 percent to the bill is customary. Sommeliers get about £1 ($1.85) per bottle of wine served. Tipping in pubs isn't done, but in cocktail bars, the server usually gets about £1 ($1.85) per round of drinks. Tipping taxi drivers 10 percent to 15 percent of the fare is standard. Barbers and hairdressers expect 10 to 15 percent. Tour guides expect £2 ($3.70), although this tip isn't mandatory. Theater ushers are not tipped.

Transit Info

For 24-hour information on London's Underground, buses, and ferries, call ☎ 020/7222-1234 or go online to www.tfl.gov.uk.

Weather Updates

For the daily London weather report before you go, check the VisitLondon Web site at www.visitlondon.com.

Toll-Free Numbers and Web Sites

Airlines

Air Canada
☎ 888/247-2262
www.aircanada.ca

Air New Zealand
☎ 800/262-2468 (U.S.)
☎ 0800/737-767 (New Zealand)
www.airnewzealand.com

American Airlines
☎ 800/433-7300
www.aa.com

British Airways
☎ 800/247-9297 (U.S.)
☎ 0345/222-111 (U.K.)
www.british-airways.com

British Midland
☎ 0800/788-0555 (U.K.)
www.britishmidland.com

Continental Airlines
☎ 800/625-0280
www.continental.com

Delta Air Lines
☎ 800/221-1212
www.delta.com

Icelandair
☎ 800/223-5500
www.icelandair.is

Northwest Airlines
☎ 800/225-2525
www.nwa.com

Qantas
☎ 800/227-4500 (U.S.)
☎ 612/9691-3636 (Australia)
www.qantas.com

United Airlines
☎ 800/241-6522
www.united.com

Virgin Atlantic Airways
☎ 800/862-8621 (continental U.S.)
☎ 0293/747-747 (U.K.)
www.virgin-atlantic.com

Major hotel chains

Hilton Hotels
☎ 800/HILTONS (U.S.)
☎ 0800/88844 (U.K.)
www.hilton.co.uk

Hyatt Hotels & Resorts
☎ 800/228-9000 (U.S.)
☎ 0845/888-1234 (U.K.)
www.hyatt.com

Le Meridien Hotels & Resorts
☎ 800/225-5843 (U.S.)
☎ 0800/028-2840 (U.K.)
www.lemeridien.com

Macdonald Hotels & Resorts
☎ 888/892-0038 (U.S.)
☎ 0870/830-4812 (U.K.)
www.macdonaldhotels.com

Moat House Hotels
☎ 800/641-0300 (U.S.)
☎ 0870/225-0199 (U.K.)
www.moathousehotels.com

Red Carnation Hotels
☎ 877/955-1515 (U.S.)
☎ 0845/634-2665 (U.K.)
www.redcarnation.com

Relais & Chateaux
☎ 800/735-2478 (U.S.)
☎ 0800/2000-0002 (U.K.)
www.relaischateaux.com

Sheraton Hotels & Resorts
☎ 800/325-3535 (U.S.)
☎ 0800/3253-5303 (U.K.)
www.sheraton.com

Thistle Hotels Worldwide
☎ 800/847-4358 (U.S.)
☎ 0800/181716 (U.K.)
www.thistlehotels.com

Major car-rental agencies

Alamo
☎ 800/327-9633 (U.S.)
☎ 0800/272-200 (U.K.)
www.goalamo.com

Avis
☎ 800/331-1212 (continental U.S.)
☎ 0990/900-500 (U.K.)
www.avis.com

Budget
☎ 800/527-0700 (U.S.)
☎ 0541/565-656 (U.K.)
www.budgetrentacar.com

Hertz
☎ 800/654-3131 (U.S.)
☎ 0990/6699 (U.K.)
www.hertz.com

National
☎ 800/CAR-RENT (U.S.)
☎ 0990/565-656 (U.K.)
www.nationalcar.com

Where to Get More Information

For general information about London, contact an office of VisitBritain (formerly the British Tourist Authority) at one of the following addresses or on the Web at www.visitbritain.com:

✔ **In the United States and Canada:** The main VisitBritain office for North America is at 551 Fifth Ave., Suite 701, New York, NY 10176-0799 (☎ 800/462-2748).

✔ **In Australia:** Level 2, 15 Blue St., North Sydney, NSW 2060 (☎ 02/9021-4400).

✔ **In Ireland:** 18–19 College Green, Dublin 2 (☎ 01/670-8000).

✔ **In New Zealand:** Level 17, NZI House, 151 Queen St., Auckland 1 (☎ 09/303-1446).

The Web gives you a great place to find information on London. For general information on London, try these sites:

✔ **www.visitbritain.com:** You may find the Web page for the official British tourism agency, VisitBritain, a good resource for visitors to London and the United Kingdom, in general.

✔ **www.visitlondon.com:** The city's official London Web page has all kinds of special information for visitors to London.

✔ **www.londontown.com:** This site features special offers on hotels, B&Bs, and theater tickets.

✔ **http://news.bbc.co.uk:** You can find national and international BBC news reports and features on this site.

✔ **www.guardian.co.uk:** *The Guardian,* London's left-of-center daily newspaper, provides up-to-the-minute online news coverage.

- ✔ **www.timesonline.co.uk:** *The (London) Times,* the oldest and most traditional of London papers, is a good source for general news and cultural information.

- ✔ **www.gaylondon.co.uk:** This site provides a useful list of gay and gay-friendly hotels, services, clubs, and restaurants.

- ✔ **www.baa.com:** You can get information on London's Heathrow and Gatwick airports on this site.

- ✔ **www.londontransport.co.uk:** This is the Web site for London Transport, which is in charge of all forms of public transportation in the city: the Tube, buses, and ferry service.

- ✔ **www.royal.gov.uk:** If you want more history, information, and trivia about the Windsors and the British monarchy, in general, check out the official Royal Web site.

Index

See also separate Accommodations and Restaurant indexes at the end of this index.

General Index

• A •

AARP, 62
About a Boy (film), 27
Absolutely Fabulous (television series), 27
Access America, 73
Access London, 63
accessibility issues, 62–66, 208–209
Accessible Journeys, 64
accommodations. *See also* Accommodations Index
  in Bath, 269
  B&Bs (bed and breakfasts), 103–104
  boutique hotels, 105
  in Brighton, 272–273
  in Canterbury, 276
  chain hotels, 105
  for children, 60
  costs of, 2–3, 39–40, 41, 43, 106–107, 109–110
  deluxe hotels, 105, 135
  finding on Internet, 107–108
  landmark hotels, 105
  list of, by neighborhood, 139–140
  list of, by price, 140–141
  maps for, 112–113, 115–121
  reserving, 108–109
  in Salisbury, 284–285
  self-catering hotels, 43, 105
  in Stratford-upon-Avon, 281
  telephone numbers for, 338
  transportation from airport to hotel, 84–88
  types of, 103–105
  VAT added to cost of, 41, 110

Ackroyd, Peter (*London: A Biography*), 26
addresses, postal areas for, 2
Admiral Duncan's, 306
Admiral Lord Nelson, 311
Admiralty Arch, 204
AE (American Express), 46, 48, 333
afternoon tea, 175–176
Ain't Nothing But Blues Bar, 303
Air Canada, 51
Air New Zealand, 51–52
Air Tickets Direct, 53
airlines, 51–54, 58, 338
airports, 45, 51–52, 78–79
Al Fayed, Dodi, 242
Al Fayed, Mohamed, 242
The Albemarle Booking Agency, 291
Albert Memorial, 19, 194, 314
Albert, Prince, 19, 314
alcohol, laws regarding, 335
Alfred the Great (king), 324–325
All Zone Visitor Travelcard, 44
Althorp, 224
American airline, 52
American Airlines Vacations, 58
American Bar, 305
American Express (AE), 46, 48, 333
American Foundation for the Blind, 64
amphibious tour, 233
Anchor Inn, 319
Andrew, Prince, 21
Anglo-Saxon kingdoms in England, 18
Anne Boleyn gate, 228
Anne Hathaway's Cottage (Stratford-upon-Avon), 278–279
Anne of the Thousand Days (film), 312
Anne, Queen, 19
Antiquarius, 244
antiques stores, 254
Anything Left Handed, 251

Apple Market, 244
Apsley House, 12, 223
architecture, 16, 19, 22–23, 222–224
art attractions, 212–214. *See also*
museums and galleries;
performing arts
art events, 32, 33, 35
Artsline, 63
Assembly Rooms (Bath), 268
ATMs, 46–47, 333
attractions. *See also* museums and
galleries; performing arts
accessibility issues, 65, 208–209
architectural, 222–224
art attractions, 212–214
in Bath, 266, 268–269
in Brighton, 270–272
in Canterbury, 273, 274–275
castles and palaces, 10, 189–191,
194–195, 228–229, 236
for children, 60–61, 218–220
costs of, 40, 42, 60
in Greenwich, 229–231
in Hampstead, 226
historic landmarks, 9–10, 209–212,
235–236
hours of operation, 261
list of, by neighborhood, 233–235
list of, by type, 235–236
literary landmarks, 215–216
maps for, 186–187, 210–211
parks and gardens, 15, 224–226, 236
in Salisbury, 282–284
in Stratford-upon-Avon, 276, 278–280
for teens, 218–219
on the Thames, 222
time spent in, 261

• *B* •

babysitters, 61, 333
BADA Antiques & Art Fair, 32
baggage, 72–73, 78–79
Baker Street, 94
ballet, 15, 297
Bank of England, 92
Bank of England Museum, 217
banks, 46, 333
Bar Rumba, 305
Barbican Centre, 92, 293, 296

Barclays Bank, 46
Bargain Alert icon, 5
bars. *See also* pubs
list of, 305–306
maps for, 300–301
Bath, 266–269
Bath Abbey (Bath), 268
bath products, stores selling, 254
Battle of Hastings, 18
Bayswater, 96, 139, 178
BBC Henry Wood Promenade
Concerts, 34
B&Bs (bed and breakfasts), 103–104
Beauchamp, 95
beer, 24–25
Belgravia, 95
Benjamin Franklin House, 216
Best of the Best icon, 5
Bethnal Green, 234
Big Ben, 192–193, 194
Black Friar, 302
Blair, Tony (prime minister), 21
Bliss the Chemist, 243
Bloomsbury, 93, 139, 178, 234
Bloomsbury Group, 93
blue shuttle bus, 87
blues clubs, 303
boat tours, 232–233
The Body Shop, 251
Boingo, 77
Boleyn, Anne (queen), 10, 18
Bond Street, 14, 250, 252
books about London, 25–26, 60–61,
89, 101
bookstores, 253, 254
Boots the Chemist, 243
Boudicca, Queen, 17, 314, 323–324
boutique hotels, 105
boxes, in theater, 291
Bracewells Bar, 305
breakfasts, 104
Brighton, 66, 270–273
Brighton Museum & Art Gallery
(Brighton), 272
Britain & London Visitor Centre, 97
British Airways, 52
British Airways Holidays, 58
British Airways London Eye, 20, 97, 188
British Library Exhibition Centre, 215
British Museum, 11, 93, 188–189, 190

British Travel International, 57
BritRail pass, 44, 265
Brixton Academy, 298
Brompton Road, 245
"Bucket of Blood", 320
bucket shops, 53
Buckingham Palace, 10, 34, 94, 101,
    189–192
Burberry, 250
bureau de change, 45–46, 334
Burlington Arcade, 251
buses
    bus tours, 231–232
    fares for, 100
    from Heathrow airport to London,
        85–86
    information about, 337
    Travelcards for, 99
    using, 100
    Visitor Travelcards for, 44, 100
business hours, 333
buttresses, 22

• *C* •

Cabinet War Rooms, 20, 209
cabs
    from Gatwick airport to London, 87
    from Heathrow airport to London, 86
    telephone numbers for, 337
    tipping in, 40
    from train stations to London, 88
    using, 101
cafes, 75–76, 145, 335
calendar of events, 32–35
Camden Place, 305
camera repair, 333
candy stores, 254
Canterbury, 273–276
Canterbury Cathedral (Canterbury),
    273, 274
The Canterbury Tales (Chaucer),
    18, 273, 275
The Canterbury Tales exhibition
    (Canterbury), 275
Carlyle, Thomas (author), 215
Carlyle's House, 95, 215
Carnaby Street, 251
cars, renting, 71–72, 265–266, 339
cashpoints (ATMs), 46–47, 333

castles and palaces, 10, 189–192,
    194–195, 228–229, 236
cathedrals. *See* churches
The Cazalet Chronicles (Howard), 26
Cazalet Chronicles (television
    series), 27
cellphones, 74–75
Central London, 89, 95–97
Central Zone Visitor Travelcard, 44
Ceremony of the Keys, 203
chain hotels, 105
Changing of the Guard, 191–192, 229
Charbonnel et Walker, 252
Charing Cross, 93–94
Charing Cross Road, 14, 94, 253
Charles I (king), 19, 311–312
Charles II (king), 19
Charles, Prince, 20, 21
Chaucer, Geoffrey (author)
    The Canterbury Tales, 18, 273, 275
    Southwark Cathedral attended
        by, 221
Chelsea, 95, 139, 178, 234, 245–247
Chelsea Antiques Fair, 32
Chelsea Antiques Market, 244
Chelsea Crafts Fair, 35
Chelsea Flower Show, 29, 33, 95
Chelsea Physic Garden, 95, 224–225
chemist's shops (drugstores),
    243, 254, 336
children
    accommodations for, 60
    attractions for, 60–61, 218–220
    babysitters for, 61, 333
    Family Travelcard for, 99
    itinerary for five-day trip with,
        260–262
    long trips with, 61
    pubs and, 145
    resources for, 59–60
    restaurants for, 60
Children's Book Centre, 247
china, stores selling, 255
Chinatown, 93
Chinese New Year, 32
chippies (fish and chips restaurants),
    173–174
Christmas lights, 35
Chunnel, 54–55

Church of St. Bartholomew the Great, 315–316
Church of St. Stephen Walbrook, 316
churches
  Bath Abbey (Bath), 268
  Canterbury Cathedral (Canterbury), 273, 274
  list of, 235, 315–318
  Salisbury Cathedral (Salisbury), 282–283
  Southwark Cathedral, 97, 221, 318
  St. Augustine's Abbey (Canterbury), 275
  St. George's Chapel, 229
  St. Martin-in-the-Fields, 204, 297, 317
  St. Paul's Cathedral, 10, 19, 92, 200–201, 315
  St. Stephen Walbrook church, 92
  Westminster Abbey, 10, 18, 206–207, 315
Churchill Arms, 302
Churchill, Winston (prime minister), 20, 314
Church's, 252
Cirrus ATM network, 46
Citibank International ATMs, 47
Cittie or Yorke, 302
city code, London (020), 2, 337
City of London, 17, 92
City of London Festival, 34
Civil War, 19
classical music, 15, 33, 34, 296–297
Cleopatra's Needle, 93
Clerkenwell, 178
Closer (film), 27
clothing stores, 254
clubs, 300–301, 303–305, 306–307
Coal Hole, 319–320
coffee bars, 175
Comedy Café, 304
comedy clubs, 304
The Comedy Store, 304
The Complex, 304
Comptons of Soho, 306
concessions (concs), 63
consolidators, 53
consulates, 334
Continental airline, 52
Continental Airlines Vacations, 58
conventions used in this book, 2–3, 5–6

cornices, 23
costs
  accommodations, 2–3, 39–40, 41, 43, 106–107, 109–110
  airfares, 52–53
  attractions, 40, 42, 60
  cutting, strategies for, 43–44
  discounts for persons with disabilities, 63
  discounts for seniors, 62
  list of, 39–40
  museums and galleries, 42, 185
  performing arts, 290
  restaurants, 2–3, 40, 41–42, 44, 146
  shopping, 42
  transportation, 39, 40–41, 44
Cottesloe theater, 294
country code (44), 2, 337
Courtauld Gallery, 214
Covent Garden
  accommodations in, 139
  attractions in, 234
  description of, 92–93
  restaurants in, 178
  shopping in, 14, 250, 253–254
Covent Garden Market, 93, 244, 253
Covent Garden Market and Piazza, 192
credit cards, 2, 47, 48–49, 333
credit-reporting agencies, 48–49
Crimean War, 312
crisis hotlines, 335
Cromwell, Oliver, 19, 313
Crown Jewels, 203
cuisine
  breakfasts, 104
  restaurants listed by, 179–181
  types of, 12–13, 23–24, 143–144
Culpeper the Herbalist, 253
currency. *See* money
Customs, getting packages through, 240–241
Customs Hall, 84
Cutty Sark (ship), 61, 230
cybercafes, 75–76, 335

• D •

dance clubs, 304–305
dance performances, 15, 297
Darling (film), 27

Davies Mews, 252
Davies Street, 252
day trips
  to Bath, 266–269
  to Brighton, 270–273
  to Canterbury, 273–276
  maps for, 264
  to Salisbury and Stonehenge, 281–285
  to Stratford-upon-Avon, 276–281
  transportation for, 263–266
daylight saving time, 88
DC (Diners Club) credit card, 2
Decorated Gothic period of
  architecture, 22
deep vein thrombosis, 73
Delta airline, 52
deluxe hotels, 105, 135
dentists, 334
department stores, 241–243, 254
department-store restaurants, 174–175
Design Museum, 217
Diana Museum, 224
Diana, Princess
  burial place of (Althorp), 224
  commemorative walk for, 101
  death of, allegations regarding, 242
  home of (Kensington Palace), 10
  marriage of, 20
  Princess Diana Memorial Playground,
    61, 194
Dickens, Charles (author)
  home of, 93, 215–216
  Nicholas Nickleby, 215
  Oliver Twist, 26, 215
  The Pickwick Papers, 215
  as social reformer, 19
Diners Club (DC) credit card, 2
dining. *See* cuisine; restaurants
disabilities, 62–66, 208–209
Disabled Traveler Fact Sheet, 63
doctors, 334
dollar signs ($), 2–3, 109–110, 146–147
doormen, tipping, 40
Doyle, Arthur Conan, 20
The D'Oyly Carte Opera Company, 295
Dr. Johnson's House, 216
Dr. Martens Department Store, 254
Dress Circle, 252
driving, 265–266

drugstores (chemist's shops),
    243, 254, 336
Duke of York Monument, 312
duty-free allowance, 240–241

• *E* •

Earl's Court
  accommodations in, 118–119, 139
  description of, 96
  gay and lesbian pubs and restaurants
    in, 66
  restaurants in, 152–153
Earl's Court Exhibition Centre, 297
Early English Gothic period of
  architecture, 22
easyInternetCafe, 76
"economy-class syndrome", 73
Edward, Prince, 21
Edward VII (king), 312
Elderhostel, 62
electricity, 334
Elizabeth I (queen), 10, 18, 206,
    327–328
Elizabeth II (queen), 20, 33, 331–332
Elizabeth, Queen (Queen Mother), 199
Elizabethan period of architecture, 23
ELTExpress, 53
e-mail access, 75–78
Embankment Gardens, 177
embassies, 334
emergencies, 334
English National Ballet, 15, 297
English National Opera, 15, 295
entertainment. *See also* performing
    arts
  clubs, 300–301, 303–305, 306–307
  events, 32–35, 66
Equifax credit-reporting agency, 49
Equinox, 304
E-savers, 54
escorted tours, 55–57, 64, 231–233
Eton College, 229
Eurostar, 54–55
events, 32–35, 66
exchange rate, 2, 45–46
exchanging money, 45–46, 88, 334
Expedia, 53
Experian credit-reporting agency, 49

• F •

families. *See* children
Family Travelcard, 99
fan vaulting, 22
Farlows, 250
Fenwick of Bond Street, 241
ferry
　information about, 337
　to London, 55
　between Tate Britain and Tate
　　Modern, 202
　to Tower of London, 204
Fielding, Henry (*The History of Tom Jones*), 125
films
　about London, 27
　London Film Festival, 35
The Filofax Centre, 251
finances. *See* money
fire. *See* Great Fire of 1666
The Firm, 11. *See also* Royals
fish and chips restaurants (chippies), 173–174
five-day trips, 259, 260–262
Flask Walk, 226
Fleet Street, 92
Flexipasses, 44
Floris, 14, 250
FlyCheap, 53
Football Association FA Cup Final, 33
The Forsythe Saga (television series), 27
Fortnum & Mason, 14, 241
Fox, Kate (*Watching the English*), 26
Franklin, Benjamin, 216
Frommer's Born to Shop London (Wiley), 26
Frommer's London from $95 a Day (Wiley), 26
Frommer's Memorable Walks in London (Wiley), 26, 101

• G •

galleries. *See* museums and galleries
gardens. *See* parks and gardens
Gatwick airport, 52, 86–87
Gatwick Express train, 86

G.A.Y., 307
Gay Times magazine, 67
Gay Village, 93
gays and lesbians
　cafes and bars for, 145
　clubs for, 306–307
　events for, 66
　neighborhoods for, 66, 93, 96
　resources for, 66–67
Gay's the Word, 67
George III (king), 328–329
George Inn, 320
George IV (king), 311, 329–330
George of Hanover (king), 19
Georgian period of architecture, 23
Georgy Girl (film), 27
Gibbs, James (architect), 317
Gielgud Theatre, 294
Gilbert Collection, 214
Glass Bar, 306
Global System for Mobiles (GSM), 74
Globe Theatre, 18, 97
Globus and Cosmos, 56
Glore Studio Theatre, 295
Golden Age, 18
Golden Hinde (ship), 222
Goldsmith, Oliver (playwright), 319
GoToMyPC, 76
Grand Circle Travel, 62
Great Fire of 1666
　architectural styles following, 16, 19
　Monument commemorating, 92, 223
Great Plague of 1665, 19
Green Park, 94, 178, 199–200
Greenline 757 bus, 87
Greenwich, 229–231, 234
Greenwich mean time, 337
GSM (Global System for Mobiles), 74
The Guided Tour, 64
Guy Fawkes Night, 35

• H •

Hall's Croft (Stratford-upon-Avon), 278, 279
Hamleys, 251
Hampstead, 226, 227, 234
Hampstead Heath, 226
Hampton Court, 234
Hampton Court Flower Show, 34

Hampton Court Palace, 10, 18, 228
Hanover Grand, 305
Harley Street Clinic, 94
Harold, King, 18
Harrods, 13, 95, 242
Harry Potter book series, 60–61
Harry, Prince, 21
Harvey Nichols, 14, 242
Hatchards, 250
Hayward Gallery, 97
Heads Up icon, 5
health issues. *See* medical issues
Heathrow airport, 51–52, 84–86
Heathrow Express, 86
Heaven, 307
Henley Royal Regatta, 34
Henry II (king), 326
Henry VII (king), 206
Henry VIII Gateway, 313
Henry VIII (king), 10, 18, 312–313,
    326–327
Hermitage Rooms, 214
Hertford House, 12
high commissions, 334
high tea, 175, 176–177
Hilditch & Key, 250
Hippodrome, 304
historic landmarks, 9–10, 209–212,
    235–236
historic pubs, 319–321
history museum, 12, 61, 95, 198
History of Britain (Schama), 25
history of London, 17–22
The History of Tom Jones (Fielding), 125
H.M.S. *Belfast* (ship), 222
H.M.S. *Cutty Sark* (ship), 61, 230
Holborn, 92, 178, 234, 247–250
Holiday Care Service, 63
holidays
    calendar of events, 32–35
    list of, 334–335
The Holland Park Theatre, 295
Hollinghurst, Alan (*The Line
    of Beauty*), 26
Holmes, Sherlock (fictional character),
    20, 94
Holy Trinity Church (Stratford-upon-
    Avon), 279
hospitals, 335
Hotelink, 86

hotels. *See* accommodations
hotlines, 335
Hotwire, 54
hours of operation
    attractions, 261
    business hours, 333
    pubs, 25, 302, 333
    shopping, 237, 333
    Tube/Underground, 99
House of Windsor, 20
Houses of Parliament, 10, 192–193
housewares, stores selling, 255
hovercraft, 55
Hoverspeed UK Limited, 55
Howard, Elizabeth Jane (*The Cazalet
    Chronicles*), 26
HSBC, 46
Hundred Years' War, 18
Hyde Park, 60, 177, 193

• *I* •

Icelandair airline, 52
icons used in this book, 5–6
Imperial War Museum, 209
Industrial Revolution, 19
information for visitors, 97, 335,
    339–340
Inns of Court, 92
insurance, 56, 72–73
Internet access, 75–78, 335
Internet service provider (ISP), 76, 77
InTouch USA, 75
iPass network, 77
The Irish Shop, 254
ISP (Internet service provider), 76, 77
Italian Gardens, 194
itineraries, 257–262

• *J* •

Jack the Ripper, 20
Jacobean period of architecture, 23
James I (king), 19
James II (king), 19, 313
Jane Austen Centre (Bath), 269
jazz clubs, 303
Jermyn Street, 14, 247, 250
Jewel House, 192

Johnson, Samuel, Dr. (lexicographer), 216, 319
Jones, Inigo (architect), 23
Jubilee Market, 244
Jubilee Walkway, 97

• K •

Kangaroo Court. *See* Earl's Court
Keith Prowse ticket agency, 291
Kensington, 96, 139, 178, 234, 247
Kensington Gardens, 60, 61, 177, 194
Kensington Palace, 10, 20, 101, 194–195
Kenwood House, 226, 297
Kenwood Lakeside Concerts, 33, 297
Kew, 234
Kew Palace, 225
Kid Friendly icon, 5
King's Dressing Room, 228
King's Head and Eight Bells, 320
King's Road, 14, 245
King's School (Canterbury), 275
kitchen in hotel room, 105, 114
Knightsbridge
    accommodations in, 118–119, 139
    description of, 95
    restaurants in, 152–153, 178
    shopping in, 14, 245, 246
Know Before You Go pamphlet, 240

• L •

Ladbroke Arms, 302–303
Lamb and Flag, 320
Lambeth, 234
landing card, 83–84
landmark hotels, 105
landmarks
    historic landmarks, 9–10, 209–212, 235–236
    literary landmarks, 215–216
laptops, 77–78
Leicester Square, 93–94, 179, 195, 234, 252
lesbians. *See* gays and lesbians
Liberty, 242–243
Liberty Travel, 57
The Library, 305
Lillian Baylis Theatre, 297
Lillie Langtry Bar, 306

Linbury Studio Theatre, 295
Lincoln, Abraham (president), 314
Lincoln's Inn Fields, 92
Lindow Man, 189
The Line of Beauty (Hollinghurst), 26
liquor laws, 335
literary landmarks, 215–216
Livingstone, Ken (Mayor of London), 21
Lloyds of London, 92
lodging. *See* accommodations
London. *See* City of London; maps; neighborhoods
London: A Biography (Ackroyd), 26
London A to Z map, 89, 185, 335
London Aquarium, 97, 219
London Brass Rubbing Centre, 205
London City airport, 52, 87
London Coliseum, 295, 297
London Dungeon, 218–219
London Eye, 20, 97, 188
London Film Festival, 35
London Lesbian and Gay Film Festival, 66
London Marathon, 32
London Open House Weekend, 35
London Parade, 32
London Planetarium, 220
London Planner booklet, 290
London Plus Pass, 44, 265
London (Rutherfurd), 25
London Symphony Orchestra, 15, 296
London Tattler icon, 5
London Transport Museum, 220
London Waterbus Co., 196
London Zoo, 196, 225
Lord Mayor's Procession, 35
lost or stolen passport, 71
lost or stolen wallet, 48–49
lost-luggage insurance, 72–73
Love, Actually (film), 27
luggage, 72–73, 78–79
Lush, 247
Luton airport, 52, 87
Lyttleton theater, 293

• M •

Madame Tussaud's, 61, 94, 196–197
magazines, 335–336

Magna Carta, 18
mail, 335, 336
A Man for All Seasons (film), 312
Map House of London, 245
maps
    accommodations, 112–113, 115–121
    attractions, 186–187, 210–211
    bars, 300–301
    Bath, 267
    Brighton, 271
    Canterbury, 274
    clubs, 300–301
    day trips, 264
    London A to Z map, 335
    neighborhoods, 90–91
    pubs, 300–301
    restaurants, 148–155
    Salisbury, 282
    shopping, 246, 248–249
    stores selling, 254
    Stratford-upon-Avon, 277
markets, 244–245, 255
Marks & Spencer, 14, 243
Mary Arden's House (Stratford-upon-
    Avon), 278, 280
Mary, Queen, 19
Marylebone
    accommodations in, 120–121, 139
    attractions in, 234
    description of, 94
    restaurants in, 154–155, 178
MasterCard (MC) credit card, 2, 48
Maupintour, 57
Mayfair, 94, 139, 178
Maze, 228
McEwan, Ian (*Saturday*), 26
MDC Classic Music, 252
MEDEX Assistance, 72
medical issues
    disabilities and, 66
    doctors and dentists, 334
    health conditions and, 73
    hospitals, 335
    insurance, 72
"Medical London". *See* Marylebone
mews dwellings, 101
Midland Bank, 46
Midnight Lace (film), 27
Millennium Bridge, 97, 200, 202, 203
Millennium Dome, 20

Mithras (Persian god), 17
money. *See also* costs; VAT (value-
    added tax)
    ATMs, 46–47, 333
    British currency, 45, 333
    credit cards, 2, 47, 48–49, 333
    exchange rate, 2, 45–46
    exchanging, 45–46, 88, 334
    lost or stolen wallet, 48–49
    traveler's checks, 47–48
The Monument, 223
More, Sir Thomas, 10
Mounted Guard Changing
    Ceremony, 192
movies about London, 27
Mrs. Dalloway (Woolf), 26
Murder One, 14, 253
Museum of Childhood, 220
Museum of Costume (Bath), 268
Museum of London, 12, 92, 212
museums and galleries
    best of, 11–12
    British Museum, 11, 93, 188–189, 190
    costs of, 42, 185
    Imperial War Museum, 209
    list of, 212–218, 235, 236
    National Gallery, 11, 94, 197
    National Portrait Gallery, 11, 94,
        197–198, 199
    Natural History Museum, 12, 61,
        95, 198
    Science Museum, 12, 95, 199
    Tate Britain, 12, 95, 201–202
    Tate Modern, 12, 97, 202
    Victoria & Albert Museum, 11–12,
        95, 206
music
    ballet, 15, 297
    classical music, 15, 33, 34, 296–297
    clubs, 300–301, 303–305, 306–307
    opera, 15, 295
music stores, 255

• *N* •

N97 night bus, 85
Nash's House (Stratford-upon-Avon),
    278, 279
National Express buses, 85–86
National Film Theatre, 97

National Gallery, 11, 94, 197
National Health System, 20
National Maritime Museum, 230
National Portrait Gallery, 11, 94, 197–198, 199
The National Trust, 63
Natural History Museum, 12, 61, 95, 198
NatWest, 46
NatWest Tower, 92
Neal's Yard Remedies, 253
neighborhoods. *See also specific neighborhoods*
  accommodations listed by, 139–140
  attractions listed by, 234–235
  best of, 16
  Central London, 89, 95–97
  City of London, 17, 92
  map of, 90–91
  shopping areas listed by, 245–254
  West End, 14, 92–95, 116–117, 150–151, 292–293
Nelson, Horatio Viscount (Admiral Lord), 311
Nelson's Column, 204, 311
New Labour party, 21
New Place (Stratford-upon-Avon), 278, 279
New Year's Day Parade, 32
New Year's Eve celebrations, 35
newspapers, 335–336
Nicholas Nickleby (Dickens), 215
night buses, 100
nightlife. *See* bars; clubs; performing arts; pubs
Norman period of architecture, 22
Northwest airline, 52
Northwest Airlines World Vacations, 58
Notting Hill, 96, 120–121, 139, 154–155, 179
Notting Hill Carnival, 34
Notting Hill (film), 27

• *O* •

Old Bailey, 92
Old Compton Street, 66
Old Operating Theatre & Herb Garret, 217
The Old Vic, 293

Olde Mitre, 302
Oliver Twist (Dickens), 26, 215
Olivier theater, 293
opera, 15, 295
Orbitz, 53
orchestras. *See* classical music
Oxford and Cambridge Boat Race, 32
Oxford Street, 14, 247, 251–252

• *P* •

p (pence), 45
package tours, 43, 57–58, 106
Paddington, 96, 139
Palace Pier (Brighton), 272
palaces and castles, 10, 189–192, 194–195, 228–229, 236
Pall Mall, 94
Parker-Bowles, Camilla (Duchess of Cornwall), 21
parks and gardens
  best of, 15
  list of, 224–226, 236
  picnics in, 177–178
Parthenon Sculptures, 188
passport, 69–71, 83–84
Passport Control, 83–84
Peacock Theatre, 297
pedestrian crossings, 102
pediments, 23
pence (p), 45
Penhaligon's, 254
Pepsi Trocadero, 198, 219
performing arts. *See also* theater
  ballet, 15, 297
  best of, 14–15
  classical music, 15, 33, 34, 296–297
  costs of, 290
  current performances, information about, 290
  curtain times for, 290
  dance, 15, 297
  opera, 15, 295
  rock concerts, 297–298
  tickets for, 291–292
  types of seats for, 291
  what to wear to performances, 290
Perpendicular Gothic period of architecture, 22
Peter Jones, 247

Peter Pan books, 60
Peter Pan statue, 194, 313–314
pharmacies, 243, 254, 336
phone calls. *See* telephone calls
phone numbers. *See* telephone
  numbers
Piccadilly Circus
  accommodations in, 139
  attractions in, 198, 234
  description of, 93–94
  restaurants in, 179
  shopping in, 247, 250
The Pickwick Papers (Dickens), 215
picnics, 177–178
Pimlico, 95, 234
Pink Paper magazine, 67
Pippa Pop-ins, 61
Pizza Express Jazz Club, 303
Pizza on the Park, 303
The Place Theatre, 297
plague (Great Plague of 1665), 19
plays. *See* theater
PLUS ATM network, 46
P&O European Ferries, 55
P&O Stena Line, 55
Poets' Corner, 206
police, 336
porters, tipping, 40
Portobello Road, 244–245
post offices, 336
postal areas, 2, 89
pounds sterling, 45, 333
Priceline, 54
prices. *See* costs
Pride in the Park, 34
Pride Parade, 66
prime meridian, 229, 231
Primrose Hill, 225
Primus, 75
Princess Diana Memorial Playground,
  61, 194
Proms concert series, 296
public telephones, 337
public toilets, 336
pubs. *See also* bars
  beer served in, types of, 24–25, 299
  children in, 145
  food served in, 145
  for gays and lesbians, 66
  historic, list of, 319–321

hours of operation, 25, 302, 333
liquor laws, 335
list of, 302–303
maps for, 300–301
pub crawl, 299
Pulteney Bridge (Bath), 269
Pump Room (Bath), 266, 268
Purcell Room, 296

• *Q* •

Qantas airline, 52
Queen Adelaide Tea Room
  (Brighton), 271
Queen Anne period of architecture, 23
Queen Charlotte's Cottage, 225
Queen Elizabeth Hall, 296
Queen Mary's Dollhouse, 229
Queen Mary's Rose Garden, 225
Queen Mother (Queen Elizabeth), 199
Queen's Gallery, 189
Queen's House, 230
QX (*Queer Xtra*) magazine, 67

• *R* •

rack rates, 2–3, 106
RADAR (Royal Association for
  Disability and Rehabilitation), 63
radio stations, 336
rail passes, 44, 265
Rail Travel for Disabled Passengers, 65
Railair Coach Link, 87
ravens at Tower of London, 203
Red Lion Public House, 320–321
Regency period of architecture, 23
Regent Street, 247, 251
Regent's Park, 94, 225
Regent's Park Open Air Theatre, 295
Rent-a-phone, 75
restaurants. *See also* Restaurant Index
  accessibility issues, 64
  in Bath, 269
  best of, 12–13
  in Brighton, 272
  cafes, 145
  in Canterbury, 276
  for children, 60
  coffee bars, 175

restaurants *(continued)*
costs of, 2–3, 40, 41–42, 44, 146
cuisine, 12–13, 23–24, 143–144
cybercafes, 75–76, 335
department-store restaurants, 174–175
fish and chips restaurants (chippies), 173–174
fixed-price meals in, 146
for gays and lesbians, 66
list of, by cuisine, 179–181
list of, by neighborhood, 178–179
list of, by price, 181–182
maps for, 148–155
picnics, 177–178
pubs, food served in, 145
in Salisbury, 284
sandwich bars, 172–173
service charges in, 42
in Stratford-upon-Avon, 280–281
teas, 24, 175–177
theatre, dining before or after, 298
tipping in, 40
VAT added to cost of, 146
wine bars, 145
restrooms, 336
Reynolds, Sir Joshua (painter), 319
Riverside Studios, 297
RoadPost, 75
rock concerts, 297–298
Roman Baths Museum (Bath), 266, 268
Roman Museum (Canterbury), 275
Roman Temple of Mithras, 92
Romans, England conquered by, 17
Ronnie Scott's, 303
Rosetta Stone, 188–189
Rotten Row, 193
Route A6 Airbus, 87
Royal Academy of Arts, 93, 212–213
Royal Academy Summer Exhibition, 33
Royal Albert Hall, 296, 298
Royal Ascot horseracing, 33
Royal Association for Disability and Rehabilitation (RADAR), 63
Royal Ballet, 15, 297
Royal Botanic Gardens, 225–226
Royal Courts of Justice, 92
Royal Doulton Regent Street, 251
Royal Exchange, 92
Royal Festival Hall, 97, 296

"Royal London" (St. James's), 94, 139, 179, 235
Royal Mews, 189
Royal National Theatre, 97, 293–294
Royal Naval College, 19, 230
Royal Observatory Greenwich, 230
Royal Opera, 15, 295
Royal Opera House, 93, 295, 297
Royal Pavilion (Brighton), 270
Royal Philharmonic Orchestra, 15, 296
Royal Shakespeare Company, 294
Royal Shakespeare Theatre (Stratford-upon-Avon), 276, 280
Royal Warrants, 14, 136, 242
Royals. *See also specific names*
expenses of, 49
list of, 323–332
popularity of, 11
Rutherfurd, Edward (*London*), 25

● *S* ●

Saatchi Gallery, 213
Sadler's Wells, 297
safety, 336
sales, 238
Salisbury, 281–285, 321
Salisbury Cathedral (Salisbury), 282–283
sandwich bars, 172–173
Saturday (McEwan), 26
Savile Row, 251
Schama, Simon (*History of Britain*), 25
Science Museum, 12, 95, 199
Scotch House, 251
Sea France Limited, 55
seasons, 28–31, 43, 106
security, airport, 78–79
Segaworld, 219
self-catering hotels, 105, 114
Selfridges, 14, 243
seniors, 62
Serpentine Gallery, 194
Serpentine lake, 193
service charges in restaurants, 42
Seven Stars, 302
seven-day trips, 259–260
Shakespeare Countryside Museum (Stratford-upon-Avon), 280

Shakespeare, William
plays, performed during Golden Age, 18
plays, seeing, 280
Shakespeare's Globe Theatre & Exhibition, 221
Southwark Cathedral, 97, 221, 318
Stratford-upon-Avon, 276–281
Shakespeare's Birthplace (Stratford-upon-Avon), 278
Shakespeare's Globe Theatre, 293, 295
Shakespearience (Stratford-upon-Avon), 280
Shepherd's Bush Empire, 298
shoe stores, 255
shopping
best of, 13–14
costs of, 42
department stores, 241–243, 254
drugstores (chemist's shops), 243, 254, 336
gay and lesbian bookstore, 67
hours of operation, 237, 333
maps for, 246, 248–249
packages, carrying home in luggage, 239–241
packages, shipping home, 239
Royal Warrants in shops, 14, 136, 242
sales, 238
sizes, conversions for, 238
stores, listed by merchandise, 254–255
stores, listed by neighborhood, 245–254
street markets, 244–245
SideStep, 53
sightseeing. See attractions
Silver Moon Women's Bookshop, 253
silver, stores selling, 255
SIM card, 74
Sir John Soane's Museum, 218
The Six Wives of Henry VII (television series), 312
606 Club, 303
sizes, conversions for, 238
Smarter Living, 54
Smith, Zadie (White Teeth), 26
smoking, 336
Soane, John, Sir (architect), 218

The Society for Accessible Travel & Hospitality, 64
Society of London Theatres, 63, 292
Soho, 93, 139, 179
Somerset House, 213–214
South Bank, 16, 97, 178, 179, 234–235
The South Bank Arts Centre, 293–294
South Bank Centre, 97, 293, 296
South Kensington, 95–96, 139, 179, 234
Southwark, 16
Southwark Cathedral, 97, 221, 318
souvenirs, 44
Speakers' Corner, 193
Spencer House, 12, 101, 223
sporting events, 32–34
sporting goods stores, 255
St. Augustine's Abbey (Canterbury), 275
St. Botolph's, 316
St. Dunstan's-in-the-West, 316
St. George the Martyr Church, 317
St. George's Chapel, 229
St. James Palace, 94, 101
St. James's, 94, 139, 179, 235
St. James's Park, 94, 178, 199
St. Margaret's Westminster, 317
St. Martin-in-the-Fields, 204, 297, 317
St. Martin's Church (Canterbury), 275
St. Martin's Court, 250
St. Mary-le-Bow, 317
St. Patrick's Day, 32
St. Paul's Cathedral, 10, 19, 92, 200–201, 315
St. Stephen Walbrook church, 92
STA Travel, 53
stalls, in theater, 291
Stanfords, 252
Stansted airport, 52, 87
Stansted Express, 87
State Opening of Parliament, 35
statues, 311–314
Stock Exchange, 92
stolen or lost wallet, 48–49
Stonehenge, 283–284
Strachey, Lytton (historian), 93
The Strand, 92–93, 139, 179, 235
Stranger's Gallery, 192
Stratford-upon-Avon, 276–281
street markets, 244–245, 255
Stuart period of architecture, 23
subway. See Tube/Underground

Summer Rites, 66
Sunday, Blood Sunday (film), 27
Sutton Hoo Treasure, 189
symphony orchestras. *See* classical
    music

• *T* •

Tate Britain, 12, 95, 201–202
Tate Modern, 12, 97, 202
taxes. *See* VAT (value-added tax)
taxis. *See* cabs
Taylors of Old Bond Street, 14, 250
The Tea House, 254
teas, 24, 175–177
teens, attractions for, 218–219
telephone calls
    cellphones, 74–75
    costs of, saving, 43
    international calls, 337
    to London from United States, 337
    public telephones, 337
telephone numbers
    directory assistance (192), 48, 337
    emergency number (999), 334
    list of, 338–339
    London city code for (020), 2, 337
    U.K. country code for (44), 2, 337
television series about London, 27
Temple of Mithras, 318
10 Downing Street, 212
terrorist bombings, 22
Thames Festival, 34
Thames River, 89, 222, 232–233
Thameslink train, 86
Thatcher, Margaret, 20
theater
    best of, 14
    City of London Festival, 34
    costs of, 40
    days of performances, 293
    dining before or after, 298
    fringe theater, 294
    locations of, 292–294
    outdoor theater, 295
    programs, cost of, 293
Theatre Museum, 218
Theatre Royal Haymarket, 294

Theatreland, 93–94, 292–293
three-day trips, 257–259
time
    for attractions, 261
    curtain times, 290
    daylight saving time, 88
    Greenwich mean time, 337
    for itineraries, 261
    24-hour clock used for, 88
Time Out magazine, 67, 290
time zones, 337
Tip icon, 6
tipping
    for barbers and hairdressers, 337
    in bars, 337
    for cab drivers, 40, 337
    for doormen, 40
    for porters, 40
    in pubs, 25, 337
    in restaurants, 40, 146, 337
    for tour guides, 337
T-Mobile Hotspot, 77
Tourist Information Centres, 97
tours. *See also* day trips
    amphibious tour, 232
    in Bath, 266–268
    boat tours, 232–233
    bus tours, 231–232
    in Canterbury, 273–274
    escorted tours, 55–57, 64, 231–233
    insurance for, 56
    package tours, 43, 57–58, 106
    in Stratford-upon-Avon, 278
    walking tours, 233
Tower Bridge, 97
Tower Bridge Experience, 224
Tower of London, 9–10, 18, 61, 92,
    203–204, 205
Tower Records, 250
toy stores, 255
tracery, 22
Trafalgar Square, 93–94, 204–205
Trafalgar Tours, 57
traffic, direction of, 102
Trailfinders, 58
train
    arriving in London via, 54–55, 88
    for day trips, 265
    rail passes for, 44, 265

train stations, Tube/Underground
    connections to, 88
Transport for London, 65, 98
transportation. *See also* buses; cabs;
    train; Tube/Underground
    accessibility issues, 65
    from airport to hotel, 84–87
    cars, renting, 71–72, 265–266, 339
    costs, 39, 40–41, 44
    for day trips, 263–266
    ferry, 55, 202, 204, 337
    to Heathrow airport, 86
    hovercraft, 55
    information about, 98, 337
    to London, 51–55
    within London, 97–102
    from train to hotel, 88
    walking, 101–102, 233
Transportation Security
    Administration (TSA), 79
TransUnion credit-reporting agency, 49
travel agencies, 53–54, 107
Travel Assistance International, 72
Travel Guard International, 72, 73
travel guides, 26, 89, 101
Travel Information Service, 64
travel insurance, 56, 72–73
Travel Insured International, 73
Travelcards, 44, 99, 100
traveler's checks, 47–48
Travelex Insurance Services, 73
Travelocity, 53
trip-cancellation insurance, 72
Tripscope, The Courtyard, 63
Trooping the Colour parade, 33
TSA (Transportation Security
    Administration), 79
Tube/Underground
    connections to train stations, 88
    from Heathrow airport to London, 85
    hours of operation, 99
    information about, 337
    as specified in this book, 2
    tickets for, 99
    from train stations to London, 88
    Travelcards for, 99
    using, 98–99
    Visitor Travelcards for, 44, 100
Tudor period of architecture, 22

• *U* •

U.K. country code (44), 2, 337
Underground. *See* Tube/Underground
Undiscovered Britain, 64
United airline, 52
United Airlines Vacations, 58
Universal Aunts, 61
Upstairs, Downstairs (television
    series), 27

• *V* •

V (Visa) credit card, 2, 48
VAT (value-added tax)
    for accommodations, 41, 110
    for books, 253
    description of, 2, 336–337
    refund for, 42, 238–239
    for restaurants, 146
Venom Club/The Zoo Bar, 304
Victoria, 140, 149, 179
Victoria & Albert Museum, 11–12,
    95, 206
Victoria, Queen, 19, 330–331
Victorian period of architecture, 23
Virgin Atlantic airline, 52
Virgin Atlantic Vacations, 58
Visa (V) credit card, 2, 48
visitor information, 97, 335, 339–340
Visitor Travelcards, 44, 100
Vivienne Westwood, 252

• *W* •

W & G Foyle, Ltd., 14, 253
walking tours, 233
walks, 97, 101–102
Wallace Collection, 214
War of the Roses, 18
Washington, George (president), 313
Watching the English (Fox), 26
Waterstone's, 14, 253
Wayport, 77
weather, 28–31, 337
welfare state, 20
Wembley Stadium, 297

West End
accommodations in, 116–117
description of, 92–95
restaurants in, 150–151
theater district, 14, 292–293
Western Union, 48
Westminster
accommodations in, 115, 140
attractions in, 235
description of, 94
restaurants in, 149, 179
Westminster Abbey, 10, 18,
206–207, 315
Wheelchair Travel, 65
Whispering Gallery, 200
White Teeth (Smith), 26
Wi-Fi (wireless fidelity) connections,
76–77
Wigmore Hall, 296
Wilde, Oscar (novelist), 122, 207
William of Orange (king), 19
William the Conqueror, 10, 18, 325–326
Williamson's Tavern, 321
Wilton House (Salisbury), 283
Wimbledon Lawn Tennis
Championships, 33–34
Windsor, 235
Windsor Castle, 10, 18, 228–229
wine bars, 145
wireless fidelity (Wi-Fi) connections,
76–77
wireless hotspots, 76–77
Wolsey, Cardinal, 18
Woolf, Virginia (novelist)
home of, 93
Mrs. Dalloway, 26
World War I, 20
World War II, 20
Wren, Sir Christopher (architect)
burial place of, 200
Church of St. Stephen Walbrook, 316
Hampton Court Palace, 228
Monument of Great Fire of London,
92, 223
St. Mary-le-Bow, 317
St. Paul's Cathedral, 10, 19, 200, 315
St. Stephen Walbrook church, 92
Stuart period of architecture, 23

• Y •

Ye Olde Cheshire Cheese, 321
Ye Olde Watling, 321
youth hostels, 75

• Z •

Zafash Pharmacy, 243
zebra crossings, 102

Accommodations Index

The Abbey Court, 111
Abbey House, 111
Adare House, 137
Aster House, 111
Astons Apartments, 105, 114
Avonmore Hotel, 114
Blooms Hotel, 137
Brown's Hotel, 135
Bryanston Court Hotel, 114
Byron Hotel, 122
Cadogan Hotel, 105, 122
Cartref House, 129
Cathedral Gate Hotel (Canterbury), 276
Claridge's, 105, 135
Claverley Hotel, 122
Comfort Inn Notting Hill, 123
Covent Garden Hotel, 123
The Cranley, 123–124
Crowne Plaza, 105
The Dorchester, 105, 135
Dorset Square Hotel, 124
Dukes Hotel, 138
Durrants Hotel, 124
Ebury House, 138
Fairways Hotel, 124
Fielding Hotel, 125
Five Sumner Place, 125
41, 105, 125
The Gallery, 126
Gate Hotel, 126
The Gore, 105, 126
Goring Hotel, 138

Grange Strathmore Hotel, 127
Harlingford Hotel, 127
Hart House Hotel, 127
Hazlitt's 1718, 105, 128
Hotel 167, 128
Hotel du Vin & Bistro (Brighton),
    272–273
Hotel La Place, 128
Hyatt, 105
Imperial Hotel, 129
"Iron Lady of Piccadilly", 132
James House, 129
Jenkins Hotel, 129
Kennard Hotel (Bath), 269
Kensington International Inn, 130
Landmark London, 130
Lime Tree Hotel, 130
Luna Simone Hotel, 131
Macdonald White Hart Hotel
    (Salisbury), 284
Marriott, 105
Mitre House Hotel, 131
The Montague, 105, 131
Morgans Hotel, 138
Number Sixteen, 132
Park Lane Sheraton Hotel, 105, 132
The Payton (Stratford-upon-Avon), 281
Pembridge Court Hotel, 138
Quaker International Centre, 132
Red Lion Hotel (Salisbury), 284–285
Regency Hotel, 133
Regent Palace Hotel, 133
Rhodes Hotel, 133
Rushmore Hotel, 138
The Savoy, 105, 134
The Shakespeare (Stratford-upon-
    Avon), 281
St. Margaret's Hotel, 134
St. Martin's Hotel, 105
St. Martin's Lane, 138
Swiss House Hotel, 134
Tophams Belgravia, 135
Twenty Nevern Square, 135
22 Jermyn Street, 136
The Vicarage Hotel, 136
Wigmore Court Hotel, 136
Willett Hotel, 137
Winchester Hotel, 137

Restaurant Index

Atlantic Bar & Grill, 306
Aubergine, 13, 147
Bar Italia, 306
Boxwood Café, 12, 156
Brasserie Max, 123
Brasserie St. Quentin, 13, 156
Burger King, 60
Café Boheme, 306
Café in the Crypt, 156, 205
Café Parlour at Sketch, 175
Capri Sandwich Bar, 173
Chelsea Kitchen, 157
Chiang Mai, 157
Cigala, 157
Claridge's, 176
Clarke's, 158
Costas Fish Restaurant, 173, 174
Criterion Grill, 13, 158
Dell Restaurant, 193
Dickens Inn by the Tower, 158
Ebury Wine Bar & Restaurant, 159
Ed's Easy Diner, 159, 219
Food for Thought, 159
Fortnum & Mason, 160, 176–177
The Founders Arms, 13, 160
The Fountain, 241
Fox & Anchor, 160–161
Fryer's Delight, 173
The Gay Hussar, 161
Geales, 173, 174
The George, 161
Georgian Restaurant, 177
Giovanni's Sandwich Bar, 173
The Globe Café, 221
Golden Hind, 174
Gourmet Pizza Company, 161–162
The Granary, 162
Hard Rock Café, 60, 162
Harper's Restaurant (Salisbury), 284
Harrods, 174, 177
Harvey Nichols, 174–175
Hathaway Tea Rooms & Bakery
    (Stratford-upon-Avon), 280
The Ivy, 12, 162–163, 298
Jardin, 128

Joe Allen, 163, 298
Ken Lo's Memories of China, 13, 163
KFC, 60
The Lanesborough Hotel, 177
Langan's Bistro, 12, 164
Maggie Jones's, 164
McDonald's, 60
Mela, 13, 164–165
Mona Lisa, 165
Moro, 13, 165
Mosaique, 165–166
Muffinski's, 176
The Museum Tavern, 166
No. 5 Bistro (Bath), 269
Noor Jahan, 13, 166
North Sea Fish Restaurant, 166–167
One Minster Street (Salisbury), 284
The Oppo (Stratford-upon-Avon), 281
The Orangery, 195
The Oratory, 12, 167
Oxo Tower Brasserie, 13, 167
Palm Court, 177
Patio, 241
Pâtisserie Cappucetto, 176
Pâtisserie Deux Amis, 176
Pâtisserie Valerie, 176
Pizza Hut, 60

Planet Hollywood, 60
Porter's English Restaurant, 13, 167–168
Portrait Restaurant & Bar, 198
Pret à Manger, 173
Rainforest Café, 60, 219
Richoux, 176
Rock & Sole Plaice, 174
R.S. Hispaniola, 168
Rules, 12, 168, 298
San Lorenzo, 169
Savoy Grill, 134
Seafresh Fish Restaurant, 174
Sea-Shell, 174
Shepherd's, 169
Simpson's-in-the-Strand, 13, 23–24, 169–170, 298
St. James's, 241
The Stockpot, 13, 170
Strand Restaurant (Brighton), 272
Sully's (Canterbury), 276
Suze in Mayfair, 13, 170
Terre à Terre (Brighton), 272
Veeraswamy, 13, 170–171
Veronica's, 12, 171
Wagamama Noodle Bar, 13, 171
Ye Olde Cheshire Cheese, 171–172
Zafferano, 172

Notes

Notes

BUSINESS, CAREERS & PERSONAL FINANCE

Grant Writing

Home Buying

0-7645-5307-0   0-7645-5331-3 *†

Also available:
- Accounting For Dummies †
  0-7645-5314-3
- Business Plans Kit For Dummies †
  0-7645-5365-8
- Cover Letters For Dummies
  0-7645-5224-4
- Frugal Living For Dummies
  0-7645-5403-4
- Leadership For Dummies
  0-7645-5176-0
- Managing For Dummies
  0-7645-1771-6

- Marketing For Dummies
  0-7645-5600-2
- Personal Finance For Dummies *
  0-7645-2590-5
- Project Management
  For Dummies
  0-7645-5283-X
- Resumes For Dummies †
  0-7645-5471-9
- Selling For Dummies
  0-7645-5363-1
- Small Business Kit For Dummies *†
  0-7645-5093-4

HOME & BUSINESS COMPUTER BASICS

Windows XP

Excel 2003

0-7645-4074-2   0-7645-3758-X

Also available:
- ACT! 6 For Dummies
  0-7645-2645-6
- iLife '04 All-in-One Desk Reference
  For Dummies
  0-7645-7347-0
- iPAQ For Dummies
  0-7645-6769-1
- Mac OS X Panther Timesaving
  Techniques For Dummies
  0-7645-5812-9
- Macs For Dummies
  0-7645-5656-8
- Microsoft Money 2004 For Dummies
  0-7645-4195-1

- Office 2003 All-in-One Desk
  Reference For Dummies
  0-7645-3883-7
- Outlook 2003 For Dummies
  0-7645-3759-8
- PCs For Dummies
  0-7645-4074-2
- TiVo For Dummies
  0-7645-6923-6
- Upgrading and Fixing PCs
  For Dummies
  0-7645-1665-5
- Windows XP Timesaving
  Techniques For Dummies
  0-7645-3748-2

FOOD, HOME, GARDEN, HOBBIES, MUSIC & PETS

Feng Shui

Poker

0-7645-5295-3   0-7645-5232-5

Also available:
- Bass Guitar For Dummies
  0-7645-2487-9
- Diabetes Cookbook For Dummies
  0-7645-5230-9
- Gardening For Dummies *
  0-7645-5130-2
- Guitar For Dummies
  0-7645-5106-X
- Holiday Decorating For Dummies
  0-7645-2570-0
- Home Improvement All-in-One
  For Dummies
  0-7645-5680-0

- Knitting For Dummies
  0-7645-5395-X
- Piano For Dummies
  0-7645-5105-1
- Puppies For Dummies
  0-7645-5255-4
- Scrapbooking For Dummies
  0-7645-7208-3
- Senior Dogs For Dummies
  0-7645-5818-8
- Singing For Dummies
  0-7645-2475-5
- 30-Minute Meals For Dummies
  0-7645-2589-1

INTERNET & DIGITAL MEDIA

Digital Photography

Starting an eBay Business

0-7645-1664-7   0-7645-6924-4

Also available:
- 2005 Online Shopping Directory
  For Dummies
  0-7645-7495-7
- CD & DVD Recording For Dummies
  0-7645-5956-7
- eBay For Dummies
  0-7645-5654-1
- Fighting Spam For Dummies
  0-7645-5965-6
- Genealogy Online For Dummies
  0-7645-5964-8
- Google For Dummies
  0-7645-4420-9

- Home Recording For Musicians
  For Dummies
  0-7645-1634-5
- The Internet For Dummies
  0-7645-4173-0
- iPod & iTunes For Dummies
  0-7645-7772-7
- Preventing Identity Theft
  For Dummies
  0-7645-7336-5
- Pro Tools All-in-One Desk
  Reference For Dummies
  0-7645-5714-9
- Roxio Easy Media Creator
  For Dummies
  0-7645-7131-1

SPORTS, FITNESS, PARENTING, RELIGION & SPIRITUALITY

0-7645-5146-9

0-7645-5418-2

Also available:
- Adoption For Dummies
  0-7645-5488-3
- Basketball For Dummies
  0-7645-5248-1
- The Bible For Dummies
  0-7645-5296-1
- Buddhism For Dummies
  0-7645-5359-3
- Catholicism For Dummies
  0-7645-5391-7
- Hockey For Dummies
  0-7645-5228-7

- Judaism For Dummies
  0-7645-5299-6
- Martial Arts For Dummies
  0-7645-5358-5
- Pilates For Dummies
  0-7645-5397-6
- Religion For Dummies
  0-7645-5264-3
- Teaching Kids to Read
  For Dummies
  0-7645-4043-2
- Weight Training For Dummies
  0-7645-5168-X
- Yoga For Dummies
  0-7645-5117-5

TRAVEL

0-7645-5438-7

0-7645-5453-0

Also available:
- Alaska For Dummies
  0-7645-1761-9
- Arizona For Dummies
  0-7645-6938-4
- Cancún and the Yucatán
  For Dummies
  0-7645-2437-2
- Cruise Vacations For Dummies
  0-7645-6941-4
- Europe For Dummies
  0-7645-5456-5
- Ireland For Dummies
  0-7645-5455-7

- Las Vegas For Dummies
  0-7645-5448-4
- London For Dummies
  0-7645-4277-X
- New York City For Dummies
  0-7645-6945-7
- Paris For Dummies
  0-7645-5494-8
- RV Vacations For Dummies
  0-7645-5443-3
- Walt Disney World & Orlando
  For Dummies
  0-7645-6943-0

GRAPHICS, DESIGN & WEB DEVELOPMENT

0-7645-4345-8

0-7645-5589-8

Also available:
- Adobe Acrobat 6 PDF
  For Dummies
  0-7645-3760-1
- Building a Web Site For Dummies
  0-7645-7144-3
- Dreamweaver MX 2004
  For Dummies
  0-7645-4342-3
- FrontPage 2003 For Dummies
  0-7645-3882-9
- HTML 4 For Dummies
  0-7645-1995-6
- Illustrator cs For Dummies
  0-7645-4084-X

- Macromedia Flash MX 2004
  For Dummies
  0-7645-4358-X
- Photoshop 7 All-in-One Desk
  Reference For Dummies
  0-7645-1667-1
- Photoshop cs Timesaving
  Techniques For Dummies
  0-7645-6782-9
- PHP 5 For Dummies
  0-7645-4166-8
- PowerPoint 2003 For Dummies
  0-7645-3908-6
- QuarkXPress 6 For Dummies
  0-7645-2593-X

NETWORKING, SECURITY, PROGRAMMING & DATABASES

0-7645-6852-3

0-7645-5784-X

Also available:
- A+ Certification For Dummies
  0-7645-4187-0
- Access 2003 All-in-One Desk
  Reference For Dummies
  0-7645-3988-4
- Beginning Programming
  For Dummies
  0-7645-4997-9
- C For Dummies
  0-7645-7068-4
- Firewalls For Dummies
  0-7645-4048-3
- Home Networking For Dummies
  0-7645-42796

- Network Security For Dummies
  0-7645-1679-5
- Networking For Dummies
  0-7645-1677-9
- TCP/IP For Dummies
  0-7645-1760-0
- VBA For Dummies
  0-7645-3989-2
- Wireless All In-One Desk Referen
  For Dummies
  0-7645-7496-5
- Wireless Home Networking
  For Dummies
  0-7645-3910-8

HEALTH & SELF-HELP

0-7645-6820-5 *†   0-7645-2566-2

Also available:
- Alzheimer's For Dummies
  0-7645-3899-3
- Asthma For Dummies
  0-7645-4233-8
- Controlling Cholesterol For Dummies
  0-7645-5440-9
- Depression For Dummies
  0-7645-3900-0
- Dieting For Dummies
  0-7645-4149-8
- Fertility For Dummies
  0-7645-2549-2

- Fibromyalgia For Dummies
  0-7645-5441-7
- Improving Your Memory For Dummies
  0-7645-5435-2
- Pregnancy For Dummies †
  0-7645-4483-7
- Quitting Smoking For Dummies
  0-7645-2629-4
- Relationships For Dummies
  0-7645-5384-4
- Thyroid For Dummies
  0-7645-5385-2

EDUCATION, HISTORY, REFERENCE & TEST PREPARATION

0-7645-5194-9   0-7645-4186-2

Also available:
- Algebra For Dummies
  0-7645-5325-9
- British History For Dummies
  0-7645-7021-8
- Calculus For Dummies
  0-7645-2498-4
- English Grammar For Dummies
  0-7645-5322-4
- Forensics For Dummies
  0-7645-5580-4
- The GMAT For Dummies
  0-7645-5251-1
- Inglés Para Dummies
  0-7645-5427-1

- Italian For Dummies
  0-7645-5196-5
- Latin For Dummies
  0-7645-5431-X
- Lewis & Clark For Dummies
  0-7645-2545-X
- Research Papers For Dummies
  0-7645-5426-3
- The SAT I For Dummies
  0-7645-7193-1
- Science Fair Projects For Dummies
  0-7645-5460-3
- U.S. History For Dummies
  0-7645-5249-X

Get smart @ dummies.com®

- Find a full list of Dummies titles
- Look into loads of FREE on-site articles
- Sign up for FREE eTips e-mailed to you weekly
- See what other products carry the Dummies name
- Shop directly from the Dummies bookstore
- Enter to win new prizes every month!

Separate Canadian edition also available
Separate U.K. edition also available

Available wherever books are sold. For more information or to order direct: U.S. customers visit www.dummies.com or call 1-877-762-2974.
U.K. customers visit www.wileyeurope.com or call 0800 243407. Canadian customers visit www.wiley.ca or call 1-800-567-4797.